The Vampire
Encyclopedia

Other titles of similar interest from
Random House Value Publishing:

The Dracula Cookbook

The Vampire Encyclopedia

MATTHEW BUNSON

GRAMERCY BOOKS
New York

This 2000 edition is published by Gramercy Books™, an imprint of Random House Value Publishing, Inc., 280 Park Avenue, New York, NY 10017, by arrangement with Three Rivers Press, a division of Crown Publishers, Inc., a member of Random House, Inc.

Gramercy Books™ and design are trademarks of Random House Value Publishing, Inc.

Book design by Mercedes Everett

Printed in the United States of America

Random House
New York . Toronto . London . Sydney . Auckland
http://www.randomhouse.com/

Library of Congress Cataloging–in–Publication Data

Bunson, Matthew.
  The vampire encyclopedia / Matthew Bunson.
      p. cm.
  Includes bibliographical references and index.
  ISBN 0-517-16206-7
  1. Vampires--Encyclopedias. I. Title.

  GR830.V3 B86 2000
  398'.45—dc21

                                           00-039366

9 8 7 6 5 4 3 2

This book is dedicated to Vincent Price.

Acknowledgments

I would like also to acknowledge the many individuals who assisted in the preparation of this work. Among them are Frank Langella; Chris Sarandon; Julie Carmen, who is truly beautiful under all that makeup in *Fright Night II*; Terry Saevig of Columbia Pictures; Jennifer Sebree of MCA Universal; Katherine Orloff, publicity director for *Bram Stoker's Dracula*; Kathy Lendech of Turner Entertainment; Ron and Howard Mandelbaum of Photofest; the free people of Romania, in particular Bogdan Vasilescu, director of the Romanian National Tourist Office in New York; Jane Freeburg, of Companion Press, Santa Barbara; Dr. Jeanne Youngson and Anne Hart of Vampires Are Us; Charlotte Simsen of the Quincey P. Morris Dracula Society; Dr. Donald A. Reed of the Count Dracula Society; Alys Lynn Mundorff; Russell Lyster; Ronald V. Borst; Sue Quiroz, assistant to Anne Rice; Abraham Pokrassa of the Roland Company; Eric Held of the Vampire Information Exchange; John Vellutini; the people and governments of Greece, Indonesia, and the Philippines; and a special thanks to Jane Meara of Crown Books, whose vision and enthusiasm made this project a delightful experience.

Introduction

The late 1980s and early 1990s have witnessed an eruption of interest in the undead greater than any other vampire craze of modern times: larger than epidemics of vampire fascination in America and Europe during the 1970s or in Paris during the 1820s when there were stage plays, comedies, musicals, and translations of John Polidori's influential 1819 short story, "The Vampyre" (and where it was said by one writer that "One can see vampires everywhere!"). In 1992 alone, there were novels, including Anne Rice's *The Tale of the Body Thief,* and several major films, including *Innocent Blood, Buffy the Vampire Slayer,* and, of course, *Bram Stoker's Dracula.* Vampire societies and organizations are thriving. Bands, playing so-called Gothic Rock, featuring "vampire" singers and musicians, blast out their throbbing, hypnotic ballads to enthralled vampire wannabes in the dark, moody bowels of clubs in American and European cities. There are vampire books, posters, toys, games, new editions of the novel *Dracula,* records, and even an Annie Lennox music video called "Love Song for a Vampire."

The Vampire Encyclopedia is intended to fill a definite need in vampirology for a handy, single-volume reference source on vampires that is interesting, comprehensive, and easy to use. The casual reader or anyone recently introduced to the world of the bloodsucker will find a detailed compendium on vampires in film, literature, folklore, poetry, art, medicine, religion, and comedy. Students of the undead will find much that is familiar and much that is new. In this book you will find traditional vampires, psychic vampires, historical vampires, and vampires in shapes only dreamed of in the nightmares of the greatest writers of the last two centuries. Above all, *The Vampire Encyclopedia* is intended to be fun, written affectionately in the spirit both of the esteemed real-life vampire hunter Reverend Montague Summers and of the multitudes of undead whom he pursued with such fanatical and righteous devotion. It remains to be seen if Dracula, Lestat, Saint-Germain, Louis, Miriam Blaylock, and all the Others of the Night will approve. Mortal readers are encouraged to write.

Throughout the whole vast shadowy world of ghosts and demons there is no figure so terrible, no figure so dreaded and abhorred, yet dight with such fearful fascination, as the vampire, who is himself neither ghost nor demon, but yet who partakes the dark natures and possesses the mysterious and terrible qualities of both.

—Reverend Montague Summers, 1928

If there is in this world a well-attested account, it is that of the vampires. Nothing is lacking: official reports, affadavits of well-known people, of surgeons, of priests, of magistrates; the judicial proof is most complete. And with all that, who is there who believes in vampires?

—Rousseau

THE
VAMPIRE
ENCYCLOPEDIA

Abbott and Costello Meet Frankenstein A 1948 Universal (International) vehicle for Bud Abbott and Lou Costello, considered the first and one of the most successful vampire comedies. Directed by Charles Barton, the film also starred some of the best-known horror stars of the era, including Lon Chaney, Jr., as the Wolfman and Bela Lugosi as Dracula. Lugosi reprised his most famous role for the first time since his 1931 *Dracula,* replacing John Carradine, who withdrew from the project. Glenn Strange, who had portrayed the creature in other films, was the Frankenstein monster. The plot, written around the frenetic comic duo, involves a plan by Dracula to find a new brain for the monster, preferably a brain that is simple and easily controlled. Wilbur Brown, played by Costello, proves a most promising victim. While focusing on the antics of Abbott and Costello, the film demonstrated the fact that Dracula could be transferred from the horror to the comedy genre. (See *Comedy.*)

Aborigines: See *Australia.*

Abruzzi Also called Abruzzo, a region in central Italy, situated on the Adriatic Sea and characterized by very rugged terrain, as the Apennine AbruzziMountains dominate the area. Mainly dependent upon agriculture, the Abruzzi inhabitants preserved elements from the ancient Roman beliefs in the return of the dead (the *lemuria*) and the Greek festival of the dead (the *Anthesteria*). On November 1, candles were placed on the graves of loved ones, and all windows and homes were kept well lighted to allow the deceased to return to their families. A meal of bread and water was set out on a kitchen table, with a lamp. According to tradition, the dead marched in procession from their graves on that date, with the souls of the good leading the way. The good were followed by those who were evil, murder victims, or condemned. Abruzzi individuals who performed certain rituals could stand at a crossroads and see the spirits, although such a sight led inevitably to madness and death. (See also *Italy.*)

Absolution: See *Excommunication.*

"Adventure of the Sussex Vampire, The" A Sherlock Holmes mystery, written by Sir Arthur Conan Doyle and originally published in the *Strand.* In this case, Holmes and Watson investigate what appears to be an instance of vampirism, involving a South American woman seen sucking blood from her young child. A paralyzed dog, South American hunting paraphernalia, a grieved husband, and a resentful first son contribute to the solution, which involves a desperate mother but no vampire. Holmes dismisses vampires during the case, stating: "Rubbish, Watson, rubbish! What have we to do with walking corpses who can only be held in their graves by stakes driven through their hearts?" (See *Holmes, Sherlock.*)

Adze A vampire spirit that dwells in tribal sorcerers among the Ewe, a people inhabiting parts of southeastern Ghana and southern Togo in Africa. The *adze* flies around in the form of a firefly but, if caught, changes into a human. It drinks blood, palm oil, and coconut water and preys on children, especially handsome ones. (See *Africa.*)

Africa: See *Adze, Asanbosam, Impundulu, Mau-Mau,* and *Ramanga.*

Aging The human process that figures prominently in vampire lore, particularly in the ability of vampires to delay such fleshly deterioration. While one of the most alluring aspects of vampires is their promise of immortality, albeit at a dreadful price, another recurring theme in the literary, historical, and cinematic treatments of vampires is the maintenance of beauty and the retardation of the aging process through vampiric practices. Historically, the most infamous figures seeking such eternal youth were Elizabeth Bathory and Gilles de Rais. Bathory (d. 1614) was a Hungarian countess who became convinced that blood was a powerful restorative, especially when extracted brutally from young girls. Thus, to preserve her youth and vigor, she bathed in the blood of maidens, hundreds of whom were slain before Bathory was tried in 1610. Similarly, Gilles de Rais (1420–1440), a marshal of France and a supposed dabbler in the black arts, committed horrible crimes against women and children in order to maintain his youth. Numerous works in film and literature have examined this idea; two of the most successful are Mary Elizabeth Braddon's "Good Lady Ducayne" and Whitley Strieber's *The Hunger.* The latter was made into a film, joining other similar cinematic projects such as *Captain Kronos: Vampire Hunter, Countess Dracula, Daughters of Darkness,* and *House of Dark Shadows.* (See also *Psychic Vampires.*)

Albania A country situated in the Balkans along the eastern Adriatic, with Yugoslavia to the north and east and Greece to the south. Its position made it susceptible to the cultural influences of its regional neighbors, and its vampire lore parallels that of other Balkan states. Several vampire types are found in Albanian traditions. One is the *vrykolakas* (*vurkolaka*), found also in Greece and exhibiting the characteristics of the Greek species. Another is called the *sampiro,* a derivation from the Slavic vampire. A lesser-known species is the *kukuthi* (also known as the *lugat*). A belief exists in northern Albanian regions that anyone killed by a vampire is unavoidably doomed to rise from the grave. The destruction of such beings is possible through the common method of piercing the heart with a stake, and hamstringing is also considered useful in the case of the *kukuthi.* There is, as well, a tradition that those guilty of a crime that went undetected in life will be condemned at their deaths to become vampires.

Algul The name given by Arabic peoples to a kind of vampire, translated from the Arabic to mean a horse-leech, or a bloodsucking *jinn,* or demon. This form of vampire became known in more common western usage as a *g*houl, a traditionally female demon that feasted upon dead babies and inhabited cemeteries. The incarnation and nature of the *algul* varied, finding expression in literature, most notably in the *Thousand and One Nights.* (See also *Amine,* for an example of an *algul,* and *Ghoul.*)

Alien Vampires: See *Science Fiction.*

Allatius, Leo One of the first important seventeenth-century writers on vampires (b. 1586), who compiled information on the Greek species, the *vrykolakas,* in his compendium on Greek superstitions, *De Quorundum Graecorum Opinationibus,* published in Cologne in 1645. While dealing in a broad sense with the legends of Greece, Allatius focused on the undead, drawing much of his knowledge from his native island of Chios. His work was very useful in preserving both the details of the *vrykolakas* and the so-called *nonocanons* (the ordinances of the Greek Orthodox church) against the vampires and vampirism. Allatius' own opinion of the *vrykolakas* held that it was "the body of a man of evil and immoral life—very often one who has been excommunicated by his bishop. . . . Into such a body the devil enters and, proceeding from the tomb, goes about mainly at night, knocking on doors and calling one of the house. If one answers, he dies the following day. A *vrykolakas* never calls twice, however, and thus the people of Chios insure their safety by waiting for a second before replying." (See also *Richard, Father François; Tournefort, Joseph Pitton;* and *Laws About Vampires.*)

All Souls' Day One of the most solemn days of the Catholic calendar, a day for commemoration of all the faithful departed, held on November 2, or November 3 if November 2 falls on a Sunday. Dating to the earliest Christian eras, the feast became popular among the Benedictine monasteries in the sixth century and was decreed officially by St. Odilo, the abbot of Cluny, in 998. A variety of beliefs were found throughout Europe concerning the return of the dead during the night hours of All Souls' Day. In Brittany, the dead supposedly visited the living, and those who in life did not join in the annual procession for the deceased, the *Tromenie,* did so after death. In Belgium, Germany, Austria, Bohemia, and elsewhere, food offerings were made for the returning dead and left on tables or in churchyards. Particularly common were the "soul-cakes," baked on November 1 and eaten the following day. (See also *Anthesteria.*)

Alnwick Castle, Vampire of A voracious vampire that terrorized the town and area around Alnwick Castle in Northumberland, England, whose predations and pestilential activities were recorded by the twelfth-century English chronicler William of Newburgh. The undead in question was, in life, a cruel and wicked man who moved from Yorkshire to Alnwick, where the local lord had granted him a position. One night, while spying his wife in adultery with a neighbor, he fell from his place on the roof and died during the night. Although given a Christian burial, he soon reappeared and began attacking villagers, spreading plague in his wake. The once populated town was emptied as the victims multiplied. A group of brave survivors finally marched on the cemetery and began digging, finding the vampire in a shallow grave. They pierced the blood-engorged body, watching in horror as blood poured out in abundance. The body was then burned, and the epidemic and deaths ceased immediately. This is an excellent example of plagues or epidemics being attributed to a revenant. (See *England, Plague,* and *William of Newburgh.*)

Alp A German vampirelike spirit associated with the bogeyman and the incubus, normally tormenting the nights and dreams of women, although men and children are also victims. The creature's physical manifestations can be very dangerous. Long connected with the nightmare, the *alp* is considered a male, sometimes the spirit of a recently deceased individual, most often an actual demon. Children can become an *alp* when a mother uses a horse's collar to ease childbirth, obviously a local custom.

During the Middle Ages, the *alp* was said to appear as a cat, pig, bird, or other animal, including a lecherous demon dog seen in Cologne, thus linking the werewolf to this legend as well. In all of its manifestations, it was known to wear a kind of hat. The spirit can fly like a bird, can ride a horse, and is credited with a certain gallant attitude, rarely forcing itself violently upon its prey. Entry is made through the victim's mouth, with the *alp* either using its tongue, becoming a mist that enters, or turning into a snake. Misery generally follows such occupation, as sexual relations with the monster are said to be terrible. The *alp* drinks blood from the nipples of men and children but especially enjoys the taste of women's milk and that of cows.

Because it is so involved in terrors of the mind and sleep, the *alp* is virtually impossible to destroy. There are, however, a number of methods available for protection and control. Women are told to sleep with their shoes at the side of their beds, with the toes pointing toward the door. The *alp* is also very protective of its hat and if it is lost loses much of its power, especially its invisibility and strength. It thus rewards generously anyone who returns the hat. The *alp* must also safeguard its eye, for in that orb resides its means to torment the sleep of a victim, an attribute steeped in the traditions of the "evil eye." (See *Germany, Incubus, Nightmare,* and *Succubus.*)

Alucard An assumed name used by Count Dracula, created by spelling his real name backward. This novelty was first employed in the 1943 Universal picture *Son of Dracula,* starring Lon Chaney, Jr. The use of this name was repeated with such regularity in subsequent works that its very appearance in a film created either a campy atmosphere or unintentional humor. (See *Comedy.*)

Aluga (Aluka) A name for a vampire or bloodsucking demon (meaning "horse-leech") derived from Proverbs (30:15), translated into the Latin as *sanguisuga* (bloodsucker). The *aluga* was probably similar to the Arabian *algul* (or ghoul) but was considered by some sources to be a formidable blood demon, possibly even the demon king of the vampires.

Alytos A Greek term meaning "undissolved," describing the remarkable physical preservation of a vampire or revenant.

America, Central: See *Civatateo, Films, La Llorona, Mexico,* and *Tlaciques.*

America, North: See *Bell Witch; Native Americans; New England; Ray Family Vampire; Rhode Island; South, American; Voodoo;* and *Weeping Woman.*

America, South: See *Brazil, Jaracacas, Lobishomen,* and *Voodoo.*

Amine An *algul* (Arabian ghoul) whose story was told in the *Thousand and One Nights.* According to the tale, a young man, Sidi Numan, weds a beautiful maiden, Amine, who eats virtually nothing except a bowl of rice, which she takes grain by grain with a knife, along with small crumbs of bread. Suspicious, Sidi learns that Amine leaves the house each night. Following her one evening, he discovers her feasting on a corpse with a fellow ghoul. Confronting her the next night at dinner, he is turned into a dog by her spell. Restored eventually by a woman learned in white magic, Sidi receives a potion that transforms Amine into a horse. The ghoul is then led to the stables. (See *Algul, Arabia, Ghoul,* and *Thousand and One Nights.*)

"Amsworth, Mrs." A famous short story written by E. F. Benson and published originally in *Visible and Invisible* in London, 1923. The story depicts a small English village where a friendly widow is actually a vampire, described as "always cheery and jolly; she was interested in everything, and in music, in gardening, in games of all sorts was a competent performer. Everybody (with one exception) liked her, everybody felt her to bring with her the tonic of a sunny day." Naturally she also brings a lust for blood, the same thirst that slew her husband, haunted the city of Peshawar, and now threatens the village of Maxley. The "one exception" is a Professor Francis Urcombe, who proves her undoing. Reprinted in collections and in anthologies of vampires tales, "Mrs. Amsworth" is considered one of Benson's best works.

Ancient Vampires: See the following: *Anthesteria; Apollonius of Tyana; Apuleius, Lucius; Assyria; Babylon; Ekimmu; Empusas; Horace; Lamia; Menippus; Mormo; Ovid; Petronius; Philinnion; Philostratus; Pliny the Elder; Polycrites; Theodore of Gaza;* and *Utukku.*

Andrew, Feast of St. Held each November 30, a feast day that was considered, along with the feasts of St. George and Easter, one of the most dreaded periods of the year in Romania. Its importance is derived from the belief that vampires were very active and dangerous in the days just before the festival, particularly on St. Andrew's Eve. The exact duration of their activities was longer or shorter depending upon the Romanian regional traditions, but throughout the land it was deemed wise to rub garlic on the doors and windows of the family residences in order to protect the inhabitants from attacks. (See *Romania.*)

Andros Vampires Supposed residents of Andros, the second largest and most northerly of the Cyclades group in the Aegean Sea. There the belief in vampires remained firm well into the twentieth century. The Greek vampire species, the *vrykolakas,* was considered quite common, and the local clergy often opened graves to seek out possible revenants. The local custom of Andros required that a corpse suspected of vampire infection be exhumed, chopped into pieces, and burned. (See also *Greece.*)

Anemia A medical condition involving the reduction of red blood cells or their oxygen-carrying pigment, hemoglobin. The presence of anemia in both humans and animals had long been held to be indicative of a major vampire infestation, as attacks by vampires were believed to be the leading cause of such a disorder. Symptoms of anemia are understandably similar to the general effects of recurring visits from a member of the undead: dizziness, shortness of breath, fainting, weakness, and extreme pallor. When such symptoms appear mysteriously or after the sudden death of a loved one, and if they are accompanied by other equally troubling signs, such as nightmares, nervous prostration, and an increasing aversion to certain herbs, sunlight, or crosses, a close examination is recommended for telltale bite marks, usually near the neck. A secondary agent is normally required to find the marks and to recognize the symptoms, as the victim is unable to see his or her own plight until it is too late.

In animals, attacks of anemia, accompanied by razor-sharp bites, can be indicative of the feasting of vampire bats. Cattle that suffer blood loss can, by tradition, be rescued by the use of the need-fire (see *Need-fire*). Humans can be saved through blood transfusions, bathing the wounds with holy water (a temporarily excruciating experience), and, of great importance, the removal of the vampire preying on the victim. It is possible to apply a red-hot iron bar with the holy water, although that is considered a dangerous procedure and is suggested only during an emergency. An excellent example of this was given in the film *Brides of Dracula* (1960), when Van Helsing (Peter Cushing) heals himself of a vampire attack. Garlic, strung about the patient's bed, has the double effect of additional protection and purification. The patients suffer nausea and discomfort during the described healing processes. (See *Protection from Vampires.*)

Animals The creatures of nature that have figured prominently in vampire lore throughout the world, sometimes in the control of the undead, sometimes becoming vampires themselves. According to the gypsies of Yugoslavia, virtually any creature can become a vampire, including horses, dogs, cats, sheep, and hens. The most feared were snakes, because of their ancient connection to Satan. The manner in which such transformations take place range from an animal serving as a victim to a vampire to the act of a dog or cat jumping over a corpse, at which time the soul of the deceased enters into the animal. Stories of vampire animals depict wolves, butterflies, birds, cats (such as those of Nabeshima), dogs (perhaps the Priculics), and the much maligned vampire bat.

Just as animals are feared, so too can they be used to combat vampires in a region. Horses are used in cemeteries to find the grave of an undead, and black dogs or even black crows are formidable vampire hunters. Romanian gypsies hold that cemeteries are patrolled by vampire-destroying white wolves. Finally, mention must be made of the supposed ability of vampires to transform themselves into animals. The Slavic tradition included cats, dogs, rats, fleas, birds, frogs, or insects. (See individual animals for details.)

Anthesteria A Greek festival held at Athens during ancient times in which it was believed that the dead returned to the city from Hades and wandered the streets. The Anthesteria was held in the month *Anthesterion* (February-March) was related to the god Dionysus, celebrating the maturing of the wine for the season and honoring the coming of spring. Throughout the joyous days the dead returned from the underworld to share in the festivities with their families, reminding them of the immortal nature of life. To placate those who might have been forgotten, the Athenians made offerings of food and drink, a gift of love as much as of fear. Nevertheless, there were spirits of a malign nature present, and to protect their houses from such evil, the Athenians chewed the leaves of the whitethorn and smeared tar on their doors. Such customs were continued by the Romans and involved the *lemuria;* they are demonstrated in such Christian festivals as All Souls' Day. (See *Greece.*)

Apollonius of Tyana A noted first-century (A.D.) philosopher and sophist, whose life was recorded in the famous *Life of Apollonius of Tyana,* by Philostratus. In the work (Book IV) was the tale of one of Apollonius' pupils, Menippus, who was saved from certain death at the hands of a female vampire species, the *empusa.* This story was the basis of the famed poem "Lamia," by Keats.

Appearance, Vampiric A clear and well-defined image, thanks in large measure to the creative talents of the Englishman Hamilton Deane, who adapted Bram Stoker's *Dracula* to the stage, and to Bela Lugosi, who performed the title role. Lugosi's costume defined the vampire, in some ways made it a caricature. Succeeding Draculas, such as those played by Christopher Lee and Frank Langella, helped to reinforce the image established by Lugosi. The male vampire is impeccably, if anachronistically, dressed in evening clothes. He is hypnotically and sensually attractive, has long white fangs (except in Lugosi's case), and becomes a monstrous creature when cornered or threatened. Female vampires are equally stereotyped: tall, deathly pale, dressed in white, irresistible, and sexually provocative, exhibiting symbols of danger and forbidden love.

The traditional folk vampires and the creatures of literature, however, are quite different and present a fascinating variety of types. The dread revenant of Europe was recognizable to villagers everywhere. It wore either its burial clothes or its shroud. Its stench from the dried blood of victims was almost as horrible as its hideous breath, described as the smell of a charnel house. Its visage was grotesque, its mouth covered with muck (like its taloned hands), but its razor-sharp, blood-smeared fangs were quite visible. Worst of all were the vampire's eyes, hypnotic, riveting, and glowing like red-hot coals, symbolizing the fact that the creature burned with a preternatural fire and a lust for blood.

In some cultures, however, the vampires were only partially human. The Chinese *kuang-shi* was covered with greenish fur, the African *adze* changed in form from a noble human to a twisted, humpbacked dwarf. Still other traditional vampires were not even remotely humanoid. Such were the cats of Nabeshima, the *bajang* of Malaysia, which was shaped like a pole cat, the killer butterflies of several locales, and not-so-deadly vampire watermelons of Yugoslavia. This last creature, coming out of Gypsy lore, perfectly demonstrates a truth about vampires in legend and literature: their appearance and powers cannot always be categorized.

Vampires can take the form of fruits, insects, chairs, houses, plants, and cars (as in Stephen King's *Christine*). The plants in H. G. Wells's "The Flowering of the Strange Orchid" and in Algernon Blackwood's "The Transfer" were both remarkably malevolent killers. There are, as well, those hungry vampires who have the characteristic of needing not flesh or blood, but the life energies of victims. Mary Wilkins-Freeman's "Luella Miller," Fritz Leiber's "Girl with the Hungry Eyes," and Harlan Ellison's "Try a Dull Knife" all depict such a fearsome being.

Apuleius, Lucius A second-century (A.D.) writer and Platonic philosopher, a native of North Africa, famed for his prose narrative work, *The Golden Ass*, called the *Metamorphoses* by the author. The story of a young man who undergoes various adventures and is turned into an ass by magic was based in part on the *Metamorphoses* by Lucius of Petrae, also considered largely biographical. Apuleius is cited as an early writer who recorded tales of vampires, including several in *The Golden Ass*. One of these is a story about Socrates, who becomes a virtual prisoner of a witch, Meroe. She pursues him after he tries to escape her powers, drawing out his blood with the aid of her sister witch, Panthia. Socrates' wound is staunched with a sponge, and he is seemingly healthy the next morning. While drinking at a stream, however, the sponge drops away from the wound and Socrates collapses, an emaciated victim of skin and bones. The tale is an excellent example of the link frequently made between witchcraft and vampirism. (See also *Ancient Vampires* and *Lamia*.)

Arabian Nights: See *Thousand and One Nights*.

Ardisson, Victor The so-called Vampire of Muy in southern France, who was arrested in 1901 for multiple illegal exhumations and violations of graves. Ardisson was unlike other notorious criminals who bore the nickname of "vampire" (such as John Haigh and Peter Kürten), as he was virtually nonviolent. He raided cemeteries purely to indulge in necrophilia on female corpses, often women he had known in life. His crimes and behavior were examined in detail by Dr. Alexis Epaulard, who in 1901 wrote a thesis on Ardisson. Ardisson was sentenced to an asylum. (See *Necrophilia.*)

Arges Castle: See *Castle Dracula.*

Armenia A region in eastern Asia Minor, a onetime Republic in the Soviet Union and an area of rich history and constant strife. Among the many stories told of vampires in Armenia, the most famous was that of Dakhanavar, who inhabited the mountains of Ultmish Altotem. The creature disliked having anyone violate his territory and hunted down those who tried to count the valleys nestled in the mountains, murdering them by sucking the blood from the soles of their feet. Two travelers outwitted him, however, by sleeping with their feet tucked under one another's heads. Unable to find the feet of either victim, Dakhanavar grumbled that he had journeyed through the 366 valleys of the mountains but had never come across anyone with two heads and no feet. With that the creature left the region.

Art There are many forms of artistic expression, some with strong commercial purpose, some with psychological intent, that illustrate the vampiric traditions. Such depictions played a major role in establishing the image of the undead in the contemporary social consciousness. Movie posters, book covers, comic books, and advertisements have all displayed vampires, especially Dracula, in lurid and sensational poses, with the intentions of attracting and terrifying the public. At the same time, however, such illustrations have reinforced widely accepted impressions of the genre, mainly the vampire's sensuality, strength, blood lust, or the many aversions common to such beings. Line drawings, etchings, and paintings have been used by publishers to heighten the atmosphere for these frightening tales and to attract readers visiting bookstores or perusing catalogs. Aubrey Beardsley's illustrations are considered superior examples of art accompanying books or stories. His drawings appeared in the *Pall Mall.* Readers of mass market or the so-called pulp paperback novels concerning the undead are quite familiar with lurid drawings or illustrations of a bloodsucker attacking its prey, a hand emerging out of a coffin, or a shadowy cloaked figure appearing just beyond the garden door, waiting to enter at the behest of its enthralled and eager victim.

A much more subtle artistic analysis of the vampire has been provided by painters who appreciate the psychological aspects of vampirism and its place in the historical contexts of various regions and peoples. Among the most notable vampire paintings are Etienne Csok's *The Vampires* (1907), Edvard Munch's study *The Resuscitated Corpse* in the Musée Wiertz, and Max Klinger's *Vampire Nightmare*.

Asanbosam A vampire found in Africa, known among the Ashanti of southern Ghana and by people in the areas of the Ivory Coast and Togo. The *asanbosam* (also *asanbonsam*) is believed to reside in deep forests, most often encountered there by hunters. It is of general human shape, with two exceptions: its teeth are made out of iron, and its legs have hooklike appendages. Anyone walking by the tree from which it dangles will be scooped up and killed. There are male, female, and small *asanbosams*. (See also *Africa*.)

Ash One of the trees commonly used in Europe for the creation of stakes required in the destruction of vampires. Ash trees were favored by the vampire hunters of northern Europe, especially in Russia and along the Baltic. According to the Roman writer Pliny the Elder, in his *Natural History*, all evil things feared ashwood. Ygdrasil, the tree upon which the world was founded (according to Norse myth), was an ash. The name was probably derived from the Norse *asha* (man) in the belief that Odin, the great god, used it to make humanity. (See *Stake, Wooden*.)

Asia: See entries concerning this vast region under the following countries and their related topics:

Borneo
Burma: See *Karens, Kephn*, and *Swawmx*.
China: See *Chang Kuei, Hsi-hsue-kuei, Iron, Jade, Kuang-shi*, and *P'o*.
India: See *Bhandara, Bhuta, Bhutastan, Brahmaparush, Chordewa, Churel, Jigarkhwar, Kali, Masan, Mmbyu, Pisacha, Pret, Rakshasa,* and *Vetala*.
Indonesia
Japan: See *Hannya*, and *Nabeshima, Cat of*.
Malaysia: See *Bajang, Bataks, Langsuir, Mati-anak, Pelesit, Penanggalan, Polong*, and *Pontianak*.
Mongolia
Nepal
Philippines: See *Aswang, Bebarlangs, Capiz*, and *Danag*.
Sumatra: See *Bataks*.
Tibet
(See also *Buddhism, Butterflies, Gods*, and *Vampire*.)

Aspen A tree found throughout Europe that was used especially during the Middle Ages for the creation of vampire-killing stakes. While other woods, such as the ash or oak, were favored in specific regions, the aspen, when available, was revered for its supposed power over evil. This belief was based largely on the tradition that the wood of Christ's cross was aspen. (See also *Cross; Crucifix;* and *Stake, Wooden.*)

Assier, Adolphe d' The author of the 1887 work *Posthumous Humanity,* which proposed the presence of an astral body as a means of explaining vampire attacks. Assier argued that the corpse of a vampire remained in its coffin while the astral form wandered and fed upon the living. The blood that it consumed was then converted to the actual body that remained in the ground through a form of spiritual diffusion. This idea has been developed in subsequent works. (See *Astral Body* and *Astral Planes.*)

Assyria The ancient Mesopotamian empire that is believed by some to be the birthplace (along with Babylon) of the original vampire traditions. (Others cite Egypt or India as the possible source.) The Assyrian tradition was considerable, stemming in part from the complex system that was in place concerning their hierarchy of spirits, particularly evil ones. There were several classes of Assyrian vampires, including the feared Seven Spirits, the *ekimmu,* and the *utukku.* The latter two were intertwined to some degree, their characteristics overlapping. It was in Assyria that the earliest writings on the undead were uncovered, including incantations and exorcisms. One of these, translated in the 1866 *Cuneiform Inscription of Western Asia,* states:

> The phantom, child of heaven,
> Which the gods remember,
> The Innin (hobgoblin) prince
> of the lords,
> The . . .
> Which produces painful fever
> The vampire which attacks man,
> The Uruku multifold
> Upon humanity,
> May they never seize him!

(See *Ancient Vampires* and *Babylonia.*)

Astral Body The name given by spiritualists or occultists to the so-called etheric body that serves as the vehicle of a person's life energy as compared to the physical body to which it is connected. At night, while one sleeps, it wanders the astral plane and is also supposedly a seat of the many desires and longings. As it survives long after the demise of the physical body, the astral body can linger on the material plane (in the world) for some time and can become a ghost, apparition, or, under rare circumstances, a vampire. There are said to be evil beings in the astral plane, capable of taking over someone's astral body and compelling him or her to evil acts akin to vampirism. Such beings can be drawn from the material plane and forced to serve a magician or sorcerer. (See *Magic*.)

Similar to this theory is the belief that a strong enough being from the astral plane is capable of entering a corpse and animating it. This created vampire then feeds the spirit within with blood. The noted supernaturalist Adolphe d'Assier had a differing view, arguing that vampires were actually astral beings that wandered about, drank blood, and then, by some unknown process, transferred the blood back to the body, which never left the coffin. The idea of spirits fit into the traditional Church declaration that vampires were either demons inhabiting a body or the spirit of an appropriately wicked person that had returned to endure the suffering of being an undead. (See *Blavatsky, Madame; Blood; Demonology; Doyle, Sir Arthur Conan;* and *Psychic Vampires*.)

Astral Planes: See *Astral Body*.

Aswang A vampire of the Philippines, believed always to be a female of considerable beauty by day and a fearsome flying fiend by night. The *aswang* lives in a house, can marry and rear children, and is seemingly a normal human during the daylight hours. At night, however, the creature is led to the houses of its victims by night birds, supposedly crying *Kikik!* (or *Kakak!*) as it flies. Its nourishment is always blood, and it feeds with its long, hollow, thin tongue inserted through the cracks in the roofs of its prey's houses. An *aswang* will feed especially on children, but not those who sleep at the edge of mats. It always preys on those who sleep in the middle and supposedly announces this as it enters the abode. The creature is recognized by its swollen appearance after feasting, so much so that it looks pregnant. Dawn marks the return of the *aswang* to its human form, possibly because of the sun or because it washes itself clean of the special ointment it uses each night to acquire its powers. If the *aswang* licks someone's shadow, that person will die soon after, and it is held to be very unlucky to see the *aswang* under the house. Garlic rubbed under the armpit acts as a repellent. (See also *Danag*.)

Athens: See *Greece*.

Australia The island continent in the Pacific, occupied in early prehistoric times by diverse aborigines, who believed in the survival of the soul after death and commonly accepted the wandering of the dead. There were also certain spirits in aboriginal lore that were to be feared, most notably the *mrart*, or ghost of a deceased member of the community or a stranger. The *mrart* was a vampirelike creature and was particularly powerful in the dark, often trying to drag victims away from a campsite. Aborigines also believed in a kind of second soul that could sometimes inhabit another person's body or could live in the bush and terrorize its living relatives. Corpses were weighted down in aboriginal burial rites, or their legs were broken. The possessions of the deceased were destroyed and his campsite abandoned. (See also *New Guinea.*)

Austria The European state long known for vampiric literature, due in part to the writings of Sheridan Le Fanu, who set his famous tale *Carmilla* (1871) in the region of Styria. There were also two cases of apparent vampire killings in the region. The first was that of Countess Elga (see *Elga, Countess*), reported in the September 1909 edition of the *Occult Review*. The other was in the late nineteenth century and involved a psychic vampire. A young girl's cruel and miserly uncle, Helleborus, had gained control of her rightful inheritance and declared in his will that he intended to leave her but a small sum. When the girl and her husband secured a lawyer, her uncle vowed revenge despite his deteriorating condition, caused by tuberculosis. The lawyer soon fell ill, and the uncle improved as the attorney's health failed. At the time of the lawyer's death, the uncle was robust and well. Soon after, however, with his source of strength gone, Helleborus had a relapse and died, his goal achieved. (See also *Bavaria* and *Germany.*)

Ayrer, Marcus Author of an early historical source on Vlad the Impaler, dated to 1488. His work is currently in the Landesbibliothek in Weimar. (See *Vlad the Impaler.*)

Aztecs: See *Mexico.*

Azzo, Count The main character of the anonymously written "The Mysterious Stranger" (1860). Known in full as Count Azzo von Klatka, he bore remarkable similarities to Count Dracula—as he resided in the Carpathian Mountains, chose women as his preferred victims, and even had power over wolves. He was described as "a man of about forty, tall and extremely thin. . . . There were contempt and sarcasm in the cold grey eyes, whose glance, however, was at times so piercing that no one could endure it long." (See *"Mysterious Stranger, The"* for details; see also *Dracula* and *Varney, Sir Francis.*)

Babylonia An ancient Mesopotamian empire centered on Babylon that overshadowed Assyria and flourished during the third millennium B.C. The Babylonians possessed a complex vampire tradition stemming from their multifaceted demonic and spirit hierarchies. The Sumerians, Babylon's earliest inhabitants, believed in three spirit classes: ghosts, semi- or half demons, and devils of the most fearsome nature. The Babylonians added to this gallery several types of vampires, the *utukku* and *ekimmu*, which, like their Assyrian counterparts, were intermingled and linked in legend. The *ekimmu* was greatly to be feared, however, for it was the spirit of an unburied person or someone who had died violently. It hunted mercilessly and was dislodged only by exorcism, usually in the form of threats. Babylonia is also notable for having produced the earliest depiction of vampires, found on a cylinder seal. (See also *Ancient Vampires.*)

Baital: See *Vetala.*

Bajang A demon vampire found in Malaysia, said to be a male (as compared with the female *langsuir*), appearing as a mewing pole cat and normally threatening children. The *bajang*, like the *langsuir*, can be enslaved and turned into a kind of familiar, or demonic servant, and is often handed down from one generation to the next, becoming a family heirloom. It is kept in a *tabong*, or vessel made of bamboo, closed by a stopper made from certain leaves, and protected by charms. While imprisoned, the *bajang* is fed eggs and milk and will turn on its owner if not provided with enough sustenance. The master of the *bajang* can send it out to inflict harm on his enemies, the victims soon suffering from a mysterious and fatal ailment. Wizards are usually the owners of the creatures.

Children were protected from the attacks of the *bajang* by amulets, and there were a number of prescribed methods for rooting out the user of the vampire. An old woman witch doctor was summoned to investigate, questioning a victim while he was in a state of delirium. Experts, called *pawang*, found the wizard in question by scraping an iron vessel with a razor in the belief that the criminal's hair would fall out. Frequently, people in villages were killed or driven away on suspicion of their guilt in such affairs. According to traditions, a *ba-*

jang came from the body of a stillborn child, compelled out of the corpse in which it was residing by incantations and spells. (See *Malaysia.*)

Balderston, John An American writer and playwright (d. 1954) who with Hamilton Deane was responsible for adapting *Dracula* (in 1927) to the American stage after its successful run in London. A journalist working in London for the *New York World,* Balderston was already a successful playwright, most notably for his *Berkeley Square,* a ghost story. His version of Deane's original play was quite different from the one that had been produced in England, with major changes in dialogue and structure. While initially reluctant to have a byline, fearing it would detract from his other work, Balderston eventually accepted co-billing with Deane. Later, Balderston participated in the negotiations that brought *Dracula* to the screen and was active as a screenwriter, working with John Hurlbut on the *Bride of Frankenstein* (1935).

Balkans: See *Albania, Bulgaria, Carpathians, Greece, Romania, Transylvania,* and *Yugoslavia.*

Baobhan-sith A Scottish bloodsucking fiend that normally disguised itself and lured unsuspecting men to their deaths. Considered part of the fairy lore of the British Isles, the *baobhan-sith* supposedly appeared in the shape of a lovely maiden dressed in green. One story, told in *The Anatomy of Puck* by K. M. Briggs, was about four hunters who took shelter for the night at a deserted shielding. To keep warm they began to dance, one of them providing mouth music. They were soon joined by four beautiful, golden-haired maidens in green, three of them dancing while the fourth joined the singer. This last man was horrified to see blood dripping from his friends, and he ran for his life, hiding with the horses until dawn. Returning to camp, he found his comrades dead, completely drained of blood. (See *Scotland.*)

Baron Vampyr, Der A novel written by Edwin Bauer and published in 1846 at Leipzig. It is notable because of the apparent influence of John Polidori's *The Vampire* (1819) and its creation at a time in Europe when the vampire was becoming a popular subject for writers and playwrights. It was described as a picture of contemporary culture. (See also *Literature.*)

Bas, Là A novel written in 1891 by J. K. Huysmans (1848–1907), translated as *Down There.* A fictional survey of the occult revival in France during the late nineteenth century, it presents several cases of vampirism, including the infamous Gilles de Rais and Sergeant Bertrand. The most compelling of his stories, however, was that of Madame Chantelouve, whom he termed a vampire. She was based on a real person, just as the character of Durtal was largely autobiographical. Madame Chantelouve, as well as her real-life model, had the capacity to feed upon the vitality of those around her, increasing her energy and strength while her victims sank into listlessness and then into an exhausted torpor. While Huysman's definition of vampirism was not highly technical, he captured the dread and the spirit of the predatory creature succinctly. (See *Psychic Vampires; Bertrand, Sergeant;* and *Gilles de Rais.*)

Bataks Known also as *battas,* a kind of witch doctor found in Sumatra, especially helpful in fighting the local species of vampire. They worked to reclaim the souls of those who had fallen under attack. As the soul departed a body threatened by a vampire, the person fell ill and wasted away. To return the soul to its rightful place, the *batak* used garlic, a soul-compelling herb, in certain prescribed supernatural rituals.

Bathory, Elizabeth Hungarian noblewoman (1560–1614) and member of the powerful Bathory family who became known as the "Bloody Countess" for her multiple murders and obsession with blood. Married to the warrior count Ferenz Nadasdy, Bathory spent many nights alone while her husband was fighting the Turks. She developed obsessive interests in her own beauty, in pleasure, in the occult, and in the most depraved kinds of sadism, which were normally manifested toward her serving girls, with whom she engaged in orgies before murdering them with the help of her lieutenants. Bathory became convinced that blood was a useful cosmetic and restorative when she hit a victim so hard that her blood splashed onto the countess's face and arms; when she washed off the blood she believed that her skin felt smoother and younger. Henceforth she drank, bathed, and showered in the blood of maidens, murdering hundreds of young girls who were brought into her service.

Exact figures on the number of her victims vary, but some accounts put the number at 610, others as few as 50. Inevitably, however, the truth became known, and in 1610 the countess and her henchmen were arrested, tried, and convicted. Her accomplices were executed or imprisoned, and Bathory was walled up in her bedroom at Castle Csejthe. Four years later the guards who attended her looked through the tiny slot used to provide her with food and discovered that she was dead. The "living vampire" was no more, although her memory was kept alive by legends and tales. Several films were made about her, including *Daughters of Darkness* (1970), *Countess Dracula* (1971), *Blood Castle* (1972), *Ceremonia Sangrienta* (1972), and *La Noche de Walpurgis* (1972). (See *Aging; Baths, Blood; Blood; Historical Vampires; Hematomania;* and *Sex and Love.*)

Baths, Blood A horrifying practice involving actual bathing or show-ering in human blood, tied to the belief that blood contained definite restorative powers and was especially beneficial for the skin. Bathing in blood found its most fiendish expression through the Hungarian countess Elizabeth Bathory in the early seventeenth century. (See *Bathory, Elizabeth.*) She was convinced that virgin's blood kept her young and drank it and sat in vats of it to rejuvenate her complexion. Maidens died horribly to provide her with this magical substance. Some were kept in cages suspended from the ceiling; the countess's henchmen used sharp points to draw blood from these young women so that Bathory could stand under the cages and be showered with the vital fluid. (See *Blood.*)

Bats: See *Vampire Bats.*

Baudelaire, Charles An influential French poet (1821–1867) who had a decisive effect on European literature in general and on the so-called Decadent Movement in particular. Much like his contempo-raries in the movement, Baudelaire was shaped by Edgar Allan Poe, with whom he identified and whose works he translated from 1852 to 1865. He, in turn, inspired numerous writers, who imitated his sensational and convention-challenging style. His one book of po-etry, *Les Fleurs du Mal* (1857, *Flowers of Evil*), was especially honored but was also condemned, leading to his conviction on obscenity charges. Six of the most offensive poems were cut, including two of his greatest works, "Le Vampire" ("The Vampire"), and "Les Meta-morphoses du Vampire" ("Metamorphoses of the Vampire"). The second work, about a dangerous seductress with a "strawberry mouth," popularized the image of the femme fatale in literature and marked the literary ascendancy of the vampire until the time of Bram Stoker and *Dracula* (1897).

> Meanwhile, from her red mouth the woman, in husky tones,
> Twisting her body like a serpent upon hot stones
> And straining her white breasts from their imprisonment,
> Let fall these words, as potent as a heavy scent:
> "My lips are moist and yielding, and I know the way
> To keep the antique demon of remorse at bay.
> All sorrows die upon my bosom. I can make
> Old men laugh happily as children for my sake.
> For him who sees me naked in my tresses, I
> Replace the sun, the moon, and all the stars of the sky!
> Believe me, learned sir, I am so deeply skilled
> That when I wind a lover in my soft arms, and yield
> My breasts like two ripe fruits for his devouring—both
> Shy and voluptuous, insatiable and loath—

Upon this bed that groans and sighs luxuriously
Even the impotent angels would be damned for me!"

When she had drained me of my very marrow, and cold
And weak, I turned to give her one more kiss—behold,
There at my side was nothing but a hideous
Putrescent thing, all faceless and exuding pus.
I closed my eyes and mercifully swooned till day:
And when I looked at morning for that beast of prey
Who seemed to have replenished her arteries from my own,
The wan, disjointed fragments of a skeleton
Wagged up and down in a new posture where she had lain;
Rattling with each convulsion like a weathervane
Or an old sign that creaks upon its bracket, right
Mournfully in the wind upon a winter's night.

> "Metamorphoses of the Vampire"
> Charles Baudelaire (1857)
> Translated by Edna St. Vincent Millay.

Bauer, Edwin: See *Baron Vampyr, Der.*

Bavaria A region in southern Germany, distinguished by the Bavarian Alps, the Bohemian Forest, and the Main and Danube rivers. The Bavarians developed a series of techniques for preventing the creation of vampires that were described by Mark Twain during his visit to Germany, including placing the dead in small huts for several days to ensure that they were not vampires (or, in a more enlightened fashion, that they were not victims of a catatonic fit). The most famous Bavarian revenant tale concerns the Specter of Kodom, a village in the region. A herdsman during his life, this vampirelike ghost began appearing to other villagers. Soon one of the villagers died, his passing blamed on the specter. Certain that still more persons would meet the same end, the Bavarians dug up the corpse and pinned it to the ground. The dead herdsman soon reappeared, however, suffocating several individuals. The body was then given to the local executioners. When stakes were driven into the corpse, it howled and threw up great quantities of blood. Amid screams and kicking, the executioner then burned the body in a field next to the cemetery. Only then did the revenant find peace. (See also *Germany.*)

Bebarlangs A tribe found in the Philippines that supposedly had members who practiced a kind of psychic vampirism. They had the capacity to send out their astral bodies to prey on fellow tribe members or on others. They fed not on blood, but on the vitality or life forces of individuals. (See *Philippines.*)

Becoming a Vampire

Methods by which a person can become an undead, as documented from traditions and customs of folklore.

Predispositions

Birth:
   Born at certain times of the year (new moon, holy days)
   Born with a red caul, with teeth, or with an extra nipple
   Born with excess hair, with a red birthmark, or with two hearts
Conceived on a holy day
Weaned too early
Suckled after weaning
Born the seventh son of a seventh son
Death without baptism
Received a curse
Mother did not eat enough salt during pregnancy
Mother stared at by a vampire while pregnant

Actions in Life Leading to Vampiric Transformation

Committing suicide
Practicing sorcery or witchcraft
Eating sheep killed by a wolf
Leading an immoral life, i.e., prostitutes, murderers, and treacherous
   barmaids
Saying a mass while in a state of mortal sin (for priests)
Being a werewolf

Death or After-Death Causes

Death at the hands of a vampire
Wind from the Russian Steppe blowing on the corpse
Having a cat or other animal jump or fly over the corpse
Having a shadow fall on the corpse
No burial or improper burial rites
Death by violence or murder
Murder that is unrevenged
Having a candle passed over the corpse
Having one's brother sleepwalk
Death by drowning
Stealing the ropes used to bury a corpse
Being buried face up in the grave (in parts of Romania)

Becoming a Vampire: See table.

Beheim, Michel A German troubadour or *meistersinger* (fl. mid–fifteenth century) who authored some of the first stories, in the form of a long poem, detailing the cruelties of Vlad Tepes (Vlad the Impaler) and his campaigns against the Ottoman Turks. Beheim was in the service of Emperor Frederick III of the Holy Roman Empire and the House of Hapsburg, writing his poem probably during the winter of 1463, when he and his master were residing at Wiener Neustadt. (See *Vlad Tepes* for details.)

Belgrade Vampire The name given to two different vampire cases that took place in Belgrade, Yugoslavia, nearly two centuries apart. The first incident was in 1732, recorded initially by Dr. Herbert Mayo in his noted 1851 work, *On the Truths Contained in Popular Superstitions.* The city and surrounding area of Belgrade were terrorized by a vampire who was responsible for several deaths and the creation of more of its kind. These other undead were destroyed, and when the coffin containing the vampire was uncovered, the body "leaned to one side, its skin was fresh and ruddy, the nails grown long and crooked, the mouth slobbered with blood from its last night's repast." A stake was driven into it, producing blood and screams. It was then burned to ashes. The "facts" of the case were attested to by three regimental surgeons, a sublieutenant, and a lieutenant colonel.

   The second case occurred in 1923. Residents of the city complained that a certain house on Bosanka Street, number 61, was haunted by a vampire. Damage was done to the house, and a procession was held within it in an attempt to expel the evil creature with holy water and prayers. Despite the intense beliefs of the locals, the haunting has been diagnosed more as a poltergeist infestation than as a vampiric one.

Bell Witch, the A famous American vampire case, so called because it involved a very malevolent spirit that terrorized the Bell family of North Carolina in the first half of the nineteenth century. The patriarch of the family was a planter who had in his employ a cruel and violent overseer with whom he quarreled incessantly. Their feud became so intense that Bell shot the overseer and was legally exonerated by a jury. A short time later the family crops failed, animals became sick, and Bell eventually went bankrupt. Moving to Tennessee did not help allay the attacks; they continued, including the disappearance of milk in the dairy herds. When the Bells moved to Mississippi, their condition worsened. The overseer reappeared, demanding the hand of Bell's daughter, Mary. When Bell refused to wed his daughter to the corpse, she wasted away and was also buried.

The assaults continued, although there is little documentation as to the final outcome.

Benson, E. F. An English writer (1867–1940) noted for his Lucia novels and horror tales, also deemed one of the foremost authors of the vampire short story in the early part of this century. His two most famous stories were "Mrs. Amsworth" (1923) and "The Room in the Tower" (1912), while two other excellent works, "Negotium Perambulans" (1923) and "And No Bird Sings" (1928), were less known and rarely in print. The former tells of an angel who takes revenge upon two men who have committed sacrilege, by adopting the shape of a horrid slug and sucking their blood. A similar monster type was repeated in "And No Bird Sings." This time the vampire is a sluglike creature of the earth. Benson's stories were collected into several anthologies: *The Room in the Tower* (1912), *Visible and Invisible* (1923), *Spook Stories* (1928), and *More Spook Stories* (1934).

I sprang out of bed, upsetting the small table that stood by it, and I heard my watch, candle, and matches clatter on to the floor. But for the moment there was no need of light, for a blinding flash leaped out of the clouds, and showed me that by my bed again hung the picture of Mrs. Stone. And instantly the room went into blackness again. But in that flash I saw another thing also, namely a figure that leaned over the end of my bed, watching me. It was dressed in some close-clinging white garment, spotted and stained with mould, and the face was that of the portrait.

Overhead the thunder cracked and roared, and when it ceased and the deathly stillness succeeded, I heard the rustle of movement coming nearer me, and, more horrible yet, perceived an odour of corruption and decay. And then a hand was laid on the side of my neck, and close beside my ear I heard quick-taken, eager breathing. Yet I knew that this thing, though it could be perceived by touch, by smell, by eye and by ear, was still not of this earth, but something that had passed out of body and had power to make itself manifest. Then a voice, already familiar to me, spoke.

"I knew you would come to the room in the tower," it said. "I have been long waiting for you. At last you have come. Tonight I shall feast; before long we shall feast together."

E. F. Benson
"The Room in the Tower"
(1912)

Berard, Cyprien: See *Lord Ruthven ou les Vampires.*

Bertrand, Sergeant An infamous criminal who was finally caught in 1849 in Paris after terrorizing the cemeteries in and around the city and earning the nickname "the Vampire." A military engineer of the 74th Regiment, Bertrand began breaking into cemeteries, desecrating tombs, exhuming bodies, and inflicting horrible mutilations upon them. Guards and caretakers spread hysteria by claiming to see shadows darting among the tombstones and declaring that the walls and iron gates should have been strong enough to keep out any mortal prowlers. Of significance, however, was the fact that when security and watches were intensified around a cemetery suffering attack, the "Vampire" moved to a new one. Bertrand was finally captured after being shot and leaving behind pieces of his uniform in his haste to escape. Traced to a military hospital, he was arrested, tried, and imprisoned for one year. His case was examined by Dr. Alexis Epaulard in his 1901 treatise on vampires. (See *Necrophilia.*)

Berwick Vampire A case of a wandering undead reported by the twelfth-century English historian William of Newburgh and taking place in the town of Berwick in the far northern area of England. A wealthy but supposedly evil man died and was buried, emerging soon after to roam the streets of the town. He apparently did not attack anyone, but his increasing state of decomposition caused a wave of panic that a plague would spread. Townsmen exhumed the corpse, which slept during the day, and cut it to pieces. (See also *Plague.*)

Bhandara Small shrines found in parts of India for the worship of a number of vampire species, particularly the *bhuta,* which are revered as virtual gods. The *bhandara* are intended to be places where the vampires can dwell and where sacrifices or oblations can be made to keep them placated. While varying markedly in shape, the shrines are designed to allow the creatures to rest without touching the ground, which they are forbidden to do because the earth is sacred. Flowers are placed at the shrine once a month. Some have cradles, perhaps hanging from ropes or chains, many with bell, knife, and a bowl of water placed within them. (See also *Bhutastan.*)

Bhut: See *Bhuta.*

Bhuta Also known as *bhut* or *bhuts,* a name that can designate in a broad sense all of the Indian vampires or malevolent spirits or signify a specific vampire species. The vampire type of *bhuta* is normally someone who suffered a violent death or died by accident, execution, or suicide. It could also represent a person who was not provided with proper funeral rites. The *bhuta* are found in cemeteries or in dark, desolate places, eating excreta or intestines. An attack by a *bhuta* can result in severe sickness or in death, although some of these creatures, such as the *bhuta* of Awadh, described as tall, white, and shining, prefer to play jokes or to impede the progress of travelers. To placate the *bhuta,* shrines called *bhandara* or *bhutastan* are built throughout India. Some sources consider the dangerous *rakshasa* to be a type of *bhuta.* (See *India.*)

Bhutastan Large temples found in parts of India, erected to honor several *bhutas* or one *bhuta* considered great or important enough to be worshiped by an entire village. Much more decorated and impressive than its smaller counterparts, the *bhandara,* the *bhutastan* customarily houses a bronze statue representing the *bhuta* residing within it. These shrines are also settings for festivals during which the vampires supposedly speak to the villagers through a dancer, who appears naked and painted in yellow, white, and red. Blood sacrifices are often made at the end of the ceremonies. (See *Bhandara* for details.)

Bibi A Gypsy being, long associated with cholera and death, honored one day a year by Gypsy tribes, particularly in the Balkans. According to the tales told of her, Bibi appears as a tall, barefoot, thin woman in a red dress and is accompanied by two small girls and two white lambs. When welcomed into a home she promises good fortune, but she curses those who reject her. Bibi strangles children, though their deaths appear to have been caused by cholera. She is one of several vampirelike women who act as vengeful spirits or are threats to children and their mothers. (See also *La Llorona, Weeping Woman,* and *White Lady, The.*)

Binding a Corpse The practice of tying the arms or legs of a corpse to prevent it from becoming a revenant and thus wandering. The exact methods of binding vary from place to place, depending upon local customs. The Finns tied the knees together, while others preferred to tie the feet. The practice of tying the mouth shut was also used in some regions. Others used coins, cotton, or garlic to prevent the deceased from biting or chewing. Such binding was not permanent, as knots could hinder the dead person's journey into the afterlife; the ropes were thus cut before burial. In Romania the ropes were buried nearby, and if they were ever used in black magic ceremonies after the burial, the corpse became one of a vampire species called the *strigoii.* (See *Becoming a Vampire, Burial,* and *Prevention.*)

Birds Animals sometimes associated with the undead because of their ability to fly or their predatory habits. The so-called vampire finches drink blood. As was true with virtually every animal, birds could become the servants of the undead or actual vampires themselves, depending upon the circumstances involved. Several species of vampire, the *aswang,* and *bruxsa,* for example, transformed themselves into large birds. (See also *Flying, Fowl,* and *Owls.*)

into a cult favorite despite its many obvious failings. Marshall, a respected actor, provided depth to the character of the vampire Mamuwalde by insisting on changes to the original script and story. An African prince (Marshall), traveling through nineteenth-century Europe to campaign against the slave trade, visits Count Dracula and is cruelly turned into a vampire. Locked into a coffin in Dracula's castle, Mamuwalde is eventually transported to modern Los Angeles and is accidentally released. He kills with regret, has sympathy for his victims, and commits suicide at the end of the film by walking onto a sunlit roof. *Scream, Blacula, Scream* was released in 1973 but was not as successful at the box office.

Blavatsky, Madame Helena Russian-born spiritualist (1831–1891) and cofounder with Colonel H. S. Olcott of the Theosophical Society (an occult philosophical-religious group). Her principal work, *Isis Unveiled* (1877), a two-volume compendium on theosophical lore, contains a story of a Russian vampire, supposedly reported by an eyewitness early in the century. A provincial governor, a jealous and cruel tyrant, forcibly wed a beautiful young girl, whom he routinely abused. Eventually falling ill, he made her swear that she would never remarry, promising to come back and do away with her if she did. After his death, she broke her promise and was betrothed to the man she had always loved. The governor, true to his word, returned to carry out his threat. Each night his risen corpse rode in a terrible black coach drawn by six black horses to her house. He would enter freely, the servants and guards either thrown aside by an electrical shock or placed under a hypnotic spell. The vampire then attacked his widow, draining her of blood and bringing her closer to death with every hideous visit. Desperate to save the woman, officials took the decisive step of exhuming the governor's body. The remains were found perfectly preserved and bloated with blood. The traditional method of staking was used, followed by an exorcism, and the young woman was saved. Blavatsky, in the same book, also examined the question of psychic vampirism, calling it "a kind of occult osmosis." She presented esoteric views for the origin of vampires on the earth as well.

Bloch, Robert Prolific American writer (b. 1917), one of the most respected in the field of horror, who has authored more than twenty works on vampires or similar creatures. He began as a student of H. P. Lovecraft, developing his reputation with stories that appeared in the magazine *Weird Tales:* "Nursemaid to Nightmares" (1942) and "The Bat Is My Brother" (1944). Other tales in other publications are "Dig That Crazy Grave" (1957), "The Cloak" (1939), and "The Living Dead" (1967). He also wrote the screenplays for the films *Asylum* and *The House That Dripped Blood*. The latter included the plot of "The Cloak," about a cape that transforms its wearer into a vampire. His best-known screenplay was for *Psycho*.

Blood A virtually universal food source for the undead, whether acquired by stealing it from blood banks, taking it from animals, or drawing it from the necks of helpless human victims. Blood has always been held to possess supernatural and mystical qualities, as it is the keeper and giver of life. To lose it, to have it taken away, signifies the irretrievable loss of vitality, essence, and strength. To receive it, through drinking or magical infusions, can restore lost power, heal mortal wounds, and grant eternal life. Little wonder that blood was the vital fluid for vampires. In fact, the association of the vampire with blood presents a complex union of ancient blood myths, death, immortality, and the very nature of human life.

A vampire's need for blood has been utilized to great effect by writers. In *Dracula* (1897), for example, Count Dracula begins as an old creature, turning gradually younger as the story progresses, thanks to the blood of the living. In modern novels the undead do not need to feed every day, and truly old vampires feast on mortals only to savor the taste or the pleasure of such a meal. Their spirits are now so strong that their blood is beyond the need for fortification from younger essences.

How does blood actually function in maintaining the vampire's existence? How is the transmutation to energy achieved? For how long must a vampire drink? How is blood associated with vampiric creations and transformations, and what alchemical events take place that allow for the conversion of blood into the traditional powers of vampires? Is vampirism a disease, a virus, a diabolical experiment gone wrong? Questions such as these, raised by philosophers, medical specialists, and spiritualists, have added a dimension of reality to the vampire over time, and the medical, physical, spiritual, and metaphysical implications of vampiric existence provide a certain luster to vampirology itself. These aspects of vampiric unlife link the creatures to the primordial questions of all human existence: the vampire appears to be the bridge between the physical and the spiritual world, between life and the grave, between death and immortality.

The mystique of blood is so powerful among the living, however, that it has produced some fascinating and disturbing social phenomena. The psychologist Ernest Jones, in his studies on dreams and the nightmare, noted that blood is one of the most important vital liquids, ranking with saliva and semen in the human unconsciousness. Throughout history, and even today, there are human beings suffering from definite needs to drink or to share blood. Deriving great psychological and sexual satisfaction from blood, such people often travel across the country, even across the world, in search of fellow blood drinkers. Among the famed historical vampires in this psychological field are Elizabeth Bathory and Gilles de Rais. While small in number, such persons epitomize the myths and the power of blood even into this era. (See also *Anemia* and *Porphyria.*)

Blood and Roses A 1960 French film originally called *Et Mourir de Plaisir* (*And Die of Pleasure*), known in its censored American release as *Blood and Roses,* directed by Roger Vadim and starring his wife, Annette Vadim, Mel Ferrer, and Elsa Martinelli. Based on Sheridan Le Fanu's story, "Carmilla," Vadim's work presented Carmilla as a woman possessed by the spirit of a vampire, placing the film in a setting of an Italian baronial estate. The lesbianism of the original, so blatant and increasingly graphic in subsequent projects, was introduced to the cinema in this work, with suggestive and surreal scenes. Two such episodes include an operation at the end of which Carmilla sees herself covered in blood, and a frozen moment as Carmilla kisses a drop of blood from the lips of her beautiful victim. (See *Karnstein, Carmilla* and *Films.*)

Blood Games The third in the series of novels about the aristocratic vampire Le Comte de Saint-Germain by Chelsea Quinn Yarbro, published in 1979. In this work the count finds himself in imperial Rome during the depraved and perilous era of Emperor Nero in the first century A.D. As with her other novels, Yarbro's careful attention to historical detail is impressive.

Blood Guilt A concept found in numerous cultures, in which revenge must be taken for the death of a relative or a loved one. The blood of the slain must be satisfied in this act of vengeance or the deceased will rise as a vampire. The relatives are also cursed, doomed to become vampires as well. These serve both as excellent incentives for revenge and retribution and as the basis for a new cycle of blood guilt instituted by the family of the next individual slain.

Bloodright The first of the pseudohistorical novels by Peter Tremayne involving Dracula and his family. Published in 1977 and known originally in England as *Dracula Unborn* and in the United States as *Bloodright: Memoirs of Mircea, Son to Dracula,* this is a fictionalized memoir of one of Dracula's male offspring who resists the efforts of his father and brother to bring him into their vampiric ranks. Subsequent novels were *The Revenge of Dracula* (1978) and *Dracula, My Love* (1980).

Blow Vampire A case reported in a village near Kadam, Bohemia, recorded in the book *Magia Posthuma,* by Charles Ferdinand de Schertz in 1706. A herdsman, Myslata of Blow, began appearing after his death, calling out the names of those he recognized in the district.

Perhaps from fright, these unfortunate individuals died a few days later, and it was deemed necessary to take the prescribed steps to rid the region of danger. The body of the Blow Vampire (also called the Blau Vampire) was exhumed, and a stake was pounded into its heart. That night, however, the vampire returned in a ghastly form, frightening several villagers to death and suffocating others. He laughed at his assailants, mocking and thanking them for providing him with a fine stick for beating off dogs. Desperate, the villagers gave the body to the executioner, who pierced it with several whitethorn stakes and burned it, all the while suffering the violent protests of the undead.

Blue Eyes A tradition found in regions of the Balkans and especially in areas of Greece held that persons with blue eyes would become vampires after death or were already members of the undead. The belief probably stemmed from the scarcity of blue-eyed people in that part of the world and was reflected in the suspicion shown to blue-eyed strangers and travelers from other lands. In Ireland, however, blue or gray-eyed people were said to be able to see ghosts. (See also *Red Hair.*)

Blutsauger A German name for the vampire, translated literally as "bloodsucker." (See *Germany.*)

Body Snatching The grisly practice of stealing or removing a corpse, usually a freshly buried one, for a variety of reasons, ranging from necrophilia to ransom demands, to the more common custom of selling the cadaver to a medical research institution. In the seventeenth to the nineteenth centuries, during which time the business flourished, body snatching was probably the cause of numerous cases of vampire hysteria, as the disappearance of corpses often took place soon after the deceased was interred.

The practice is believed to have originated in France, spreading elsewhere when it was learned how profitable the business could be. Medical schools, allowed to use very few corpses for teaching anatomy, kept themselves supplied with fresh bodies by purchasing corpses from body snatchers, known as "resurrection men." When the number of stolen corpses multiplied in England, guards were placed over new burial sites. Deprived of their usual sources, the "resurrection men" took to murdering people such as prostitutes and the sick to keep their customers happy. The most infamous case of this kind was recorded in 1827. Two men in Edinburgh, named Burke and Hare, killed guests in the latter's boardinghouse and then sold their bodies to Dr. Robert Knox. After they were caught, Burke was hung. Hare and Knox were spared by a legal technicality.

Bonfinius, Antonio A court historian (fl. mid–sixteenth century) to the Hungarian King Matthias II, who authored a very detailed version of the life of Vlad Tepes (Vlad the Impaler) in 1543. His account is particularly useful in preserving details about Vlad's last years and his death.

Borneo The largest Island of the Malay Archipelago and one of the biggest islands in the world. The vampire tradition of Borneo is largely the result of cultural diffusion from Malaysia, but there is an interesting variety of beliefs in some regions of the island concerning the body and the spirit. A corpse is allowed to rot and decompose to the point of total elimination of the flesh so that the soul, connected to the body, can develop into a fully formed spirit. This formation is believed to take place in direct proportion to the degree of decay taking place. As the process takes some time, the soul is homeless, wandering about and hovering near the sites of the living, to which it is naturally drawn. In this form the spirit poses a threat to those alive because it is capable of inflicting diseases. When the body is reduced to bones, the spirit, complete, no longer seeks the living.

Bottling a Vampire The most respected and powerful means of destroying vampires in Bulgaria, although it can be accomplished only by a well-trained sorcerer as it is dangerous and requires a powerful will, an experienced hand, and an excellent sense of balance. A sorcerer, armed with an icon (a holy picture or relic) and carrying a bottle, lies in wait for the local undead, ambushing it and then driving it across rooftops, through houses, and even up trees. No respite is granted by the determined magician, who forces the monster away from all shelter. Faced with the icon, the vampire is finally forced to enter the bottle, a favorite form of vampire food (in the case of the Bulgarian *ubour*, manure is recommended) having been inserted into the bottle as an additional lure. Once the vampire is inside, a cork is placed on the top of the bottle, which is sealed with a small piece of icon. The sorcerer then screams in victory, hurling the bottle into the middle of a roaring flame, thus accomplishing the vampire's final destruction. This supposed method of imprisonment is probably derived from the magical bottling of imps, demons, or the *jinn* (genies). A similar practice is used in Malaysia with the *bajang*. (See also *Magic.*)

Bradbury, Ray American writer (b. 1920), prolific in the fields of science fiction, horror, the unusual, and nostalgia. Many of his stories are now considered classics and have been collected into anthologies or made into films. His treatment of vampires has been marked as unique, capturing the grotesque while imbuing the characters with genuine pathos. Among his best in this genre are "The Crowd" (1943), "The Man Upstairs" (1947), "The Exiles" (1951), and the excellent "Pillar of Fire" (1948).

Brahmaparush A particularly cruel vampire species found in parts of northern India that enjoys consuming human beings. The creature drinks blood from the skull of the victim, eats the flesh from the skull, and dances with the body's intestines wrapped like a turban around its head. (See *India.*)

Bram Stoker's Dracula A major film, directed by Francis Ford Coppola and released by Columbia Pictures in 1992. *Bram Stoker's Dracula* is successful because of its superb special effects, of course, but also because of its courage in handling the very demanding themes of the original novel: the inherent sexual component; the redemptive power of love; the mystique of blood; the inevitable triumph of good over evil; and the struggle between the forces of light and darkness in every human soul. The cast includes Gary Oldman (Dracula), Anthony Hopkins (Van Helsing), Winona Ryder (Mina), Sadie Frost (Lucy), Keanu Reeves (Jonathan Harker), Richard E. Grant (Seward), Cary Elwes (Holmwood), and Bill Campbell (Quincey P. Morris). It marks the first time cinematically that every major character from the novel has been presented.

The association of the historical Vlad Tepes with the Dracula in the Stoker novel forms the focal point around which the movie revolves. From the opening sequence the audience sees that this Dracula once lived, and his subsequent rebirth as the King Vampire is the result of his conscious rejection of God after the death of his great love Elisabeta at the moment of his victory over the Turks. Flashbacks throughout the rest of the film serve as ominous reminders of the dark, hellish, and tragic past of the prince. As in the novel, the early scenes in the film are the most interesting and visually arresting. The aged Dracula moves through his ruined but once beautiful fortress in eerie scenes that render homage to F. W. Murnau's *Nosferatu* (1922) and Tod Browning's *Dracula* (1931); all the while Oldman makes the role hauntingly his own. Of particular note are the vampire women, the most riveting of *lamias,* who seduce and feast, albeit briefly, on Jonathan Harker before receiving an infant from their horrifying master.

Once Dracula reaches England, the plot moves subtly but successfully away from the novel. The prince and Mina meet and fall in love. Their tenderness contrasts sharply with the vampirization of Lucy (a grand performance by Frost). Leading the forces of good is, of course, Van Helsing, whose driven, often frenzied labors barely overcome the blood-link of Mina and her prince, a tie that extends back centuries, as Vlad has once more found his Elisabeta. Fun, campy at times, and a visual feast, *Bram Stoker's Dracula* will be ranked as one of the greatest interpretations of the 1897 masterpiece and a memorable contribution to the vampire cinema.

"Braut von Korinth, Die": See *Goethe.*

Brazil: See *Jaracca* and *Lobishomen.*

Bread, Blood The custom found in parts of Poland centuries ago, where bread was supposedly made from the blood of a vampire. Considered a powerful means of protecting one's family from attacks of the un-dead, the bread was made by gathering a small amount of blood from inside the coffin of a destroyed vampire, normally possible because of the great amounts of blood that were said to gush from the body. The liquid was then mixed with flour and baked into a kind of bread. Consuming it was said to make a person invulnerable to a vampire.

Breath, Vampire One of the traditional means of identifying a member of the undead. The breath of the vampire, particularly those found throughout Europe, is commonly held to be obscene, described most often as "reeking like a charnel house." The reasons for this are obvious, of course, as the vampire's diet consists mostly of blood (depending upon the species), and there is little incentive for the creatures to take measures to improve their hygiene or to brush their teeth. The vampire of fiction and films generally has unremarkable breath. Count Dracula, as described by Bram Stoker in *Dracula* (1897), possessed terrible breath.

Breslau Vampire A revenant that appeared in the city of Breslau, Poland, the onetime capital of Lower Silesia in 1591 to 1592, re-corded by the seventeenth-century writer, Henry More, in his *An Antidote to Atheism.* This particular case was a demonstration of the creation of vampires by suicide and improper burial. A shoemaker in Breslau killed himself by slitting his own throat. His wife, discovering the body, washed him and dressed the corpse in such a way as to be able to claim that he had died of apoplexy, avoiding the shame of suicide. He was thus given a Christian burial despite the rules for-bidding the religious interment of suicides. As weeks passed, how-ever, the shoemaker was seen, sometimes during the day and often at night. Parts of the city were thrown into panic by the revenant, who would appear at bedsides or in meeting places. At first the residents tried to pretend the terror was not real, but the violence of his attacks increased. The authorities exhumed the body, cut it up, burned the pieces, and dumped the ashes in the river.

Bride of the Isles: See *Vampire, The (Planché).*

Brides of Dracula The sequel to the very successful *Horror of Dracula* (1958) made by Hammer Films in 1960, it did not star Christopher Lee as Dracula. In *Brides of Dracula,* the evil count has been destroyed, but his followers are still around, in this case the vampire Baron Meinster (David Peel). His opponent is the redoubtable Van Helsing (Peter Cushing), and the title is derived from the baron's efforts to create a virtual harem of vampire brides, stalking his victims at a girls' academy. His plans are ruined by Van Helsing, whom he nearly kills (see *Anemia*). The climax involves a burning windmill turned to take the shape of a massive cross. The film was significant in its presentation of symbolic incest (Meinster kills his mother, making her a vampire), in the idea of vampires turning into bats, and in the continued presence of Van Helsing as a formidable foe of the undead.

Brittany: See *All Souls' Day.*

Browning, Tod American director (1882–1962) noted for his 1931 Universal film *Dracula.* Browning began as a circus clown and actor, turning to directing in 1917. While successful in mainstream films, he was most known for his work in horror, displaying an eye for the monstrous or the macabre that was considered daring, even shocking, in his time. Chief among his "grotesque" projects was the 1932 film *Freaks. London After Midnight* (1927), starring Lon Chaney, Sr., epitomized Browning's genuine talent for evoking atmosphere. Browning chose Chaney as the star of his *Dracula,* but Chaney died in 1930, before production, a loss from which Browning never recovered artistically. The *Mark of the Vampire* followed *Dracula* in 1935 but was not as profitable. His last film was the 1939 *Miracles for Sale.*

Bruxsa A feared female vampire species found in Portugal. The *bruxsa* exhibits many characteristics of the *aswang* of the Philippines. Normally transformed into vampiric form through witchcraft, she leaves her home at night and flies in the shape of a large bird. Tormenting travelers is one of her frequent activities, and much of her nourishment is taken from her own offspring, whose blood she drinks. There are no known ways to destroy the creature, the customary methods proving unsuccessful.

Buckinghamshire Vampire A case of a revenant that occurred in the English county of Buckinghamshire in 1196, reported by the chronicler William of Newburgh. In this case, the wandering dead man, while aggressive, was not particularly powerful. His attacks on his wife and family were easily repulsed, so he took to abusing household pets or nearby animals. Local villagers also saw him, however, some during the day. So alarming did his presence become that

Church authorities were summoned. The bishop, reluctant to burn the body, placed an absolution on the corpse instead, a measure that proved successful.

Buckthorn The common name given to trees (or shrubs) of the genus *rhamnus*, also called Christ's thorn. Branches of the buckthorn are said to be useful as means of keeping away evil and are hung throughout areas of Europe from the gates of houses. It was used by the ancient Greeks to protect homes from the wandering dead during the festival of Anthesteria and was thus later associated with safeguarding a residence from vampires.

Buddhism: See *China; Demonology; Gods, Vampire; Japan; Mongolia; Nepal;* and *Tibet.*

Bulgaria A country in the Balkans, the home of the *ubour,* an undead type distinguished by two chief characteristics. It possesses only one nostril and has a barb or sting at the end of its tongue. Vampirism in Bulgaria stems from a number of causes, including dying suddenly and violently, committing suicide, having a cat or another animal jump over a corpse, or having a person who, by force of will, refuses to depart his material existence. Signs of a developing vampire are a hole in the tombstone above the grave and severe bloating before burial. For forty days after interment, the Bulgarian creature remains bloated, composed of blood and a jellylike substance, a skeleton forming only after that period. After that time, however, it rises from the grave and appears as a normal person.

Its activities include the usual mischief (freeing cattle and throwing household items), but it is also cruel, choking people, tormenting the living, and smearing cow manure on everything. It eats dung and regular food and does not require blood from the living except when food is scarce. Protection from it can be obtained by placing a sunflower at the door of the house, by burning candles, and by building a fence around its grave. Destruction is generally the task of the so-called *vampirdzhija* (vampire killer), a sorcerer skilled in detecting and removing the threat to the community who makes good money for his services. The hole in the tombstone is filled with dirt and poisonous herbs, and the corpse is pierced to allow gases to escape. A ritual, actually a "second burial," can also be tried. The corpse is simply reburied. The most dramatic process of destruction is bottling, during which the vampire is forced into a bottle and then burned in a fire. Wolves can be used to discover the undead. (See *Magic* and *Witchcraft.*)

Bullets: See *Silver Bullets.*

Bunnicula A 1979 book for children, written by Deborah and James Howe, presenting the vampire rabbit, Bunnicula. His predatory habits are not quite traditional, as he sucks the juice from garden vegetables. Bunnicula returned in several sequels: *The Celery Stalks at Midnight* and *Nighty-Nightmare*. This charming creation is an excellent demonstration of the pervasive nature of the vampire/Dracula motif in contemporary society and the early age at which children are introduced to it.

Bürger, Gottfried German poet (1747–1794), a founder of the Romantic movement, who was one of the first great writers to introduce the vampire to literature and to examine the idea of the "demon lover" in his ballad "Lenore" (1773). A spectral romance, the work tells of a ghostly rider who arrives in the place of a maiden's long-lost lover, who had gone off to battle. She rides with him across a cruel, eerie landscape, lit by moonlight and lightning. Passing a host of specters, they arrive at a churchyard where the coming of dawn reveals that the rider is Death, a skeleton with scythe and hourglass, crumbling in the rays of the sun. "Lenore" was very influential with the Romantic movement but was not published in England until 1796. (See *Literature*.)

Burial: See following entries: *Becoming a Vampire; Binding a Corpse; Body Snatching; Candle; Carpet; Cemetery; Charnel House; Christianity; Coffin; Cremation; Earth; Embalming; Excommunication; Food Offerings; Hawthorn; Jumping over a Corpse; Knots; Necrophilia; Oil, Holy; Piercing a Corpse; Premature Burial; Preventing a Vampire; Prone Burial; Protection from Vampires; Roses; Seeds; Shrouds; Spikes; Stake, Wooden; Suicides; Thorns; Water, Holy; Wine; Wool;* and individual entries.

Burma: See *Karens, Kephn,* and *Swawmx.*

Butterflies An enormous and varied insect group comprising, with moths, the order *Lepidoptera*. Butterflies have been connected with death and the undead throughout the world. In parts of Asia, there was a tradition that vampires could assume the form of a butterfly, a belief probably stemming from stories about a species of moth in Malaysia that is a bloodsucker. In Japanese legend, the butterfly is a representative of good, the symbol of the souls of the dead. It is also a messenger of the underworld, carrying into the next life the spirits of the holy dead. Among the Slavs, and in the Balkans, the soul supposedly took material shape when departing the body, and one of its forms was the butterfly. The Serbian vampire could turn into a butterfly.

Byron, Lord Known in full as George Gordon Noel Byron, sixth Baron Byron, the English Romantic poet (1788–1824), considered one of the most influential of his era, the epitome of the Romantic movement. He is associated with vampiric literature through his writings and his dealings with Dr. John Polidori. In 1816 Byron traveled with Polidori to Italy, via Switzerland, meeting with Percy Bysshe Shelley in Geneva. It was during this visit from Byron that Mary Shelley created Frankenstein. Byron began a story as well, preserved only as a fragment of a novel. Three years later, in April 1819, the *New Monthly Magazine* published a story, "The Vampyre," under Byron's name. Byron denied authorship, and in the next issue Polidori declared that he was the true author, having based his tale on the story begun in Geneva. According to critics and contemporaries, the character of Lord Ruthven, the evil vampire in the work, was derived from the figure of Byron. The poet was thus a major contributor to the image of the vampire as it evolved in nineteenth-century literature, for "The Vampyre," along with "Varney the Vampire" (1845) and "Carmilla" (1872), gave shape to the appearance, nature, and concept of the literary undead (see *Gothic*). Aside from his fragmentary piece for a novel, Byron also composed the well-known poem "The Giaour," in 1813.

Cadet Buiteux, Vampire A French drama that opened in Paris in August 1820, written by the playwright Désaugiers. When published later that year, the libretto bore the motto *Vivent les morts!* ("Long Live the Dead!"). (See *Plays.*)

Calendar: See *All Souls' Day; Andrew, Feast of St.; Anthesteria; George, Feast of St.; Lemuria; Saturday; Season of the Dead;* and *Soul-cakes.*

Caligula Roman emperor (d. A.D. 41), known in full as Gaius Caligula (ruled A.D. 37–41), whose demented and cruel reign culminated in his assassination. According to whispered rumors that became legend, Caligula returned as a revenant, haunting the Lamia Gardens and the Esquiline Hill on which he was buried. Taken there after his murder, he was given a hasty half cremation and placed in a shallow grave. Although Caligula was later exhumed and cremated properly, stories were told that he wandered the gardens, and the hill acquired an evil reputation as a result. (See *Italy.*)

Callicantzaro A terrible creature found in Greece, linked to vampires and recorded by the sixteenth-century writer Leo Allatius. The *callicantzaro* (plural *callicantzari*) is a child born during the time of holiness between Christmas and Epiphany (perhaps even later), who must leave his or her family to live most of the year in the underworld. From Christmas to New Year's Day, however, the creature comes back to earth to terrorize people, especially hoping to devour its brothers and sisters. Its exact nature varies from region to region, changing according to village lore. It can be large or small, appearing most often with a black face, red eyes, ears like a donkey, and sharp fangs. Little relief is found in death, for it is known to return as a vampire. One method of saving a child from becoming a *callicantzaro* is to singe the toes and the feet. (See *Greece.*)

Calmet, Dom Augustine French cleric and theologian (1672–1757), noted for his prolific writings on the Bible and his famous treatise, *Traite sur les Apparition des Espirits, et sur les Vampires* (*Treatise on the Appearance of Spirits and on Vampires*), published in 1746. One of the earliest experts on the undead, this Benedictine monk taught at the Abbey of Moyen-Moutier and was largely responsible for disentangling the vampire from association with demons and demonology. He devoted a sizable portion of his work to the subject of the undead, which he had studied for years. In a commonsense fashion, Calmet defined vampires as "men who have been dead for some time . . . and these issue forth from their graves and come to disturb the living, whose blood they suck and drain," adding that if the hysteria of the undead was false, it should be exposed as a superstition. (See also *Allatius, Leo; Rohr, Philip;* and *Zopfius, Johann Heinrich.*)

Candle A source of illumination that has served traditionally as a powerful item used to ward off evil. While the light of the candle is not painful to the undead, it does represent, symbolically, the rays of the sun and is linked spiritually to the Light of Christ, hence its presence in Christian ceremonies, including exorcism. Throughout Slavic regions candles were placed in a grave to provide illumination to the deceased on its path into the next world. In Romania a candle was used along with a towel and a coin as one of the main preventatives against vampirism. (See *Preventing a Vampire.*)

Cannibalism Also known as anthropophagy, the practice of eating human flesh by other humans, deriving its name from the Spanish form of the language of the Carib Indians of the West Indies. Cannibalism is associated with vampirism in several ways. Among primitive cultures in Africa, Melanesia, Australia, New Zealand, North and South America, and Asia, it was pursued where meat animals were scarce. Cannibalism was commonly part of the rituals that followed battles, as well as an aspect of important ceremonies and the funerals of great warriors or chieftains. The practice was adopted in order to allow members of the community to partake of the vital essence, strength, or virtues of the victim being consumed. The ceremonial consumption of the dead is known as endocannibalism. Such eating was done with great respect and honored the deceased. Another, grosser form of cannibalism was practiced by deranged members of the civilized societies of the world, persons who murdered for various lunatic reasons. They often drank the blood of the corpses and then ate various parts. (See *Historical Vampires.*)

Capes More properly black capes, often with red lining, one of the most well-known and hence caricatured possessions of vampires on stage, screen, or in the popular imagination. The cape provides the important symbolism of wings, bat wings in particular, heightened by trimming the edges in the style adapted by the modern Batman. The image of the cape as part of a vampire's wardrobe did not play a major part in Bram Stoker's novel *Dracula* (1897) but was a conscious device instituted by Hamilton Deane, who brought the work to the stage for the first time in 1924. Deane recognized that the cape would provide a powerful visual impact on the audience. His decision was totally successful, and henceforth, the actors portraying Dracula made the cape an essential part of their costumes. Bela Lugosi first wore a cape on screen in the 1931 *Dracula* and was buried in it in 1956. (See also *Appearance, Vampiric.*)

Capiz A province in the Philippines in the northern region of Panay Island, considered the traditional home of the *mandurugo*.

Captain Kronos: Vampire Hunter A 1974 Hammer Films production, also known as *Kronos*, released by Paramount, starring Horst Janson in the title role, Wanda Ventham, and Caroline Munro (who also appeared in *Dracula A.D. 1972*). Directed by Brian Clemens of *Avengers* fame, this action-oriented vehicle, suffused with dark humor and atmosphere, follows the exploits of a trained vampire killer and his learned associate, a humpbacked expert on the undead. *Captain Kronos* mixes such concepts as the Karnsteins (see *Karnstein, Carmilla*) and energy draining, presenting vampires who suck the youth out of their victims rather than the traditional blood. (See *Films.*)

Caribbean: See *Loogaroo; South, American; Voodoo;* and *West Indies.*

"Carmilla" The 1872 novella or short story, written by the Irish author Sheridan Le Fanu and published originally in his collection of tales, *In a Glass Darkly.* "Carmilla" is one of the most significant vampire stories ever created and one of the seminal works in all of vampire literature. With its brilliant style, horrifying but subtle sensuality, daring use of vampiric lesbianism, and application of fresh Gothic atmosphere, it revised the structure of the undead tale, influencing countless other writers, including Bram Stoker, who acknowledged his own debt to Le Fanu in the writing of *Dracula* (1897). Le Fanu clearly researched the legends pertaining to the undead, using them not as inhibiting factors in his work, but as colorful, liberating devices to add authenticity and harsh elements of realism to his often super-natural, otherworldly passages. The character of Carmilla Karnstein remains the preeminent female vampire.

The story begins with reminiscences of the heroine, Laura, con-cerning her childhood, recalling the nightly visitations to her home in Styria of a woman who caused puncture wounds on her neck. Some twelve years later, Laura comes to the aid of a beautiful young lady who has survived a wagon wreck. Her name, she says, is Carmilla, the same woman of Laura's dreams, who also bears a striking resem-blance to a portrait of Countess Mircalla Karnstein in Laura's house, painted in 1698 (many years before). Laura and Carmilla are soon involved in a close relationship, Laura growing weak and exhausted with each passing day, enduring the torment every night of a phan-tom or a cat coming into her room. Her ultimate death is prevented by the arrival of a family friend, a general, who lost his own daughter to a woman named Millarca. It is soon apparent that Millarca, Mir-calla, and Carmilla are one and the same. Found in the ruins of the once proud castle of the Karnsteins, Carmilla is staked, decapitated, and cremated, her legacy described by Laura: "To this hour the image of Carmilla returns to memory with ambiguous alternations . . . and often from a reverie I have started, fancying I heard the light steps of Carmilla at the drawing room door." (See *Karnstein, Carmilla.*)

Carniola Vampire: See *Grando.*

Carpathians A large mountain chain in Central Europe, stretching into Poland, the former Czechoslovakia, the former Soviet Union, Hun-gary, and Romania. It is associated most closely with vampire lore in the region of Transylvania in modern Romania. The novel *Dracula* (1897), by Bram Stoker, was crucial in bringing the Carpathians (and Transylvania especially) to wide public attention, placing Castle Drac-ula there, accessible only by traversing high, jagged, and rugged roads and crossing the Borgo Pass, where the English real estate agent, Jonathan Harker, had his first encounter with the disguised Count Dracula. As presented by Stoker, the Carpathians are forbidding, gloomy, riddled by superstition, and the abode of one of the world's most horrible fiends: Dracula. (For a vampire case involving the Carpathians, see *Elga, Countess;* see also *"Mysterious Stranger, The."*)

Carpet An item used in parts of the Balkans and among some Slavic peoples as a preventive for vampirism during burial. Considered a form of corpse binding, the practice of wrapping a body in a carpet served to restrain the corpse and to restrict its movements, much as the tying of the legs or knees. Carpet wrapping was found in Bulgaria and Russia, perhaps stemming from Turkish or Asian influences. (See also *Binding a Corpse.*)

Carradine, John American-born actor (1906–1990), generally acknowledged to be a talented performer, who nevertheless appeared in some of the worst films ever made, particularly in the field of horror. Carradine was a Shakespearean-trained actor, displaying his genuine skills in such projects as *Stagecoach* (1939) and *The Grapes of Wrath* (1939). He first played Count Dracula in 1944, in the *House of Frankenstein,* substituting for the better-known Dracula, Bela Lugosi. Interestingly, with his height, thin appearance, and mustache, he more closely resembled Bram Stoker's original creation than anyone before him. The success of the *House of Frankenstein* led to the *House of Dracula* (1945), which was well received despite the poor quality of the film. While Carradine pulled out of *Abbott and Costello Meet Frankenstein* (1948), he returned to the role of Dracula on stage in the 1950s. A sign, perhaps, of things to come was provided during a performance in Detroit when the props and equipment failed, turning the production into a farce. After the final curtain, Carradine added to the hilarity of the audience by rising from his coffin and declaring: "If I'm alive, what am I doing here? On the other hand, if I'm dead, why do I have to wee-wee?" He often repeated this line in the henceforth appalling vampire films in which he took part: *Billy the Kid vs. Dracula* (1966), *Blood of Dracula's Castle* (1967), the Mexican *Las Vampiras* (*Vampire Girls,* 1967) and *La Señora Muerte* (*Madame Death,* 1968), and the terrible Filipino project, *Vampire Hookers* (1979). (See also *Films.*)

Carrot Seeds One of the grains used in parts of Europe as protection from vampires. They are either strewn in the grave or along the road to the cemetery in the belief that the undead must stop and count each one before proceeding. Variations on this idea include the belief that the seeds will be counted only one grain at a time or eaten one grain at a time, one per year. (See also *Seeds.*)

Castle Dracula An infamous residence of Vlad the Impaler (1431–1476), constructed near the Transylvanian border on a commanding hill to the north of the town of Curtea-de-Arges. Probably built in the fourteenth century and known by several names, including Castle Agrish and Castle Poenari, it passed through many hands until 1456, when its remains came to Vlad Dracula. Deciding to rebuild the fortress, he used slave labor to provide stones from the remains of another castle cross the Arges River. According to legend, thousands died in this enforced construction. After his death, the castle was used mainly as a prison, coming under the control of the Hungarians in the sixteenth century before being abandoned. Subject to numerous legends and folk tales, Castle Dracula influenced Bram Stoker, who chose it as his model for the home of Count Dracula in the novel, emphasizing its inaccessibility, loneliness, and ambiance of terror.

Catina, Ion Romanian playwright (fl. mid–nineteenth century) who authored a two-cat stage play on Vlad Tepes (Vlad the Impaler) in 1847. It was never produced because the play's content was deemed unsuitable by the government.

Cat of Nabeshima: See *Nabeshima, Cat of.*

Cats Animals long associated with the uncanny, the mysterious, witchcraft, and magic. During the Middle Ages and in the subsequent witch crazes of Europe, cats were viewed as direct links to evil, serving supposedly as familiars, or demonic servants. They were put on trial, tortured, and eventually executed by hanging for their participation in heresy and crime. Not surprisingly, the same environment of suspicion that surrounded them was revived with the vampire hysteria of the seventeenth and eighteenth centuries. Vampires could supposedly transform themselves into felines, and thus the animals were kept away from corpses lest they jump over them and transform the deceased into a revenant. In some parts of Europe a dead cat, stretched out at the bottom of a door, prevented a vampire from entering, presumably on the assumption that the same powers that gave life to a corpse could work in reverse.

Throughout Asia, the same interweaving of cats into vampire lore is evident. In Japan there were the cats of Nabeshima, while in China the same taboo about jumping animals was prevalent. There the tiger was also believed to possess what was known as soul-recalling hair. The *bajang* of Malaysia appeared as a mewing pole cat, while the *chordewa* of Bengal sent out her soul in the shape of a deadly black cat. Finally, victims of the *pelesit* cried out in delirium about cats. (See also *Animals* and *"Carmilla"*.)

Cattle Domesticated animals found virtually everywhere in Europe, largely defenseless and hence victims of vampire attacks, thus providing evidence of a local vampire infestation. Deaths in the cattle population through severe blood loss or anemia in the survivors could

convince ranchers that vampires were at work. A solution traditionally used was the need-fire, a ritual involving the running of herds
around flames. (See *Need-fire.*) Cattle are also susceptible to the feeding of vampire bats, whose presence is detectable by the amounts of
ammonia in their urine deposited after feeding. This kind of assault
was presented in the novel and film version of *Nightwing* by Martin
Cruz Smith. (See *Anemia, Animals,* and *Vampire Bats.*)

Caul The amnion of the embryo, or the amniotic membrane that sur-
rounds an unborn child. Folk beliefs about the caul varied around the
world. Some cultures believed that it was bad luck to be born with it;
others claimed it indicated good fortune. Cauls were sold from time
to time, especially to sailors, who claimed that wearing one provided
protection from drowning. In Romania a man who knew that he had
been born with a caul left instructions that after his death he should
be treated as a member of the undead. Among the Kashubes, a Slavic
tribe in the Ukraine, it was held that a red caul, caused by hemor-
rhages, indicated a predisposition to vampirism. To prevent this and
to provide protection from attack, the caul was preserved and dried
and eventually crumbled into the child's food.

Cemetery The abode of the dead, the name meaning a sleeping place.
Along with the dark, dank tombs, castles, and dismal swamps or
marshes, cemeteries are considered the most likely habitation of vampires. The vampire in film, curiously unaffected by the cross-shaped
tombstones clearly visible, is often depicted stalking through a deserted burial ground. This image became a virtually required element
in the productions of Universal Pictures in the 1930s and 1940s. (See
Detecting the Vampire.)

Chaldaea: See *Babylonia.*

Chaney, Lon An American actor (1883–1930) called the "Man of a
Thousand Faces," who became one of the greatest stars of the silent
screen. Known for his total devotion to a role, his grotesque makeup,
and his ability to twist his features into nearly unrecognizable shapes,
he created such memorable characters as the Phantom of the Opera
and the Hunchback of Notre Dame. His only appearance as a vampire
came in the 1927 *London After Midnight,* in which he played a police
inspector in the disguise of an undead. He was director Tod Browning's first choice to play Dracula for the screen, but Chaney's death
interfered, and the role went to Bela Lugosi. Based on his makeup in
London After Midnight, Chaney's interpretation of Dracula would have
been radically different from Lugosi's. His son, Lon Chaney, Jr.,
starred in *Son of Dracula* (1943). [See *Dracula (1931),* Film.]

Chang Kuei The victim in a Chinese vampire tale set in 1751, told in G. Willoughby-Meade's *Chinese Ghouls and Goblins* (1928). Chang Kuei was a courier bearing a message from Peking to the provinces. While passing through the region beyond Liang Hsiang, he encountered a severe storm. Fortunately he found a small hut inhabited by a young girl, who invited him inside and stabled his horse nearby. That night she admitted him to her bed, promising to waken him before dawn. When he finally did stir, it was many hours past sunrise. He found himself numb with cold, stretched out on a tomb, his horse tied to an adjoining tree. When interrogated by the local magistrate as to why he was late with the dispatch, he told of his terrible experience. The tomb was opened, and the body of the girl was discovered perfectly preserved. The authorities burned the corpse.

Charms Items worn to ward off evil or to bring good luck, or any action or recitation of a formula that casts magic or has a desired effect. Used against all things evil or against black magic, charms have also been weapons of protection against the undead. In Malaysia, the species of the *bajang* and *pelesit* were countered by drawings often worn by villagers. Children were shielded from the *bajang* by wearing an armband made of black silk. Among the Gypsies of Europe and India, charms were common, varying from simple tigers' teeth worn around the neck to holy water and iron rings set with pearls. Gypsies also wielded steel needles, used to stab a vampire in the stomach, thus causing it to dissolve. Socks stolen from a dead person were also considered powerful. (See also *Preventing a Vampire, Protection from Vampires,* and *Socks.*)

Charnas, Suzy McKee American feminist writer (b. 1931) who first earned notoriety with her science-fiction novel, *Walk to the End of the World* (1974), followed by *Motherlines* (1978). Aside from her vampirelike tale, "The Ancient Mind at Work" (1979), and the children's work, *The Silver Glove* (1988), she is most known for her book *The Vampire Tapestry* (1980), in which she created the memorable vampire Weyland.

Charnel House A place or structure set aside specifically for the bones of the dead, differing from cemeteries or churchyards in that it did not always require formal burials. With the exception of those charnel houses established as an abode for revered and holy monks or clerics, many such places were often dreary dumping grounds for lost souls, those outside of society or deemed unclean. In Russia, pits known as *ubogie doma* were used for the *inovercy* (unclean dead), a practice continued until the late eighteenth century and after that in secret. In Bavaria, huts were filled with recently deceased to ensure that they were dead and not in simple states of catalepsy or developing into vampires. Obviously charnel houses were foul-smelling, filthy breeding grounds for diseases, deemed the perfect homes for vampires, who relished the darkness, the general absence of Christian symbols, and the rarity of human visitation. Barbara Hambly in *Those Who Hunt the Night* (1988) staged a very memorable scene in the skeleton-filled catacombs beneath Paris, the home of an aged undead. (See also *Cemetery.*)

Chastelard: See *Swinburne, Algernon.*

Chetwynd-Hayes, Ronald English-born writer (b. 1919), author of numerous books and stories in the supernatural, horror, and science-fiction genres. *The Monster Club* (1975) is considered his best work, containing his well-known story "The Werewolf and the Vampire" (1975), touching upon the complicated nature of monster intermarriage. His other vampire tales include "The Door" (1973), "The Labyrinth" (1974), *The Partaker* (1980), *Dracula's Children* (1987), and *The House of Dracula* (1987).

Chiang-shi: See *Kuang-shi.*

Children With the exception of the aged or the infirm, the most defenseless of human victims, whose deaths are the saddest results of vampiric infestation. When returning from the grave as undead, they are also truly dreadful creatures, whose mercilessness is often tinged with a kind of poignant longing for their lost lives. Throughout the world, children are the preferred prey for many vampire species, particularly the risen forms of mothers who died in childbirth, or malevolent females. These types include the *aswang, civatateo, langsuir, penanggalan,* the White Lady, La Llorona, and witches everywhere. Vampire children are found most often where premature birth and stillbirth are greatly feared. The *mati-anak* (or *pontianak*) of Malaysia is the stillborn child of the *langsuir.* Among the Gypsies, if a child dies before baptism, it returns to suck from the breast of its mother and can be staved off by taking earth from the grave, placing it in a cloth, and sleeping with it under a pillow.

The most harrowing child vampires in fiction were created by Anne Rice (Claudia in *Interview with the Vampire,* 1975), Stephen King (the children on the bus in *'Salem's Lot,* 1975), and Manly Wade Wellman (the schoolboys in "School for the Unspeakable," 1937). A very effective segment was written by Bram Stoker in *Dracula,* in which the vampire Lucy hunts the young as the "Bloofer Lady." Children's culture today exhibits many examples of the presence of the vampire motif. The introduction is made at an early age: children watch the Count on Sesame Street, eat Count Chocula cereal, read the book *Bunnicula,* and dress up as Count Dracula on Halloween. They graduate to the well-known vampire films shown throughout the year on television and thus, even before reading *Drac-*

ula or any other novel, have acquired a definite understanding of what a vampire is and how it functions. (See also *Comic Books.*)

Children of Judas An evil clan of vampires found in Serbia, Bulgaria, and Romania, distinguished by their red hair. They are known mainly by oral traditions and are considered the worst of the Balkan undead, the spawn of Judas Iscariot, whose hair was supposedly red. The children of Judas possess the awful power of draining a victim with a single kiss or bite, leaving a scar in the shape of XXX, signifying the thirty pieces of silver given to Judas for betraying Christ. (See also *"Kiss of Judas, A."*)

China A country rich in legends, superstitions, and customs, often connected with Buddhist and Taoist lore. The name *kuang-shi* (or *chiang-shi*) was used to describe the most feared vampire type in China, a demon distinguished by its glaring red eyes and sharp fangs and talons. White or greenish white hair covered its body. This vampire sometimes had the ability to fly, to appear as a mist or vapor, and even to become invisible. Such species of undead could be created through a number of means, all of which were to be avoided strenuously. If the skeleton or the skull of a corpse remained undecayed, the *p'o* (or lower soul) could become a vampire. Animals could not be allowed to jump over a corpse, and direct sunlight or moonlight were to be kept away from a dead body because the rays were considered capable of infusing the corpse with a supply of *yang* (a positive force), thereby fortifying the lower soul, which then required human blood to keep the body incorrupt. Garlic, incense, and strong, pungent odors were used to protect individuals from attack, another similarity to European traditions.

Numerous tales abound concerning the Chinese vampires and ghosts. One of the best is of a temple haunting that supposedly took place in 1741. A shepherd, looking for somewhere to stay after tending his flock, asked permission to sleep in an old temple dedicated to three heroes. Although told by the local inhabitants that it was the abode of ghosts, he moved in anyway, gathering his sheep onto the veranda. Around midnight he heard a rustling under the pedestal of the three statues, and out of the ground arose a horrible creature, with eyes like lightning and a body covered in green fur. Attacking the creature with his whip, he discovered his weapon was useless. The shepherd barely escaped the monster's clutches, climbing a nearby tree and hanging on until dawn, when the fiend, seemingly unable to leave the temple, returned to the earth. The local magistrates, summoned by the shepherd, uncovered a large twisted body with green hair, which they burned, despite a putrid black vapor, the cracking of its bones, and the blood, which gushed forth from the remains. Two key sources on this and other legends from China are

G. Willoughby-Meade's *Chinese Ghouls and Goblins* (1928) and J. J. M. de Groot's *The Religious System of China* (1910). (See also *Asia, Hsi-hsue-kuei, K'uei, Nepal,* and *Tibet.*)

Chios Also Khios, a mountainous island in the Aegean Sea, held to be the birthplace of Homer. The inhabitants believed in the vampire species the *vrykolakas,* their views preserved by the native writer Leo Allatius. To prevent a corpse from becoming a *vrykolakas,* a cross of cotton or wax was placed on the lips of the deceased, and during the funeral the priest added a shard of pottery on which was inscribed "Jesus Christ conquers." It was said that the *vrykolakas* would issue from its grave and knock at doors, calling out the name of someone in the household. If a response was given, the person died the next day. As the *vrykolakas* never called twice, the people of Chios always waited for a repetition of their names before answering.

Chordewa A witch found among the Oraons, a hill tribe of Bengal, capable of turning her soul into a type of black vampire cat. In that form she found her way into the homes of the sick and dying, eating the person's food and licking their lips, thus dooming them. The *chordewa* in cat form could be identified by its peculiar mewing and the superhuman effort required to catch the creature. Any injury inflicted on the cat was immediately discovered on the witch as well, and should the cat be captured, the witch fell into a coma, remaining in that state until the feline was freed and able to reenter her body. Often, women suspected of being such a creature were burned.

"Christabel": See *Coleridge, Samuel Taylor.*

Christianity The main enemy of all evil, vampires included, which, ironically, helped to give shape to the European understanding of vampirism. As was the case with witchcraft, the Christian church considered vampires to be the creatures of the devil (the Greek church stressed that they were bodies inhabited by demons). Chief among the earliest Christian documents concerning vampires was the *Malleus Maleficarum,* published in 1485, which proclaimed that the devil used corpses to inflict grievous harm on mankind. In this tradition, and derived from the rapidly growing legends or customs of the dead, learned theologians authored pseudoscientific treatises, collecting hearsay, doctrine, and often pure fantasy into lengthy works that came to be accepted as fact. Church leaders, having fostered widespread hysteria, were seemingly the only officials capable of dealing with the crisis as terrified villagers turned to clerics to serve as their vampire hunters.

Other ways in which doctrine "created" members of the undead included baptism (unbaptized persons were believed to come back as revenants), excommunication, beliefs concerning suicide, burial requirements, heresy, and adherence to the sacraments. Failure to be good members of the Church caused a person to become a vampire. Fortunately, Christianity possessed the greatest weapons available against bloodsuckers: crosses or crucifixes, incense, the consecrated host, holy water, prayers, the mass, absolution for excommunicants, and the personal faith of ordained clerics. The eighteenth century, however, witnessed a gradual secularization of the war against the undead as local townspeople and villagers, familiar with the stories of the vampire, took matters into their own hands. While Christianity declined as the exclusive combatant of vampires, its weapons nevertheless remained intact, becoming essential elements of the symbolism of the entire field. The new kind of vampire hunter was made clear in Bram Stoker's *Dracula* (1897)—Dr. Abraham Van Helsing leads the forces of light as a man of science, spirituality, and conscience. He is not a servant of the Church, but a supporter of good in general. (See also *Allatius, Leo; Calmet, Dom Augustine; Davanzati, Giuseppe; Rohr, Philip;* and *Zopfius, Heinrich.*)

Churches Places of Christian worship important to the genre, as they are held to be sanctuaries where any living person is safe from vampire attack, their boundaries delineating holy ground. These churches are also filled with the most powerful weapons against the undead: the cross, holy water, and the consecrated host, as well as prayer books, the Bible, incense, and candles. Just as a consecrated church is impenetrable ground for vampires, a desecrated one is most appealing to the undead. Such a building serves like a magnet in attracting the fell creatures of the earth. The inherent risk of an evil being inhabiting a ruined church, however, is seen in the film *Taste the Blood of Dracula* (1969), when Dracula (played by Christopher Lee) is trapped and destroyed by the lingering spirit of goodness. Recent trends in films and literature have reexamined the long-standing idea of churches and sanctuaries. Anne Rice's vampire Lestat and his mother sleep beneath the altar in a church near Paris, and in *Nightlife,* the vampiress, played by Maryam d'Abo, enters sacred ground to the consternation of her compatriots. (See also *Excommunication.*)

Churel Also called *churail,* a vicious and vengeful ghostlike vampire found in India; normally a woman who died while pregnant during the Dewali Festival or while unclean at any time. The *churel* is horrible in appearance, possessing pendant breasts, sharp long teeth, thick ugly lips, unkempt hair, and a black tongue. She is also white in front and black behind. She hates life, saving her greatest spite for her relatives. Prevention is possible by burying her facedown or filling the grave with stones or thorns and strewing the ground where she died with mustard seeds. Prior to her burial, small nails are driven through her forefingers and thumbs, and her big toes are welded together with iron rings. Cremation is possible, but a ball of thread is burned with the body so that she will remain busy unwinding it and thus forget about her family. (See *India.*)

Civatateo A type of witch-vampire found among the Aztecs of Mexico, coming to the attention of the Europeans in the sixteenth century as a result of the Spanish Conquest. Said to be the servants of the gods Tezcatlipoca (a moon deity) and Tlazolteotl (also associated with the moon), the *civatateo* were also given the honorific title of *civapipiltin* (princess), as they were noblewomen who had died in childbirth. They supposedly returned to the earth to wander on broomsticks, haunting crossroads and holding a type of sabbat. Crossroads were consequently avoided at night, and great offerings of food were placed in shrines there to placate the creatures who otherwise might attack the living. Children were their favorite victims, dying horribly of a type of wasting disease. The *civatateo* were described as hideous, with white faces, their arms and hands covered in a white chalk called *ticitl,* crossbones painted upon their tattered dresses. (See *Mexico.*)

Coffin Known in the funeral business as a casket, the coffin probably came into use among primitive peoples as a means of protecting a corpse from being consumed by wild animals or as part of evolving mortuary practices, as in ancient Egypt. The coffin also accentuated the separation of the deceased from society. Lavish and ritualized entombment was conducted by the great civilizations of the ancient world, but it was only in the seventeenth century that coffins became common for all classes of society. The connection of vampires with their coffins is a vague one. Bram Stoker, in his 1897 novel *Dracula,* emphasized that the count had to return to one of his coffins filled with his native Transylvanian soil. This idea was soon adopted as a chief vampiric habit, reproduced in numerous films and writings and now part of the contemporary image of the undead. (See also *Earth.*)

Coin According to Greek and Roman custom, it was necessary for the deceased, traveling through the underworld, to cross the river Styx, reachable only by a ferry steered by the dread boatman, Charon. The coin was put into the mouth to pay for the trip. It was also believed to offer protection from evil, as it prevented a spirit from entering a body. This practice continued in Romania, where a coin was included in a grave, with a candle and a towel, to keep the body quiet in the earth.

Coleridge, Samuel Taylor English poet and philosopher (1772–1834), author of the poem "Christabel" (1797), and an associate of Southey and Wordsworth, with whom he published *Lyrical Ballads* (1798), the most important single work of the Romantic movement. It included the famed "Rime of the Ancient Mariner," which vampirologists such as Devendra P. Varma say exerted an influence on Bram Stoker in the portion of the novel *Dracula* (1897) recounting the count's journey to England by sea. In the writing of "Christabel," Coleridge may have relied upon the imagery of Gottfried Bürger's "Lenore" (1773). "Christabel" is richly decorated with a vampiric motif, presenting a young maiden whose energy and will are attacked by another beautiful maiden. It is ranked as one of the great early examples of vampire literature. (See *Literature.*)

Collins, Barnabas The main character of the television series "Dark Shadows" (1966–1971, 1990–1991) and its film version. Barnabas is one of the most popular figures in the world of vampires. As portrayed by the actor Jonathan Frid and, according to critics, less successfully in the new series by Ben Cross, the character was beloved for his charm, sadness, and immense pain, the result of being forced to live as a vampire. Barnabas earned a niche in the hearts of traditional viewers of daytime television. Originally intended to be a Gothic soap opera, "Dark Shadows" suffered from atrocious ratings until its creators decided to introduce a vampire to the sedate area of Collinsport, an undead tormented by a curse placed upon him centuries before and desperate to become a normal human being. Most of Barnabas's adventures in the series centered on his stay in Collinsport or on his efforts to be healed of his need for blood. After the program first went off the air, Barnabas's popularity continued through numerous novels, comic books, syndication of the show, and clubs. (See *"Dark Shadows"*; see also appendix 4 for a list of related clubs or societies.)

Comedy A form of entertainment that has united with the vampire genre, with some surprising successes and many stunning failures, particularly in the vampire cinema. Direct, intentional vampire comedies, with bloodsuckers as central parts of the plot, have proven immensely profitable and have resulted in several classics of the genre. The first of these comedies was *Abbott and Costello Meet Frankenstein* (1948), followed years later by segments in *Vault of Horror* (1973) and *The Magic Christian* (1969), finding fullest expression in *Dance of the Vampires* (1967) and *Love at First Bite* (1979). Sadly, the lowlights of vampire comedy far outnumber the high. In the 1980s, for example, there was a string of campy films assailed by critics who found them unworthy of both the undead and comedy, charging that they diluted the inherent dread of the vampire and the place of the vampire film as a legitimate horror art form. Among the worst of the vampire comedies were *Once Bitten* (1985), *Vamp* (1986; with Grace Jones), *My Best Friend Is a Vampire* (1987), *Vampires on Bikini Beach* (1988), and *Transylvania Twist* (1989; with Robert Vaughn).
Another form of vampire comedy is the use of subtle elements of black humor or even outright slapstick in a mainstream horror film,

book, or short story, which can be effective in relieving an audience's tension and can make the reader or viewer more responsive to the poignancies of a tale or to progressively more shocking and outrageous scenes. The first technique was used by Ronald Chetwynd-Hayes in his short story "The Vampire and the Werewolf" (1975), while the second technique was adopted in the films *Fright Night* (1985), *The Lost Boys* (1987), and *Fright Night II* (1990). Many films, of course, have been unintentionally humorous, starting out as regular horror projects but degenerating into stunningly awful spectacles. The acknowledged star of the unintended vampire comedy was John Carradine, who appeared in such memorable bombs as *Blood of Dracula's Castle* (1967), *Billy the Kid vs. Dracula* (1966), and *Vampire Hookers* (1970). Some international productions have achieved the same level of unintended humor, most notably the Mexican films featuring vampire-fighting wrestlers. Other recent vampire comedies include *Innocent Blood* (1992) and *Buffy the Vampire Slayer* (1992).

Comic Books The inevitable combining of film with literature, creating vampire characters and stories that have often gone well beyond the intentions of the original authors, according to some critics, to the detriment of the horror genre in general and the vampire world in particular. Bram Stoker's *Dracula* was first transferred to the illustrated form in 1953, with issue number twelve of *Eerie* by Avon Periodicals. There followed other vampire tales, but the Comics Code Authority of the 1950s found the material morally objectionable, banning the undead until 1962, when Dell, which did not adhere to the code, issued a new work on Dracula.

Among the companies engaging in publishing vampire comics were Dell, Marvel, DC, and NCG. They established a sizable variety of bloodsuckers, conspicuous for their irresistible charm or beauty, voluptuousness, excellent musculature, and frequent absence of clothing. Along with Dracula (who bears virtually no similarity to the Stoker original), other well-known vampires of the comics include Lilith—Daughter of Dracula, Satana—the Devil's Daughter, Morbius . . . the Living Vampire, and Vampirella. *Weird Tales* and *Tales from the Crypt* (EC Comics) both had vampire stories in illustrated form. One of the most memorable was "Midnight Mess," which appeared in a 1953 issue of *Tales from the Crypt* and in the film *Vault of Horror* (1973). The main character wanders accidentally into a nest of vampires, ending upside down with a spigot in his neck, while the undead exclaim as they fill their glasses with his blood: "Nothin' like the *real* stuff!" (See also *Films.*)

Conde Dracula, El A 1970 film, largely a Spanish production, directed by Jesus (Jess) Franco, starring Christopher Lee, Herbert Lom, and Klaus Kinski. Known in the United States as *Count Dracula*, in Germany as

Nachts, Wenn Dracula Erwacht (*Nights, When Dracula Awakes*), and in England as *Bram Stoker's Dracula,* this was intended to be the most ambitious and faithful adaptation of the 1897 novel *Dracula* ever filmed, with careful attention paid by Lee to his overall appearance and costume. While Lee portrays Dracula with both subtlety and control, the rest of the film is a disappointment. Its significance, however, is in its desire to adhere to the original story rather than mirror Hamilton Deane's play. (See *Films.*)

Consecrated Host: See *Host, Consecrated.*

Corpse: See *Becoming a Vampire, Body Snatching, Burial, Cannibalism, Detecting the Vampire, Excommunication, Exhumation, Preventing a Vampire,* and *Sacrifices.*

Corpse Binding: See *Binding a Corpse.*

Corpse Piercing: See *Piercing a Corpse.*

"Count Dracula" A 1978 British Television (BBC) adaptation of the novel *Dracula* (1897), seen as a miniseries and presented to the American television audience on public television stations. Starring the suave actor Louis Jourdan, it was distinguished by an excellent production and a high degree of faithfulness to the original material, containing even the grim scene of three women vampires feasting on the baby brought to them by Dracula. This segment was considered too shocking for the American public television audience and was cut from the U.S. version. (See *Films.*)

Countess Dracula A 1971 Hammer Films production featuring the notorious Countess Elizabeth Bathory (d. 1614), starring the well-known horror star Ingrid Pitt, with Nigel Green and a young Lesley-Anne Down, and directed by Peter Sasdy. The title is misleading, as the countess was not a vampire in the usual cinematic sense but was chosen to pander to an audience more familiar with Hammer's legitimate Dracula entries. *Countess Dracula* focused on Bathory's psychological obsession with blood, emphasizing her mental deterioration while interweaving metaphysical or supernatural facets concerning the power of blood to keep her youthful. One of the first projects to examine the "Bloody Countess," the film was unequal to the monstrous figure that it portrayed and was hampered by a poor script and production. (See also *Daughters of Darkness.*)

Count Yorga, Vampire A low-budget 1970 American International film, starring Robert Quarry and directed by Bob Kelljan. Supposedly made for as little as $20,000, *Count Yorga, Vampire* was very successful, shocking American audiences with its cruel ending, its violence beyond even the heights achieved by Hammer Films, and the representation of female vampires who are no longer serene, beautiful bloodsuckers, but slightly decayed ghouls more at home in a George Romero film. The production begins by following Yorga's coffin from a docked freighter to his new abode in Los Angeles. From there he descends upon an unsuspecting city. The count is remarkably anachronistic in his clothing and speech; nevertheless, his victims are unable to comprehend that he is precisely what he appears to be, a vampire. He is aided by the disbelief of the living despite the blood-drained bodies and disappearances. They turn too late to the traditional weapons against the undead. An even better-made sequel, *The Return of Count Yorga*, was released in 1971. (See *Films*.)

Crawford, F. Marion American writer (1854–1909), born in Italy, well known in vampire circles for his acclaimed story "For the Blood Is the Life" (1911) and his less known "The Screaming Skull" (1908). Crawford was also noted for his tale "The Upper Berth," not about the undead, but one of the most terrifying short stories ever written. He lived for years in India and was a Sanskrit scholar. *Wandering Ghosts*, published in 1911, included "For the Blood Is the Life" and six other tales, establishing, albeit posthumously, his place in horror literature. (See *Literature*.)

> The Thing seemed to be trying to climb to its feet, helping itself up by Holger's body while he stood upright, quite unconscious of it and apparently looking toward the tower, which is very picturesque when the moonlight falls upon it on that side.
> "Come along!" I shouted. "Don't stay there all night."
> It seemed to me that he moved reluctantly as he stepped from the mound, or else with difficulty. That was it. The Thing's arms were still around his waist, but its feet could not leave the grave. As he came slowly forward it was drawn and lengthened like a wreath of mist, thin and white, till I saw distinctly Holger shook himself, as a man does who feels a chill. At the same instant a little wail of pain came to me on the breeze—it might have been the cry of the small owl that lives among the rocks—and the misty presence floated swiftly back from Holger's advancing figure and lay once more at its length upon the mound.

> F. Marion Crawford
> "For the Blood Is the Life" (1911)

Cremation The burning of a corpse, hopefully to reduce it to ashes, the most extreme but successful method for destroying a vampire. Cremation as a weapon against the undead was often used as a last resort in Europe, a reluctance stemming from the teachings of the Church that bodies should not be burned and the belief that staking or, in some cases, the lifting of the ban of excommunication should be sufficient. Additionally, the actual process of cremation was a major undertaking, even for those with an executioner, proper materials, and a limitless supply of wood. Corpses require great temperatures, oxygen, and constant heat to be reduced to ashes, demands that villagers could not meet. Such conflagrations were rare in the ancient world and reserved for the highest classes; in India, the poorer classes simply dumped their dead in the Ganges.

When, as was recorded in many chronicles, stakings and prayers proved ineffective, cremations were applied. In Greece and Bulgaria they were often used when it was agreed that the deceased was a prime candidate for vampirism, serving then as a preventive. The details varied from place to place, some holding that the body should be cut to pieces first, others insisting that beheading take place or that the pieces be boiled in wine, oil, or holy water. Much importance was placed by the Russians in capturing and killing any animal or insect that emerged from the flames, for to fail in this would begin the cycle of death all over again. A compromise of sorts was reached by the Bulgarians, who combined the best aspects of staking and burning by pounding a red-hot stake into the heart. (See also *Destroying the Vampire, Fire,* and *Preventing a Vampire.*)

Crete A large island in the Mediterranean Sea, home of some of the world's oldest civilizations. Its vampire beliefs were largely formed through the influence of Greece, developing certain traditions about the species of vampires, the *vrykolakas,* that endured into the twentieth century. The Cretan vampire was created by persons who had led evil lives or especially those excommunicated before death. After their burial, their bodies were deemed inhabited by a demonic spirit, which then wandered about terrorizing the islanders during a forty-day period. It could be frightened away by gunfire, but after forty days the spirit was considered indestructible. Certain priests were summoned to lay the fiend to rest for a fee before the end of the forty days, using the recitation of prayers and commandments. Fortunately, this final demise of the *vrykolakas* brought an end as well to other vampires created by its bloody activities, setting off a chain reaction of annihilation. (See *Greece* and *Vrykolakas* for other details; see also *Katakhana.*)

Croatia Known in the Croatian as Hrvatska, a region in northwestern Yugoslavia, its historical capital at Zagreb, and comprising the areas of Slavonia, Dalmatia, and much of Istria. It has been influenced by the culture of the Balkans and the Adriatic, including Italy. This is seen in its vampire customs, particularly the various names found in

Croatia for the undead: *tenjac, vukodlak, kosac, prikosac,* and the Italian *lupi manari,* each with different Slavic or Italian origins and meanings. Croatian vampires were said to rise from the grave at night, attacking people in a district, especially those with whom they had quarreled in life, preferring to eat their hearts and intestines or to drink their blood. They were most often hunted during epidemics (see *Plague*) and could be identified by the sounds that they made at night, said to be similar to those of a donkey or a dog. They also made the *vresket* sound, a word translated properly as crying or shouting. Blackthorn stakes were weapons against them, but so too were most sharp objects, including axes, useful for decapitation. A priest, holding candles and sprinkling holy water, then said prayers over the grave. (See also *Yugoslavia.*)

Croglin Grange, Vampire of One of the most sensational and famous cases of undead attack, gaining considerable notoriety because of its plausible circumstances and its original appearance in the memoirs of Augustus Hare, *The Story of My Life* (published 1896–1900), as told to him by one Captain Fisher. Croglin Grange was an old family estate in Cumberland, England, owned by the Fisher family. After moving to Thorncombe, near Guildford, they rented the one-story house to a trio of two brothers and a sister. The siblings became quite popular in the district, enjoying their accommodations. One summer evening, however, the sister, having retired, could not sleep, as it was very warm. She chose instead to watch what was a beautiful night. Suddenly, she became aware of two lights moving among the trees between the lawn of the house and the churchyard. The two lights, she realized, were attached to some fearful creature that began walking across the grass to the house. Seized by an uncontrollable terror, she could only follow its terrifying progress, waiting for it to go around the house. When the creature seemed to turn, "she jumped out of bed and rushed to the door, but as she was unlocking it, she heard scratch, scratch, scratch upon the window and saw a hideous brown face with flaming eyes glaring at her." Hiding in her bed, she watched helplessly as the creature clawed its way into her room, grabbed her hair with its long, bony fingers, and sank its teeth into her neck.

Screaming at last, she summoned her brothers, who arrived after the monster had fled. It was pursued by one of the brothers until it disappeared into the churchyard wall. While her wound was healing, the family doctor recommended a trip to Switzerland. Before long, however, she dismissed the incident as the activity of an escaped lunatic and urged a return to the Grange. There all went well for several months, but on one March evening she awoke to the same dreadful scratching at the window. Looking out of the top windowpane, as the rest of the window was now always shuttered, she saw the same evil face and burning eyes. This time she screamed, and her well-armed brothers charged out the front door, shooting at the creature as it fled over the lawn. Confident that they had hit it in the leg, the brothers marched to the vaults of Croglin Grange, finding all but one of the coffins broken and mutilated. Inside the coffin was a hideous brown and mummified monster, its leg damaged by a pistol shot. The brothers burned the vampire.

Hare's account of the Fisher story has been attacked by critics as pure fantasy, the most outrageous of the many "tall tales" included in the memoirs. While no place called Croglin Grange has ever been located, the spot where the story supposedly took place is probably the very real Croglin Low Hall. (See also *England.*)

Cross A traditional weapon against the undead (and evil in all forms), differentiated from the crucifix by the fact that it does not have upon it the representation of the crucified Christ. It is still deemed generally powerful, however, and is the most common form of protective device, especially as improvisation can provide one quickly—in the form of two swords held in the cross insignia, candlesticks, arms, even taped tongue depressors. Crosses have been used in burial practices throughout Europe, hung outside of doors or at windows to block the entry of evil beings, and worn around the neck as a very personal amulet or shield.

It has been pointed out by vampire hunters of history, films, and literature, or by vampires themselves, that the strength of the cross rests not in its substance, but in the power it emanates, in its symbolism, magnified by the will and by the faith of the wielder. Without a firm belief in the triumph of good over evil, it will be effective only against the weakest of the undead. Truly formidable or ancient vampires have been known to throw crosses aside or burn or crush crosses held before them. Contemporary characters, in fact, such as Anne Rice's vampires or Whitley Strieber's Miriam Blaylock in *The Hunger*, are unaffected by crosses of any kind. Dracula is held at bay in many cinematic productions only by a consecrated host. Theoretically, any great symbols of good, especially relics, can be used against the undead; Stars of David, Buddhist prayer wheels, or Tibetan *yamas* are as potent as crosses. Questions remain, of course, as to whether a cross or Christian item would be efficacious against a Jewish or Chinese vampire. The perils of applying the wrong symbol were displayed in the comedy *Dance of the Vampires* (1967), in which a Jewish man returning from the dead stalks a young girl, who seeks safety behind a cross. Seeing it, he only laughs, commenting as he lunges for her neck: "Heh, have you got the wrong vampire!" (See also *Christianity, Churches, Garlic, Icon, Protection from Vampires,* and *Water, Holy.*)

Cross, Ben: See *"Dark Shadows"* and *Nightlife.*

Crossroads The juncture of two roads, so called because of the cross shape that is produced. Crossroads have long been held to be sites better avoided at night, the belief traditional in Europe, India, and among the Aztecs of Mexico. At such places, it was said, evil things lurked. Witches held their sabbats there, and ghosts often materialized. In England suicides were buried at crossroads, often with stakes in their hearts, as older customs proclaimed that the spirits of suicides haunted the crossroads until they could find peace through decent burial; the stake was used to keep them pinned in their graves. Among the Russians, the undead waited at crossroads, drinking the blood of the unsuspecting who chanced by. Similarly, in Ceylon, forms of female demons, including one who drank elephant blood, stood waiting in the gloom of the night at crossroads. On the positive side, vampires theoretically found the choice of four paths to be confusing, standing in the middle of the road pondering the proper direction until dawn, at which time they were forced to hurry back to their graves.

Crow A partially migratory black bird, similar to ravens, magpies, and jays. Because it is a predatory creature and a carrion eater, the crow is considered a harbinger of death, most notably in India. They are also viewed as opponents of the undead, a belief stemming from their carrion-eating habits. As is true with virtually all animals, however, they can be controlled by vampires or, according to Gypsy tradition, can become members of the ranks of the undead. (See also *Birds.*)

Crucifix One of the great symbols of good, a form of a cross but bearing upon it the form of the crucified Christ. While adhering to the basic characteristics of the simple cross, the crucifix is considered more powerful, hence more deadly to the undead, because of its heightened symbolism. The burns received by vampires from a crucifix are more severe. (See also *Christianity; Churches; Garlic; Host, Consecrated; Protection from Vampires;* and *Water, Holy.*)

Csejthe Castle A mountaintop fortress, located in Transylvania, overlooking the village of Csejthe. It was the residence of Countess Elizabeth Bathory (d. 1614), who used its dungeons and torture chambers to conduct orgies with and mutilations and murders of young girls. Fittingly, after her condemnation by a noble court in 1610, she was walled up in her bedroom at Csejthe, dying there four years later.

Cuntius, Johannes: See *Pentsch Vampire.*

Curse A verbal invocation or appeal for an injury, evil, or death to befall a person, place, or thing; also the state of having misfortunes placed upon an individual. Curses normally involve the intervention of God, the devil, or the casting of magic in intercessions. Curses are considered one of the main ways by which people become revenants.

Christianity has long practiced the most solemn form of curse imaginable, the excommunication, an act by which an individual is removed from the community and is denied participation in the sacraments of the Church. Excommunication forces the damned soul to remain in the body or to wander as a revenant or, even worse, to endure a tortured existence as a full-fledged vampire until absolution is granted. Curses are also used as weapons against the undead, working often in conjunction with charms. Romanian Gypsies, for example, destroyed vampires by declaring: "God send you burst!" (See also *Becoming a Vampire.*)

Cushing, Peter English actor (b. 1913) known to horror fans as the star or costar of some of the genre's best films. During the early 1960s and 1970s, he embodied Dr. Van Helsing, the great enemy of Dracula and his minions. Cushing worked for many years as a supporting actor, rising to prominence with Hammer Films in their successful *Curse of Frankenstein* (1957), teamed with Christopher Lee as the monster. The following year he played Van Helsing for the first time in the *Horror of Dracula* (1958), presenting the character as the complex man of spirit and science intended by Bram Stoker in the novel *Dracula* (1897). So well did he reprise the role in *Brides of Dracula* (1960) that the villain, the blond effete Baron Meinster (David Peel), was overshadowed throughout the picture. Cushing returned to vampire films in 1970 in *Incense for the Damned*, with Patrick Macnee, and the *Vampire Lovers*, part of Hammer's Karnstein Trilogy, with Ingrid Pitt. The next year saw *Twins of Evil*, where Cushing played Gustav Weil, the head of a band of Puritan witch-hunters. Returning at last to the role of Van Helsing, he was paired with Lee in *Dracula A.D. 1972* (1972) and *Satanic Rites of Dracula* (1974), neither film really doing justice to their stars. His most bizarre appearance as Van Helsing came in 1974's *Legend of the Seven Golden Vampires*, advertised as "the first King-Fu Horror Spectacular!" (See *Films.*)

Daggers Sharp weapons that served in some regions of Europe as devices against the undead. They were blessed and used to impale a suspected corpse or to hamstring it and thereby prevent its rising from the grave. (See also *Destroying the Vampire.*)

Dakhanavar: See *Armenia.*

Dalmatia: See *Croatia.*

Danag A Filipino vampire held to be very ancient as a species, responsible for having planted taro in the islands long ago. The *danag* worked with humans for many years, but the partnership ended one day when a human cut her finger and a *danag* sucked her wound, enjoying the taste so much that it drained her completely. (See *Philippines.*)

Dance of the Vampires A 1967 black comedy film, directed by Roman Polanski, ranked with *Love at First Bite* (1979) as one of the most entertaining satires of the vampire genre, despite its near total failure at the box office. Intended to be a pastiche of Hammer Films productions, and a parody of the vampire film in general, *Dance of the Vampires* fails to sustain humor throughout, but its successful moments, sumptuous details, and generally excellent performances make it more enjoyable and offer a more terrifying atmosphere than many serious projects. Its main characters are Professor Abronsius (Jack MacGowran) and his faithful but dim assistant, Alfred, who travel across Europe in search of vampires to destroy. While visiting a Transylvanian-like town, they develop suspicions that the undead are about, their fears confirmed when a young woman, Sarah (Sharon Tate), disappears. Going to the castle of Count Krolock (Ferdy Mayne), an obvious vampire, they undergo a series of adventures while attempting to rescue the damsel, including dancing at a ball at which vampires from many regions are in attendance. They barely escape over a snow-filled landscape, unknowingly transporting a vampire with them, an ending used in subsequent films. A legal battle developed between Polanski and his co-producer Martin Ransohoff over the American release, as the latter made cuts in the original, which was shown as *The Fearless Vampire Killers or: Pardon Me, But Your Teeth Are in My Neck* or, more commonly, *The Fearless Vampire Killers.* (See *Comedy, Cross,* and *Films.*)

Daniels, Les American writer best known for his series of novels about the vampire Don Sebastian de Villanueva: *The Black Castle* (1978), *The Silver Skull* (1979), *Citizen Vampire* (1981), and *Yellow Fog* (1986). In Don Sebastian, Daniels created one of the most evil figures in all of vampire literature. Much like the works of Anne Rice and Chelsea Quinn Yarbro, Daniels's writings are rich in historic detail, compensation for a villain who is utterly reprehensible.

Darkangel, The A fantasy science-fiction novel (1982) by Meredith Ann Pierce, set on the moon in the distant future. A blend of Gothic, fantastic, and fairy-tale elements ("Beauty and the Beast"), the novel tells of a vampire who finds itself on the moon, now with an atmosphere and inhabited by specially adapted human beings. Critically acclaimed, *The Darkangel* continued the successful integration of the vampire into the science-fiction genre. (See *Science Fiction.*)

Darkness It is in darkness that a vampire of contemporary imagination must function, residing in a dank subterranean place, a coffin, or a darkened house or castle. The legendary (folk) undead were not always rendered helpless or destroyed by light or sunshine. Russian and Polish vampires operated from noon until midnight, for example. Darkness, associated with the nightmare and the traditional time of evil, was usually the preferred time of vampiric attack. This concept, developed by writers, and especially by Bram Stoker in *Dracula* (1897), was transferred to the screen and became one of the main characteristics of the cinematic vampire. (See also *Sunlight.*)

"Dark Shadows" The most successful and beloved television series featuring a vampire, running on ABC from 1966 to 1971 and on NBC briefly from 1990 to 1991 as part of an intended revival. "Dark Shadows" first appeared in June 1966 on daytime television, as a Gothic-style soap opera, hampered initially by poor ratings. The producer, Dan Curtis, then introduced Barnabas Collins (played by Jonathan Frid), a 175-year-old vampire, and the public, largely schoolchildren and housewives, was riveted. The series focused on the Collins family, a wealthy clan in Collinsport, Maine, and their large estate on Widow's Hill, run by Elizabeth Collins Stoddard (Joan Bennett). Barnabas was awakened after a long period of slumber, finding himself in modern times. He became a mysterious member of the family, trying to discover a way to cure himself of his terrible affliction. Many episodes of the often complicated story line took place in historic (Colonial) Collinsport, explaining how Barnabas became a vampire. Other plot developments involved werewolves, a blond witch, and a warlock.

"Dark Shadows" went off the air in 1971, but the series was already honored by many fan clubs and societies. Its popularity was maintained by comic books, syndication, novels (featuring Barnabas and the werewolf, Quentin), video releases, and two feature films, *House of Dark Shadows* (1970) and *Night of Dark Shadows* (1971). In 1990 NBC attempted to bring back the characters in a new series. Barnabas was played by Ben Cross and Elizabeth by Jean Simmons. Additional cast members were Barbara Steele, Joanna Going, and Stefan Gerasch. While developing a small, devoted following, the new version suffered from low ratings and was canceled. (See appendix 4 for "Dark Shadows" clubs and associations.)

Daughters of Darkness A 1971 German-European film, known also as *Le Rouge aux Levres* (*The Lips of Red*), starring Delphine Seyrig, Daniele Ouimet, and John Karlen (originally of "Dark Shadows") and directed by Harry Kumel. A mainly intellectual and erotic examination of the famed Countess Elizabeth Bathory, *Daughters of Darkness* transports the countess into the twentieth century, presenting the ideas of blood, vampirism, lesbianism, and sadism in a work of Gothic expressionism. The countess (Seyrig) and her lover, Ilona (Andrea Rau), arrive at a deserted hotel in Ostend, encountering a honeymoon couple, Stefan (Karlen), a sadist, and Valerie (Ouimet). While Valerie becomes entranced by Elizabeth, Stefan accidentally kills Ilona. The couple is soon drawn into a relationship with the blond, death-white countess, who is recognized by a porter as having been a guest some forty years before. Valerie is the countess's true object, introduced to her vampiric world after sharing in Stefan's murder and in the drinking of his blood. The ending, in which the countess is hurled through a car window in a crash and impaled on a branch, is seemingly out of place in the otherwise dreamlike ambiance of the film. (See *Films.*)

Davanzati, Giusseppe Archbishop of Trani (1665–1755), respected theologian and the author of the well-known vampire treatise, *Dissertazione sopra I Vampiri* (1744), published at Naples. An Italian, Davanzati studied at the universities of Naples and Bologna, earning considerable notoriety for his genius and gaining the favor of several popes. He served as the papal representative to Emperor Charles VI and was then made an archbishop. His *Dissertazione* was compiled as a result of concern expressed in Rome (1738–1739) about the apparent outbreak of vampirism in the diocese of Olmütz. In the treatise, Davanzati accepted the long-standing view that vampires had their origin in the demonic, presenting the "factual" cases that had recently been studied in Germany from 1720 to 1739. His writings were the inspiration for the Italian opera *I Vampiri*, written by Silvestri di Palmi and performed in 1800. (See also *Christianity.*)

Dawn With the exception of vampires in Poland and Russia and certain other unique cases, dawn has always been the time at which the undead retire, the signal for their retreat being the crow of a cock. Any direct attack launched against a vampire, therefore, should be made after dawn, a rule frequently forgotten or broken by the vampire killers. In the cinema, daybreak has been used to great effect, with numerous films adopting the natural phenomenon to create a fiery climax. (See also *Sunlight* for an examination of the effects of the sun on vampires.)

Deane, Hamilton Irish actor, producer, and playwright (d. 1958) who was responsible for bringing Bram Stoker's *Dracula* (1897) to the stage, thus helping to create the public image of the vampire that has endured ever since. Deane worked for a time as a bank clerk before making his stage debut in 1899, a member of the Henry Irving Vacation Company. An acquaintance of Bram Stoker, he began looking for a way to adapt the novel to the stage. By 1920 he was the eminent owner of the Hamilton Deane Company but was unsuccessful in finding a writer to make the adaptation. Finally, in 1923, while ill, he himself penned the three-act play *Dracula*. The play opened in 1924 in Derby, proving a hit, with Deane taking the part of Abraham Van Helsing. Three years later the play moved to London and the same year was on its way to America. Now forever connected to the legendary count, Deane finally played the title role himself in 1939, giving his last performance as Dracula in 1941. He introduced the black cape and evening dress to the role and had a nurse at the theater to treat the fainthearted. [See *Dracula*, (*Deane*) for other details.]

Dearg-due Also *dearg-dul*, a dreaded creature of Ireland, whose name means "Red Blood Sucker." An ancient vampire dating perhaps to pre-Celtic or early-Celtic days, it is greatly feared. The only way to curb its predations is to pile stones upon any grave suspected of housing such a beast. The most famous tale of the *dearg-due* is the story of a beautiful woman supposedly buried in Waterford, in a small churchyard near Strongbow's Tree. Several times a year she rises from the earth, using her stunning appearance to lure men to their doom. (See also *Ireland*.)

Decapitation The removal of a human head, one of the more effective if grim ways of destroying a vampire. The use of decapitation in the battle against the undead stems probably from the belief that the vampire cannot exist without its head or its heart, being unable to regenerate either. Beheading is normally accomplished by wielding a sexton's blade, after giving warning that the stored-up blood in the corpse will literally explode everywhere. Reburial often includes specific steps to make certain that the head does not come in contact with the vampire's neck, to avoid reattachment. The *nachzehrer* is rendered permanently helpless by placing the head away from the body, separated by a wall of dirt. Lithuanians put the head at the body's feet; others stick it behind the buttocks. It should not be positioned near the arms or the vampire will return, holding its head in its arms. (See *Destroying the Vampire*.)

de Launay, Gabrielle One of the saddest and most romantic cases of a revenant, ending in a trial in Paris in 1760. Gabrielle de Launay was a beautiful young lady, the daughter of the president of the Tribunal of Toulouse. She desperately loved an officer, Maurice de Serres, but was forbidden to marry him by her father, who did not wish her to go to the Indies, where de Serres was being sent. Two years later word arrived that the officer had been killed. Convinced of her love's death, Gabrielle was persuaded to marry President du Bourg, a man thirty years her senior. Five years passed, and Gabrielle, never happy, finally died. At the same time, de Serres, who was not dead as reported, returned to Paris, where he learned of her passing. He bribed the sexton of St. Roch Cemetery, where she was buried, to allow him to view the body. Overcome with grief, de Serres suddenly seized the corpse and ran off, forcing the sexton to reinter an empty coffin and to keep silent, lest the authorities learn of his crime. Another five years passed, and du Bourg, who kept the anniversary of Gabrielle's death, was traveling through Paris when he spotted his dead wife. She drove away quickly, but he saw the coat of arms of de Serres upon her coach. Du Bourg undertook to prove that Gabrielle was alive, impersonating the spouse of de Serres, one Julie de Serres. His claim was proven by his small daughter, and the High Court ordered Gabrielle to return to her husband, declaring that she had not died but had been in a catatonic state. Du Bourg awaited his wife's arrival, watching in horror as she staggered into the mansion. She had taken a swift-acting poison, dying at his feet as she declared: "I restore to you what you have lost." At the same instant, de Serres killed himself.

De Masticatione Mortuorum The name given to two popular vampire treatises, translated roughly as *On the Masticating Dead*. They were written by Philip Rohr, published in 1679 at Leipzig, and by Michael Ranftius, published in 1728 also at Leipzig. Like the other pseudo-scientific works of the era, such as those by Calmet, Allatius, and Zopfius, the treatises did much to spread the vampire hysteria in the sixteenth century. (See also *Manducation*.)

Demon-Lover, The: See *Fortune, Dion.*

Demonology: See *Demons* and *Magic.*

Demons Evil beings who roam the earth and the various planes of existence, seeking to bring about misfortune, the fall of humanity, and the spread of chaos. Demons have been found in virtually all of the world's ancient civilizations or religious systems, including those of Hinduism, Buddhism, Greece, Rome, and Judaism. A most highly developed system of demonic belief was found among the Assyrians and Babylonians of Mesopotamia, out of which came one of the main links between demons and vampires. Much of Judaic and Christian demonology came from this ancient tradition. Vampires were ranked with demons as the chief agents of sin, a philosophy that became official Church doctrine in the Middle Ages. Devil worship, witch-craft, vampirism, and demonology were grouped together as evils to be purged by mankind. Many theologians, especially those in the Greek church, held that demons created vampires by entering and animating corpses. Just as women were tortured and burned as witches, so were corpses exhumed, examined, and likewise set on fire in an effort to rid the body of the infesting fiend. Vampires from all over the world are considered actual demons, including some of the many Asian species: *bhayankara, kuang-shi, langsuir,* and the *mmbyu.* (See also *Female Vampires, Incubus, Satan, Succubus,* and *Witchcraft.*)

Deneuve, Catherine: See *Hunger, The.*

Denmark Part of the widespread area of northern Europe where the be-lief in the *mara* prevailed. The *mara* (mare) generally represented the active terror of the night (the nightmare), an incubus or succubus, and an oppressive or crushing weight during the sleeping hours. Among the Danes it assumed certain specific characteristics. A female, vam-pirelike creature that adopted human form in the day, often marrying unsuspecting males who were soon strangled, the *mara* was very dan-gerous because of her ability to function on several levels of conscious-ness and unconsciousness. She could be seen and repulsed by stretching out a knife, pointed upward; when she descended the knife jabbed her, forcing her to flee. (See *Mara* for other details.)

de Rais, Gilles: See *Gilles de Rais.*

Derleth, August American writer (1909–1971), contributor of more than one hundred stories to the magazine *Weird Tales,* who made his debut at the age of seventeen with his "Bat's Belfry" (1926). An admirer of H. P. Lovecraft, in 1939 he founded the publishing com-pany Arkham House, devoted to fantasy literature and to the spread of Lovecraft's fame. Aside from his authoring novels about Wiscon-sin's Sac Prairie and detective stories, his reputation was based on horror, including numerous vampire tales. After premiering with his undead in "Bat's Belfry," Derleth continued writing for *Weird Tales,* often using the pseudonym Stephen Grendon, under which his best-known story, "The Drifting Snow," appeared in 1939. Other vam-piric works included "Those Who Seek" (1932), "The Satin Mask" (1936), "Keeper of the Key" (1951), and "The Occupant of the Crypt" (1966) with Mark Schorer. (See *Literature.*)

Dervishes Members of a Muslim religious body (*a tariqah*) that was established in the twelfth century. Often mendicant in behavior and life-style, dervishes were long credited with certain powers over evil spirits and the undead. In the Balkans they were called vampire killers by more gullible segments of the population, who were easily impressed by them and their equipment: rods with sharp points (*'shish*) or long sticks with a small ax at the top. As was true with other *vampirdzhija* (vampire hunters or killers), they could make good money destroying revenants troubling a village or district.

de Sade, Marquis Known in full as Donatien Alphonse François, comte de Sade, one of the most infamous libertines in history (1740–1814), whose life-style and writings spawned the word *sadism*. A French nobleman, he possessed an insatiable appetite for sexual perversion, earning imprisonment in Milan, Vincennes, the Bastille, and finally a lunatic asylum at Charenton. While incarcerated, de Sade authored novels that gave literary embodiment to his prodigious licentiousness. Among them were *Justine, ou les malheurs de la vertu* (*Justine, or the Misfortunes of Virtue*) and *Juliette*, both of which contained scenes of vampirism. In *Justine*, the comte de Gernade enjoys watching his victims bleed and other characters are quite vampiric, while in *Juliette* are to be found the Russian monster, Minski, a cannibal, and Cordelli, a necrophile. De Sade's twisted habits convinced many writers to include him on lists of living vampires of the past. He was also a figure in Les Daniels's novel *Citizen Vampire* (1981). (See also *France*.)

Desmodus rotundus: See *Vampire Bats*.

Desmodus rufus: See *Vampire Bats*.

Destroying the Vampire: See table.

Detecting the Vampire: See table.

"Devil Is Not Mocked, The" A short story published in the magazine *Unknown Worlds* in June 1943, written by Manly Wade Wellman. This work presents the events that might have surrounded the occupation by German soldiers of Castle Dracula in Transylvania during World War II. The main character, a general, is invited into the fortress by a pale figure dressed in black. His men are soon massacred by werewolves and vampires, the general dying at the hands of his host, who reveals himself as the historical Dracula. The story was the basis of an episode of the television horror anthology series "Night Gallery." A similar work, *The Keep* (1981), was written by F. Paul Wilson.

Dhampir The name given by the Slavonic Gypsies to the child of a vampire; a person possessing certain unique powers in combating his undead sires and relatives. The title and characteristics change from region to region. Traditionally, the male Gypsy vampire had an insatiable need to have sex with his widow, doing this before anything else. It was possible that his spouse could become pregnant, giving

Destroying the Vampire

Methods by which such creatures can be annihilated throughout the world, designed for specific species and to be used in any combination with care.

Common Methods

Staking: The most commonly used method in the world.

Beheading: Avoid splattering of blood.

Sunlight: Some aged and powerful vampires are immune.

Cremation: Found throughout the world; scatter the ashes.

Piercing with a sword: A blessed sword should be used.

Immersing in water: A bathtub can be used, but body disposal may prove a problem.

Drenching in garlic and holy water: Large amounts have to be hauled to the gravesite to assure a clean kill; oil, wine, or vinegar can also be used.

Touching with a crucifix: Destroys a young vampire but is normally used only as a repellent.

Trapping in the grave: Iron bits, red peas, rice (for Chinese species), roses, garlic, stones, and holy water can be used.

Extracting the heart: Can be very messy.

Less Common Methods

Stealing the left sock: Useful for only a few species; fill a sock with soil, grave dirt, or rocks, and throw outside of village limits, aiming for a river.

Injecting with holy water: Demands close proximity to vampire.

Magic: Use only a trained sorcerer.

Bottling: Hire a professional Malaysian or Bulgarian sorcerer.

Breaking the spine: Follow by decapitation or other methods.

Using a *dhampir*: Some *dhampirs* are disreputable and untrustworthy because of their vampire lineage.

Using animals: Cocks, dogs, and white wolves recommended.

Boiling the heart: Use in conjunction with heart extraction; vinegar, oil, or wine can be used.

Using Sabbatarians: Only if they wear their clothing in particular fashion.

Detecting the Vampire

Clues to the presence of the undead, particularly to large infestations of the creatures.

At the Grave or Cemetery

Finger-size holes
Disturbed earth
Constant mists
Disturbed coffins
Moved or fallen tombstones
Broken or fallen crosses
Footprints leading from grave
No birds singing
Dogs barking (or refusing to enter cemetery)
Geese screaming when near a suspected grave
Horses shying from grave
Groaning sounds heard from under the earth

Signs in Possible Victims

Sleeplessness
Nightmares
Anemia
Bite marks, usually on neck*
Exhaustion
Nervousness and irritability
Sleepwalking
Difficulty in breathing
No appetite
Weight loss
Aversion to garlic

Signs on a Corpse or in a Coffin or Tomb

Open eyes
Ruddy complexion
Fangs
Bloated body
New nails or long hair
Long, talonlike nails
Flexible limbs
Lack of decomposition
Blood around the mouth Blood in the coffin or tomb
Overly protective caretaker
Sense of impending doom about the corpse
Other similar corpses nearby
White liver (when examined)
Open mouth

Suspected Vampire's Appearance or Habits

Fangs
Red eyes
Long nails
Paleness
Reluctance to enter house without invitation
Hairy palms
Aversion to bright lights
No appetite
Never seen during day hours (not always true with some species)

Signs in Possible Victims	Suspected Vampire's Appearance or Habits
Strange dental growths	Possesses remarkable strength and dexterity
Photosensitivity	Has quiet footstep
	Possesses knowledge about botany, with a large collection of soil in house or in vicinity
	Resides in abode deemed evil by others
	Strange clothing habits
	Evidences enormous sexual appeal
	People who know him/her frequently die
	Rarely, if ever, discusses religion
	Really bad breath

* Note: Not all victims are bitten on the neck, as some vampires feed from the feet, between the breasts, over the heart, from the nipple, or between the eyes. Also, not all vampires need blood.

The Vampire Hunter's Kit

The following items should be procured by any prospective vampire slayer. Custom dictates that these be carried in a black bag or similar receptacle.

Stakes	Rope
Mallet	Saw
Mirror	Crowbar
Cross	Pistol
Garlic	Flashlight
Holy wafer (optional)	Neck brace or iron collar (optional)
Holy water	
Knives	

birth. The offspring was often called a *dhampir* but was also known to other Gypsy groups as the *vampir* (if male), *vampuiera* (if female), *vampijerovic,* or *lampijerovic.* Some believed that the child was always a male; others claimed that it was short-lived because of a jellylike body, or that it could not come from the family of an Orthodox or Muslim cleric, or that it was a normal human.

Dhampirs were very effective in detecting and destroying their vampiric families. They were found in Serbia and elsewhere in parts of Yugoslavia, many making comfortable livings as vampire hunters. Only they could see the bloodsuckers (Serbian undead being invisible), and they performed bizarre rituals, whistling, running about, undressing, and using shirtsleeves as a kind of telescope. Wrestling furiously with an invisible foe, the *dhampir* finally declared dramatically that the feared vampire was dead. A large fee was then collected. The last known *dhampir* ceremony was held in 1959 in the Yugoslavian province of Kosovo. (See also *Silver Bullets.*)

Diphylla ecaudata: See *Vampire Bats.*

Dirt: See *Earth.*

Dissertatio de Vampyris Also *Dissertatio de Vampiris,* a pseudoscientific treatise by Johann Heinrich Zopfius and the lesser-known Francis von Dalen, translated as *Dissertation on the Vampire* and published in 1733. It was one of the more popular and authoritative treatises on the undead of the eighteenth century, containing the now famous declaration:

> The vampires, which issue forth from their graves at night, rush upon people sleeping in their beds, suck their blood and destroy them. They attack men, women and children, sparing neither age nor sex. People attacked by them complain of suffocation and a great interception of spirits; after which they soon die. . . . Those who are killed by them, after death, become vampires. . . .

Dog, Fetch A natal spirit that was believed to follow and aid a Sabbatarian, a person born on Saturday, throughout his or her life, empowering them to cure disease and to have great success in fighting the undead, particularly the *vrykolakas* of Greece. Its name was derived from the preferred shape that the spirit (fetch) adopted, although the Icelandic fetch (the *fylgja*) could also appear as a bird, horse, wolf, bear, or dragon. According to custom, while fighting the *vrykolakas,* the Sabbatarian became invisible to everyone except the little dog.

Dogrose A wild rose (species *Rosa canina*) found in parts of Europe and Asia, with thorns and white or pink flowers. As was true with most varieties of rose, the dogrose was used as a preventive to vampirism.

The Wallachians placed its vines in the grave or coffin, its thorns clinging to the corpse's shroud. Thus pinned, the body was supposedly unable to rise. (See also *Roses.*)

Dogs Animals that have been counted both among the servants and the enemies of the undead; ranked with other species, particularly cats, as creatures to be kept away from a recently deceased person as they might jump over the corpse and thus create a revenant. The vampire is able to transform itself into a dog, often a big, black one, and can control hounds as part of its power over animals. Additionally, it is held that dogs themselves may become vampiric beings. The 1978 film *Dracula's Dog,* starring Jose Ferrer, Reggie Nalder, and Michael Pataki, presents the idea of the count having a loyal pet; at the end a vampire puppy is loose in the woods. On the other hand, among the Gypsies, it was held that black dogs were opponents of vampires. The hounds were highly capable of detecting the presence of the undead, attacking them with success.

Dolphin, Dr. David A professor of chemistry at the University of British Columbia, who in 1985 presented a theory that the victims of the disease porphyria during the Middle Ages may have been responsible for the spread of the vampire legend and hysteria. Their symptoms, Dolphin argued, made them appear like the undead, with their photosensitivity, aversion to garlic, hairiness, and elongated teeth. They supposedly took to drinking blood in the desperate effort to alleviate their suffering from the terrible disease by introducing its required elements (heme) into their systems. Covered by the press with headlines that were both sensational and partly comical, the hypothesis created a major stir in the medical field, particularly among the physicians involved in treating porphyria and its victims. Numerous experts attacked Dolphin's hypothesis, either pointing out the flaws in his reasoning or complaining about the negative publicity generated by the controversy, as well as the unfortunate perpetuation of traditions and legends. (For other details, see *Porphyria.*)

Doppelsauger: See *Dubbelsüger.*

Doyle, Sir Arthur Conan Scottish-born writer (1859–1930), world famous for his literary creation Sherlock Holmes. A graduate of the University of Edinburgh, he practiced medicine until 1891, by which time Holmes had made his appearance (in the 1886 *A Study in Scarlet*) and was solving cases in the *Strand* magazine on a regular basis. The only case in which Holmes investigated an apparent vampire was "The Adventure of the Sussex Vampire," although other writers invented several works in which the detective encountered Count Dracula. Interested greatly in the paranormal and in the supernatural, Conan Doyle also wrote two vampire tales: "John Barrinton Cowles" (appearing in an 1894 collection of works) and the more well-known "The Parasite" (1891). (See also *Literature.*)

Dracula The name of both the Transylvanian ruler Vlad Tepes (Vlad the Impaler) and the infamous vampire of the 1897 novel by Bram Stoker. Dracula was based on the title Dracul, given to Vlad's father, Vlad II, meaning the "Devil" or the "Dragon." (Dracula means simply "Son of Dracul." Its more proper spelling is Draculea.) Dracul was used to describe Vlad II's activities, although there are two historical views as to why it was adopted in popular usage. The first argues that the enemies of Vlad used the term to mean "Devil," thus associating him with evil and diabolism. Another theory postulates that the name came from Vlad's dragon-stamped currency and his membership in the Order of the Dragon, which included the wearing of the dragon symbol on his clothing and on his banners. His son, Vlad III, who became known locally as Tepes, the "Impaler," apparently earned the name by being his father's son and not for any conspicuous crimes. Dracula as a name was probably not used locally, as it did not appear on documents intended for Romanian consumption, even though Dracula was Vlad's preferred signature, Dracul having potentially evil connotations among his people. The name was expedited by foreigners, such as the Venetians, who knew Vlad as Dragulia, in an effort to attach his name to cruelty and wickedness. Virtually forgotten by the West, Vlad came to the attention of Bram Stoker, who was researching Romanian legends for his novel. He found the name perfectly suited his vampire, given the ruler's reputation for bloodthirstiness. There is, however, no link in Romanian folklore between Vlad and vampirism. (See *Vlad Tepes.*)

Dracula The character Count Dracula, as he is portrayed in films. Some critics have argued that Bram Stoker would be horrified at many of the films supposedly based on his renowned 1897 novel. Nevertheless, Dracula has proven remarkably durable in cinematic history, changing radically over the years and assuming varied incarnations. Unfortunately, the count, as he appeared in the novel, has not been presented definitively in film, although a number of efforts have been made to do so, most notably *El Conde Dracula* (1970), starring Christopher Lee, and *Bram Stoker's Dracula* (1992). The character has been based rather on the Hamilton Deane–John Balderston play, although the first known version of *Dracula* was the 1922 *Nosferatu* by F. W. Murnau. Of great influence was the 1931 Universal release *Dracula*, starring Bela Lugosi, an actor who became the most famous and recognizable Dracula, in a film that set the tone for many of the depictions of the count. Universal, however, then moved farther away from both the novel and the play, ending with a comedy, *Abbott and Costello Meet Frankenstein* (1948).

After nearly a decade in which the only memorable Dracula was the Turkish *Drakula Istanbulda* (1953), the vampire returned in brilliant Technicolor in the person of energetic and impressive Christopher Lee, in Hammer Films' *Horror of Dracula* (1958). Initially faithful in spirit to Stoker and Deane, they, too, made substantial changes to Dracula. The final Lee picture, *The Satanic Rites of Dracula* (1974), was, in many ways, an artistic disaster. Lee, of course, emerged as the finest representative of the count, adding depth and genuine style to the role, a marked improvement on Lugosi's more theatrical and static interpretation. A clutch of other actors have assumed the cloak of the King of Vampires, including Jack Palance, Louis Jourdan, Klaus Kinski (in a remake of *Nosferatu*), Gary Oldman, and the sensual Frank Langella. In 1992 the count returned to the screen in *Bram Stoker's Dracula*, directed by Francis Ford Coppola, a work that will probably be remembered as one of the finest versions of all time. (See also *Films*.)

Dracula The character of Dracula as he was first presented in Bram Stoker's great 1897 novel, *Dracula*, and in the subsequent creations of modern authors. Count Dracula of Bistritz is one of the major figures in horror, the prototypical bloodsucker—a villain of incalculable ego with an utterly evil and diabolical disposition—who dominates the pages of the novel despite his infrequent appearances after the early chapters. The inheritor of the "best" qualities of the literary vampires Lord Ruthven, Varney, and Azzo, with the sensuality of Carmilla, the count represents the undeniable attraction of evil and is a classic demonstration of sexual symbolism in the literature of the repressed Victorian age.

His allure remains despite the passage of time or the seemingly unappealing characteristics given to him by Stoker. He was portrayed as being dressed completely in black, with a strong face, thin nose, heavy mustache, sharp teeth, pointed ears, hairy palms, long nails, and fetid breath. Additionally, he possessed powers that have become synonymous with the attributes of all undead in the contemporary imagination. He casts no shadow, has the strength of twenty men, grows younger on the blood of his victims, controls the elements (such as fog, thunder, and rain), controls many animals (including the owl, bat, moth, fox, wolf, and rat), and can travel on moon rays as elemental dust or as a mist. Despite these impressive abilities, he is quite limited. Only with an invitation can he enter an abode, he cannot pass running water save at high or low tides, can shape-shift or transform only at noon or at sunset except when he is in his coffin, and must sleep in a coffin filled with his native soil. Dracula also recoils before the cross, garlic, or the holy wafer.

Destroyed in the last pages of *Dracula*, the count proved such an intriguing (and profitable) character that a resurrection of some kind was inevitable; but only a few of the numerous novels featuring

Dracula are viewed to be of any lasting significance. The most interesting of these present the original tale from his perspective or give him a kind of "historical lineage." Among such works are the writings of Raymond Rudorff, Peter Tremayne, and Fred Saberhagen, as well as Jeanne Youngson's "Count Dracula and the Unicorn" (1978). (See also *Literature.*)

Dracula **(Novel)** The 1897 novel by Bram Stoker, published in London by Archibald Constable and Company. Ranked as the greatest work of the genre (fans of *Interview with a Vampire* or *'Salem's Lot* would disagree), and one of the foremost pieces of horror literature, it is also considered the final achievement of Gothic writing that established forever the vampire as part of the popular folklore of the West. In *Dracula,* Stoker created the paramount villain of the age, a character who has become an enduring fixture of film and theater.

In the tradition of Wilkie Collins, Stoker utilized the narrative device of presenting his story through a series of journal entries, diary accounts, newspaper reports, phonograph recordings, and letters. Such a device, of course, required him to write in a variety of styles, as he had to adopt the persona of each character, with their specific attributes and mannerisms. In this he was utterly successful, weaving a complex tale that is both riveting and full of surprises. It is generally agreed, however, that the novel's best moments come at the beginning, in the journal entries of Jonathan Harker, detailing his harrowing experience in Castle Dracula, where the reader is introduced to the count in hair-raising detail. For the audience of the time, such episodes as Dracula scaling the castle wall, the three vampire women, and the discovery of the count in his coffin by an aghast Harker were wildly terrifying. The pace and content of the middle portions do not equal the early chapters, but Stoker was careful to pursue the development of his major players, particularly Lucy Westenra, Mina Harker, Dr. Seward, and Abraham Van Helsing. This deliberate literary structuring makes the outrages committed by the count even more malevolent, while serving as the source for intense scholastic and psychological scrutiny of the work and Stoker himself, particularly in the second half of the twentieth century.

Second in popularity to Harker's account of his Transylvanian sojourn is the brilliant climax, following the pursuit of Dracula from England to his homeland, where he is destroyed under the very shadow of his castle. Particularly impressive is the use of hypnotism by Van Helsing, utilizing the mind link between Mina and Dracula to track the count's movements. Contrary to popular mythology, Dracula is not impaled with a stake or exposed to the rays of the sun. He is stabbed in the heart by a bowie knife wielded by Quincey P. Morris, the only American in the book, and has his throat slit by a Gurkha knife (a *kukri*) in the hands of Jonathan Harker.

The result of the evolution of the vampire story, *Dracula* is a combination of the writings of Polidori, Le Fanu, Rymer, and the anonymous author of "The Mysterious Stranger" (1860). While it owed much to these preceding works, the novel has served as the basis for the vampire literature that followed it. It has been imitated, pastiched, even mimicked, but *Dracula* remains the ultimate novel of the undead, and in those other efforts that try both consciously and unconsciously to avoid similarities, the ghost of the King Vampire lurks hazily upon the page. *Dracula* was an immediate sensation, with public reaction generally highly favorable. Even the more conservative, religiously oriented publications of the time liked its basic moral message of good triumphing over evil. Translations followed, the first being in Russian, and new editions appear frequently, most recently as part of the promotion for the film *Bram Stoker's Dracula* (1992). (See also *Stoker, Bram*, for other details; see also under the numerous films based on the novel and under entries related to vampiric attributes, methods of protection, prevention, and destruction for the immense impact of *Dracula* on vampire lore.)

***Dracula* (1931)** The famed Universal screen adaptation of the Hamilton Deane–John Balderston play, starring Bela Lugosi in a career-defining performance, with Edward Van Sloan, Dwight Frye, and Helen Chandler and directed by Tod Browning. *Dracula* is one of the most important films in vampire cinema, influencing the way in which the count was forever after depicted, shaping the general style of succeeding Universal projects and proving the financial potential of horror and the undead at the movies. The result of the success of the play *Dracula* in America, the film version was put in the hands of Browning, who initially wanted Lon Chaney as his vampire but settled on Bela Lugosi, who had played the role on stage (as had Van Sloan, in the role of Van Helsing).

By today's standards, *Dracula* is quite disappointing, hampered by static photography, Lugosi's theatrical performance, and the painful absence of meaningful action. While relying heavily upon the play, Browning did achieve superb atmosphere. Intended for the cinema of the time, the film worked in 1931 precisely because it was not excessively shocking to audiences quite unprepared for graphic violence or tension. Significantly, whereas the other works of the period, such as *London After Midnight* (1927), ended with the monstrous threat proven to be unreal or a hoax, *Dracula* sustained its supernatural elements, adding to the overall effectiveness of the treatment.

Largely forgotten except by film students or movie buffs was the parallel release in 1931 of a Spanish-language version, filmed on the same set but starring a different cast, as dubbing techniques had not yet been perfected. This was an effort to capitalize on the sizable Spanish-speaking audience. *Dracula* in the Spanish version was directed by

George Milford and starred Carlos Villarias as "Conde" Dracula, with Barry Norton and Lupita Tovar. The only known complete print of this version was, for many years, in Havana, in the possession of the Cuban Film Archives, but the film was recently released in America on videocassette. (See also *Dracula,* the character, and *Films.*)

***Dracula* (1973)** An MGM television film, actually airing in 1974 because of an initial preempting in October 1973, starring Jack Palance, Simon Ward, Fiona Lewis, and Nigel Davenport, written by Richard Matheson, and directed by Dan Curtis. While changes were made in the story line, this was a generally faithful adaptation of the Bram Stoker original, memorable for its Yugoslavian and English location shots and for the performance of Palance as the count. Curtis created a film rich in mood, but the script downplays the supernatural power of the vampire, so that even after being bathed in sunlight, Dracula is merely paralyzed and then staked, instead of deteriorating as in other films. Palance portrays Dracula as a combination of ferocity and personal revulsion at the existence to which he is condemned. As the spear descends, he displays relief that he will, at last, find peace, a significant departure from the novel. (See *Films.*)

***Dracula* (1979)** A Universal film, starring Frank Langella, Sir Laurence Olivier, Kate Nelligan, and Donald Pleasance, the screen adaptation of the enormously popular revival of *Dracula,* which opened on Broadway in 1977. This version is one of the most effective ever produced, thanks to the sensual, complex performance of Frank Langella (re-creating his stage role) and the chemistry he developed with Nelligan (Lucy Seward) and Olivier (Van Helsing). Directed by John Badham, *Dracula* retained all of the Gothic terror of the novel and original play while emphasizing the seductive horror of the count. Effective scenes include Dracula scaling the walls of Dr. Seward's sanatorium, Mina's return as the "Bloofer Lady," and the transformation of Carfax Abbey into the vampire's lair. John Williams's score and the sumptuous sets add to the eerie ambiance while injecting just the right amount of camp. (See *Films.*)

***Dracula* (Deane)** The famous stage presentation of Bram Stoker's novel *Dracula* (1897), later adapted to the American theater and serving as the basis of the 1931 Universal film *Dracula.* The earliest theatrical version of the work was by Stoker himself, performed on May 18, 1897, under the title *Dracula, or the Undead,* at the Lyceum Theatre. It was a dull presentation intended really to copyright the original story. While a play was inevitable, the stage presentation involved an imposing challenge, given the narrative's first-person structure, varied locations, and multiple characters. The actor and producer, Hamilton Deane, tried unsuccessfully for years to find a writer for a play, finally penning it himself in 1923 while in bed with a severe cold.

Retaining the basic plot of the novel but reducing it in scope and characters, the play *Dracula*, in three acts and an epilogue, was set in London in "the Study of Jonathan Harker's house on Hampstead Heath," "Mrs. Harker's boudoir," "the Study of Jonathan Harker's house," and, in the epilogue, "The coach house of Carfax Abbey." Starring Edmund Blake as Dracula and Deane as Van Helsing, the play opened in June 1924 at the Grand Theater to a warm public reaction, moving to London in 1927, where on February 14 it premiered at the Little Theater with Raymond Huntley as Dracula, Bernard Jukes as Renfield, and Dora May Patrick as Mina. The play's success allowed it to move to the Duke of York's and the Prince of Wales Theatre. Assailed by critics, it was nevertheless an immense hit, kept so by Deane, who hired nurses to attend any member of the audience who might feel faint from fright.

In 1927 the American rights to the show were purchased by Horace Liveright. John Balderston, an American writer, was hired to make *Dracula* appealing to a United States audience. His adaptation, virtually a complete rewrite, switched the characters of Mina and Lucy, placed the events in Dr. Seward's library, in Lucy's boudoir, back in the library, and in a secret vault, and set the story in contemporary England. Opening in October 1927 at New York's Fulton Theatre, the new version had Jukes again as Renfield, Edward Van Sloan as Van Helsing, and introduced as the new Dracula, Bela Lugosi. The play took the country by storm, requiring the formation of additional companies to handle the demand for performances. Deane finally played the vampire in 1939, fulfilling a longtime dream—an irony, considering that he based the character Dracula on himself.

Still an immensely popular play, *Dracula* has been revived countless times by professional and amateur companies. Among the actors who have assumed the role of the count are John Abbott, Louis Hayward, Hurd Hatfield, John Carradine (including a memorable performance in Detroit), and Frank Langella. Hamilton Deane's play, more than Bram Stoker's novel, has helped to establish the nature, shape, and image of Dracula in the public's imagination. From Universal's 1931 release to Hammer's horrors, to the 1979 film version of the Broadway revival, the play has served admirably as a basis for the vampire cinema. (See also *Plays.*)

Dracula (**Nantucket**) A revival of the Hamilton Deane–John Balderston play, *Dracula*, which was a huge success on Broadway in 1977. The production was undertaken in 1973 by the Nantucket Stage Company of Nantucket Island, Massachusetts, directed by Dennis Rosa, and moved to Broadway in October 1977, where it was distinguished by elegant sets and the riveting performance of Frank Langella, who went on to star in the 1979 Universal version. (See also *Plays.*)

Dracula A.D. 1972 A 1972 Hammer Films production, originally known as *Dracula Today,* starring Christopher Lee (as Dracula), Peter Cushing (as Van Helsing), Stephanie Beacham, and Caroline Munro and directed by Alan Gibson. While reuniting Lee and Cushing, this effort to bring the count into a modern setting has been criticized as the least effective of the Hammer vampire films (with the exception of *The Satanic Rites of Dracula,* 1973), precisely because it abandoned the Gothic elements of the original projects. Dracula is resurrected in 1972 London through a black mass conducted by a young descendant, Johnny Alucard, who later becomes a vampire. Swearing vengeance upon the family of Van Helsing, Dracula stalks Jessica Van Helsing, granddaughter of the original professor's grandson (Cushing). Now in the twentieth century, the count nevertheless does not leave the ruined church in which he has settled. It is there that he is confronted by Van Helsing's grandson, once again destroyed, ironically on the grave of his old nemesis. (See *Films.*)

Dracula Archives, The A 1971 novel by Raymond Rudorff, written in a style closely resembling that of Bram Stoker's *Dracula,* connecting the two infamous historical figures Vlad the Impaler and Elizabeth Bathory with Count Dracula. An attempt to explain the origins of the count, the book follows the two lines of Vlad and Elizabeth, intertwining them, culminating with the creation, through mystical means, of Dracula, actually Vlad, his body resuscitated and inhabited by the spirit of Stephen, a descendant. There follow the events of Bram Stoker's novel. *The Dracula Archives* was the first effort to provide the count with a "historical" lineage, the idea being used by such subsequent writers as Peter Tremayne (in his novels) and Gail Kimberly (*Dracula Began,* 1976).

Dracula Has Risen from the Grave A 1968 Hammer Films production starring Christopher Lee, Rupert Davies, Veronica Carlson, and Barry Andrews, picking up the story where it left off in *Dracula—Prince of Darkness* (1966), with the count trapped beneath a frozen stream near his castle. Directed by Freddie Francis, the film focuses this time on two lovers, Maria (Carlson) and Paul (Andrews), with Lee's role reduced, in part as a result of the same budgetary restrictions that had plagued the episodes that preceded it. The count is accidentally revived by blood pouring into the stream; thus does he escape his watery grave. Unable to enter his abode because of a golden cross placed upon the door by the local monsignor, Dracula swears revenge, attacking the cleric's niece, Maria. Before dying, the monsignor explains to Paul how to destroy the fiend, but the self-declared atheist refuses to say the required prayers after staking Dracula. In a revisionist and intriguing scene, Dracula pulls out the stake, only to die later, impaled upon the cross of the monsignor, while the priest who accidentally brought Dracula to life utters the necessary prayers. Highly profitable, the film paid for the next installment, *Taste the Blood of Dracula* (1969).

Dracula, My Love The third novel by Peter Tremayne featuring Count Dracula, published in 1980. In this account, Dracula, still in Transylvania, brings a destitute Scottish woman to his castle to fill the position of governess. The two become romantically involved, with the count displaying a capacity for love.

Dracula, or the Undead A stage presentation written by Bram Stoker and performed on May 18, 1897, at the Royal Lyceum Theatre, a few days after the publication of Stoker's novel *Dracula*, on which it was based. The earliest stage version of the novel, it was probably intended as a means of insuring the copyright of his fictional creation. The play was four hours long, in five acts, with a prologue, substantial changes having been made to convert it. The performance provided little drama, despite the efforts of the members of the Royal Lyceum Theatre group, foreshadowing the major difficulties that would be encountered in transferring *Dracula* from the novel to the stage. (See *Plays.*)

Dracula—Prince of Darkness A 1966 Hammer Films production, directed by Terence Fisher, marking the return of Christopher Lee as Count Dracula, for the first time since his vampiric debut in the 1958 *Horror of Dracula*. The film also starred Andrew Keir, Barbara Shelley, and Philip Latham. It has been criticized for its less than original plot, the minimal use of Lee, and the absence of dialogue for the count, limitations with regard to Lee that were caused by budgetary demands. The plot presents four travelers who find their way to Castle Dracula, one of them dying at the hands of Klove (Latham), the count's servant. The corpse is then strung up over the coffin bearing Dracula's ashes, its blood pouring onto the remains, thereby reviving him. The moment—one of the goriest scenes in Hammer history—is very effective, making the rest of the film rather anticlimactic. There follows the usual hunting of the remaining guests, rescued by the spirited performances of Andrew Keir as Father Sandor, the vampire killer, and Barbara Shelley as Helen, a visitor who becomes a sexually unhinged vampiress. In a nice innovation, Dracula is defeated by drowning, falling beneath the ice of a frozen stream. The next episode was *Dracula Has Risen from the Grave* (1968).

Dracula's Daughter A 1936 Universal production, directed by Lambert Hillyer, the sequel to the 1931 release, *Dracula*. Starring Gloria Holden, Otto Kruger, Irving Pichel, and Edward Van Sloan (who returned as Van Helsing), *Dracula's Daughter* was supposedly based on Bram Stoker's "Dracula's Guest" (published in 1914), although there is virtually no similarity between the story lines. It presents the premise that Dracula somehow had a daughter, Countess Marya Zaleska (Holden), a reluctant inheritor of her father's vampirism, abetted by her ghoulish-looking servant, Sandor (Pichel). She tries to cure herself of her condition, falling in love with Dr. Jeffrey Garth (Kruger), Van Helsing's pupil, who she believes can help her. She is unable to resist her impulses, however, vampirizing a young girl in a scene of subtle, implied lesbianism. Convinced that she cannot reverse her plight, she invites Garth to join her in "eternal life," abducting his fiancée when he refuses. The countess dies in Transylvania, impaled by an arrow intended for Garth. A sophisticated film for its time, *Dracula's Daughter* is considered by many critics to be markedly superior to *Dracula*. (See *Films*.)

"Dracula's Guest" An early chapter from the novel *Dracula* by Bram Stoker, written with the rest of the work but omitted from the final version published in 1897 because of limitations of space. "Dracula's Guest" was published only in 1914, appearing in *Dracula's Guest and Other Weird Tales*. While not considered a short story in the traditional sense, it is nevertheless quite self-contained. Whether on its own or, as would have been preferred by many critics, left as part of the original novel, it is very effective, serving as an eerie introduction to the supernatural elements of the novel and the power of the count himself. Jonathan Harker, in a foreshadowing of the terror of Castle Dracula, is stranded in a storm, finds the haunted tomb of Countess Dolingen of Gratz, and barely survives an encounter with an unearthly wolf. An inscription on the Countess's tomb reads *THE DEAD TRAVEL FAST*, a line from Bürger's "Lenore" (1773).

Draculea The preferred name used by Vlad Tepes (Vlad the Impaler, 1431–1476), meaning "Son of Dracul" (Son of the Devil or the Dragon), the nickname given to his father by the Romanians. Draculea appeared on documents signed by Vlad, although he also wrote Drakulya and Dragulya, among others. The name is involved in the continuing debate on the part of linguistic scholars attempting to disentangle the origins of Dracula in history and in legend. (See also *Vlad Dracul*.)

Dragon, Order of the A late medieval order, established in 1418 to honor those Christian leaders or rulers who had proven themselves great foes of the enemies of Christianity, particularly heretics and the Turks who were threatening Europe at the time. Members were traditionally invested by the Holy Roman Emperors at Nürnberg and faced certain obligations, including the wearing of dark, penitential colors on Fridays and leading exemplary and devout lives. In 1431,

Vlad II of Transylvania, the father of Vlad Tepes (Vlad the Impaler), was admitted to the order's ranks, subsequently using the dragon symbol on his banners and coinage. This, possibly, is the origin of his name, Vlad Dracul (also translated as Vlad the Devil), but the precise roots are still debated by scholars. The Romanians and historians considered him either a devil (the dragon was associated with Satan at the time) or as the holder of the devil's symbol. Vlad Tepes was subsequently known as Vlad Dracula (or Draculea), the Son of Dracul, inheriting his father's penchant for cruelty. Peter Tremayne, in his novel *Dracula's Revenge* (1978), proposed a connection between the dragon and the ancient cult of Draco in Egypt, whose members practiced the black arts in order to achieve immortality. Dracula was supposedly a descendant of that powerful society.

Drakula A silent picture made probably in 1921 by the Hungarian film producer Karoly Lajthay. Few details are available about the film, and it is not known with certainty whether it focused on the fifteenth-century Transylvanian ruler Vlad Tepes (Vlad the Impaler), called Dracula or Draculea, or was an adaptation of the Bram Stoker novel *Dracula*. If it was based on *Dracula*, it would rank as one of the earliest films to present the count or to bring vampires to the screen. The clear first work on Stoker's creation was F. W. Murnau's *Nosferatu* of 1922. (See *Films.*)

Drakula Istanbulda A 1953 Turkish film, translated as *Dracula in Istanbul,* directed by Mehmet Muhter and starring Atif Kaptan. A little-known project, it presented a loose version of Bram Stoker's novel *Dracula,* set in Istanbul. In the film, the evil count, according to the villagers around the Carpathian castle, is directly descended from Vlad Tepes (Vlad the Impaler, Dracula). *Drakula Istanbulda*'s importance is derived from the portrayal of Dracula by Kaptan. For the first time since the 1922 *Nosferatu* by F. W. Murnau, a vampire was seen on the screen with sharp fangs, a feature used subsequently in virtually every vampire film, particularly the creations of Hammer Films. (See *Films.*)

Draskylo A Greek term meaning "to step across" or "stepping across," referring to the fear of animals jumping over a corpse; a phobia of the region directed especially at cats. The act was believed to create a vampire of the corpse. Another variation on this fear was called *pernáei apano apo* (passing over). (See *Jumping over a Corpse.*)

Dress, Vampire: See *Appearance, Vampiric.*

Dreyer, Carl Danish-born director (1889–1968), one of the finest film-makers of his era, whose distinctive style included authentic sets, long close-ups, and limited action, as well as a type of static photography. Among his best films were *La Passion de Jeanne d'Arc* (1928, *The Passion of Joan of Arc*), *Ordet* (1955, *The Word*), and *Vredens Dag* (1943, *Day of Wrath*). His effort to undertake a vampire film resulted in *Vampyr* (1932), loosely based on Sheridan Le Fanu's "Carmilla."

"Drifting Snow, The" A 1939 short story by August Derleth, published originally in *Weird Tales,* under the pseudonym Stephen Grendon. Noteworthy for the use of nature—snow—as the eerie, evil environment for vampiric killings, "The Drifting Snow" is set in an isolated house during a snowstorm, relating a woman's obsession about the windows, always curtained after nightfall, particularly the west windows. Her fears, she explains to her young relatives, are based on the death of her father, lost in the drifting snow after seeking a servant girl he had seen outside, despite the fact that she had been dead for a year. The girl lured him to his death, returning with him to haunt the snow around the house.

Drowning One of the ways in which a person can become a revenant or vampire. The belief in this transformation is grounded in the fact that drowning, much like suicide or murder, normally occurs suddenly, cutting short a person's life, shocking the soul, and allowing an evil spirit or demon to enter the corpse and use the body as a vampire. This belief was common among the Croatians and in other Slavic territories. The undead, of course, encounter great difficulties with water and are unable to cross running streams or rivers. (See *Becoming a Vampire*.)

Dubbelsüger Also called the *doppelsauger,* a type of vampire found in northern Germany, in the region of Hannover, among the Germanized Slavs (Wends). Its name means "doublesucker," so called because of the idea that a child, once weaned, will become a vampire after death should he or she nurse again. Awakening after their passing as a vampire and while still in the coffin, the *dubbelsüger* will eat the fleshy parts of its breasts, thereby drawing out the life essence from a surviving family member through a kind of sympathetic magic. Its presence is detectable by the wasting away of a living relative and by certain telltale signs on the body, such as lips that have not decayed. Methods of prevention include placing a gold coin between the teeth or a half round board under the chin to separate the head and the chest (the lips and the breast). Additionally, the burial garment should not come in contact with the lips. When taking the body of a suspected *dubbelsüger* out of the house, the coffin is passed under the movable sill of the front door, which is replaced and made very tight, prohibiting the body's return, for it must enter by the same route by which it left. Its destruction is possible by slicing off the back of the neck with a spade, an act usually accompanied by a bone-chilling cry from the corpse. (See *Germany*.)

Dumas, Alexandre Known also as Dumas père, to differentiate him from his son, Alexandre Dumas fils. One of the great writers of the nineteenth century and author of *The Three Musketeers* and *The Count of Monte Cristo*, Dumas (1802–1870) also wrote a play, *Le Vampire*, in collaboration with Maquet, opening at the Parisian Theatre Ambigu-Comique on December 20, 1851. It was based on *The Vampyre* (1819) by John Polidori and included the increasingly well-known Lord Ruthven, Polidori's vampire character. This production was Dumas's contribution to the numerous vampire plays that were found throughout Paris, one of which (a revival of the successful 1820 Charles Nodier play, *Le Vampire*, at the Porte-Saint-Martin), in 1823, he mentioned in his *Memoirs*. His account, considered a livelier portion of the *Memoirs*, contained a detailed description of the play and Dumas's critique of the performance, as well as a conversation with a neighbor in which the work of Calmet on the undead was mentioned and the reality of vampires proposed. Dumas's play was presented as a "Drama Fantastique en Cinq Actes, en Dix Tableaux." He also wrote a short story, "The Pale-Faced Lady" (1848) about a vampire in the Carpathians.

Dummolard, Martin A late-nineteenth-century mass murderer in France, known as the "Monster of Montluel," whose crimes were made more macabre because of the control exercised over him by his obese mistress, one Justine Lafayette. After meeting Justine while in her Lyon boardinghouse, the youthful, handsome Dummolard fell completely under her spell. They were both necrophiles, Dummolard drinking the blood of his victims and bringing home the fleshiest portions of his kills to serve up for Justine. Despite the terror that broke out in Montluel, he was able to murder some eighty girls. The capture of Dummolard and his mistress in 1888 was followed by a sensational trial. Justine was guillotined, and Dummolard was confined to an asylum. He died early in this century and is ranked as one of the most hideous of the so-called vampires of history. (See also *Historical Vampires*.)

Earth Dirt, soil, associated with death and undeath. According to folklore, a vampire returns to its grave or resting spot once a day, normally at dawn, although there is nothing to support the notion that a revenant is compelled to this activity, nor much information pertaining to the widely accepted idea that a vampire must sleep in its native soil. Dirt was sometimes placed in a body's mouth to prevent its rise from the dead, a preventative measure, essential in the case of the *estrie*.

The importance of native earth was introduced to great effect by Bram Stoker in the novel *Dracula* (1897). Stoker emphasized Dracula's need to reside during the day in a coffin filled with his native Transylvanian soil. This, of course, provided Stoker with an excellent literary device, as the heroes were forced to hunt for and locate the count's coffin before sunset. Adopting the concept for her own writings, Chelsea Quinn Yarbro conceived a variation for her characters, in that the vampire Saint-Germain and his associates wander about during the day with their native soil in the heels of their shoes.

Egypt One of the world's first great civilizations developing along the Nile River in northern Africa. According to many vampirologists and writers, Egypt was also the birthplace of the vampire. Egypt has thus been the scene of many fictional works, its ageless pyramids, its mystical rites, and its lost lure serving as the perfect backdrop for the creation and spread of vampires. Ancient Egypt early on developed a rich, complex, and highly positive view of death and the afterlife.

The overall positive concept of eternal life, however, and the blissful abodes offered to the dead who were found worthy of them shielded the Egyptians from the terror and horror concerning death as experienced by other cultures. Most corpses were called "beloved Osirises," in fact. Mortuary cults, especially those of the pharaohs or important queens—which featured recitation at the tombs of the royal personages, with the offering of food and wine, along with prayers and the recitation of the names of the dead—might have provided the first hint of vampirism to later scholars. Another aspect of Egyptian belief that prompted vampiric consideration was the *ka*, the astral being who was deemed a companion to each human being while he or she lived. This *ka* guided the person while he or she was alive, but then became powerful in the tomb, leading the soul, the *ba* or *khu*, into eternity. The *ka* was maintained in the tomb by offerings, and heads were placed outside of each tomb to allow the *ka*, which was able to move about, to find its own resting place again.

It should be noted that the Egyptian fear of being forgotten by later generations was quite strong. The recitation of the name of the deceased kept that individual functioning and active in eternity. Prayers, offerings, chants, rituals, and gifts for the deceased were purchased by the people before they died, so that they could be properly embalmed for the tomb and then remembered. The Egyptians believed that if a person's name was forgotten, that individual perished forever. In some parts of Egypt today the family members of a deceased visit the tomb and talk to the person, reciting ills and troubles or the good fortune of the clan.

With the fall of the New Kingdom in 1070 B.C., eras of occupation by foreign kings began. The Babylonians, Libyans, Nubians, and eventually the armies of Alexander the Great marched across Egypt, bringing their own legends and traditions. The Ptolemys ruled Egypt (after Ptolemy, the general of Alexander the Great) until Rome conquered Cleopatra and Marc Antony. Thus the Greek, Babylonian, and other customs were adopted and incorporated into the older philosophical systems of Egypt.

Egypt, however, remains enduring in its mysterious evocation of spirits, rites, and mysteries, and many writers have incorporated the vampire legend into its setting. The most recent and most notable of such writers is Anne Rice, with her Vampire Chronicles, especially Book III, *The Queen of the Damned* (1988), in which vampires begin and the King and Queen of the Undead are established in Egypt. Peter Tremayne, in *The Revenge of Dracula* (1978), has Dracula belonging to an ancient cult of immortals, the Egyptian cult of Draco, devoted to magic and achieving power through eternal life. Finally, Chelsea Quinn Yarbro dates her formidable character Le Comte de Saint-Germain to a time of great antiquity, recounting his days in Egypt in the novel *Out of the House of Life* (1990).

Ekimmu One of the most fearsome creatures of the ancient world, found among the Assyrians and Babylonians, a departed spirit, the soul of a dead person who was unable to find peace. The creature wandered over the earth, waiting to attack. Its characteristics were very similar to the *utukku,* although the *ekimmu* was more widely known and more dreaded. There were many ways in which a deceased could become an *ekimmu,* including violent or premature death, dying before love could be fulfilled, improper burial, drowning, dying in pregnancy, starvation, improper libations or food offerings, and the failure, for various reasons, to be buried at all.

Elga, Countess A supposed vampire in the Carpathian Mountains, whose predations cause the castle of her father, Count B____, to be burned by the local populace. The initial account of the conflagration was reported in the *Neues Wiener Journal* in Vienna on June 10, 1909. It detailed how villagers, suffering the deaths of children at an alarming rate, decided that the count, who had recently died, had returned as a vampire and was residing somewhere in his castle, a fortress originally built as a defense against the Turks. In the *Occult Review* of September 1909, however, an article, ''An Authenticated Vampire Story,'' offered the theory of vampirologist Franz Hartmann that the count was not the vampire, but that it was his daughter, Countess Elga, who had been killed in a horse riding accident sometime before her father's death. Hartmann's hypothesis was supported by a story from an occultist journal editor who visited the castle before its destruction. He experienced several episodes of hauntings and apparitions that centered around a painting of the countess.

Embalming The process by which a body is treated with chemicals and subjected to extensive treatment by specialists with the aim of rendering it inert and thus partially preserved. Dating to the early periods of ancient Egypt, as far back as the old kingdom, 2575–2134 B.C., embalming has been used by many cultures. It is a very effective method of preventing vampirism, as it removes most of the vital organs of the deceased, including the intestines and the blood, while cutting into the corpse itself, an action that is believed to neutralize many of the traditional requirements for the transformation of the body into vampiric form. The complexity and time-consuming nature of embalming made it impractical for mass burials or for burials in poor, rural areas in the world prior to the twentieth century. (See also *Burial.*)

Empusas Vile, vampirelike creatures in Greek mythology, usually members of the wicked hordes in attendance to the mysterious goddess of magic Hecate. They served with the *mormos* and were described as demons who could assume from time to time the guise of flesh and blood. The most famous account of their activities was recorded by Philostratus in his *Life of Apollonius of Tyana.* It told of the handsome youth Menippus, who was enticed by an *empusa* disguised as a Phoenician woman. Confronted by Apollonius, the *empusa* revealed itself and admitted to fattening up Menippus so that she might devour him. The *empusas* were also mentioned by Aristophanes.

Encore un Vampire A vampire comedy produced in 1820 at Paris, published by Emile B. L. It was one of the earliest and most successful vampire farces that appeared in the French theater following the spread in popularity of John Polidori's *The Vampyre* (1819) and the adaptation of the work onto the stage. (See *Plays.*)

Energy Draining: See *Psychic Vampires.*

England The island nation had few original vampire traditions but nevertheless made significant contributions to the development of the vampire. Early stories of the undead in England remain largely undocumented, but influences in ancient times certainly came from the Celts and the Romans. It has been stated by scholars that the first poem on the undead in the isles was the "Vampyre of the Fens," an Anglo-Saxon work that is otherwise unknown. The Anglo-Saxon invasion of the isles, coupled with Norse domination for many years, introduced Scandinavian and Germanic traditions of the undead.

Once accepted by the English, vampires received considerable mention in the writings of medieval chroniclers, such as William of Malmesbury, William of Newburgh, and Walter Map. There followed, however, centuries of quiet, broken in the eighteenth century by English translations of the stories of vampires from the Continent and the account of "The Travels of Three English Gentlemen," published in 1745. Since that time some of the most intriguing of all vampire cases have come from the isles, including the Croglin Grange and the Highgate Vampire. English literary figures such as Byron, Coleridge, Southey, and others created memorable works in vampire literature, while the two Irish writers, Bram Stoker and Sheridan Le Fanu, had their renowned works, *Dracula* (1897) and "Carmilla" (1872) respectively, published in London. (See also *Films, Ireland, Scotland,* and *Wales.*)

Epidemics: See *Plague.*

"Episode in Cathedral History, An": See *James, M. R.*

Erasmus Franciscus: See *Grando.*

Erestun: See *Heretics* and *Russia.*

Eretica A formidable Russian vampire species, associated with the traditions in the region that heretics became members of the undead after death. The *eretica* (plural *ereticy*) was a woman who sold her soul to the devil during her lifetime, returning after she had died and assuming, during the day, the guise of an old woman in rags. By nightfall she gathered with fellow *ereticy* in ravines, where they held a sort of sabbat. She was active only in the spring and in the late fall, sleeping at night in the coffins of those who, in life, had been impious. To fall or sink into one of the graves containing an *eretica* caused a person to waste away. Most dangerous of all was seeing the evil eye of the creature, as to do so brought about a slow, withering death. The *eretica* could be destroyed by staking and burning. (See *Heretics* and *Russia.*)

Eric, Stanislaus: See *"True Story of a Vampire."*

Estonia A region situated along the Baltic Sea to the north of Latvia, historically part of Livonia. The Estonians had several species of vampires, largely the result of external influences, especially Russian. The rarest of the undead in Estonia was the *vere-imeja* (bloodsucker). The

Estonian species, the *veripard* (blood beard), was essentially a manifestation of a nightmare, tormenting people during the night and pressing down upon them. Another type of Estonian undead, the *vampiir*, was probably another foreign tradition that found only limited acceptance in the region.

Estrie A feared Hebrew spirit connected both with demons and witches, always a female and invariably assuming the shape of a vampire. The *estrie* was held to be one of the incorporeal spirits of evil that had taken flesh and blood, living among humanity in order to satisfy its appetite for blood. Children were its favorite prey, although men and women were attacked as well. It could change its appearance at will but reverted to its demonic shape while flying about at night. If injured or seen in its natural state by a human, the *estrie* had to acquire and eat some of the person's bread and salt or it would lose its powers. When prayers at religious services were offered for a sick woman suspected of being the vampire, no one in the congregation said "Amen." At the burial of a possible *estrie*, the body was examined to see if the mouth was open. If so, the creature would continue its activities for another year. Dirt, placed in the mouth of the corpse, made the vampire inactive.

Eternal Life: See *Immortality*.

Et Mourir de Plaisir: See *Blood and Roses*.

Europe: See the following entries: *Abruzzi, Albania, Art, Austria, Bavaria, Belgrade, Breslau, Brittany, Bulgaria, Christianity, Crete, Croatia, Denmark, England, Estonia, Finland, France, Germany, Greece, Hungary, Iceland, Ireland, Italy, Laws About Vampires, Lithuania, Macedonia, Poland, Portugal, Romania, Russia, Santorini, Scandinavia, Scotland, Silesia, Spain, Styria, Transylvania, Wales, Yugoslavia*, and individual subjects.

Eve of St. George: See *George, Feast of St.*

Ewers, Hans Heinz German writer (d. 1943) known for his sympathetic views toward nazism. His graphic and, for the time, shocking visions of vampirism made his works largely unappealing but earned them a place among the truly grim vampire writings. His 1911 novel *Alraune* presents a psychosexual monster with vampire traits, the result of the insemination of a Berlin prostitute by a sex murderer. The female Alraune is a life-consuming creature who feeds on the antihero, Frank Braun, until she is finally destroyed. Even more bizarre is the 1922 *Vampire,* again featuring Frank Braun, this time afflicted with a mysterious malady from which he finds relief only in the company of women who leave him within a few days. Only one, an old lover, stays with him; he drinks small amounts of her blood while in a trance. (See also *Literature.*)

Excommunication One of the most severe punishments that can be exacted by the leaders of a church against their own members. As defined by canon law, excommunication is the exclusion of someone from the communion of the faithful, rendering them unable to participate in church activities, to receive the sacraments or, according to some traditions, to find release after death until such time as some kind of penance has been performed and absolution granted. The soul thus endures eternal suffering, and there is no peace in death. Some doctrines, particularly those of the orthodox church, held that a corpse would remain incorrupt until such absolution was given, a concept that had a major role in the dissemination of stories about vampires. A logical extension of this belief was the terrifying notion that preserved bodies were the perfect vessels for possession by evil spirits. Demons thus animated the corpse, which emerged from the grave, wandering about to find nourishment: blood from the living. It became customary to exhume those persons who had been dead for a while to check on their states of decomposition. In time, vampirism and excommunication became quite intertwined in folklore. Conversely, the Roman Catholic church was often of the view that a body that did not decay was evidence of a degree of sanctity. (See also *Greece* and *Vrykolakas.*)

Exhumation The disinterring or digging up of a corpse, deemed an important early step in the detection and destruction of vampires. A suspected corpse was disinterred for examination purposes, the investigator looking for obvious vampiric characteristics. Such an act was mentioned in numerous firsthand accounts or chronicles. In the region where the Greek church had an influence on the populace, exhumations were undertaken by local priests to determine the degree of putrefaction of a corpse that had been buried for three years. If the remains were deteriorated properly, then the soul had left the world. If not, especially if the body appeared preserved, some evil influence was thought to be at work and appropriate actions followed. In North America, from colonial times into the nineteenth century, many persons in the East accepted the idea that mysterious diseases were being caused by vampire infestations. Deaths from tuberculosis, credited to vampires because of the symptoms of wasting away, coughs, and contagion, made many persons exhume the recently deceased to see if the heart of the corpse was bloodless and rotting. If the organ contained blood, it was assumed that the dead was feeding on new victims and that it was necessary to burn the heart. (See also *Detecting the Vampire.*)

Family The relatives of a vampire, usually the first victims of its attack. It was widely accepted among the Slavs, Greeks, and others that a risen undead always moved first against his or her own family. This was out of aggressive feelings, jealous hatred that they should be among the living, and the comparative defenselessness of relatives in the face of the unexpected appearance of a recently departed loved one. Also adopted was the idea that a curse (of which vampirism is ranked by many) would continue to plague an entire clan or line. Soon after one person died, other family members fell ill with a mysterious ailment, dying and joining their relative in an unearthly cabal. In literature this idea was presented in numerous works, including Victor Rowan's "Four Wooden Stakes" (1925). (See also *Children, Exhumation,* and *Ray Family Vampire.*)

"Family of the Vourdalak": See *Tolstoy, Alexis.*

Fangs The elongated canine teeth of the vampire, often seen bared in a hideous grimace as they sink into the neck of a hapless victim. Fangs are another example of the way in which writings and films have made an otherwise unrelated characteristic one of the most recognized aspects of the living dead. In folklore, there is virtually no significant mention of fangs. In fact, the tongue, provided with a point or a barb, was more common, especially in Bulgaria, Russia, and among the eastern Slavs. It was in literature that the vampire was first provided with fangs, an attribute that emphasizes its terror, savage demeanor, and cruel method of drinking blood. Varney and Count Dracula both had long, sharp teeth, while the 1922 film, *Nosferatu,* with Count Orlock, showed a fiend with rodentlike fangs. The visual power of these was not pursued by Universal Pictures; thus Bela Lugosi was never seen gulping down his sanguinary meal. *Drakula Istanbulda* (1953) gave fangs to its bloodsucker, and Hammer Films' monsters always had beautiful white canines. Plastic or wax teeth are now essential items in a vampire costume at Halloween. (See *Hypnotism*; see also *Porphyria*.)

Fealaar, Vampire of A Scottish story found among the Highland people, reported in *Selected Highland Folk Tales* by R. Macdonald Robertson. The tale gives an account of two poachers who took refuge in an old house near Fealaar, between Athall and the Braemer country. As the door was locked, they entered through the window. Deciding to get some water, one of the men put his leg over the windowsill to leave but was suddenly seized and bitten by something that drank his blood. Yanking his leg away, the man fell back into the shelter. He later searched the area for some kind of animal. Nothing was discovered, but the men saw in the distance white-winged objects and blue lights. The bitten man was scarred for life, and the site acquired a terrible reputation, haunted, it was said, by a vampire. (See also *Will-o'-the-Wisp*.)

Fearless Vampire Killers: See *Dance of the Vampires*.

Female Vampires Also known as vampiress, vampira, or a lamia, the female vampire is found throughout the world in many shapes and disguises. See the following entries: Vampires—*Amine, Asanbosam, Aswang, Bruxsa, Chordewa, Churel, Civatateo, Danag, Estrie, Hannya, Hecate, Jigarkhwar, Kali, La Llorona, Lamia, Langsuir, Leanhaum-shee, Lilith, Loogaroo, Mandurugo, Mara, Moroii, Nadilla, Old Hag, Penang-galan, Strix, Succubus, Sundal bolong, Toad Woman,* and *White Lady, The.* Films—*Black Sunday; Blood and Roses; Brides of Dracula; Countess Dracula; Dance of the Vampires; Daughters of Darkness; Dracula's Daughter; Hunger, The; Lifeforce; Lust for a Vampire; Mark of the Vampire; Nightlife; Twins of Evil;* and *Vampire Lovers.* Literature—"Amsworth, Mrs."; Baudelaire, Charles; Benson, E. F.; Bürger, Gottfried; "Carmilla"; Gautier, Théophile; Goethe; *Hunger, The*; James, M. R.; Lee, Tanith; Leiber, Fritz; Le Fanu, Sheridan; Poe, Edgar Allen; Rice, Anne; "Room in the Tower, The"; "Tomb of Sarah"; Vampirella; Williamson, J. N.; and Yarbro, Chelsea Quinn. (See also *Witchcraft*.)

Fevre Dream A highly successful 1982 work by George R. Martin, presenting the vampire Joshua York, set on the Mississippi River during the steamboat era. The title is derived from the boat built by York and his mortal partner, Abner Marsh, a ship captain. Rich in historical detail and color, the novel focuses on York's efforts to hunt down his enemy, the leader of a group of evil vampires, the descendants of Cain. (See also *Literature*.)

Films: See table.

Films

Movies with a star (✪) are covered in detail in a separate entry. Those with a cross (†) star Christopher Lee.

✪ *Abbott and Costello Meet Frankenstein* (U.S., 1948)
After Dark (U.S., 1987)
Ahkea Kkots (South Korea, 1961)
L'Amante del Vampiro (Italy, 1961)
Anak Pontianak (Malaysia, 1958)
Andy Warhol's Dracula (U.S./Italy, 1974)
Angeles y Querubines (Mexico, 1972)
Ataque de los Muertos, El (Spain, 1973)
Ataud del Vampiro, El (Mexico, 1958)
Atom Age Vampire (Italy, 1960)
Attack of the Giant Leeches (U.S., 1959)
Baul Macabro, El (Mexico, 1936)
Beiss Mich, Liebling (Germany, 1970)
Beverly Hills Vamp (U.S., 1989)
Billy the Kid vs. Dracula (U.S., 1966)
✪ *Black Sabbath* (Italy, 1963)
✪ *Black Sunday* (Italy, 1960)
✪ *Blacula* (U.S., 1972)
Blood (U.S., 1973)
Blood and Roses (France, 1960)
Blood Bath (U.S., 1966)
Blood Beast of Terror (U.K., 1969)
Blood Castle (Spain/Italy, 1972)
Blood Drinkers (Philippines, 1961)
Blood of Dracula (U.S., 1957)
Blood of Dracula's Castle (U.S., 1967)
Blood of Frankenstein (U.S., 1970)
Blood of the Vampire (U.K., 1958)
Blood Spattered Bride, The (Spain, 1974)
Blood Thirst (Philippines, 1965)
Bloodless Vampire (U.S., 1965)
Body Beneath, The (U.K., 1970)
Bowery Boys Meet the Monsters, The (U.S., 1954)
Bram Stoker's Dracula (U.S., 1992)
✪ *Brides of Dracula* (U.S., 1960)
Buffy the Vampire Slayer (U.S., 1992)
✪ *Captain Kronos: Vampire Hunter* (U.K., 1974)
Capulina Contras Los Vampiros (Mexico, 1972)
Capurcita y Pulgarcito (Mexico, 1962)
Carry on Screaming (U.K., 1966)

†   *Castello dei Morti Vivi, Il* (Italy, 1964)
    Castillo de los Monstruos, El (Mexico, 1958)
    Ceremonia Sangrienta (Spain, 1973)
    Chantoc contra el Tigre y el Vampiro (Mexico, 1971)
    Chappaqua (U.S., 1966)
    Charro de los Calaveras, El (Mexico, 1967)
    Chemins de la Violence (France, 1972)
    Children of the Night (U.S., 1991)
    Chi Osu me (Japan, 1971)
    Chosen Survivors (U.S., 1973)
✪† *Conde Dracula, El* (Italy/Spain/U.K. 1970)
    Condemned to Live (U.S., 1935)
    Count Downe (U.K., 1973)
✪ *Count Dracula* (U.K., 1978)
    Count Erotica, Vampire (U.S., 1971)
✪ *Count Yorga, Vampire* (U.S., 1970)
✪ *Countess Dracula* (U.K., 1971)
    Creatures of the Prehistoric Planet (U.S., 1969)
    Crime Doctor's Courage (U.S., 1945)
    Curse of the Undead (U.S., 1939)
    Curse of the Vampires (Philippines, 1970)
✪ *Dance of the Vampires* (U.K., 1967)
    Danza Macabra, La (Italy, 1963)
    Dark Vengeance (U.S., 1980)
    Daughter of Darkness (U.S., 1990)
✪ *Daughters of Darkness* (Belgium, 1971)
    Dead Men Walk (U.S., 1943)
    Dead of Night (U.S., 1977)
    Deathmaster (U.S., 1972)
    Dendam Pontianak (Malaysia, 1957)
    Devil Bat (U.S., 1941)
    Devil Bat's Daughter (U.S., 1965)
†   *Devils of Darkness* (U.K., 1965)
    Devil's Wedding Night (Spain, 1973)
    Diary of a Madman (U.S., 1963)
    Disciple of Death (U.K., 1972)
    Disciples of Dracula (U.S., 1975)
    Dr. Terror's Gallery of Horror (U.S., 1967)
†   *Dr. Terror's House of Horror* (U.K., 1964)
✪ *Dracula* (U.S., 1931)
    Dracula (U.K., 1969)
✪ *Dracula* (U.S., 1973)
    Dracula (Canada, 1973)
✪ *Dracula* (U.S., 1979)
✪† *Dracula A.D. 1972* (U.K., 1972)
    Dracula Business, The (U.K., 1974)

Dracula contra el Doctor Frankenstein (Spain, 1972)
✪† *Dracula Has Risen from the Grave* (U.K., 1968)
† *Dracula, Père et Fils* (France, 1976)
✪† *Dracula–Prince of Darkness* (U.K., 1965)
✪ *Dracula's Daughter* (U.S., 1936)
Dracula's Dog (U.S., 1977)
Dracula's Great Love (Spain, 1972)
Dracula's Lusterne Vampire (Switzerland, 1970)
Dracula's Widow (U.S., 1988)
Dracula, the Dirty Old Man (U.S., 1969)
Dracula vs. Frankenstein (U.S., 1971)
✪ *Drakula* (Hungary, 1921)
✪ *Drakula Istanbulda* (Turkey, 1953)
Drakulita (Philippines, 1969)
Dugong Vampira (Philippines, 1970)
Echenme al Vampiro (Mexico, 1963)
† *Ercole al Centro Della Terra* (Italy, 1962)
Every Home Should Have One (U.K., 1970)
Evils of the Night (U.S., 1985)
Face of Marble (U.S., 1946)
Fade to Black (U.S., 1980)
Fantasmagorie (France, 1962)
Fee Sanguinaire, La (Belgium, 1968)
First Man in Space (U.K., 1959)
Fluch der Grünen Augen, Der (Germany, 1963)
Frankenstein, el Vampire y CIA (Mexico, 1961)
✪ *Fright Night* (U.S., 1985)
Fright Night II (U.S., 1989)
Frightmare (U.S., 1983)
Frisson des Vampire, Le (France, 1970)
Ganja and Hess (U.S., 1973)
Garu the Mad Monk (U.K., 1970)
Gli Amante d'Oltre Tomba (Italy, 1965)
Gran Amor del Conde Dracula, El (Spain, 1973)
Grave of the Vampire (U.S., 1972)
Graveyard Shift (U.S., 1987)
Guess What Happened to Count Dracula? (U.S., 1972)
Hand of Night (U.K., 1966)
Hannah, Queen of the Vampires (Turkey/U.S., 1972)
Happening der Vampire (Germany, 1971)
Hardy Boys and Nancy Drew Meet Dracula, The (U.S., 1977)
Hija de Dracula, La (Spain, 1972)
Historical Dracula, The (U.S./Romania, 1976)
Hombre que Vino de Ummo, El (Spain/Italy/Germany, 1969)
✪† *Horror of Dracula* (U.K., 1958)
Horror of the Blood Monster (U.S., 1970)

✪ *House of Dark Shadows* (U.S., 1970)
House of Dracula (U.S., 1945)
House of Dracula's Daughter (U.S., 1973)
House of Frankenstein (U.S., 1944)
House on Bare Mountain (U.S., 1962)
House that Dripped Blood (U.K., 1970)
Huella Macabra, La (Mexico, 1963)
✪ *Hunger, The* (U.S., 1983)
I, Desire (U.S., 1982)
I Drink Your Blood (U.S., 1971)
I Married a Vampire (U.S., 1983)
Imperio de Dracula, El ((Mexico, 1967)
Incense for the Damned (U.K., 1970)
Innocent Blood (U.S., 1992)
† *In Search of Dracula* (Sweden, 1971)
Invasion de los Muertos, La (Mexico, 1972)
Invasion de los Vampiros, La (Mexico 1962)
Isla de la Muerta, La (Italy, n.d.)
Isle of the Dead (U.S., 1945)
It Lives By Night (U.S., 1974)
It! The Terror Beyond Space (U.S., 1958)
Jonathan (Germany, 1970)
✪ *Keep, The* (U.S., 1983)
Kiss Me Quick (U.S., 1963)
Kiss of the Vampire (U.K., 1963)
Kuroneko (Japan, 1968)
Kyuketsuki Gokomidore (Japan, 1969)
Lair of the White Worm (U.K., 1988)
Last Man on Earth, The (Italy, 1954)
Last Rites (U.S., 1980)
Leech Woman (U.S., 1960)
Legacy of Satan (U.S., 1973)
Legend of the Seven Golden Vampires (U.K., 1974)
Lemora, the Lady Dracula (U.S., 1973)
Let's Scare Jessica to Death (U.S., 1971)
✪ *Lifeforce* (U.K./U.S., 1985)
Living Dead at the Manchester Morgue, The (U.K., 1974)
Llamada del Vampiro, La (Spain, 1972)
London After Midnight (U.S., 1927)
✪ *Lost Boys, The* (U.S., 1987)
✪ *Love at First Bite* (U.S., 1987)
Loves of Dracula, The (U.S., 1979)
✪ *Lust for a Vampire* (U.K., 1970)
Maciste Contre Il Vampiro (Italy, 1961)
Mad Monster Party (U.K., 1967)
† *Magic Christian, The* (U.K., 1969)

Pontianak Kembali (Malaysia, 1963)
Queen of Blood (U.S., 1966)
Red Blooded American Girl (Canada, 1989)
Reine des Vampires, La (France, 1968)
Retorno de Walpurgis, El (Spain, 1973)
Return of Count Yorga, The (U.S., 1971)
Return of Dracula (U.S., 1958)
Return of Dr. X (U.S., 1939)
Return of the Blood Beast (Italy, 1965)
✪ *Return of the Vampire, The* (U.S., 1944)
Rockula (U.S., 1990)
Sadique aux Dents Rouges, La (Belgium, 1970)
Saga de los Draculas, La (Spain, 1973)
✪ *'Salem's Lot* (U.S., 1979)
Sangre de Nostradamus, La (Mexico, 1960)
Sangre de Virgenes (Mexico, 1968)
Santo Cycle (Mexico, 1962–1973)
✪† *Satanic Rites of Dracula, The* (U.K., 1974)
Saturday the 14th (U.S., 1981)
✪† *Scars of Dracula* (U.K., 1970)
† *Schlagengrube und das Pendel, Die* (Germany, 1968)
† *Scream and Scream Again* (U.K., 1970)
Scream, Blacula, Scream (U.S., 1973)
Sexy Prohibitisimo (Italy, 1964)
Son of Dracula (U.S., 1943)
Sonho de Vampiros, Um (Brazil, 1968)
Sorella di Satana, La (Italy, 1965)
Spermula (France, 1976)
Spider Woman Strikes Back, The (U.S., 1946)
Spooks Run Wild (U.S., 1941)
Star Virgin (U.S., 1980)
Strage dei Vampiri, La (Italy, 1962)
Subspecies (U.S., 1990)
Sumpah Pontianak (Malaysia, 1958)
Sundown (U.S., 1990)
Taste of Blood, A (U.S., 1967)
✪† *Taste the Blood of Dracula* (U.K., 1969)
† *Tempi duri per i Vampiri* (Italy, 1962)
Tender Dracula (France, 1973)
Terror Nello Spazio (Italy, 1965)
† *Theatre of Death* (U.K., 1966)
Thing, The (U.S., 1951)
Thing, The (U.S., 1983)
Thirst, The (Australia, 1979)
To Die For (U.S., 1989)
To Die For 2: Son of Darkness (U.S., 1991)

Track of the Vampire (U.S., 1966)
Transylvania 6-5000 (U.S., 1989)
Transylvania Twist (U.S., 1989)
✪ *Twins of Evil* (U.K., 1971)
L'Ultima Preda del Vampiri (Italy, 1960)
Understudy: Graveyard Shift II, The (U.S., 1988)
Vaarwhel (Netherlands, 1973)
Valerie a Tyden Divu (Czechoslovakia, 1969)
Vamp (U.S., 1986)
Vampira (Old Dracula) (U.K., 1975)
Vampiras, Las (Mexico, 1969)
Vampire (U.S., 1979)
Vampire, Le (France, 1945)
Vampire, The (U.S., 1957)
Vampire at Midnight (U.S., 1988)
Vampire Bat, The (U.S., 1933)
✪ *Vampire Circus* (U.K., 1971)
Vampir-Cuadecuc (Spain, 1969)
Vampire de Dusseldorf (Italy/France, 1964)
Vampire Hookers, The (Philippines, 1979)
✪ *Vampire Lovers, The* (U.K., 1970)
Vampire Nue, La (France, 1969)
Vampire People, The (Philippines, 1966)
Vampires (U.K., 1974)
Vampire's Ghost, The (U.S., 1945)
Vampire's Kiss (U.S., 1988)
Vampires on Bikini Beach (U.K., 1988)
Vampiri, I (Italy, 1957)
Vampiro, El (Mexico, 1959)
Vampiro del Autopista, El (Spain, 1970)
Vampiro dell'opera, Il (Italy, 1961)
Vampiro para dos, Un (Spain, 1966)
Vampiro Sangriento, El (Mexico, 1961)
Vampira 2000 (Italy, 1972)
✪ *Vampyr* (France, 1932)
Vampyres (U.K., 1975)
Vampyros Lesbos (Spain, 1970)
Vault of Horror (U.K., 1973)
Velvet Vampire, The (U.S., 1971)
Vierges et Vampires (France, 1971)
Viol du Vampiri, Le (France, 1968)
Wicked, The (U.S., 1987)

Fingernails An often overlooked characteristic of the undead, despite the popularly conceived notion that the nails of the vampires are long, sharp, and as hard as iron. Their extreme length probably developed in legend as a result of the exhumations that frequently took place in parts of Europe in the hunt for revenants—corpses, bloated and hideous, had long nails, as these grew even after death. Count Dracula is described by Bram Stoker as having nails that are "long and fine, cut to a point," adding to his animallike appearance. Count Orlock, in *Nosferatu* (1922), had long, tapering, inhuman nails.

Finland Known in the Finnish as Suomi, one of the northernmost countries in the world, situated between Sweden, Norway, and Russia. The myths and songs of the ancient Finns, gathered in the nineteenth century into the *Kalevala*, include a mythological framework that has a well-defined concept of the underworld, called *Tuonela* or *Manala*. Its rulers were Tuoni and his wife, Tuonetea, joined by their frightful daughters and the terrible Kalma, the personification of death. Kalma reigned over graves and was named after *kalma*, the odor of a corpse. Guarding her abode was Surma, a monster with sharp fangs who drinks, like his mistress, the blood of humankind. The Finns often impaled corpses to keep them from becoming vampires. Many Finnish tribes attributed illness to the spirits of deceased who had been murderers in life or victims of violent death. Old maids also fell into this group. (See also *Scandinavia*.)

Fire A powerful force for good against evil, differentiated from cremation in that it is not always applied ceremonially but is often improvised or is an act of nature. Flame or fire is revered by alchemists, hermeticists, and sorcerers as a symbol of God. It has the capacity to purify and to cleanse, purging evil or disease from a person or a place. Just as it was used to save towns and villages from the plague, so it has been a most dramatic method of attacking the undead. Fire clearly threatens the vampire, although the creature is able to recover from severe burns through its regenerative strength. This has been demonstrated effectively in literary treatments of the vampires, remarkably so in Anne Rice's *Interview with the Vampire* (1976). A now familiar and almost caricatured image in films is that of large crowds of angry peasants with flaming torches marching on the castle of the local vampire. Usually, as in *Scars of Dracula* (1970), the only thing the peasants achieve is to so enrage the vampire that he or she takes vengeance upon the village. The use of fire should thus be adopted carefully, with cremation—the reduction of a vampire's body to ashes—always preferred.

Fishnets An item used in many Gypsy villages, particularly among the Doms, to protect against attack. Fishnets were dropped over the doors of houses with the knowledge that vampires who sought entrance would be compelled to count all of the knots in the net before setting about feeding. This action was similar to the placing of knots in graves to distract the vampires.

Fleas One of the insects or animals believed by many cultures, particularly the Slavs, to be a form into which a vampire could change itself. Part of the reason for this belief stemmed from the bloodsucking activities of fleas and their connection with filth. Ironically, the flea was a dangerous carrier of disease in many cultures, especially the plagues that were so crucial in nurturing vampire hysteria over the centuries. The Russians held that when burning the corpse of a vampire, care should be taken not to allow any animals to escape from the body, including the flea, as such an escape would allow the vampire to be reborn.

Flies Insects long associated with disease, filth, and demonry that are often controlled by more powerful members of the undead. There is also a belief in some areas that vampires can transform themselves into flies, an idea stressing the diabolical nature of the vampire and its obvious ties to Satan, or Beelzebub, lord of the flies. The Russians made certain that when cremating a revenant all insects that flew out of the fire were captured and burned, to avoid the start of a new vampire cycle. (See also *Animals.*)

Flückinger, Johann An Austrian army surgeon who, in 1732, with his fellow medical officers, published a sensational report on a vampire epidemic in Serbia. Flückinger was one of several officials sent from Belgrade to investigate stories that vampires were active in the area around Meduegna. As a result of their findings, the group issued a detailed account of the vampires, focusing on individual cases, including that of Arnold Paole. Signed on January 7, 1732, the report stated categorically that the undead did exist and that they were spreading throughout the German-speaking world. These declarations, naturally, caused an enormous uproar, inspiring articles and learned treatises in an effort to explain the phenomenon. On March 4 of that year, the *London Journal* printed an almost complete translation of the account, marking the introduction of the word *vampire* into common English. A title given to the report was *Visum et Repurtum.* (See also *Paole, Arnold.*)

Flying An activity associated with witchcraft and sorcery, undertaken by magical means, usually spells or enchanted items such as broomsticks. While mastered by males (called warlocks or wizards), flying has been linked traditionally to females. An extension of the often misogynist views of women held by some Western and Asian cultures, flying women are part of vampiric lore from Europe to China and Malaysia. A few of these vampiresses are the *aswang, danag,* and *mandurugo* of the Philippines; the *langsuir* of Malaysia; the *bruxsa* of Portugal; and the *civipipiltin* of pre-Columbian Mexico, who rode on actual broomsticks. The *loogaroo* of the West Indies is believed to shed its skin and to fly about as a burning ball. In most cases the flying forms an essential part of the tradition concerning these types of vampires, as they reach their victims in this manner, landing on rooftops or entering through windows, a clear embodiment of the *mara* (mare) of the nightmare, the succubus who torments the nights and dreams of men. Another way in which a vampire is said to fly is through transformation into a bat or into other creatures, such as birds, butterflies, and insects.

Food The sustenance of the vampire, generally assumed to be blood but often varying, as the vampires of folklore enjoy a diverse, if not disgusting, diet. The Indian *bhuta* and the *ubour* of Bulgaria will eat manure or excreta, the latter also able to consume regular food. Other food eaters are the *ekimmu* of Babylon and Assyria. The undead of the Gypsies will return home, demand a meal, and then complain to their widows all night: "This food is no good, bring me something else." Blood is thus not always absolutely vital to vampires. Bulgarian monsters drink blood only when food is scarce. Count Dracula epitomizes the general eating habits of the literary and cinematic vampire, stating everything with the now famous line: "I never drink—wine." Blood remains their main repast, although some vampires have drunk wine in an effort to disguise their true nature among the living, vomiting the liquid later, as it cannot be digested. Unique among vampires are those that feed from the psychic energies of those around them.

Food Offerings The placing of food in front of or in a gravesite in an effort to placate or honor the dead, thereby ensuring their peace and contentment. Libations were also used to satiate the needs of an undead that has been plaguing an area. Funeral feasts at which large amounts of food were consumed, with a place often set for the deceased, were common among the primitive peoples of Europe and elsewhere. Food offerings were made at tombs stretching through the ages, from ancient Egypt to Assyria to Greece. It has been argued by some vampire experts that the Egyptian *ka* (astral companion) would be forced to leave its tomb and wander among the living if denied its traditional meals. An interesting variation on food offerings is found in India, where shrines, called *bhandara* or *bhutastan,* are used to provide the *bhuta* with a home and with a constant food source so that they will not molest mortals. (See *Food.*)

"For the Blood Is the Life" One of the most well-known vampire short stories, written by F. Marion Crawford, published posthumously in 1911 and reprinted in numerous anthologies. Ranked as a classic of the genre, the tale is set in Italy, an area with which Crawford was very familiar. It tells of a young Gypsy girl, Cristina, who is spurned by a handsome youth, Angelo, whom she loves. She later dies at the hands of thieves. Such a violent death and unrequited love bring her back to feed on Angelo until her destruction. The mound in which she was hidden retains a terrifying aura, remaining forever a haunted and sinister place. Functioning on several levels of horror, "For the Blood Is the Life" is among the best written and most developed of the traditional vampire stories of this century.

Fortune, Dion Well-known and respected psychologist, writer, and specialist in matters of the occult or paranormal. Born Violet Firth (1891–1946), Fortune authored several important works, including *The Mystical Qabalah* and *Psychic Self-Defense* (1930). In the latter she covered the subject of psychic vampirism quite extensively, recounting a psychic attack that she endured from a principal, and elaborating on her theories pertaining to this form of vampiric activity. Her chapter on this concept is considered by occult experts to be one of the finest ever composed. She also authored a novel, *The Demon Lover* (1927), the story of Veronica Mainwaring, a young woman who has mediumistic powers, falling under the influence of a cruel occultist, John Lucas. Fortune also wrote the vampire short story "Blood Lust" (1926).

Forty Days A time period of biblical origin that has been associated through legend with the life span of a vampire. According to Bulgarian traditions, the *ubour* (undead) takes shape over a forty-day period, during which time the corpse remains bloated, its bones reduced to a jellylike substance. Only when the forty days have elapsed does a skeleton form again, and the vampire emerges looking like a normal human being. Among certain Gypsy tribes, such as the Orthodox Christian clan in the Raska region of the Balkans, it was said that their undead, more like ghosts, haunted the cemetery at night, but only for forty days. (See *Life of a Vampire.*)

"Four Wooden Stakes" A short story by Victor Rowan that appeared in 1925 in *Weird Tales*. Attacked by some critics as too conventional, it is hailed by others as a wonderfully vivid and horrifying old-fashioned vampire story. Set in England, it centers on a young man summoned by Remson Holroyd, a college friend, to the Holroyd country estate where the entire Holroyd family is rapidly dying out through some mysterious malady. The deaths began with the passing of the grandfather, who had suffered from an attack of vampire bats while in South America. Remson's father died next, followed by his two brothers. The visitor soon discovers that he and Remson are next, catching the now monstrous grandfather drinking from Remson's neck and finding on his own neck two dots rimmed with blood. Going to the family crypt, the friends open the four coffins of the recently deceased and confirm their fears. The appropriate title is derived from their solution to the vampiric presence.

Fowl Domesticated birds, either hens or cocks, ranked with all birds in the prohibition against animals either jumping or flying over a corpse lest the deceased return as a revenant. Fowl figured also in certain rituals to appease vampires or to aid in curing a victim of recent vampirism. In India, a person made sick by a vampire had a cock passed in front of his or her face three times. The bird's neck was then twisted until blood spurted on the patient, who then had the blood rubbed all over his or her body. Similarly, the Russians wrung a fowl's neck and then cut off the head for the same purpose. After a cross was scraped into the ground, the knife used for the decapitation was buried at a crossroads. In each of these methods the aim was to appease the vampire so that it would move on, properly satisfied with the death of the animal. Of course, fowl, like most creatures, could become vampires themselves, or their shapes could be used by the undead to prey upon the unwary. (See also *Birds.*)

France A country that, like the British Isles, possesses virtually no original vampire traditions, although it has a long line of so-called historical vampires—maniacs who drank blood and engaged in crimes so hideous that even vampires would blanch at their retelling. The absence of a specific body of original beliefs is curious, especially given the Germanic and Roman influences that shaped Gallic culture, so much so that the learned vampirologist Montague Summers declared that the absence may have been deliberate. There are, however, some cases that are quite late historically but can be classified as genuinely intriguing. The two best known are Gabrielle de Launay and the Marquis de Morieve. Of course, the living vampire of the French past remains the most examined aspect of Gallic vampirism. Among the most famous are the Marquis de Sade, Sergeant Bertrand, Antoine Leger, Alexandre Simon, Victor Ardisson, and Gilles de Rais.

Novels in which the characters journey to France, especially to Paris, include Anne Rice's *Interview with the Vampire* (1975) and *The Vampire Lestat* (1984); Barbara Hambly's *Those Who Hunt the Night* (1988); Michael Romkey's *I, Vampire* (1990); Les Daniels's *Citizen Vampire* (1981); and Chelsea Quinn Yarbro's *Hotel Transylvania* (1978). As a result of the popularity of John Polidori's *The Vampyre* (1819), the French theater was overwhelmed by stage versions during the middle of the nineteenth century, with such productions as those of Charles Nodier and Alexandre Dumas père. In this century, the vampire cinema witnessed the creation of the euphemistically known Sex Vampire, thanks to the French director Jean Rollin. In a number of works, including *La Vampire Nue* (1969), *Le Frisson des Vampires* (1970), and *Vierges et Vampires* (1971), Rollin served up gratuitous sex, thin plots, and extensive use of erotic, surreal imagery. While grouped in their original releases with French pornography and low-budget science-fiction flicks, Rollin's films nevertheless influenced many European directors during the 1970s, including Jesus Franco and Jean-Louis Van Belle. (See *Laws About Vampires* and *Salic Law;* see also *Ardisson Victor; Bertrand, Sergeant; de Launay, Gabrielle; de Sade, Marquis; Garnier, Gilles; Gilles de Rais; Leger, Antoine;* and *Morieve, Marquis de.*)

Frankincense An aromatic resin or gum taken from several types of trees found in East Africa. It is turned into a kind of incense, traditionally one of the gifts brought to the infant Jesus by the Magi. In Dalmatia and Albania frankincense was used by the clergy to bless daggers or knives intended as stakes or weapons in fighting the undead. (See *Incense.*)

Frid, Jonathan Canadian-born actor identified closely by the public with Barnabas Collins, the vampire character that he played in the ABC television series "Dark Shadows" (1966–1971). Frid received a master of fine arts degree in directing from the Yale Drama School and had Shakespearean training. He was introduced in 1967, capturing the hearts of viewers and emerging as the main character of the show. His performances were marked by a blend of ferocity, passion, and revulsion at his own fate. He was the recipient of many letters from female fans, offering their own necks to him, among other things. A revival of the series was attempted in 1990–1991 by NBC, but the consensus of opinion among "Shadows" fans was that Frid remains the definitive Barnabas. He still attends "Dark Shadows" conventions and stars in a successful one-man show.

Fright Night A 1985 Universal film starring Chris Sarandon, William Ragsdale, Roddy McDowall, Stephen Geoffreys, and Amanda Bearse. Deftly mixing gore and comedy, this is one of the great special effects–laden vampire flicks of all time, replete with flying monsters, disintegrating bodies, and disco-dancing undead. The suave vampire Jerry Dandridge (Sarandon) descends upon an unsuspecting city, moving in next door to a nosy teenager, Charlie (Ragsdale), who witnesses Dandridge's appalling appetite for young women. Threatened with death, Charlie turns to the only person he thinks can help, a burned-out host of B horror movies on a local television station, Peter Vincent (McDowall). At first disbelieving, Vincent learns the hard way the reality of the undead, joining Charlie in hunting Dandridge after the youth's girlfriend is kidnapped. The confrontation in the vampire's lair is wild and bloody, full of shocks and gruesome images. Dismissed by critics as a teenage thriller, it was successful enough to ensure a sequel, *Fright Night II*, a box-office disappointment despite the return of McDowall and Ragsdale and the outstandingly sensual performance of Julie Carmen as Regine, Dandridge's vengeful sister. (See also *Comedy* and *Films*.)

Frogs Amphibian creatures, one of the animal species into which vampires are supposedly able to transform themselves. In Wallachia it was claimed that red-haired men returned as undead who could turn into frogs, preferring to suck the blood of beautiful girls.

Frog Woman: See *Toad Woman* and *Weeping Woman*.

Frye, Dwight American stage and screen performer (d. 1944) who earned enormous notoriety as the deranged Renfield, the slave of Count Dracula in the 1931 film, *Dracula*. A successful actor on the New York stage, he was married to the actress Laura Bullivant, then moved to Los Angeles after theater opportunities declined. Able to project wide-ranging emotions, he became stereotyped as Renfield, a fly-eating maniac, and his future role options narrowed considerably. His equally outstanding, unhinged performances in *Frankenstein* (1931) and *The Vampire Bat* (1933) cemented Hollywood's perception of him. Frye re-created the Renfield role in a 1941 revival of the stage play in Los Angeles but was forced to supplement his income as a machinist during World War II. (See *Renfield*.)

Funerals: See *Burial*.

Garlic An occult food, a pungent herb that has wide use against evil and is now synonymous with protection against vampires, so much so that it is heavily caricatured. It is also an anticipated item in the vampire hunter's kit. The origins of garlic's reputation for being beneficial stretch all the way to ancient Egypt, where it was believed to possess healing powers. Vampirologists, scholars, and even cooks note that it is a virtually universal weapon against vampires. In China and Malaysia it is rubbed on the heads of children to prevent attack, while in the Philippines the chosen spot is the armpit. *Bataks* of Sumatra use it as a kind of soul-recalling herb, helpful in returning a soul to a sickly person's body. In Slavic lands, as everyone knows, it is hung from doors and windows or worn around the neck, a curious if not antisocial activity. Many unfortunate children have been forced to play and work with cloves hanging from their clothing, a precaution that kept everything at bay, including playmates.

In Slavic villages and elsewhere, cloves were stuffed into the mouth, ears, and nostrils of a corpse to ensure that no evil could enter. It was also smeared over the eyes. Following the destruction of a vampire through staking or decapitation, it was poured into the mouth. Additionally, it is highly aromatic. This reek, functioning in much the same way as buckthorn (whitethorn), leeks, or incense, is deadly to evil, which flees before it or cannot cross a threshold over which it is rubbed or hung. The scent of garlic is deemed preferable to other choices at one's disposal: burned animal parts, decayed food, or human feces. Each of these has been used in various areas, but garlic, easy to find and simple to keep, is always the first choice. (See *Protection from Vampires.*)

Garnier, Gilles A late-sixteenth-century French mass murderer, considered in his day to be a kind of werewolf. He murdered young girls or women and then ate them, drinking their blood for nourishment. What made him particularly horrifying was his habit of choosing prime cuts from his victims, which he then took home to his wife. Condemned, Garnier was executed. (See also *Historical Vampires.*)

Gaspar of Heltai A late-sixteenth-century Hungarian songwriter, author of a song in Hungarian on Vlad Tepes (Vlad the Impaler), published at Cluj in 1574. Like other compositions from the period, which took a decidedly hostile view toward Vlad, this work helped to present the ruler as a villain, befouling Vlad's reputation in the West.

Gautier, Théophile French poet, novelist, and critic (1811–1872) called Le Bon Theo, an influential figure in French literature. An adherent for many years of the Romantic movement, Gautier was the author of such well-known novels as *Mademoiselle de Maupin* (1835) and *Le Capitaine Fracasse* (1863). An interest in the supernatural led him to compose the tale *"La Morte Amoureuse"* ("The Dead Lover"), which first appeared in the *Chronique de Paris* on June 25–26, 1836. Titled in English "Clarimonde" and "The Beautiful Vampire," this brilliant story tells of a young priest, Romuald, who becomes enamored of a beautiful courtesan, Clarimonde. She dies, however, returning from the grave to visit him each night. For three years he serves during the day as a priest and at night is a wild, passionate lover in the arms of his undead mistress, surrendering amounts of his blood for her favors. An older priest learns of his affair and leads Romuald to Clarimonde's grave. Exhuming the body, the old priest sprinkles holy water upon the corpse, which crumbles to dust. (See also *Literature*.)

Gayal Also *ut*, a kind of Indian vampire-ghost, the spirit of a man who dies unmarried or without a male heir, thereby depriving him of a person who can properly perform the funeral rites. When returning, the *gayal* focuses his ire upon the sons of other individuals as well as his own relatives. These threats thus ensure that the dead man's distant kin or even his neighbors will complete all of the necessary funeral rituals. Among the Punjabis, the *gayal* is given a small platform, with a hemispherical depression in which is poured milk and Ganges water as a kind of sacrifice. Lamps are placed around it. Mothers in the region hang a coin around the necks of their sons to protect them from attack. (See *India*.)

George, Feast of St. An important religious festival in Eastern Europe, celebrated on April 23 and honoring St. George. Known also as the "Great Martyr," George was a beloved saint, considered the patron not only of England, but of numerous other countries as well, and the patron of cattle, horses, wolves, and all enemies of witches and vampires. St. George's Eve was considered the most dangerous night of the year, as the powers of evil and vampires were at their height. People hid in their houses with every antivampire weapon they could muster. They placed thorns upon the thresholds, painted tar crosses on their doors, lit bonfires, put thistles on windows, and spread garlic everywhere. In Romania the lights in homes were extinguished, prayers were recited throughout the night, and naked blades were positioned under pillows. Bells rang until dawn in parts of Swabia. Should the night pass without incident, the saint's feast was celebrated with enthusiasm the next day. Houses were garlanded with flowers, such as roses, replacing the thorns and the garlic. Bram Stoker, having researched vampire lore for his novel *Dracula* (1897), used the dread of peasants on St. George's Eve to warn Jonathan Harker that at midnight "all the evil things in the world will have full sway."

Germany A country with a highly varied vampire tradition, reflecting the diverse history of the region and the many cultures that have had a hand in the formation of that nation's character. Aside from the Slavic species of vampires found in the eastern regions, the Germans have been faced with such dangerous types as the *nachzehrer*, the *neuntöter,* the *alp,* and the little-known Prussian variety of the *gierach.* Among the various antivampiric activities conducted there was the placing of nets or stockings in a grave, as the vampires in northern Germany were compulsive untiers of knots. The Silesians buried their suspected dead facedown to avoid its potentially dangerous gaze. The Germans also made a lasting contribution to vampirology in the numerous treatises written by "experts" on the undead during the seventeenth and eighteenth centuries. These included the works of Michael Ranft, Johann Christopher Rohl, Johann Stock, and Johann Zopfius. They were largely responsible for introducing the vampire to European theater. A similar achievement cinematically was made in 1922 by the director F. W. Murnau, with his *Nosferatu,* one of the great vampire films of all time. Werner Herzog's *Nosferatu the Vampyre* (1979), was a remake of Murnau's masterpiece. (See also *Ewers, Hans Heinz.*)

Ghoul A cemetery-infesting demon, known in the Arabic as *algul,* a name derived from the word *horse-leech,* a kind of bloodsucking *jinn.* The ghoul appears most frequently as a woman, half human, half fiend, sometimes marrying an unsuspecting man who learns, perhaps too late, of her nocturnal eating habits. Found usually in cemeteries at night, they lure travelers to their deaths, enjoying above all the taste of warm human blood. When in human form they can bear children but are distinguished by their apparent lack of appetite when presented with regular human food, eating only a few grains of rice as they prefer to wait until nightfall, when they are able to sneak away to their repasts in graves. The ghoul received development in Arab myth and in the *Thousand and One Nights,* with such stories as those of Amine and Nadilla. Ghoullike creatures are found in various countries, including Japan and the Philippines. In the latter they are said to munch on the recently dead, the sound of their chewing explaining the strange noises often emanating from burial grounds. (See also *Kasha.*)

"Giaour, The": See *Byron, Lord.*

Gilles de Laval: See *Gilles de Rais.*

Gilles de Rais Also known as Gilles de Laval (1404–1440), a marshal of France and a national hero of the Hundred Years War, who, as a result of his supposed cruelty, cannibalism, satanism, sadism, and assorted sexual perversions, became one of the most notorious murderers of all time, a historical vampire, and the basis of the story of "Blue Beard." A brilliant soldier and nobleman, Gilles fought alongside Joan of Arc against England, earning the rank of marshal at the age of twenty-four. An inheritor of a vast fortune, he was subject to incredibly extravagant tastes as well as an interest in alchemy, sorcery, and other forbidden black arts. Coupled with the enemies he had made for himself at the royal court, these interests brought him to virtual financial ruin. Accused finally of countless murders, particularly of young boys who had disappeared from the areas around his estates, he was brought to trial and tortured. The resulting confession produced appalling revelations of brutality, vampirism, and sadism. Executed for his crimes, he has been considered by some a victim of political intrigue, his schizophrenia, financial waste, and bizarre sexual habits aiding in his own destruction. (See also *Historical Vampires.*)

Glass Phials Containers or vessels of glass used in ceremonies and rites to trap evil spirits or vampires. Such uses for the phials probably had their origins in the legends of the Middle or Near East, moving to the West over a period of time during the Middle Ages. A recurring theme in legends is that of the imp or *jinn* that is forced into a phial and later released, usually giving a reward to the individual who frees it. While the *bajang* of Malaysia is controlled in bamboo, glass phials are used in the dangerous business of bottling a vampire in Bulgaria.

Gleaner A Dutch journal, known originally as the *Glaneur Hollandois,* that helped to spread vampire stories in the eighteenth century. In 1732 it published a copious list of vampire cases in Eastern Europe— Hungary, Serbia, and Moravia in particular—recommending that those who did not believe them or were interested in learning more should consult the numerous other treatises on the subject that had been written by German theologians, scientists, and academicians. The *Gleaner* thus not only added to the hysteria of the time but legitimized the pseudoscientific writings of supposed vampire experts. (See also *Mercure Galant.*)

Gods, Vampire Dreadful deities of merciless bloodthirstiness, beings that possess distinctly vampirelike characteristics. Like death itself, the vampire god is found in the earliest, blackest, and most dreadful memories of humanity. The terror of the night, of blood-drinking divinities, and of losing one's life to an utterly evil creature are found in countries all over the world. Such gods probably helped give substance to legends and to circulating tales of vampires, over time becoming all but forgotten by modern generations, except as the dimmest of collective recollections. Through the ages these divine beings came leering into human nightmares, propagated now in stories and films.

By far the most impressive pantheons of vampire gods are found in Asia. The earliest of these awesome deities was found in the Indus Valley, according to some scholars as early as the third millennium B.C. Once established, the concept of vampire gods spread to surrounding regions and soon, with developing religions, so too did their power. They were normally depicted with fangs, red eyes, and an insatiable appetite for blood and were dressed with such adornments as human heads, skulls, and other organs. The most famous ancient goddess of this type was Kali in India, who is still appeased by offerings of blood, today from animals, but in the past from humans.

The vampire god epitomizes the eternal nature of the undead and the general powerlessness of primitive man to oppose them. Only a great Hindu or Buddhist saint could hope to defeat such foes, short of divine intervention from a good god or the powers of light. As humanity developed homocentricity, the vampire slowly lost its omnipotence in direct proportion to the learning and wisdom of mortals. Thus, vampire hunters could seek out and destroy the undead, whereas earlier generations would have worshiped them. This contrast in the ancient and modern views is clear in *Dracula* (1897). The count, in his ancient home, is able to compel and terrorize the local population, one still enshrouded in ancient beliefs and traditions. Once he leaves his homeland, however, he finds that science and reason are as fierce enemies as their practitioner, Abraham Van Helsing. Dracula is routed by the forces of light, but, like the old gods themselves, the evil that he represents threatens to burst forth again, for it can never be completely expunged or forgotten.

Goethe In full, Johann Wolfgang von Goethe, a German poet, dramatist, and novelist (1749–1832). Among his vast and brilliant writings was a contribution to the fledgling but growing vampire theme in literature, *"Die Braut von Korinth"* (1797, "The Bride of Corinth"), a ballad of lasting influence. The work made vampires a legitimate and respected subject for literary treatment. 'Die Braut von Korinth'' was based on the classic tale by Phlegon of Tralles of the maiden Philinnion. In Goethe's version, the girl dies of grief because her parents refuse to allow her to marry her love, Machates. She returns as a kind of corpse-bride, finding emotional and sexual freedom only in death and undeath. Another probable influence on Goethe was the story of Menippus and the *empusa,* told in Philostratus' *Life of Apollonius of Tyana.* (See also *Literature.*)

Gogol, Nikolai Russian dramatist and novelist (1809–1852) who made the first major contribution to the vampire genre in Russian literature with his 1835 story "Viy." Essentially more humorous than horrifying, "Viy" tells of the so-named King of the Gnomes. In it are several vampire characters, such as a dog that transforms itself into a beautiful girl, stealing babies and drinking their blood. Another is the evil daughter of a wealthy Cossack near Kiev, who is under the power of Viy and rides a phantom horse. She lures men to their deaths and tempts the philosopher Homa Brut. (See also *Literature* and *Russia.*)

"Good Lady Ducayne" A short story written by Mary Elizabeth Braddon (1837–1915), published in *Strand* magazine in February 1896. "Good Lady Ducayne" was only one of Braddon's many works, which include the very popular novel, *Lady Audley's Secret* (1861–1862). Not a traditional vampire tale, it relates the activities of Lady Adeline Ducayne in her efforts to preserve her already ancient life. She hires young ladies-in-waiting who never remain with her long, as they suffer ill health and die under mysterious circumstances. Bella Rolleston enters the lady's service and, while in Italy, begins deteriorating physically. Her death is prevented only through the vigilance of a young doctor, who discovers the lady's secret of longevity. (See *Literature.*)

Gothan, Bartholomeus A German printer who, around 1480 or 1485, published an account on the activities of Vlad Tepes (Vlad the Impaler). Originally from Magdeburg, Gothan moved to Lübeck in 1484, then to Sweden in 1486, where he founded a printing press in Stockholm. His account, called by scholars an incunabulum, was probably first printed in Lübeck or possibly in Augsburg, Leipzig, or Nuremberg. Written in Low German to make it accessible to the towns of the Hanse (north German) region, it helped spread much of the accepted idea concerning Vlad's cruelty. The title of the work was "About an Evil Tyrant Named Dracole Wyda MCCCCLVI Years after the Birth of Our Lord Jesus Christ, This Dracole Wyda Carried out Many Terrible and Wondrous Deeds in Wallachia and Hungary."

Gothic Literature A romantic form of writing that flourished in the late eighteenth and throughout the nineteenth centuries, having a decisive role in the formation of the vampire image. Called Gothic because of its reliance on medieval ruins, castles, and monasteries, it was distinguished by its use of mystery, gloomy atmosphere, and touches of the supernatural. In England the Gothic novel was popularized by Horace Walpole's *Castle of Otranto* (1765), which was followed by the works of Mrs. Ann Radcliffe, Matthew Gregory Lewis, and Charles Robert Maturin. It was inevitable that the vampire should attract the attention of Gothic writers. Early vampire contributions included Goethe's "Die Braut von Korinth" (1797), Bürger's "Lenore" (1773), and Southey's "Thalaba the Destroyer" (1801).

The arrival of the undead in popular literature came in 1819, with the publication of John Polidori's *The Vampyre; a Tale*. Polidori's creation, Lord Ruthven, remains one of the most influential vampires in literature because of his synthesis of traditional vampiric characteristics with the classic Gothic villain. He drinks blood and is clearly a living dead, but gothically he is cruel and rapacious, the traditional rake of the eighteenth century in the vein of other Gothic villains.

Based on Lord Byron, Ruthven revolutionized the image of the vampire, who heretofore had been represented as a peasant in rural areas. Such lower-class bloodsuckers were uneducated, dirty, and unappealing. The vampire depicted in the novel was aristocratic, comfortable in upper society, and at ease in settings that could be identified by readers of the time. Such placement in the contemporary world added to the frightening nature of the tale by increasing plausibility and would be used again by Bram Stoker in his novel *Dracula* (1897). Thus was born the so-called Byronic vampire, a handsome, sexually alluring being who brings the hauntings and the torments of the past into the present, all the while committing unspeakable crimes without remorse.

The next notable Gothic work on the vampire was *Varney the Vampire* (1847), almost certainly by James Malcolm Rymer. The debt owed by Rymer to Polidori was paid in part by Rymer's naming of a minor character, Count Pollidori. Varney is even more reprehensible than Ruthven, taking what he desires in the true Gothic fashion—only in this case it is blood. He also has an obsession with money. Another combination of folklore and literary traditions, Varney reinforced the aristocratic nature of the Gothic vampire that was to remain constant throughout the nineteenth century. The vampire of Sheridan Le Fanu's "Carmilla" (1872) is a noblewoman, but her attacks are more subtle and seductive than those depicted in earlier works, Varney's sensual assault on Flora in chapter XX of *Varney the Vampyre* notwithstanding.

These works influenced and paved the way for *Dracula*, considered the greatest Gothic vampire story and the last expression of Gothic literature. In *Dracula* Stoker established a formidable Gothic villain in the count, but at the same time Dracula is a supernatural being, whose powers and attributes are seen by the reader only after he has been well developed as a peculiar if not repugnant character. *Dracula* is also a Gothic work in the style of *Jane Eyre* and *Middlemarch* in that it forces its audience to concentrate not only on terror and the morbid, but on the social issues of the era. (See also *Literature* and *Rice, Anne*.)

Grain: See *Seeds*.

Grando Also called the Carniola Vampire, an active creature that terrorized the district of Kranj (Carniola) near the city of that name in Yugoslavia. The story first appeared in the commentary of Erasmus Franciscus for the 1689 work *Die Ehre des Herzogthumus Krain* by Baron Valvasor. Grando, a peasant landowner, died and was buried in a customary fashion, returning a short time later as an apparent undead. So numerous were his attacks that Church authorities were summoned. The exhumed body was quite preserved, marked, however, by a quizzical smile, at least until a crucifix was held over it—then it frowned, tears rolling down its cheeks. After commending the soul to God, the officials decapitated the corpse.

Grant, Charles American writer (b. 1942) of horror and fantasy, noted for his incisive manner of examining the inner workings of the mind. Among his novels are *The Nestling* (1982), *Night Songs* (1984), and *The Pet* (1986), as well as several stories set in the town of Oxrun Station in New England. His treatment of the vampire includes "The House of Evil" (1968), "Crystal" (1986), and the well-known "Love Starved" (1979), along with *The Soft Whisper of the Dead* (1979). In the latter he adopts a nineteenth-century literary style, telling of a nobleman's vampiric attempts to take over Oxrun Station through hypnotism. (See *Literature.*)

Grave Desecration: See *Bertrand, Sergeant* and *Necrophilia.*

Graves The burial sites of the dead, normally holes in the earth, although the term can be applied to tombs and sepulchers. As graves are most frequently the place in which a dead person becomes a vampire, they are closely identified with the discovery of the predatory undead. Around the grave of a suspected vampire will be found numerous holes, approximately the width of a man's finger, the means by which the creature issues forth at night in a mistlike form. The earth around or over the coffin is also frequently disturbed, a state explained by the constant movement of the undead below the surface. Vampire hunters look to the grave immediately upon starting their investigations, sometimes throwing holy water, boiling oil, or vinegar upon the dirt, at other times using the horse method of detection—by leading a virgin horse around the cemetery, the vampire's resting place can be discovered through the response of the animal. One other event that convinces the hunters that evil is afoot is the moaning, groaning, and munching sound that reportedly issues from the graves, said to be the living dead busy at work eating themselves, their grave clothes, or other corpses. (See *Detecting the Vampire.*)

Greece One of the great vampire countries, the home of an abundance of undead, where the war between the living and the unliving has long been waged. Greece serves as one of the foremost models for extensive vampire lore, with travelers such as Montague Summers, Leo Allatius, and Pitton de Tournefort recording the destruction of various specimens. Another source, Father Francis Richard, wrote of the vampires on the island of Santorini, evidence of the degree to which Greek thinking spread throughout the Aegean. Greek undead date back to the ancient world, with such foul creatures as the *lamia,* *empusa, ephialtae,* and the *mormo.* Blood and the return of the dead figured quite prominently in classical writings, as is seen in the *Iliad,* when Odysseus filled a pit with blood to empower the spirits of Hades and thereby learn of the future.

Christian Greeks retained belief in the return of loved ones, revenants who were generally not feared and who were treated with respect. Various regional words such as *tympanios* were applied to them, as the word for vampire was unknown. In time, Slavic influences from the Balkans made their mark, working in conjunction with the precepts of the Greek Orthodox church to alter the populace's view of the undead. The Greek church taught that excommunication caused the corpse of one so cursed to remain incorrupt until the lifting of the ban. There resulted a confusion among the people in that excommunication was seemingly the cause of vampirism—the body, left incorrupt, was an active vessel for an evil contaminent. So risen, the undead was called a *vrykolakas,* the Slavic word for "werewolf" that became directly associated with vampires out of the belief that all werewolves were vampires after death. The Church issued decrees to clarify the situation, with little effect. It was declared that there was a difference between excommunicants and the *vrykolakas;* simply because a body remained incorrupt did not mean that it was a vampire. A *vrykolakas,* church leaders said, was created by demonic infestation. As local clergymen routinely exhumed suspected corpses after set periods of time to determine their degrees of decomposition, such pronouncements did not clear up the matter at all. It was assumed by the villagers that excommunicants came back as vampires, joining the long list of other candidates: suicides, unbaptized, immoral persons, those who had a cat jump over their corpses, and witches, all of whom came to be called *vrykolakas.* (See also *Alytos, Ancient Vampires, Andros Vampires, Anthesteria, Chios, Crete, Draskylo, Excommunication, Icon, Incense, Jumping over a Corpse, Macedonia, Morlacchi, Samos Vampire, Santorini,* and *Vyrkolakas.*)

Grettis Saga The latest of the Icelandic sagas, dated to around 1320, translated as *The Saga of Grettir the Strong.* The saga is a treasure house of folklore, centering on the heroic deeds of the outlaw Grettir. Among his adventures is the freeing of Iceland from the ravages of the ghost of Glam, a warrior who has returned to threaten the countryside. He puts the fiend to rest but is cursed, a demonstration of the fear of the Norse for the dead. (See also *Iceland.*)

Guzla, La A series of ballads written by the French dramatist, historian, and author Prosper Mérimée (1803–1870), but published in 1827 under a pseudonym. *La Guzla* was a literary hoax, perpetrated upon France and the rest of Europe, the second such prank by Mérimée, who had previously created the collection of plays *Le Théâtre de Gazul*

(1825); published as translations of the work of a Spanish actress. The idea of the *Guzla* began with Mérimée's continuing interest in folk poetry and his acquisition of two volumes of Serbian verses. Desiring to visit Illyria, he discovered that he could not afford to go and decided to pay for the trip by composing his own Illyrian ballads. Named after a Serbian musical instrument, *La Guzla* was supposedly written by an outlaw poet named Hyacinth Maglanovich, the work "discovered" by an Italian traveler. It deceived most of the scholars of the day and was received quite favorably as a selection of Illyrian poems collected from Dalmatia, Bosnia, Croatia, and Herzegovina. All but one of the thirty-two translations were created by Mérimée, an immense achievement. The poems dealt with revenge, murder, and vampires. Among the colorful vampire characters depicted were the Bey of Moina and "the Cursed Venetian."

Gypsies Nomadic people found virtually everywhere, including Australia, but most numerous in Europe, where they have been stereotyped mercilessly in a great many vampire and werewolf films, depicted as fortune-tellers and ignorant and superstitious peasants. They were also deemed victims of vampiric evil, as in the novel *Dracula* (1897) by Bram Stoker. In actual fact, the Gypsy culture is both an ancient and a proud one, and these ever-roaming people have made many positive contributions to vampiric lore, perhaps playing a major role in spreading the fear of the undead throughout the world. As the *Rom* (the broad term used by the Gypsies for themselves) date back to India, they probably brought with them the extensive vampire traditions of that nation when they migrated westward, either through Egypt and North Africa or via the northern route into Europe. Gypsies have often been viewed as social outcasts by their host countries and have been blamed for a variety of crimes or evils, usually without substantiation. They are, thanks to the preservation of customs and traditions, great repositories of knowledge concerning the undead. The useful but generic term for the Gypsy vampire is *mullo*. Its characteristics vary widely in the different regions of Europe, as Gypsy communities have absorbed some elements of the area in which they reside, even becoming devoted Christians or Muslims. There is, however, a nearly universal terror of the dead among them, and the return of a loved one was believed to bring about the most evil consequences. Swedish Gypsies held that their undead could transform into horses or birds, while Muslim Gypsies in Yugoslavia believed that both pumpkins and watermelons could turn into vampires if kept for too long. (See *Mullo* for details.)

Haarmann, Fritz A German mass murderer (1879–1925), nicknamed the Hanover Vampire, who with two accomplices was responsible for the deaths of at least twenty-four and perhaps as many as fifty young men. One of the worst killers of the century, Haarmann was known as a vampire because of his cannibalism and habit of biting his victims on the throat. A child molester, he spent time in an insane asylum after discharge from the army but after being released rejoined the army, this time serving with an elite unit, distinguishing himself during World War I. A civilian again during Germany's postwar era, he opened a cook shop and worked as an informer. Already a murderer, in 1919 he met Hans Grans, a fellow homosexual, who came to dominate him, leading him into their ventures in the tawdry underworld of Hanover's homosexual community. Here Haarmann found an endless supply of prey, bringing young men home with him and murdering them in a grisly fashion, all under Gran's watchful eye. Another mysterious accomplice aided in body disposal. The victims' clothing was sold in the store, and most horrible of all, Haarmann sold body parts for human consumption. Finally captured by the police, who had visited his lodgings on previous occasions, bodies hidden just feet away, he confessed his crimes in minute detail, proclaiming his sanity but declaring that he committed the crimes while in a trance. Executed in April 1925, Haarmann received a kind of immortality. His brain was removed by officials and given to scientists at Göttingen University to be studied. (See *Historical Vampires.*)

Haigh, John An infamous mass murderer (d. 1949) known as the Vampire of London and Acid Killer. This case shocked the British public when the details of his crimes came to light. A onetime choirboy, John George Haigh was the son of a fanatically pious and puritanical family that forced him to lead a life utterly devoid of social activities and filled with the threat of eternal punishment for sin. In this environment he grew up repressed, becoming fixated on religion and blood, with an increasingly uncontrollable urge to drink blood. By the time he was finally caught in 1949, he had murdered nine people. In each case he drank the blood of his victims, including that of a young girl.

Assuming that he could not be prosecuted if there were no bodies, he routinely disposed of the corpses in drums of sulphuric acid, for which he earned the nickname Acid Killer. What made Haigh so horrible in the public's mind was his absence of remorse, his seemingly normal physical appearance, and the detailed, often unbelievable accounts of his crimes, told in an inhuman matter-of-fact style. Of gruesome interest was his own recitation of his early life, including his experiences as a junior organist for Wakefield Cathedral, where he spent hours gazing at the statue of the bleeding Christ, dying on the cross. Haigh was also distinguished by the apparent absence of a motivational sexual content in his cravings, a characteristic commonly exhibited by other serial killers. (See *Historical Vampires.*)

Hair: See *Kuang-shi, Palm Hair,* and *Red Hair.*

Hamilton, George: See *Love at First Bite.*

Hammer A tool intended to drive or pound something, in the case of the undead usually a wooden stake. The hammer, seen hanging in the air and then descending upon a stake, which plunges into the heart of a vampire, is a recurring theme in film. It is certainly an image closely linked with the dedicated vampire hunter. In "The Mysterious Stranger" (1860), nails are pounded into the coffin of Count Azzo, and in "Carmilla" (1872) the vampire is staked. Hammer Films made the most of the hammer and stake, repeating their use in numerous films, but two of the most powerful scenes of a staking were in the television film *'Salem's Lot* (1979), and the movie *Bram Stoker's Dracula* (1992). The symbolism of the tool is derived from the association of the hammer with the thunder god of the Teutons and the Norse deity Thor, whose powerful weapon was a terrible foe of all evil. (See also *Stake, Wooden.*)

Hannya Perhaps the most feared demon in the extensive pantheon of monsters and fiends of Japan. Its most common manifestation is in the feminine form, although there are male *hannya*. It is said that a *hannya* was once a truly beautiful woman who, for various reasons, became insane and ultimately possessed by a demon. She was transformed into a hideous creature, often identified with the ghoul, drinking blood and eating children. Infants were a special treat, although the No drama of Japan depicted young men as the favorite victims of a particularly vindictive female *hannya*. Some of Japan's most disturbing and frightening examples of monster art present the *hannya* in many of its hideous forms. (See *Japan.*)

Hanover Vampire: See *Haarmann, Fritz.*

Hare, Augustus: See *Croglin Grange, Vampire of.*

Harenburg, John Christian An early-eighteenth-century German writer and expert on vampires. He was the respected author of several learned treatises on the undead, the most renowned being the 1739

Von Vampyren (*On the Vampires*). It was considered by scholars of the period to be built on the writings of other vampirologists such as Rohr, Rohl, Stock, and Zopfius. Harenburg also wrote *Philosophicae et Christianae Cogitationes de Vampiris* (1739, *Philosophical and Christian Thinking on the Vampire*), and was mentioned in Sheridan Le Fanu's "Carmilla."

Harker, Jonathan One of the main characters of Bram Stoker's novel *Dracula,* in many ways the central hero of the story who serves to introduce the reader to the absolute evil that is Count Dracula. Harker fulfills the essential role in the tale of the Gothic hero: he is young, handsome, sexually unthreatening to the heroine, and the main rival of the villain for the affections of the woman they both desire. Ultimately triumphant, he rescues his love from evil clutches and marries her, embarking upon a long, happy, and uninteresting life. The essential Englishman, Harker embodies accepted English values, ideas that are tested severely from the very start of the tale. His English courtesy actually saves him, as he is unable to refuse a rosary from a terrified villager, wearing it despite his non-Catholic upbringing. Ironically, while he is trapped in the castle of Dracula, the rosary brings him comfort and a sense of protection. Confronting evil and the seductive, hypnotic aspects of vampirism, he is nearly killed, his unguided attempts at destroying the count proving futile. Barely escaping with his life, he finds a mentor in Dr. Van Helsing and goes on to play a leading role in the defeat of the monster who so shamed him. As the obvious love interest to Mina (Lucy in subsequent films), Harker was retained in the stage and screen adaptations of *Dracula*. In most versions he is presented as a good, if not naive person, utterly out of his depth, saved by the experience and wisdom of Van Helsing. [See also *Dracula*, (*Novel*).]

Hartmann, Franz An early-twentieth-century Austrian physician who was also a leading investigator into the occult and the undead, earning considerable notoriety for his 1896 work, *Premature Burial*. In it he argued that throughout history untold people had been declared dead incompetently, leading to the most tragic consequences. Detailing some seven hundred cases of premature burial, he recommended that anyone interred without proper embalming be provided with a bottle of chloroform in the coffin. In this fashion, if the individual wakes to find that he or she is underground, the easy way out is available. As the subject was linked to vampirism, his researches, while focusing on the morbid or the grotesque, presented a possible series of explanations for vampire traditions. Hartmann was also a frequent contributor to the journal *Occult Review*. His articles focused on the paranormal, particularly episodes of vampirism, the most famous being that of Countess Elga. Although dismissed by many serious specialists as a crank, he nevertheless helped preserve some of the most interesting vampire tales of the nineteenth century. One of them, known as "Uncle Helleborus," was an excellent example of psychic vampirism. (See also *Austria.*)

Hawthorn A hardy, thorny shrub or small tree, a member of the rose family with white or pink flowers, blossoming in clusters and followed by small red, blue, or black fruits. The wood of the hawthorn tree is one of the great natural antivampire elements, used in parts of Europe, especially among the Slavs, to make stakes for destroying the undead. It has been called the symbol of "good hope" because it signals that winter has ended and spring has begun. In ancient times hawthorn was worn by Athenian women at weddings and was considered by the Romans a charm against witchcraft and sorcery. In England the hawthorn is not to be brought into a house, especially if it is in flower. Its entry must be followed by the act of throwing the hawthorn back out the front door. In Bosnia, guests at wakes concealed twigs in their clothes, dropping them in the street as they left so that the deceased, if he or she had become a vampire, would pick them up and be too distracted to follow the living home. Hawthorn was sharpened into stakes and pounded into the ground near graves to pierce a vampire as it rose from its earthly resting place. The thorns of the shrubs were placed in shrouds or in coffins to stab and pin the revenant to the ground.

Hearts One of the great seats of life, from which blood issues forth, giving energy and strength to the body. It is the accepted source of power for the undead, and its removal or destruction will do much to slay the vampire. The heart, therefore, is often the focal point of attack by vampire hunters, whether through staking, piercing, or being torn away with merciless, righteous force. While some areas prefer decapitation as a method of slaying, most regions, in Europe particularly, adhere to the idea that a heart must be removed or mortally damaged. A demonstration of the heart's importance is found in Romania, where the *strigoii* is believed to possess two hearts, the second providing the creature with its diabolical unlife. When punctured, this organ will spout blood high into the air.

The prescribed methods for purging the heart are varied. In Serbia it was cut out, boiled in wine, and placed back into the cavity. In areas where the Greek church held sway, the heart was removed by the town butcher, who had the nasty task of rummaging through the corpse as the initial incision was made in the stomach and not in the chest. His groping in decayed remains, disguised to some degree by incense fumes, finally ended when the heart was found and literally ripped out—an idea that would have horrified other groups, such as the Yugoslavian Gypsies, who believed that contact with vampire blood caused madness. Other people simply burned the heart, while in Romania a stake or needle, often heated, was inserted, rendering the organ useless to evil entities with designs on the corpse. (See also *Blood, Destroying the Vampire, Sacrifices,* and *Stake, Wooden.*)

Hecate A goddess of the ancient world, held by the Greeks to be the patroness of magic and spells, later revered and feared as a deity of the underworld, the so-called Queen of the Phantom World. Her name meant "She Who Works Her Will," and she was often depicted as triple-formed, with three bodies standing back to back to back so that she could observe all directions from a crossroad. Her association with vampirism, particularly with the drinking of blood, probably stemmed from her involvement in dark magic, known as the magic of the left-hand path, and the foul nature of her servants. Among her evil entourage were the demons known as *mormos* (singular *mormo*) and the fiendish phantomlike vampires called *empusas* (singular *empusa*). Hecate, whose position in witchcraft and magic has remained constant over the centuries, was an influential figure in linking vampires with sorcery and evil magical rites.

Hematomania A psychological fixation on blood from which an individual derives satisfaction of a kind of erotic blood lust. Such forms of gratification, called also hematodipsia, are generally rare but constitute a condition for which there are numerous historical and modern examples. Elizabeth Bathory, the Marquis de Sade, and Gilles de Rais were obsessed to varying degrees with the sexual aspects of bloodshed. Today many persons wander cities and countries in search of blood donors, as researched by Carol Page, author of *Blood Lust* (1991), a study of modern vampires, seemingly ordinary people who drink human blood. According to her figures, there are nearly fifty thousand "vampires" in the United States today. Dr. Jeanne Youngson has also interviewed these self-proclaimed vampires. (See *Blood* and *Historical Vampires.*)

Herbs: See *Garlic.*

Heretics Adherents to a theological teaching or doctrine condemned as false by recognized ecclesiastical authorities. Heresy has been evident over the centuries in numerous religious belief systems around the world, but historically it has been most often associated with the Christian church, with such heretical groups as the Donatists, Pelagians, Arians, and Albigensians. Stern measures were taken at times to purge these heretics from the body of the Church, ranging from the Inquisition to the individual punishment of excommunication. Through the latter pronouncement, the idea was fostered that excommunicants would be liable to transform into vampires. Nowhere was this more true than in Russia, where several vampire types were named for heretics: *eretik, erestun,* and *eretica.* These were persons who had deviated from the teachings of the Russian Orthodox church, dabbled in black magic, practiced witchcraft, or sold their souls to the devil during their lifetimes. (See also *Christianity, Excommunication, Inovercy,* and *Russia.*)

Hiadam Vampires Also Haidam, several vampires found in a village near the Hungarian border, who in 1720 were investigated by the officials of the Holy Roman Empire. The result was one of the best-documented cases of vampirism of the time. It began one night at dinnertime when a soldier, billeted with a farming family, watched a stranger come into the house and take a place at the table—to the total horror of the silent hosts. The following morning the farmer was found dead. Finally the family told the soldier that the stranger had been the farmer's father, dead for ten years. The trooper naturally reported this incident to his friends, and word reached the local general, Count de Cadreras, who undertook a formal investigation. Depositions were gathered, and the father was exhumed, his corpse discovered perfectly preserved. Soon others came forward to report on other vampires: one had been dead for thirty years and had killed three family members; another, dead sixteen years, had sucked the blood and life out of two of his sons. It was decided that each of these creatures had to be destroyed. The farmer's father was decapitated, the second had a nail driven into his skull, and the third was cremated. A full account of these events was sent to Emperor Charles VI. Shocked, he ordered another investigation, this time by lawyers, surgeons, and theologians. The count later described the case to a member of the faculty at the University of Fribourg.

Hide Various kinds of animal skins used in some regions, particularly by the Gypsies, to cover a grave or a body during the process of impalement. They believed that any vampire hunters coming in contact with the blood of a vampire would almost certainly go insane and thus avoided touching blood at all costs. By tradition, there were two methods at their disposal: the first was to place a hide over a suspected grave and then to pound poles or stakes into the earth to impale the rising dead; the second was to drape or wrap the actual corpse with the hide and then hammer a stake into its heart. The covering ultimately served a practical purpose as a corpse in the state of decomposition can become bloated with gases, literally exploding when pierced, covering anyone in the vicinity with foul liquids and blood. (See also *Destroying the Vampire.*)

Highgate Vampire The modern case of hysteria, in which it was widely reported that a vampire was living in Highgate Cemetery, London. An example of continuing public fascination with the undead, the

Highgate Vampire first came to the public's attention in March 1970, when the *London Evening News* reported that around one hundred people had taken part in a hunt the previous night for a vampire within the dark, moody confines of the cemetery. The focus of the media attention turned to David Farrant and Allan Blood, vampire experts who led the search. Both were convinced that a vampire was sleeping in one of the vaults and were determined to find it and kill it. While blamed for the desecration of tombs and arrested for trespass, Farrant was acquitted on the grounds that the cemetery was open to the public. As is typical of such incidents, stories based on rumor and on unconfirmed sightings soon spread, and the tabloids and newspapers ran exploitative reports. No vampire was ever publicly discovered. One witness reported seeing a gaunt man in black leave the cemetery at night, and a nearby young woman was supposedly a victim of the Highgate Vampire. Another expert, Sean Manchester, conducted his own investigation of the affair.

Historia Rerum Anglicarum A chronicle of England written around 1196 to 1198 by William of Newburgh. Translated as *History of English Events,* the work covers the years 1066 to 1198 and is an extremely valuable source on English domestic history. It has been criticized, however, for its overreliance on oral traditions, legends, and hearsay. The *Historia* is cited as one of the foremost medieval accounts of vampires, containing several interesting episodes in Buckinghamshire, Berwick, Alnwick Castle, and Melrose.

Historical Vampires: See table.

Historie von Dracole Wayda Also *Historie von Dracule Wajde* (History of Prince Dracula), a German pamphlet published in Leipzig in 1493 on the life of Vlad Tepes (Vlad the Impaler). While the actual authorship remains unknown, it has been argued by one scholar that it was published by Martin Landsberg. This pamphlet differs from other works on Vlad in that it presents him in uniform and depicts him as less than handsome. It is currently in the State Public Library, Saltykov, Shchedrin, St. Petersburg.

Hodder, Reginald English writer of the early twentieth century whose novel, *The Vampire* (1912), is considered a minor classic in the genre. It tells of a woman who is the leader of an occult society, compelled to vampirize other persons in an attempt to sustain her dwindling vitality. Her vampirism is of a psychic nature, transmitted through a powerful talisman. Much of the plot revolves around the device's seizure by evil forces who intend to use it for their own plans of domination. (See also *Fortune, Dion,* and *Psychic Vampirism.*)

Historical Vampires

Name	Activities or Crimes
Ardisson, Victor (early twentieth century)	Illegal exhumation and necrophilia, the "Vampire of Muy"
Bathory, Elizabeth (1560–1614)	Sadism, vampirism
Bertrand, Sergeant (mid–nineteenth century)	Corpse mutilation and necrophilia, the "Vampire of Montparnasse"
de Sade, Marquis (1740–1814)	Extreme sexual deviance, sadism
Garnier, Gilles (late sixteenth century)	Blood drinking, lycanthropy, cannibalism
Geisslerin, Clara (late sixteenth century)	Witchcraft, vampirism, and cannibalism
Gilles de Rais (1404–1440)	Sorcery, necrophilia, sadism, vampirism, and cannibalism
Haarmann, Fritz (1879–1925)	Vampirism, corpse mutilation, cannibalism, and selling of body parts, the "Hanover Vampire"
Haigh, John (d. 1949)	Murder and vampirism, the "Vampire of London"
Kurten, Peter (1883–1931)	Rape, murder, vampirism, the "Vampire of Düsseldorf."
Leger, Antoine (d. 1824)	Rape, murder, vampirism, and cannibalism
Verzini, Vincenzo (late nineteenth century)	Murder, corpse mutilation, and vampirism

(See also *Ivan Vasilli, Living Vampires, Moroii, Necrophilia,* and *Necrosadism.*)

Holly The name given to a broad genus of shrubs or trees, extending into some 295 species, including the well-known Christmas hollies. They are distinguished usually by greenish flowers with red or black berries. The Christian custom of decorating houses and churches with holly probably stemmed from the Roman use of the shrub during the festival of Saturnalia or from the Teutonic beliefs concerning herbs, plants, and nature. Holly is thus ranked as a beneficent tree and has been used as a protective device against the undead, hung at windows or on doors.

Holmes-Dracula File, The A 1978 novel by Fred Saberhagen, continuing the story of Dracula begun in his *The Dracula Tape* (1975), in which he brings together Sherlock Holmes and Count Dracula. Shocking, even horrifying, to faithful readers of both Arthur Conan Doyle and Bram Stoker, *The Holmes-Dracula File* is based on the premise that Holmes is the half nephew of the count, the result of an affair between the future detective's mother, a harlot, and Dracula's younger brother. Sherlock has an evil vampire twin and loses his mother, who, having become an undead, is staked by her husband and the eldest son, Mycroft. Dracula, meanwhile, is challenged by the villainous Dr. Seward but is aided by his love, Mina Harker. The novel is typical of Saberhagen's cleverly and deliberately convoluted plots, intertwining two distinct literary creations in a bizarre tale.

Holmes, Sherlock. The most famous of all fictional detectives, created by Sir Arthur Conan Doyle and first appearing in the *Strand* magazine in 1891. Holmes never investigated a real vampire, but he did solve a case involving apparent vampirism in "Adventure of the Sussex Vampire." Later writers in the twentieth century brought Holmes into battle with the undead, even if Sir Arthur Conan Doyle did not. Their works have taken the detective into frightening and bizarre situations. In 1978 Loren D. Estleman wrote *Sherlock Holmes vs. Dracula*, while that same year Fred Saberhaben produced the shocking *The Holmes-Dracula File*, which depicts Holmes as the half nephew of Dracula.

Holy Water: See *Water, Holy.*

Horace A great Latin lyric poet (65–8 B.C.) whose verse made him one of the most respected literary figures in early imperial Rome. While not composed specifically on the subject of the undead, Horace's poetry included tremendous sensuality and veiled references to being bitten in his *Carmen* (I.XIII.11,12):

> I burn, when in excess of wine
> He sails those snowy arms of thine,
> Or on thy lips the fierce fond boy
> Marks with his teeth the furious joy.

(See also *Poetry.*)

"Horla, The": See *Maupassant, Guy de.*

Horror of Dracula The first great Dracula film from Hammer Films, re-leased in 1958, starring Christopher Lee, Peter Cushing, and Michael Gough, directed by Terence Fisher. The epitome of the Hammer Films style of moviemaking, this colorful, gory, sexy, and well-paced work began the long line of very popular Dracula and vampire productions for the studio. Coming on the heels of *Curse of Frankenstein* (1957), the *Horror of Dracula* (also *Dracula*) established Hammer's place in the hor-ror cinema. It introduced Lee as the ultimate Dracula and made fangs, red eyes, great amounts of blood, and an overt sexual component an essential part of subsequent vampire films.

As directed by Fisher, this is a version of Bram Stoker's 1897 novel, but it relies in large measure on Hamilton Deane's play. Jonathan Harker is not presented as a naive Englishman. Instead he is here a devoted disciple of Van Helsing, entering Dracula's castle knowing full well who and what the count is. Fisher assumed that the audience would recognize immediately the basic plot and char-acter of Dracula without need for additional explanations. Lee enters the scene as a subtly ominous host, making his sudden transforma-tion into a red-eyed monster a short time later all the more shocking. Harker is killed and vampirized by the count, eventually finding re-lease by Van Helsing's hand. Desirous of taking as his bride Lucy, Harker's love, Dracula departs his castle, passing Van Helsing on the road. While the doctor brings news of Harker's death to Arthur Holm-wood (Gough) and his wife, Mina, Dracula is claiming Lucy as his own. Dying from his embraces, she returns as a vampire but is de-stroyed by Van Helsing and an utterly horrified Holmwood. His cre-ation killed, the count next chooses Mina Holmwood, seducing her in very effective scenes. Her death is prevented by Van Helsing, who chases Dracula to the vampire's castle and there confronts him. The climax of the film is quite spectacular, with Van Helsing leaping across a table to tear down a curtain, revealing the rays of the sun. Dracula, caught in the sunlight, dissolves to dust, a stunning conclu-sion that posed certain problems in producing a sequel. (See *Films.*)

Horse An animal often held to be instrumental in finding the resting places of vampires. In Albania a white horse was led into a cemetery suspected of housing an undead, where the animal was forced to trod on graves. The horse absolutely refused to step over ground that sheltered the hunted monster. Investigation for other telltale vampire signs followed. Elsewhere in Europe, the ritual adhered to these broad lines but with specific changes. In some places the horse had to be black, without any color blemishes. Further, it was supposed to be a mount that had never stumbled and was ridden by a virginal youth. The horse, on occasions, was also required to be virginal. While custom holds that a horse will not cross a vampire's grave, the Gypsies stated that the fiend could be destroyed by walking a steed several times over a suspected burial plot, compelling the horse to do so if necessary. The undead, however, can transform themselves into horses, usually black, and horses can also become vampires, at which time they are no longer satisfied with apples or sugar cubes. (See also *Animals.*)

Horseshoes A symbol of good luck found in numerous countries, from Scotland to India. In England it was widely held that a horseshoe in a house or on a door was a potent preventive against attacks by witches or warlocks. A similar view was found in the Scottish countryside, while greater emphasis was placed in Italy and in Spain on forked pieces of coral, the shape being more important than the material used, in this case coral replacing iron. From these antiwitch properties came the broad acceptance of horseshoes as devices of felicity. They can be used in an attempt to keep vampires at bay, the bane that they represent against evil extending even to the undead. (See also *Charms.*)

Horwath, Adam A late-eighteenth-century Hungarian playwright, author of a play on Vlad Tepes (Vlad the Impaler) that presented the nobleman as a villain. Published in 1787 at Györ, the work was first performed in Buda on July 15, 1790, and published in rewritten form as a three-act drama at Pest in 1792. The plot revolves around Dracula's revenge on the Hungarian leader Janos Hunyadi, for the murder of his father and brother. Dracula betrays Hunyadi to the Serbians and their despot, Brancovic. This was one of the earliest-known dramatic presentations of Vlad. (See also *Plays.*)

Host, Consecrated More properly known as the Holy Eucharist, the Catholic sacrament in which bread and/or wine are consecrated in commemoration of the passion and death of Jesus Christ. The wine becomes His Blood, and the host, usually a thin wafer made according to traditional design and materials, is honored as His Body. Of all of the weapons used against vampires, the host is surely the most powerful and the most feared by all forms of evil. Its application, however, is understandably rare, as during the Middle Ages, even into the twentieth century, the Eucharist was carefully protected, normally kept in a tabernacle or locked cylinder. Great reverence must be maintained lest the sacrament be desecrated. The specific uses for the host are manifold. It can be wielded as an impenetrable shield or a burning weapon or it can be broken into four pieces and placed in the rough shape of a cross in a coffin full of earth, thereby eliminating the box as a resting place for the vampire. (See also *Protecting a Vampire.*)

Hotel Transylvania The first in a series of novels by Chelsea Quinn Yarbro, published in 1978, introducing the character Le Comte de Saint-Germain, an ancient vampire who wanders the world and is presented in various historical periods. *Hotel Transylvania* places the count in 1743 Paris, the plot revolving around his struggle with a cult of Satan worshipers and his efforts to rescue his lover from their clutches. The novel establishes Saint-Germain as the hero, his sanguinary habits a minor offense compared with the twisted, vile activities of the mortals whom he encounters.

House of Dark Shadows A 1970 MGM-distributed film that brought to the screen the popular television show "Dark Shadows," starring Jonathan Frid, Joan Bennett, Grayson Hall, and John Karlen. The vampire Barnabas Collins (Frid) is awakened from his resting place by a greedy treasure hunter, workman Willie Loomis (Karlen), and returns to his family home of Collingwood. There, accepted by his modern relatives as a lost cousin, Barnabas establishes his lair, terrorizing the countryside with his nocturnal feedings. Dr. Julia Hoffman (Hall) learns of his real nature and tries to cure him, nearly succeeding until jealousy intervenes, as the vampire chooses as his bride another woman (Kathryn Leigh Scott). The entire production is moodily effective, energized by Frid's now familiar performance, reliable special effects, and the supporting cast. A memorable scene involves the trapping of a female vampire by cross-wielding police, a new concept in law enforcement. Dan Curtis, creator of the television show, directed.

Hsi-hsue-kuei A Chinese name for a vampire. It is translated as "suckblood demon." (See *China, Kuang-shi,* and *K'uei* for other details.)

Huber, Ambrosius A late-fifteenth-century printer of Nuremberg, who in 1499 published a pamphlet on Vlad Tepes (Vlad the Impaler). One of the works that helped to present Vlad to the West as a savage, wild tyrant, the pamphlet included a woodcut depicting the ruler dining in the midst of numerous impaled victims. The text then added to this grim scene by recounting his habits of impaling people and roasting their heads in kettles, as well as cooking children and making their parents eat them.

Hubner, Stephen The so-called Vampire of Treautenau, a Slavic village, who killed several people sometime between 1730–1732. Hubner's case was remarkable in that he attacked not only human beings, but cattle as well, supposedly strangling them. The supreme court of the district investigated the murders and found sufficient cause to exhume the body of Hubner, even though he had been dead for five months. He was perfectly preserved as a corpse. Giving the body to the public executioner, the magistrates ordered it decapitated and cremated. As a precaution, the corpses buried near Hubner were also burned.

Huet, Pierre-Daniel French bishop of Avranches and Soissons (1630–1721) who included in his *Memoirs* a discussion of vampires, one of the earliest church writers to examine the undead. Taking his holy orders in 1676, Huet was a leading classical scholar of the time, his interests extending as well into astronomy, anatomy, Arabic, and mathematics. The section of his *Memoirs* devoted to vampirism was based on his own theological views and the reports provided to him by Father François Richard, himself a recognized authority, thanks to his many years of service on Santorini, the most vampire-infested place on the planet. Huet's account included Greek customs of burning the dead, the belief that wicked persons had their bodies taken over by the power of the devil, and the curious custom of cutting off a corpse's feet, nose, hands, and ears and then hanging these around the dead person's elbow as a preventive.

Hungary A country described by the early-twentieth-century expert Montague Summers as sharing with Greece and Slovakia the reputation of being heavily infested with vampires. Indeed, it was in Hungary that the undead first came to the general attention of Europe, owing to the numerous cases that took place in villages and throughout the countryside during the seventeenth to eighteenth centuries. These were examined as fact by such journals as the *Gleaner* (*Glaneur Hollandois*) and the *Mercure Galant,* as well as in the treatises of German experts and theologians, including Philip Rohr, Dom Augustine Calmet, and Karl Ferdinand de Schertz. The incessant nature of these reports caused both secular and Church authorities to investigate, the latter inquiry forming the basis of de Schertz's book, *Magia Posthuma.* Among the notable were the cases of the Hiadam Vampire and Arnold Paole, the latter by far the most talked about vampire in the eighteenth century. The most common species found in Hungary is the *vampir,* similar in all respects to the regular Slavic variety, destroyed by a stake through the heart. More obscure is the *liderc nadaly,* whose predations are ended by a nail through the temple. The land of the Magyars, Hungary gave to the world the word *vampire,* which has origins in the Magyar tongue. A country of firsts in vampiric traditions, Hungary is also the home of possibly the earliest vampire film, the 1921 silent picture, *Drakula*, although it is unclear whether the work was about Vlad Tepes (Vlad the Impaler) or a version of Bram Stoker's novel *Dracula*. (See also *Liebava Vampire*.)

Hunger, The A 1981 novel by Whitley Strieber (of *Wolfen* and *Communion* fame), the basis for the 1983 film of the same name. *The Hunger* brings vampirism into the modern age but presents it through the near eternal creature Miriam Blaylock, not so much a vampire as another species entirely. After losing her lover, she sets out to find his replacement, choosing a female doctor involved in research on immortality. Placing herself at the disposal of the doctor, Miriam allows herself to be studied, all the while seducing the scientist, drawing the mortal inexorably into her own eternal life. The climax is startling, emphasizing the cycle of life, death, unlife, and love. (See also *Literature* and next entry.)

Hunger, The The 1983 MGM film version based on the 1981 novel by Whitley Strieber. Starring Catherine Deneuve, Susan Sarandon, and David Bowie, it presents the ancient vampire Miriam Blaylock, who grants a kind of immortality to her lovers. Directed by first-timer Tony Scott, *The Hunger* is a visually arresting work, detailing the relationship between Miriam (Deneuve) and a doctor (Sarandon), who is fascinated by the sudden, unstoppable aging of Miriam's husband (Bowie). After his departure, Miriam chooses this woman to be her next lover. Deneuve is stunning as the immortal. Flashbacks show her origins in ancient Egypt; her age is made clear by the resting place of Bowie, a box stashed away with dozens of others, each containing the body of a previous lover. Unable to die, but aging forever, they spend eternity in a box, whispering to themselves. (See *Films*.)

Huntley, Raymond English actor (b. 1904) who portrayed Count Dracula when the Hamilton Deane play *Dracula* opened in London in February 1927. A young performer of only twenty-two, he joined the Deane company while it was on the road. He was expected to supply his own costumes—various styles of evening dress. After playing very successfully in London, he was the first choice of the American producer Horace Liveright to re-create the role on the New York stage. After turning down the offer, Huntley was replaced by Bela Lugosi. Later he did accept the role in the traveling American production. Ironically, while Lugosi was forever typecast, Huntley escaped the vampire's clutches professionally, going on to a very respected and enduring career in the English theater. Huntley's Dracula makeup included a wig, with streaks of gray that were swept upward, a subtle touch that accentuated the Mephistophelian nature of the character. [See *Dracula (Deane)*.]

Hupfuff, Matthias An early-sixteenth-century publisher who in 1500 printed a pamphlet in German on Vlad Tepes (Vlad the Impaler) that continued the spread of tales concerning his bloodthirsty rule and extreme cruelty. Published at Strasbourg, the work contained a well-known woodcut depicting Vlad eating amid hundreds of victims dangling from the spikes on which they had been impaled. Copies can be found at the Staatsbibliothek, Berlin; the Royal Library, Copenhagen; and the Biblioteca Centrala Bucaresti, Bucharest. (See *Vlad Tepes*.)

Hydra Known in the Greek as Idhra, an island in the Aegean Sea, just off the Argolis Peninsula in Greece. It was said in Greek folk tales to have once been infested by a multitude of vampires. So troublesome and undesirable did they become that a local cleric used prayers and exorcisms to banish all of them to the distant isle of Santorini, which soon acquired the reputation of being the most vampire-infested place in the world. (See also *Greece*.)

Hypnotism A feared power of the undead that allows them to place a victim under their sway and to enter or depart an abode of the living, passing the most alert of guards. The vampire's hypnotic abilities are usually bent toward a specific person chosen to be the evening's prey. Meeting the intended victim in some public place, the vampire begins its campaign of suggestion and seduction, usually entering the chambers of the prey after having been invited in some hours before. There, using its burning eyes, the vampire compels the poor mortal into welcoming its murderous advances. The incisors tearing into the soft flesh of the neck appear to have an anesthetic effect. Mass suggestion is also possible by an especially strong vampire. An intriguing case of this was presented in the tale of the Russian governor who returned from the grave, as told in Madam Blavatsky's work *Isis Unveiled*. Another aspect of hypnotism is the placing of a command in the mind of a victim—this person then being driven to leave his or her abode to be with the vampiric lover. Hypnosis has been seen in many films, erotically in the 1979 *Dracula* with Frank Langella, and humorously in the 1948 *Abbott and Costello Meet Frankenstein*. The most memorable episode of hypnosis used against a vampire was in Bram Stoker's novel *Dracula*. Mina is hypnotized by Dr. Van Helsing, who uses her psychic connection with Dracula to track the vampire's movements. (See *Threshold*.)

I Am Legend: See *Matheson, Richard.*

Iceland The island nation that has had its share of warriors returned from beyond in the shape of spirits or revenants. This could be prevented by piercing the feet of a corpse before burial to keep the body from wandering. Someone who died while seated was taken out of the house still in the chair, a hole kicked in a wall to make sure the deceased had no way of remembering the door out of which he was taken. Icelandic revenants have the curious habit of climbing onto roofs to kick at shingles. They can be quieted by decapitation, coupled with reburial. The head should be placed beneath the corpse. Iceland also had a belief in Sabbatarians (those born on a Saturday), holding that such persons are aided by a fetch or natal spirit, called *fylgja,* in the shape of a dog. (See also *Grettis Saga* and *Scott, Sir Walter.*)

Icon Also *ikon,* a sacred object found in the lands under the influence of the Eastern Christian church; it is a pictorial representation of Christ, the Virgin Mary, or other holy person. Made usually of wood, the icon's picture is generally a mural painting or a mosaic. Given particular veneration by the faithful, icons are a symbol of goodness, long viewed as an indispensable aspect of worship in the Eastern Christian church. Thus they are frequently used weapons against vampires, as common in some regions as crosses or crucifixes in the West. The icon figures in the Bulgarian practice of bottling vampires, wielded by a magician who uses it to drive the undead into a container, which is then topped with a cork. A piece of an icon is placed on the cork and the entire vessel is thrown into a fire to be consumed.

Ignatius Day A feast held in honor of St. Ignatius of Antioch, who perished in the Colosseum approximately A.D. 107, eaten by lions. The date of the festival varies; in the West it is October 17, previously February 1, while in the region of the Eastern church it is usually December 20. Among the Wallachians the day was celebrated by the killing of a pig. The animal's lard was then smeared over certain body parts to prevent vampire attack and to ensure that a person would not become a vampire.

Ignis fatuus: See *Will-o'-the-Wisp.*

Immortality Eternal life, the prime allure of the vampire and one of the reasons for its enduring popularity. The fact that the undead are immortal is not universally documented in folklore, but their eternal nature is well established in fiction, with such figures as Saint-Germain, Lestat, and Dracula. The idea of living forever is appealing to anyone who recognizes the transitory nature of human life. It has been an ancient quest, sought after by magicians and alchemists. Except for those cursed by God or certain semimystical personages such as the historical Saint-Germain, it has unfortunately proven elusive. The vampire, however, has cheated death, even though its continued existence comes at a dreadful price—drinking the blood or feeding off those who were once equals in the mortal struggle. While their existence is dark and grim, filled with dangers on all sides, vampires appear to gain a sort of ironic victory, especially when compared with the slow, lingering deaths awaiting other humans.

Impundulu A voracious witch's servant (also called a familiar) found in the eastern Cape region of Africa, usually owned by a female witch, who passed it on to her daughter, a leading reason why the female offspring of witches seldom married. The *impundulu* (plural *iimpundulu*) appeared to its mistress in the form of a handsome young man who then became her lover. Sent out to bring suffering and death, it was merciless, relentless, and insatiable. The witch really had no choice but to use it to kill, as the creature was always hungry for blood, both from humans and cattle. To fail in satisfying the *impundulu* could bring about a terrible death for the owner. Entire families and herds were wiped out as the familiar sucked the blood of victims, bringing a wasting disease, coughing, an inability to breed (known as *iphika*), and sudden death. The quick demise was called being slain by the "bird of heaven," as a sharp, unbearable pain was felt in the chest or the head. When it was not handed down directly, the *impundulu* was called an *ishologu,* an ownerless fiend that acted on its own. (See also *Bajang* for a similar creature.)

I'm Sorry the Bridge Is Out, You'll Have to Spend the Night A 1970 musical comedy written by Sheldon Allman and Bob Pickett, originally starring Peter Virgo, Jr., Gloria Dell, and Tony Lane. A spoof of the entire horror genre, the production featured not only Dracula and his wife, Natasha, but Dr. Frankenstein, his monster, and the hunchbacked Igor. The loose plot centers around a young couple who wander into Dracula's castle after a storm washes out a bridge. Songs include "The Brides of Dracula" and Renfield's appropriate piece, "Flies." The play, which opened in Los Angeles, developed the musical and comedic potential of horror but never found a cult following, as did *The Rocky Horror Picture Show.* A recent musical on vampires was *Rockula* (1990).

In a Glass Darkly: See *"Carmilla"* and *Le Fanu, Sheridan.*

Incense An aromatic substance composed of grains of resins, sometimes mixed with spices, that is burned or sprinkled on lighted charcoal in a censer, thereby creating a sweet-smelling to powerfully pungent odor. Incense has been used in major religious services over the centuries to serve as an oblation, a means of symbolizing the ascent of prayer to heaven, or to drive out demons from a person or a place. In fighting the undead, it ranks with garlic as a preventive to vampirism, often driving away the undead or counteracting their stench, and was burned at times in excessive amounts during ceremonies where vampires were being destroyed. The best witness to this was Joseph Pitton de Tournefort, who in his account of his journeys in the Levant described the Greeks exhuming the rotting corpse of a suspected *vrykolakas*. Nauseating amounts of incense were used to mask the body's smell, although the aroma may also have been intended to drive away the evil spirit inhabiting the undead. In Romania, it was sprinkled or shoved into the ears, eyes, and nostrils of a deceased, thereby preventing the entry of a resuscitating spirit, something also done with garlic.

Incorruptibility of Corpses The mysterious preservation of a corpse or the absence of decomposition, a common characteristic mentioned in historical accounts about vampires. By accepted custom, vampirism leaves the body in a preserved state until it is destroyed. While the Western Christian church acknowledged that a body's lack of corruption is a symbol of holiness, as in the case of saints, the average person should deteriorate. The failure of the body to do so could be taken to mean that for various reasons an evil agent was at work, a view held especially by the Eastern Christian church. One of the other commonly believed causes of incorruption was excommunication, as doctrine and folklore stated that a body would remain incorrupt until absolution was granted. This naturally led to the belief that excommunicants returned as vampires, their corpses waiting vessels for vampires. Devils and demons made corpses incorrupt to serve as vessels for wicked deeds. Medical specialists today point out that there are many natural causes for the preservation of bodies, from excessive dryness to deep burials. (See also *Santorini.*)

Incubus A type of male demon, the masculine to the feminine *succubus* (see also), that visits women during the night to torment them and to have sexual intercourse. Its name is derived from a combination of *incubare* (to lie upon or weigh down) and *incubus* (nightmare). It possesses attributes similar to the nightmare and the vampire: nightly visitations, the draining of life and strength, extreme sexual desire, and the habit of crushing its victim. Further, like the vampires found among the Gypsy or Slavic communities, the incubus can father children, only such offspring are demons, witches, or hideously deformed humans, while the undead often produce *dhampirs,* powerful warriors against the vampire. (See also *Alp.*)

India A place of ancient and multifaceted cultures and religions, including Buddhism, Islam, Sikhism, Christianity, Jainism, and Hinduism, each with its own legends and tales of the dead. While opinions naturally vary, many scholars and vampirologists now believe that the vast world of the vampire began in India, in the bloody gods and legends of the ancient Indian peoples. (Some say Egypt, but other places are also suggested.) Vampires probably did start in the Indus Valley, sometime in the third millennium B.C., in the shape of deities who were often depicted as bloodthirsty and merciless embodiments of primordial fears: death, disease, nature, blood, and the night. In turn, these ideas and fears helped shape the vampire terror in surrounding lands, including Tibet, Nepal, China, Mongolia, and other parts of Asia. Trade, cultural and religious diffusion, even wars, carried Indian tales to other lands, ultimately reaching Europe, which had its own traditions of blood and death. The Gypsies, the great nomadic people, added their own contributions to the recounting of such tales, as they came originally from India, spreading across the entire world.

Throughout the diverse territories of the country, from Madras in the south to Rajasthan and the Himalayas in the north, there is an abundance of vampires or vampirelike beings, one to suit every conceivable taste. These were joined by ogres, ghosts, animal spirits, evil sorcerers, Hindu and Buddhist saints, demons, trolls, and other mythical beings. The word *bhuta* has been used to describe all forms of Indian vampires, although many folklorists refer to it as a specific type of vampire. Other types include *rakshasa, jigarkhwar, hanh saburo, hant-pare, hantu-dor dong, mah'anah, pacu-pati, penanggalan, pisacha,* and *vetala.* (See also *Cremation; Gods, Vampire;* and *Incense.*)

Inovercy A Russian word meaning a follower of a different faith or creed, specifically someone who does not adhere to the teachings of the Russian Orthodox church and is thus doomed to come back as a vampire after death. In old Russia, or Czarist Russia, such persons were generally persecuted against by both the government and society. It was assumed that the *inovercy* died while in a state of sin and were quite possibly in league with the devil or practiced sorcery, in which case they had to be heretics. Thus, after death, they were labeled *založnye pokojniki,* the unclean dead, not entitled to a decent burial. Their bodies were dumped in large pits or in charnel houses, called *ubogie doma,* and funerals were not allowed until the seventh Thursday after Easter. When droughts or other natural disasters struck, Russian villagers often abused the corpses of the *inovercy* to convince them to stop bringing bad luck. While the *ubogie doma* were outlawed in 1771, the practice continued in the villages for many years. (See also *Heretics.*)

Interview with the Vampire The 1976 novel by Anne Rice that has become the most popular vampire story of the late twentieth century, joined by other entries in her Vampire Chronicles (*The Vampire Lestat*, 1985, *Queen of the Damned*, 1988, and *The Tale of the Body Thief*, 1992). In this first novel of the series, Rice created an alluring, plausible, and compelling world in which vampires exist, flourish, and die in the midst of the living. The central character is Louis, a comparatively young vampire who narrates his life story to a journalist in San Francisco. Much of the story takes place in the early nineteenth century in New Orleans, where in 1791 Louis is transformed into an undead by Lestat, an enigmatic, often brutal vampire who figures most prominently in Rice's other novels. Joined by the vampire-child Claudia (one of the most tragic figures in all of vampire literature), Louis journeys to Europe to find others of his own kind. *Interview with the Vampire* works on many levels, from the purely literary to the morbid and disturbingly eerie, the innermost thoughts and feelings of the living dead revealed in stunning imagery and prose.

Invitations: See *Threshold.*

Ireland It is, in legend and lore, the land of banshees, faeries, elves, leprechauns, and vampires, receiving cultural imprints from the Celts, the Norsemen, Christianity, and the English, despite centuries of Anglo-Irish conflict. The Celts were firm believers in their blood-drinking ceremonies and in their traditions of the blood of heroes. Vampire beliefs in Ireland, however, were a late development, coming probably during the first days of Celtic migrations. The two best-known vampirelike beings in the isle are the *dearg-due* and the *leanhaum-shee.* The latter is the "fairy mistress," not described specifically as a vampire but engaging in decidedly vampiric activities, particularly toward her lovers; the former is the "red blood sucker." A *dearg-due* is supposedly buried in Waterford, near Strongbow's Tree, in a small churchyard. Ireland is also held in high regard by readers of vampire literature and by the literate in general for being the home of two of the genre's greatest figures, Bram Stoker and Sheridan Le Fanu.

Iron According to Roman custom, iron in the form of nails was taken from coffins and used as a charm against demons or evil spirits, particularly those beings that entered houses at night. Iron's primary value against vampires was in China, where it was often placed with red peas, rice, or by itself around the suspected grave of the dreaded *kuang-shi,* to trap it beneath the ground.

Isis Unveiled: See *Blavatsky, Madame Helena.*

Italy The onetime home of the Roman Empire and later the heart of Christendom, one of the main places from which opposition to the undead originated and has been led. The Christian, later Catholic, church, with its hierarchy in the Vatican, helped to give shape in the West to many of the most important and most recognizable elements of vampire lore, from bloodsuckers' inherently evil natures to their fear of the cross, holy water, communion, and the saints. Italy has no modern indigenous vampire species, although there are many customs related to death, the dead, ghosts, or returning spirits. For example, Abruzzi, a region in central Italy, has very interesting concepts related to the departed coming back once a year, on November 1. These beliefs are related to surviving elements of the ancient Roman religion, including the *lemuria,* as well as the *anthesteria* of the Greeks. The ancient Romans had an extensive number of vampirelike spirits, such as the *lamia, mormo, lemures, larvae, empusas,* and, of course, the *striges* or *strix,* a night owl associated with a night demon that sucks the blood of children. These beings, while passing into Christian lore, did not become established in folklore as they did in Greece, the Balkans, and elsewhere. The entity most like the vampire in Italian tradition is the witch *(striga),* usually an old hag who, in the pattern set by the *strix,* will attack children with her curses, causing them to waste away. A complicated series of rituals are followed to be rid of her, but the surest remedy is to rely upon the powers of the Church.

While Italian horror films are not held in high regard in most international cinematic circles, the Italians have nevertheless distinguished themselves with a number of excellent pictures, directors, and performers. Italian horror has been characterized as suffering from excess spectacle, lurid sets and plots, overacting, and scenes of terrible sadomasochistic indulgence. When directed with skill and used with a masterful purpose, these elements have combined to create memorable productions. In 1957 Riccardo Freda directed *I Vampiri,* starring the queen of Italian B movies, Gianna Maria Canale, in a version of an immortal who maintains her youth with blood, à la Elizabeth Bathory. It was released a year before *Horror of Dracula* by Hammer Films and can be declared the forerunner of the subsequent vampire films by European and American studios. By far the greatest of the Italian vampire films was *La Maschera del Demonio,* also called *Black Sunday* (1960), directed by Mario Bava and starring Barbara Steele, another favorite of Italian audiences. Bava later directed *Black Sabbath* (1963) and *Hercules in the Haunted World* (1962). Other Italian contributions have included *La Danza Macabra* (1963);

Gli Amanti d'Oltre Tomba (1965, *The Faceless Monster*); *La Sorella di Satana* (1965, *Revenge of the Blood Beast*); *La Notte dei Diavoli* (1967), a remake of the Wurdalak segment in *Black Sabbath;* and the films starring Walter Brandi: *L'Ultima Preda del Vampiro* (1960, *The Playgirls and the Vampire*), *L'Amante del Vampiro* (1961, *The Vampire and the Ballerina*), and *La Strage dei Vampiri* (1962, *Slaughter of the Vampires*). (See also *Films, Literature,* and *Verzeni, Vincenzo.*)

Iudicium aquae: See *Water* and *Vampires.*

Ivan Vasilli The name of a Russian steamer built in 1897 that was the supposed home of an insatiable murderous vampirelike phantom. The story of the so-called vampire ship first appeared in the book *Invisible Horizons* by Vincent Gaddis. Starting in 1903, the crew began to have weird experiences; they were seized by a sudden bone-numbing cold, inexplicable bouts of paralysis, and sensations of uncontrollable terror. A glowing or luminous mist in the shape of a human being would become visible on the decks, and the dread of seeing it became increasingly acute as crew members died or deserted out of fear. Three captains committed suicide, and before long no replacement sailors could be found. The ship was finally burned, and the prayers of the surviving crew members included the hope that the vampire would die with the *Ivan Vasilli*. This story is somewhat similar to that of the crew on board the *Demeter* in *Dracula*, the novel published in 1897, the same year this steamer was built.

James, M. R. A great writer of ghost and horror stories (1862–1936) during the Edwardian era who utilized his extensive knowledge of ancient and medieval history and lore to create such genuinely terrifying tales as *Casting the Runes*. A lifelong academic, Montague Rhodes James served as a fellow of King's College, Cambridge, in 1887 and became provost of Eton College in 1918. An ardent admirer of Sheridan Le Fanu, he was responsible for the publication of a collection of Le Fanu's stories in *Madame Crowl's Ghost* (1923). His own writings were gathered in several books, including *Ghost Stories of an Antiquary* (1905), *More Ghost Stories of an Antiquary* (1911), *A Thin Ghost* (1919), and *A Warning to the Curious* (1925).

James authored several vampire tales: "Count Magnus" (1904), "Wailing Well" (1928), and the classic, "An Episode of Cathedral History" (1919). "Count Magnus" tells of an English traveler who learns too much about a Swedish nobleman, dying horribly at the hands of the count and his odious henchman. "An Episode of Cathedral History" presents the creepy vampiric haunting of a church in Southminster; a clever ecclesiastical period piece, the story continued James's tradition of creating plots in which some evil from the past comes to life or is summoned into the present.

> The season was undoubtedly a very trying one. Whether the church was built on a site that had once been a marsh, as was suggested, or for whatever reason, the residents in the immediate neighbourhood had, many of them, but little enjoyment of the exquisite sunny days and the calm nights of August and September. To several of the old people—Dr. Ayloff among others, as we have seen—the summer proved downright fatal, but even among the younger, few escaped either a sojourn in bed for a matter of weeks, or at the least, a brooding sense of oppression, accompanied by hateful nightmares. Gradually there formulated itself a suspicion—which grew into a conviction—that the alterations in the Cathedral had something to say in the matter. The widow of a former old verger, a pensioner of the Chapter of Southminster, was visited by dreams, which she retailed to her friends, of a shape that slipped out of the little door of the south transept as the dark fell in and flitted—taking a fresh direction every night—about the Close, disappearing for a while in house after house, and finally emerging again when the night sky was paling. She could see nothing of it, she said, but that it was a moving form: only she had an impression that when it returned to the church, as it seemed to do in the end of the dream, it turned its head: and then, she could not tell why, but she thought it had red eyes.
>
> M. R. James
> "An Episode in Cathedral History" (1919)

Japan The island nation that was said to have been created by brother and sister deities, Izanagi and Izanami, who stirred up the ocean to create a landmass on which they could embrace. These divine associations epitomize the mythology and folklore that permeate much of Japan's history. In their vast pantheon of creatures, there are beings of exquisite goodness and a seemingly endless array of grotesque monsters of evil. Among these are demons (such as the *oni*), ghosts (*oiwa*), imps (the *kappa*), and assorted trolls, ogres, magical animals, and ghost gods. They appear in art and literature with greater regularity than in any other country in the world. The Japanese initially did not need classical vampires, preferring instead bloodsuckers or children eaters, who were unusual and very often luridly humorous. Skeletons, often representing death or the Buddhist concept of the wheel of life, were particularly feared. The most dreaded of all demons or fiends, however, was the *hannya*, a female baby eater and a man-hater. Her dreadful appetite was shared by the *kasha*, or ghoul, a creature so awful that when a ghoul couple produce a normal child they pray and hope that it dies so they can have a tasty meal. With growing interest in Western culture and ideas in Japan, it was inevitable that the more commonly accepted image of the vampire should take hold. In film, the Japanese have accepted the European vampire, making their own contribution to the genre with the 1971 production *Lake of Dracula*, known in the original Japanese as *Chiosu Me* (*Bloodthirsty Eyes*). Other Japanese vampire films include *Onna Kyuketsui* (*Vampire Man*, 1959), *Kuroneko* (1968), and *Kyuketsuki Gokomidore* (1969).

Jaracacas One of the species of vampire found in Brazil, normally appearing in the shape of a snake feeding from the breasts of nursing mothers. Children are pushed out of the way by the creature, which keeps them quiet by shoving its tail into their mouths. (See also *Brazil*.)

Java An Indonesian island south of Borneo and southeast of Sumatra in the Indian Ocean. The most feared Javanese vampire is known as the *sundal bolong* (meaning "hollowed bitch"), a female creature, the result of the suicide and return of a woman raped and impregnated by evil men. Her chosen victims are young men to whom she appears dressed in white. She lures them to their deaths, draining them of their blood. Java is also associated with vampirism in the traditional presence of several species of vampire bats on the island.

Jewett Vampire: See *Ray Family Vampire*.

Jigarkhwar Also *jigarkhor*, a type of witch or sorceress found in the Sind region of India, exhibiting vampire traits and most noted for her ability to extract a person's liver through a powerful, piercing stare and incantations. Usually a woman, the creature renders a person unconscious and removes the organ, which takes the shape of a pomegranate seed, hidden for a time in the magician's calf. The liver is thrown on a fire, expands, and is eaten, at which time the victim dies. Rescue is possible by finding the *jigarkhwar*, ripping the seed out of the leg, and returning it to the proper person, who then swallows it. The power of the witches can be broken by branding them on both sides of the head, filling their eyes with salt, and hanging them in an underground chamber for forty days. A former *jigarkhwar* can detect her own kind.

Jones, Ernest Leading psychoanalyst (1897–1958), a close associate of Sigmund Freud, and author of the influential treatise *On the Nightmare* (1931). A member of the Royal College of Physicians, London (as of 1904), he held various posts in that city before meeting Freud in 1908 at the first psychoanalytic congress in Salzburg. Jones was especially interested in psychoanalyzing folklore and literature. One of his numerous works, *On the Nightmare* was a detailed and comprehensive analysis of the folkloric and psychological nature of the nightmare. Included was an examination of the vampire. He states that they are distinguished by two basic emotions, love and hatred. Love compels the vampire to visit relatives first, especially wives or husbands, while guilt and a thirst for revenge prompts hatred. The vampire is also associated with key elements of the nightmare, including the *succubus, incubus,* and the *mara.* (See also *Nightmare.*)

Judaism: See *Aluga, Crucifix, Dance of the Vampires, Demons, Estrie, Female Vampires, Lilith, Motetz Dam, Satan,* and *Succubus.*

Judas, Children of: See *Children of Judas.*

Jumping over a Corpse The tradition that an animal or person passing over a dead body may cause it to become a vampire. A virtually universal fear, it stems from the idea that the spirit of the deceased can snatch a portion of the life of an animate creature and use it to ignite a kind of unlife in the grave. The taboo is found in most Slavic territories, and even in China, although the specifics of how a body may be transformed into a vampire vary. Generally, any animals, usually dogs or cats, are capable of corpse jumping, but people, bats, birds, and insects should be restrained as well. In China, the tiger was said to possess what was known as soul-recalling hair, while the Romanians were particularly fearful of the black hen. The two most unique methods of restoring life are a candle (a flame being considered alive) and wind. The latter, coming off the Russian Steppes, was dreaded by Russian villagers. The ways to prevent corpse jumping are obvious, but they are not always easy to accomplish. For example, the Slavs hold that the windows and doors of the house must be kept open as long as a corpse is present to ensure that the spirit has the opportunity to depart, thus allowing access to insects and other creatures, with potentially terrible or unforeseen consequences. (See *Preventing a Vampire.*)

Juniper The common name for a wide number of species of evergreen trees and shrubs, a genus of the cypress family, possessing berrylike fruits and needle- or scale-shaped leaves. Its oil is used for medicine and perfume. Among some Gypsies, particularly those of the Muslim faith, it was held that keeping a piece of juniper in a house protected the family from vampires. Additionally, should such a monster gain entry, the presence of the wood kept it from doing any real harm. (See also *Wood.*)

Ka The ancient Egyptian name for an astral being that was considered the guiding force for all human life. The *ba*, the soul of an individual, remained close to the *ka* in the grave. The term for death in ancient Egypt was "going to one's *ka.*" Mortuary practices were said to focus on guiding the *ba* safely to the *ka*, as the former could be led astray by evil influences.

According to custom, the *ka* resided in the tomb and was sufficiently corporeal to partake in the provisions that were placed there at the time of burial or offered in the mortuary cult ceremonies conducted each day on the site. Such offerings were intended to ensure that the *ka* did not have to wander to other sites in search of sustenance. The notion of the *ka* leaving the tomb was perhaps the basis for the popular belief that vampires began in Egypt. (See *Egypt.*)

Kali A formidable goddess of India (the evil aspect of the supreme goddess Devi), who is the destructive yet nurturing black earth mother, presiding over violent death, plagues, and all forms of annihilation. Kali is depicted most often as a blood-drenched creature with dark hair, protruding tongue, and four hands, each holding either a sword, shield, severed hand, strangling noose, severed head, or nothing. Her arms are upraised to give reassurance to her followers, and except for a garland of skulls and girdle of hands, she is naked. The goddess is closely associated with blood, resulting from her battle with the demon Raktavija. In fighting him, she faced one thousand new versions of the demon every time a drop of his blood struck the ground. To defeat Raktavija, she gored him with a spear and drank his blood. Thus some of her statues show her holding a demon's head. The followers of Kali sacrifice goats at her temple, particularly in the famed temple of Kalighat in Calcutta. Others, more extreme, were the Thugs or Thugees, who murdered as many as thirty thousand people. They garroted and strangled their victims as ritual sacrifices, breaking their bones for easier burial. While purged in the nineteenth century by the British, the Thugees made death and blood a lasting aspect of Kali worship. (See *Gods, Vampire.*)

Karens A tribe found in Burma noted for the power of its wizards, who possessed the skill of resuscitating corpses by grabbing the souls of sleeping persons and placing them in the dead bodies. As the sleepers died, the dead returned. This process could be interrupted, however, by another sorcerer, who snared the soul of a second sleeper, putting it into the body of the original one, the second victim dying as the first one awoke. What made this series of rituals so peculiar was the fact that it could go on endlessly, as feuding wizards moved souls from body to body in a kind of eternal game. A good night's rest was presumably rare among the uninitiated Karens. (See also *Kephn.*)

Karloff, Boris Born William Henry Pratt in London, Karloff (1887–1969) became the acknowledged king of the horror film, earning screen immortality through his two great roles: the monster in Universal's *Frankenstein* (1931) and the ancient Egyptian mummy in *The Mummy* (1933). The star of such subsequent successes as *Bride of Frankenstein* (1935) and *Son of Frankenstein* (1939), Karloff entered the vampire genre with *House of Frankenstein* (1944), a Universal film combining Dracula (John Carradine), and Wolf Man (Lon Chaney, Jr.), and the Monster (Glenn Strange). Karloff portrayed the maniacal Dr. Niemann, who revives the count by removing from the vampire's chest an offending stake. Another project was *Black Sabbath* (1963; in the Italian, *I Tre Volti Della Paura, The Three Faces of Fear*). The last of the film's three stories is "The Wurdalak" based on the work by Alexis Tolstoy.

Karnstein, Carmilla More properly Mircalla Karnstein, the character created by Sheridan Le Fanu in his masterpiece, "Carmilla" (1872). Also known as Millarca, she is a sensual, voluptuous, and essentially lesbian vampire, one of the most memorable figures in horror literature. Carmilla is described as slender and graceful, with "languid—very languid" movements, "her eyes, large, dark, and lustrous." She attaches herself to female victims, draining them slowly of life. She also appears as a cat. An influential literary figure, she reappeared in films where her sexual powers and tantalizing but fatal beauty were emphasized. Among the films presenting adaptations or variations on the Carmilla theme are *Vampyr* (1932) by Carl Dreyer; *Blood and Roses* (1960) by Roger Vadim; the Spanish *Maldicion de los Karnsteins (Curse of the Karnsteins,* 1963); *Captain Kronos: Vampire Hunter* (1974); the so-called Karnstein Trilogy by Hammer Films; and Shelley Duvall's "Nightmare Classics" for American television.

Karnstein Trilogy: See *Vampire Lovers, The; Lust for a Vampire;* and *Twins of Evil;* see also *Films.*

Kasha Evil Japanese ghouls that are feared for their voracious appetites for corpses. Because of the Japanese custom of cremation, the *kasha* must steal a corpse before it can be burned, larceny that often requires the theft of the coffin as well. To prevent this, a guard is placed over the dead and noises are made during the night to discourage the ghoul from racing away with a loved one. (See *Japan.*)

Kashubes A Slavic people found in northern Europe, specifically along the Baltic Sea in Poland, in the region of West Prussia, also known as Kashubian Poland. The Kashubes migrated in large numbers to Ontario, Canada, where they preserved their language, traditions, and customs, including their extensive vampire lore. Their vampire is called a *viesczy,* a name derived from a term for sorcerer or witch. Aside from the magicians and witches, the *viesczy* can be a person born with a caul or with teeth. Upon death, they can be detected by a bright redness of the face and their open left eye. The vampire usually begins its career by chewing on itself, so the Kashubes put a brick under the chin to keep the mouth closed. Other preventives include placing nets, flax seed, poplar crosses, and sand in the coffin. Nets are used, as the knots compel the deceased to sit forever and untie them. Other preventative measures include yanking an infant's teeth and drying out the caul before crumbling it into a child's food. If left to its own devices, this vampire will massacre the surviving family. It is suggested that should the net be insufficient, decapitation be used, with the placement of the head under the corpse's arm. As with the *upyr* and *upior,* the *viesczy* wanders about during the day.

Katakhana: See *Crete.*

Keats, John Famed English lyric poet (1795–1821), one of the foremost Romantic writers. In his tragically brief life, Keats created some of the most memorable and beautiful poetry in the English language, including "Ode to a Nightingale," "Ode on a Grecian Urn," "Ode to Melancholy," and the unfinished narrative, "Hyperion." Fascinated by romantic medievalism, he penned "La Belle Dame Sans Merci" (1819), which is included in the list of great vampire writings and a work that is superb both in its first and revised editions. Keats also composed "Lamia" (1820), a vast poetic work that appeared in *Lamia, Isabella, The Eve of St. Agnes and Other Poems,* published just before his trip to Italy in a desperate attempt to revive his deteriorating health. He died in Rome. "Lamia" was based on the story of Menippus, recorded by Philostratus in his *Life of Apollonius of Tyana.* (See excerpt; see also *Literature* and *Poetry.*)

She took me to her elfen grot,
 And there she gazed and sighed deep,
And there I shut her wild wild eyes
 So kiss'd to sleep

And there we slumber'd on the moss,
 And there I dream'd—Ah! woe betide!
The latest dream I ever dream'd
 On the cold hill side.

I saw pale kings, and princes too
 Pale warriors, death pale were they all,
They cried—"La Belle Dame sans Merci
 Hath thee in thrall!"

I saw their starved lips in the gloam,
 With horrid warning gaped wide,
And I awoke, and found me here
 On the cold hill side.

And this is why I sojourn here,
 Alone and palely loitering,
Though the sedge is wither'd from the lake,
 And no birds sing.

> Keats
> "La Belle Dame Sans Merci" (1819)
> (Revised Version)

Keep, The A 1981 novel by F. Paul Wilson, the basis for the 1983 film of the same name. *The Keep* presents a unique variation on the vampire theme, serving as a modern amalgamation of fantasy, horror, Gothic literature, and the lingering horror of nazism. A detachment of Wehrmacht soldiers arrives at the Dinu Pass, taking up position inside a vast fortress, a castle embedded with 16,807 nickel crosses. The novel is vastly superior to its cinematic treatment as it expands on the essential concepts of good and evil. Nazi soldiers unleash a terrifying vampirelike creature named Molasar that had been imprisoned in the castle for eons. *The Keep* is considered a type of allegory on Bram Stoker's novel *Dracula*.

Keep, The The 1983 cinematic version of the novel by F. Paul Wilson, starring Scott Glenn, Jurgen Prochnow, Alberta Watson, and Gabriel Byrne, directed by Michael Mann. Generally faithful to the original work by Wilson, *The Keep* suffers from a lack of definition and poor editing, relying instead on superbly grisly special effects and a moody score by Tangerine Dream. A World War II German army unit headed by a disillusioned officer (Prochnow) arrives at the Dinu Pass in

Romania, taking up position in a huge fortress that was built backward, clearly intended to keep something within it rather than to repel attackers from the outside. Ignoring the warnings of the caretaker, the soldiers try to steal the silver crosses embedded in the wall, releasing an unspeakably evil being, an ancient creature who wipes out the entire command, including additional SS troops.

Kephn A demon found among the Karen tribes of Burma, linked to sorcery and wizards, appearing in the shape of a floating wizard's head and stomach. Its preferred meal is the human soul. The description of the *kephn* is very similar to the *penanggalan* of Malaysia.

King, Stephen American writer (b. 1947), the most prolific and most successful writer of horror in this century, authoring a long list of enormously popular short stories and novels, including *Carrie, It, The Stand,* and *The Dark.* While creating some startlingly horrible monsters, King has also examined traditional terror themes, such as the vampire and the werewolf. Lycanthropy was covered in *Silver Bullet. 'Salem's Lot,* an extremely effective novel concerning the descent of a European vampire, Barlow, into an unsuspecting town, was published in 1975. *Christine* (1983) presents the proposition that even automobiles can be touched by the supernatural as a roadster is transformed into a vampirelike entity. Other vampire stories or novels by King include "Jerusalem's Lot" (1978), "One for the Road" (1977), "The Oracle and the Mountain" (1981), *Pet Sematary* (1983), "Popsy" (1987), *The Tommyknockers* (1987), and "The Night Flier" (1988).

Kinski, Klaus Polish-born actor (1926–1991) known for his intense performing style and his choice of demanding and varied roles. After working in numerous European films, he had a brief but memorable appearance in *Doctor Zhivago* (1965), later earning international acclaim as the deranged conquistador in *Aguirre, The Wrath of God* (1972). In 1971 he portrayed Renfield in *El Conde Dracula,* adopting a restrained style that actually enhanced the character's dementia. Eight years later he assumed the virtually career-defining role of Count Orlock in Werner Herzog's *Nosferatu the Vampyre.* His hypnotic performance presents a powerful counterbalance to the desirable Dracula of the cinema; his vampire is loathsome, pestilential, and incredibly sad. Kinski also had a role in the obscure Italian-French vampire film, *Nella Stretta Morsa del Ragno* (1971; *In the Grip of the Spider.*)

Kisolava Vampire: See *Plogojowitz, Peter.*

"Kiss of Judas, A" An imaginative short story written by "X.L.," a pseudonym for Julian Osgood Field (d. 1928), published originally in the *Pall Mall Gazette* with an illustration by Aubrey Beardsley, reprinted in the collections of the works of X.L., *Aut Diabolus Aut Nihil* (1894). "A Kiss of Judas" is based on the legend of a vampire clan known as the Children of Judas, evil bloodsuckers who are the descendants of Judas, draining the blood of their victims in one gulp, leaving the mark *XXX* on their necks. The work cleverly adds the requirement that to kill a person the Child of Judas must first commit suicide and then make a bargain with Satan, who allows them to return in the vampiric form best suited to seduce and destroy the intended victim. Normally the chosen person deserves death. In this case the villain, Isaac Lebedenko, a foul person with a hideous face, dies and is reincarnated as a beautiful woman. His target is Colonel Dick "Happy" Rowan. The climax is highly dramatic.

Kiss of the Vampire A 1963 Hammer film, starring Clifford Evans, Noel Willman, Isobel Black, and Jennifer Daniel, directed by Don Sharp. Known also as *Kiss of Evil*, this was not a part of the Hammer Dracula cycle but was a single production, telling of a cult of vampires who appear normal during the day but acquire their fangs at night. *Kiss of the Vampire* examines the links of pagan, primitive orgies and rituals with the release of Victorian sexual repression, a recurring theme in the company's work. These rites are used by a villainous family and their followers, headed by Ranva (Willman). They are opposed by Professor Zimmer (Evans), an obsessed father whose daughter died at their hands. (See *Films.*)

Kithnos Vampire A mischievous and rude undead named Andilaveris, who plagued the small Aegean island of Kithnos. Most of the vampires on the isle had been destroyed through the centuries or prevented by the placing of little crosses of wax over the mouths of the recently dead, on the assumption that Satan and his minions could not enter the corpse. Andilaveris, whose story was known well into the nineteenth century, was the one great exception. His nightly activities included wandering the streets of the village of Messaria, eating and drinking enormous amounts of food and smashing plates and glasses. More of a nuisance than a threat to the living, he nevertheless threw the island into a panic, as the inhabitants refused to go outdoors from dusk until dawn. The most outrageous act committed by Andilaveris was to climb onto the roof of the church to urinate on anyone passing below. Because he was a *vrykolakas*, he was confined to his grave on Fridays; thus the priest, sexton, and several others used that day to open his tomb, remove his body, and ferry it across the water to the nearby uninhabited island of Daskaleio. There Andilaveris could do no harm. He was trapped, unable to pass over water.

Kleist, Henrich von: See *Marquise of O.*

Knots While not a devastating item in the arsenal of vampire preventives, knots, especially in northern Germany, are a convenient weapon against vampires who have an uncontrollable urge to occupy themselves with untying any knots laid before them. Thus ropes with knots were placed within graves to distract the vampires. Knots have served as shields against sorcery and bad luck in many cultures, having the property of tying ill chance and evil. Some cultures bound the arms, legs, and mouths of corpses to ensure that they did not rise, but often there was a prohibition against including knotted ropes, in the belief that such items might hinder the deceased's progress into the next world. The ropes were thus cut and removed before burial. The Romanians buried their ropes near the grave. In the regions under the influence of the Greek church, the use of knots was discouraged as they supposedly kept a body from decomposing, trapping the spirit inside. Where knots, nets, or stockings were placed in graves, there was a belief that the revenant, upon waking, would see them and begin working. He was allowed to untie only one knot a year, a task that took eternity to complete. (See also *Fishnets.*)

Kozlak A Dalmatian term for "vampire," found most commonly in the region of Split. Its origins and specific meaning are quite obscure, even though it is used more regularly than other Dalmatian titles, such as *vampir.* It may be derived in some way from the name *vukodlak,* which is prevalent among the Croats.

Kresnik Also *krsnik,* a kind of vampire fighter found in Istria in Slovenia, the bitter enemy of the *kudlak,* the local vampire. The root of the word is *krat,* meaning a cross, implying that the *kresnik* was aided by the forces of light, and was a local representative of good. Similar to the *dhampir,* the *kresnik* was the result of the folkloric development of the shaman, someone who fulfilled the role of protector for the inhabitants and their homes. Every town or community had a *kresnik,* just as it had its own *kudlak.* The two were always embroiled in titanic struggles in which the combatants changed into animal shapes, pigs, oxen, and horses. Good was recognizable by its white color, although the fighters could transform into a dramatic wheel of fire. Invariably the *kresnik* defeated the *kudlak,* as the foes of God could never hope to overcome the true agent of light. Variations on these warriors were found in Slavic lands. In Hungary, the *kresnik* was called the *talbos,* with the main purpose of defending vital crops.

Krvoijac A name used infrequently among the Bulgarians for a vampire, the more common names before *vampir* or *ubour*. The *krvoijac* displays the same characteristics as other Bulgarian undead, remaining in the grave for forty days while the skeleton forms, the bones remaining in a gelatinous state during that period. It is destroyed by chaining it to the grave with wild roses strewn about the ground or planted in the earth above the coffin. (See *Bulgaria.*)

Kuang-shi The feared vampire demon of China, also called the *chiang-shi* or *kiang-si.* This nasty creature, the result of demonic inhabitation of a corpse, is tall, with white or greenish white hair all over its body. Long and sharp claws, terrible eyes, and fangs make its appearance terrifying. Older specimens also have the ability to fly. The *kuang-shi* can be trapped in its grave by sprinkling rice, iron, and red peas on the ground above it. A common means of destroying it is lightning, a method of annihilation left in the hands of nature or the gods. Numerous stories concerning the demon exist in Chinese folklore. (See *China* for other details.)

Kudlak An Istrian (Dalmation) or Slovenian name for the *vukodlak,* a kind of vampire, the exact opposite and most bitter enemy of the *kresnik.* Where the *kresnik* was the representative of goodness and light, the *kudlak* symbolized evil and darkness. Every village had both these figures, with the *kudlak* variously described as an evil wizard (*strigon*), shaman, or vampire, representing traditional threats to the living, such as pestilence, misfortune, or the loss of crops. Generally the *kudlak* was most dangerous after death, and steps were taken to prevent the return of such an individual, either by impaling the corpse on a hawthorn stake or by slashing the tendon below the knees before burial. Attacking the innocent or the defenseless, the *kudlak* was always opposed by the *kresnik.* The two entered into terrible struggles, both assuming animal shapes, such as the horse, pig, or ox. Invariably the *kudlak* lost to God's representative. The creature was always identified by its color, black.

K'uei A broad Chinese term denoting the undead, believed to have been persons who had not lived with sufficient goodness to earn an entry into the bliss of the afterworld. Deprived of a happy afterlife, they are said to be both angry and vicious, taking out their aggressions on sinners, for it is with them that they feel a close kinship. The *k'uei* have been described as skeletal beings with hideous demonic faces. They must always move in a perfectly straight line. Screens, placed just inside a doorway, are said to be the most effective barrier against them, as they cannot maneuver around the corner and, thus frustrated, move on to another location. The *k'uei* is quite different from the *kuang-shi* and is also ranked as a general evil spirit.

Kukudhi An Albanian name for the final stage in the development or transformation of the vampire. According to custom in some regions of Albania, an undead takes time to grow fully into the shape and powers of a vampire, becoming stronger the longer it survives. The last period is called *kukudhi* in Albania, and upon reaching this state the vampire is able to live at home during the day, no longer required to return to its grave, and is even able to travel to other lands, supposedly as a merchant. (See *Life of the Vampire.*)

Kürten, Peter The so-called Vampire of Düsseldorf (1883–1931), responsible for murdering or assaulting twenty-nine people during a reign of terror that lasted for years, ruining the city's reputation among Europeans. The son of an alcoholic and a long-suffering mother, whom he revered, Kürten worked as a truck driver, appearing as a boring, bespectacled little man with a mustache and neat clothes. As was true with other mass murderers, beneath this quiet demeanor lurked a remorseless killer. His victims were strangled and raped, then had their throats slit and their blood consumed by Kürten, who sought to find some release from his unstoppable cravings. Eventually marrying a woman who fulfilled his need for a mother figure, he was a devoted husband by day, setting out at night on his ghastly adventures. His murders probably would have continued had he not confessed his crimes to his astonished wife. Picked up by the police after his wife turned him in, he was tried, convicted, and sentenced to death, never appealing his conviction. Adding to the horror surrounding Kürten were his letters to the parents of the victims, in which he described how some humans were alcoholics, whereas he needed blood. The inspiration for the Fritz Lang masterpiece *M* (1931), Kürsten made the statement: "You cannot understand me. No one can understand me." His story was told in the 1964 French-Italian film, *Le Vampire de Düsseldorf,* directed by and starring Robert Hossein. (See also *Hematomania* and *Historical Vampires.*)

Kurzman and Damian Also Cosmos and Damian, two saints of the Christian church, especially the Eastern Orthodox church, honored because of their powers over the undead. While exact dates of their lives are relatively unknown, they are considered early Christian martyrs, killed at Cyrrhus, where a basilica was erected in their honor. Numerous legends related stories of their work as doctors practicing medicine as a form of charity. Both are thus patrons of doctors and healing. The powerful Medici family donated vast amounts to their cult, several members of the line bearing the name Cosimo (Cosmos). Among the Slavs, the saints are not doctors but magicians, expert in aiding all who suffered vampire attacks. In the West their feast day is celebrated on September 26, in the East on either July 1 or November 1.

Lake of Dracula The best Japanese vampire film ever produced, released originally in 1971 as *Chiosu Me* (*Bloodthirsty Eyes*) and known in the United States as *Lake of Dracula* or, less commonly, *Dracula's Lust for Blood*. Starring Mori Kishida, Midori Fujita, and Sanae Emi, and directed by Michio Yamamoto, this is an essentially derivative work, a pastiche in some ways of the Gothic productions of Hammer Films. The plot focuses on the golden-eyed son of Dracula by a Japanese woman. Having died and returned as a bloodsucker, he vampirizes the sister of the heroine but is destroyed during a struggle with the hero, a doctor. The villain falls upon a wooden post and is impaled. A recurring image in *Lake of Dracula* is a beautiful lake under a blood-red sky. (See also *Japan.*)

La Llorona "The Weeping Woman," the name given to a legendary Mexican figure who appears dressed in white and is found in folk tales in a wide variety of countries (including Mexico and Costa Rica) and U.S. states, including California, Arizona, Texas, and Colorado. The tales have produced scholarly study over the years in an attempt to define their origin. By tradition La Llorona was originally a beautiful young woman in early colonial Mexico, betrayed by her lover. He left her to marry another woman, despite the fact that she had borne him three children. Attending his wedding uninvited, she was so overcome by grief and despair that she returned to the residence he had bought for her and stabbed her children to death. Sensing the enormity of her crime, she fled the scene, screaming and crying. Executed, she was soon joined in death by her lover, who committed suicide. From that time on she began to appear as La Llorona, a beautiful seductress who lured men to their deaths in perpetual revenge against all males. Variations on this theme are found in many regions. There is a clear similarity between "The Weeping Woman" and the Aztec goddess Cihuacoatl or the goddess Coatlicue. The latter always appeared in white and was heard wailing in the night. The essential body of the legend, however, is more European than Aztec, and it has been suggested that the tale began in Europe and was carried to the New World by the Spanish during and after the Conquest. It is known that a ghost story of the White Lady (*Die Weisse Frau*) was at least as old as the late fifteenth century, and it was probably even older than that. (See also *Native Americans.*)

Lamia A kind of legendary female vampire, generally held to be stunningly attractive and highly dangerous to males and children. A *lamia* can also be used to refer to any female bloodsucker. According to one legend, Lamia was the queen of Libya, whose children were slain by the goddess Hera and who, in revenge, thereafter roamed the world, sucking the blood of infants. Other traditions state that in the ancient world she was a species of demon, with the power to remove her eyes and a desire to entice men to their deaths, usually by devouring them in a most gruesome fashion. The *lamiae* (plural) were also called *larvae* and *lemures*, sometimes confused with the *empusa* and used by nannies to frighten unruly children. Horace wrote of a *lamia* in his *Ars Poetica*. The *lamia* has been the inspiration for female vampires throughout literary history, such as Keats's "Lamia," Whitley Strieber's Miriam Blaylock in *The Hunger*, and J. N. Williamson's series of novels featuring Lamia Zacharius.

Lampir A Bosnian term for "vampire," seen most often during periods of severe epidemics, one of several types of undead in the region. Edith Durham, an English anthropologist, reported her experience in Bosnia in a 1923 article for the journal *Man:* "A recent case (told me in 1906) was when there was an outbreak of typhus. . . . A young man was first to die. His wife sickened and swore that her husband had returned in the night and sucked her blood, and said, 'He is a lampir!' The neighbors, filled with fear, begged the authorities to permit them to dig up and burn his body. Permission was refused, and a panic ensued. The *lampir* was seen and heard by many people, and there were fifteen deaths." Burning is the prescribed method for destroying this species.

Langella, Frank: See *Dracula (1979)*.

Langsuir A flying vampire of Malaysia, said always to be a female of stunning beauty. A woman can become such a creature if she dies in childbirth or from the shock of hearing that her child has been stillborn (the child is transformed into the vampire known as the *pontianak*). Her death can come before or after childbirth, and she emerges as a *langsuir* before a period of forty days has elapsed. She can be identified by her incredibly long nails, green robes, and long black hair, which hangs down to her ankles. The hair is supposedly that long to conceal a hole in the back of her neck, through which she drinks the blood of children. She also craves fish, and she and her vampiric companions can be seen at the mouths of rivers, waiting to steal fish there. It is possible to prevent transformation into a *langsuir* by placing a number of glass beads into the mouth of the corpse or by putting a hen's egg under each armpit and needles in the palms of its hands. The needles do not allow the woman to wave her arms or close her hands to fly, nor can she open her mouth to let out her terrible wail, called the *ngilai*. Once a woman has become a vampire, the best way to be rid of her is to capture her, cut her nails, and stuff her tresses into the hole in her neck. Once this is accomplished, she will become tame, ceasing her devilish activities. She can even marry and have children, living for many years as a normal person. Merrymaking and dancing are out of the question, however, as these will cause her to revert to her fiendish state, flying off into the night with devilish glee.

Lapps Also Laplanders, the indigenous inhabitants of Lapland, the vast territory stretching across northern Europe within the Arctic Circle, including parts of Norway, Sweden, and Finland. An essentially nomadic people, they follow the herds of reindeer, fishing and hunting. The late arrival of Christianity (full conversion came only in the eighteenth century) helped to preserve much of their traditional culture, including their customs concerning death. It was common for the person preparing a corpse to receive from relatives of the deceased a brass ring, which was fastened to the right arm in the assumption that it would serve as a talisman for the preparer against the dead person's spirit, sometimes a vengeful one.

Larvae A name used to describe evil spirits of the ancient world, onetime mortals who returned to wander the earth and bring torment upon the living, especially during the Roman festival of Lemuria each May. It has also been used as a title for the female vampire type found in the ancient world, called the *lamia*. Philostratus called the *lamiae* by the name *larvae* in his *Life of Apollonius*. They were also mentioned by the Protestant theologian Louis Lavater, in his writings.

Lavater, Louis A late-sixteenth-century Protestant theologian and an expert on the undead. The foremost researcher on vampires among the Protestants, Lavater authored the treatise *De Spectris, Lemuribus, et magnis atque insolitis Fragoribus* (Geneva, 1575), translated into the English as *Of Ghosts and Spirits Walking by Night* (London). Its principal value is the compilation and presentation of extensive materials on vampire species in the ancient world. He wrote about such types as the *maniae, lamiae,* and *larvae.*

Laws About Vampires Decrees or royal proclamations intended to curb the activities of the undead or to censure those who exceeded the law in rooting them out. From time to time during the Middle Ages and beyond, it became necessary to take steps against villagers who were literally hysterical with terror concerning vampires. Such laws were promulgated by the Salian Franks, the Carolingians (including Charlemagne), Stephen Dusan (ruler of Serbia from 1331–

1355), and the Wallachian ruler of Romania in the early nineteenth century. In each case it was ordered that the populace must cease exhuming bodies to impale and cremate them, forbidding as well the use of magical means to destroy vampires and urging the populace not to follow the clergymen who led these hunting parties. As such pogroms often led to the death of innocent persons, the laws had a practical value. The general view of law was the same for vampires as it was for witches: "You shall not permit a sorceress to live" (Ex. 22:18).

Leanhaum-shee The Irish name for the fairy mistress, a deadly seductress, described in folklore not as a vampire but engaging in vampiric activities. She used her incredible beauty to lure men to her side, where her irresistible charms placed them under her spell. From then on the victim was drained slowly of life, wasting away as his essence was consumed by his demonic lover. The only means of breaking her powerful grip was to find a substitute, someone who could unwittingly become her next prey. The original victim could then escape. (See also *Dearg-due.*)

Lee, Christopher English actor (b. 1922) best known for his numerous performances as Count Dracula in the long-running Hammer Films cycle. To many, Lee more than Bela Lugosi remains the ultimate vampire king, distinguishing himself with a brilliant horror career as well as with many appearances in mainstream films. The son of an Italian contessa and a colonel in the King's Royal Rifle Corps, Lee made his motion picture debut in the 1947 *Corridor of Mirrors*, securing small roles throughout the early 1950s. In 1957, however, the six-foot-four-inch actor was chosen to play the title monster in *The Curse of Frankenstein*, Hammer's mammoth hit, opposite Peter Cushing, with Terence Fisher directing. The following year the trio created Hammer's first vampire film, the ground-breaking *Horror of Dracula* (1958).

Extremely prolific, Lee appeared in a host of horror films throughout the late fifties, sixties, and into the seventies. He returned to Dracula in 1965 with *Dracula—Prince of Darkness*, but his status as a major star limited the screen time that Hammer could afford to give him. His last portrayal of Dracula came in the 1974 *Satanic Rites of Dracula*. Lee also played vampires in films made throughout Europe, the most notable being *El Conde Dracula* (1972). His autobiography, *Tall, Dark and Gruesome*, was published in 1974.

Lee, Tanith A highly innovative English writer of horror, science fiction, and fantasy (b. 1947), the author of absorbing and beautifully composed tales with devastating imagery. Originally a scriptwriter, Lee won instant acclaim with her first adult novel, *The Birthgrave*

(1975), acquiring a wide following in the United States. In 1979 she penned the short story "Red As Blood" for the magazine *Fantasy and Science Fiction*, a tale that introduces the vampire element into the Snow White tradition. The following year her most famous vampire work was published, *Sabella or the Blood Stone*, a novel about an alien creature living on Mars of the future who inhabits the body of a young girl. Another significant short story is "Bite Me Not, or, Fleur de Feu" (1984), a superb fantasy about a young girl, Rohise, who falls in love with Feroluce, a vampire prince of the air. Her other vampire writings include *Kill the Dead* (1980), "Cyprian in Bronze" (1980), "Sirriamnis" (1981), "A Lynx with Lions" (1982), "Nunc Dimitis" (1983), "The Vampire Lover" (1984), and "Quatl-Sup" (1985).

Le Fanu, Sheridan In full, Joseph Sheridan Le Fanu (1814–1873), an Irish writer who had a major influence on the development of the ghost story, earning lasting fame for his two great works: "Carmilla" and "Green Tea" (both 1872). Le Fanu was a member of an old Huguenot family and a grandnephew of the English dramatist and politician Richard Brinsley Sheridan. Educated at Trinity College, he served as editor of several newspapers, including the *Dublin University Magazine*, in which much of his own fiction was published anonymously. From 1845 to 1873 he authored fourteen novels, including *The House by the Churchyard* (1863) and *Uncle Silas* (1864). Probably his most famous short story was "Carmilla," the vampire work published in the noted collection *In a Glass Darkly* (1872). Married in 1844, he became a recluse after the sudden death of his wife in 1858, preferring to write horror and ghost tales while in bed. Revered by many writers of the supernatural in the early twentieth century, such as E. F. Benson and Algernon Blackwood, he was called the "Master" by M. R. James. (See also *Literature.*)

> I now write, after an interval of more than ten years, with a trembling hand, with a confused and horrible recollection of certain occurrences and situations, in the ordeal through which I was unconsciously passing; though with a vivid and very sharp remembrance of the main current of my story. But, I suspect, in all lives there are certain emotional scenes, those in which our passions have been most wildly and terribly roused, that are of all others the most vaguely and dimly remembered.
> Sometimes after an hour of apathy, my strange and beautiful companion would take my hand and hold it with a fond pressure, renewed again and again, blushing softly, gazing in my face with languid and burning eyes, and breathing so fast that her dress rose and fell with the

tumultuous respiration. It was like the ardour of a lover; it embarrassed me; it was hateful and yet overpowering; and with gloating eyes she drew me to her, and her hot lips traveled along my cheek in kisses, and she would whisper, almost in sobs, "You are mine, you *shall* be mine, and you and I are one for ever." Then she has thrown herself back in her chair, with her small hands over her eyes, leaving me trembling.

J. Sheridan Le Fanu
"Carmilla" (1872)

Leger, Antoine A French mass murderer (d. 1824) who specialized in both vampirism and cannibalism. He would lie in wait in the woods for victims, choosing young women who wandered by. After raping and killing them, he customarily ripped out their hearts, which he then proceeded to eat. A blood drinker as well, he was finally caught and brought to trial. When asked why he drank human blood, Leger replied simply that he was thirsty. He was guillotined. (See *Historical Vampires.*)

Leiber, Fritz A great master of fantasy, horror, and science fiction (b. 1910). Originally an actor on stage and in film, Leiber was first published in 1939, embarking upon a long career that earned him a Life Achievement Award in 1976 at the Second World Fantasy Convention. Among his numerous creations are the Lankhmar in Nehwon books, featuring Fafhrd and Grey Mouser, and a vast number of short stories and novels, especially horror, such as *Conjure Wife* (1943) and *Our Lady of Darkness* (1977). Several of his tales have presented his interpretation of vampires: "The Girl with the Hungry Eyes" (1949), "The Dead Man" (1950), "Ship of Shadows" (1961), and "Dr. Adam's Garden" (1969). "The Girl with the Hungry Eyes" presents a female vampire with an all-consuming psychic appetite. "Ship of Shadows" won Leiber the prestigious Hugo Award.

Lemon A fruit that has been used to ward off evil in Saxony, Germany. It is a principal means of disposing of the Saxon vampire species the *neuntöter* and is placed in the creature's mouth. The use of the lemon is late, however, as it was unknown to the Greeks or Romans and became familiar to the Germans only in the Middle Ages.

Lemuria The Roman festival of the dead, held each May over a four-day period; marked by great solemnity for, according to Roman belief, the dead returned to walk upon the earth. Originating probably in the

Greek festival of Anthesteria, the Lemuria was described by the writer Ovid in his *Fasti,* stressing the terrible nature of the ceremonies involved, for the spirits of the deceased had to be appeased. The wandering dead were known as *lemuria,* said to be those persons who were wicked in life or had not received a proper burial, usually improper cremation or, worst of all, no burial beneath the ground. Those evil dead were also grouped together as the *larvae.* Such persons, transformed into hideous creatures, inflicted harm and misery upon the living, haunting the homes and possessions of former friends and family. By custom, the rites of the Lemuria were always held at night.

Lestat In full, Lestat de Lioncourt, the literary creation of Anne Rice who first appeared in her *Interview with the Vampire* (1976), subsequently assuming a major role in the next entries in her Vampire Chronicles, *The Vampire Lestat* (1985), *Queen of the Damned* (1988), and *The Tale of the Body Thief* (1992). Known to many of his fellow vampires as the "Brat Prince," Lestat has emerged as one of the foremost characters in horror. By his own account he was the son of a French marquis, becoming a member of the undead by the fangs of a powerful alchemist vampire named Magnus. His early unlife was spent offending the vampire community of Paris, before embarking on a long voyage of self-discovery for "Those Who Must Be Kept," the queen of the undead and her consort. Lestat is irreverent and outrageous but equally moral in his own fashion—he will not drink the blood of the innocent. He describes himself as six feet tall, with thick blond hair, gray eyes, a short nose, and a mouth that is well shaped but too large for his face. His frequent companion in modern times has been Louis, his own creation. Lestat has his own fan club, "Anne Rice's Vampire Lestat Fan Club." (See "Vampire Societies and Organizations" in the appendixes.)

Liddell, Henry An early-nineteenth-century poet who in 1833 authored the memorable ballad "The Vampire Bride," published originally in his *The Wizard of the North, The Vampire Bride, and other Poems* (1833, London). It tells of a knight playing a game of quoit (casting rings or ropes to hook them over a stake or over a similar object), who throws his ring (perhaps his wedding ring) onto a finger of a statue of Venus. Later he is unable to remove the ring from the very crooked finger of the statue. That night an evil spirit uses his mistake as a declaration of his desire to have an immortal bride, claiming the knight as her own. After a brief struggle, the vampire bride is repelled. (See also *Poetry.*)

Liderc nadaly: See *Hungary.*

Liebava Vampire A revenant found in the small town of Liebava, in Moravia, during the early eighteenth century, reported by Dom Augustine Calmet, as told to him by a priest who was traveling through the region. The cleric accompanied a Monsignor Jeanin to Liebava to investigate reports of a vampire that had circulated among the villagers. According to their study, a resident died and returned to torment Liebava for some four years, before a Hungarian traveler learned of the fiend and put his skills to the service of the townspeople. The Hungarian mounted the clock tower of the local church and waited for the vampire, taking the shroud that the revenant abandoned while making its nightly rounds. Climbing back onto the tower with the shroud, the Hungarian watched the vampire searching frantically for its shroud and called to it. Taunting the creature, the Hungarian demanded that it climb the steep stair of the clock tower to retrieve it. The furious undead was on the verge of reaching the top when the Hungarian gave it a vicious blow. The revenant was then decapitated with a sexton's spade. The figure of the Hungarian remains somewhat mysterious—was he an actual vampire hunter or an audacious merchant, the type frequently encountered in Russian folk tales? (See also *Hungary.*)

Life of a Vampire The amount of time that the undead are granted to wander the earth. It is often assumed that once created, a vampire will live forever unless somehow destroyed. This view is only partially supported by folklore. For example, many Muslim Gypsies believe that the vampire will live only for several months, while other Gypsies proclaim that it wanders for only forty days. In Serbia and in Albania it is held that the undead must be destroyed within thirty years or it will become human, traveling the world under a new name. Immortality, however, remains one of the principal allures of vampires, so it is natural to assume that they are eternal, spending centuries secretly feeding upon mortals, existing among them and observing the passing of years as the living note the coming of days. In fiction there is no limit generally as to how old a vampire can be, a consensus being that with each century of unlife the creature grows stronger, tempered by the acquisition of wisdom and possibly by the development of a kind of ennui or *weltangst*, a world-weariness that can culminate in suicide through self-immolation or by exposure to the sun.

Lifeforce A 1985 English film, starring Steve Railsback, Peter Firth, Mathilda May, Frank Finlay, and Patrick Stewart, directed by horror maven Tobe Hooper. A special effects–dependent fusion of vampires and science fiction, with added elements of the old Dr. Quartermass movies, *Lifeforce* follows the mayhem wrought by three space vampires brought to earth after being found during an expedition to Halley's comet. The chief astronaut (Railsback), haunted by memories of the murderous flight home, becomes the main hunter of the trio after they escape from their holding lab. Aided by an SAS officer (Firth) and a scientist (Finlay), the astronaut watches wholesale carnage in England and confronts the female vampire in St. Paul's, while all of London writhes in horror outside. The film is based on a novel by Colin Wilson.

Lilith The Queen of the Night, portrayed in Hebrew legend as the first woman, created to be the wife of Adam, but with such an evil spirit that she departed Adam's side to dwell with the forces of darkness. Also known as Lili, she probably originated as Lilitu, one of the seven Babylonian evil spirits incorporated into Hebrew lore. Variations on her story relate that she was Eve, having sinned and been ejected from Eden and fleeing into the air to prey on children. Another version portrays her as the queen of *succubi,* leader of the night demons who prey on men, drawing out their seed and often their blood in the hope of causing misery and death. Lilith has a special hatred for children, as her own were twisted, misshapen, and wicked. In corporeal form, she appears as a beautiful woman with an abundance of sharp black hair on her legs. Characters similar to Lilith are found in tales all over the world. (See also *Succubus.*)

Lilitu A Babylonian demon, often considered an evil spirit of the night. Lilitu probably had an influence in the formation of the Hebrew legend of Lilith.

Linden The common name for the members of the Tilia family of trees, found in the world's northern regions. It is marked by fragrant cream and gold flowers. Linden ranks with hawthorn, maple, and aspen as prime wood for making stakes used to impale and destroy vampires. (See also *Wood.*)

Linen Seeds The seeds of flax, used in many European countries as a means of limiting the activities of the vampire. Sprinkled along walkways or on graves, the linen seeds force the vampire to become distracted, as a revenant must pick up each individual seed before continuing with its activities. Usually the vampire is prohibited from being able to pick up more than one seed a year; thus it is condemned to a useless activity and deterred from harming the living.

Literature: See table.

Literature

Major works in vampire literature since 1800.

Date	Title	Author
1800	"Wake Not the Dead"	Johann Ludwig Tieck
1805	*The Marquise of O*	Heinrich von Kleist
1818–21	*The Serapion Brethren*	E.T.A. Hoffmann
1819	"The Vampyre; A Tale"	John Polidori
1820	*Lord Ruthven ou Les Vampires*	Cyprien Berard
	Smarra, ou les Demons de la Nuit	Charles Nodier
1827	*La Guzla*	Prosper Mérimée
1833	"Viy"	Nicolai Gogol
1836	"La Morte Amoureuse"	Théophile Gautier
1838	"Ligeia"	Edgar Allan Poe
1847	*Varney the Vampyre*	James Malcolm Rymer
	"Family of the Vourdalak"	Alexis Tolstoy
1848	"The Pale-Faced Lady"	Alexandre Dumas
1860	"The Mysterious Stranger"	Anonymous
1870	*Vikram and the Vampire*	Sir Richard Burton
1872	"Carmilla"	J. Sheridan Le Fanu
1875	*The Vampire City*	Paul Feval
1881	"The Man-Eating Tree"	Phil Robinson
1887	"The Horla"	Guy de Maupassant
1894	"The Parasite"	Sir Arthur Conan Doyle
	"Kiss of Judas"	X.L.
	"The True Story of a Vampire"	Count Eric Stenbock
1897	*Dracula*	Bram Stoker
1900	"The Tomb of Sarah"	F. G. Loring
1904	"Count Magnus"	M. R. James
1907	"A Vampire"	Luigi Capuana
1911	"For the Blood Is the Life"	Marion Crawford
	Alraune	Hans Heinz Ewers
1912	"The Room in the Tower"	E. F. Benson
	"The Transfer"	Algernon Blackwood
	The Vampire	Reginald Hodder
1919	"An Episode in Cathedral History"	M. R. James
	"Mrs. Amsworth"	E. F. Benson
1922	*Vampire*	Hans Heinz Ewers
1925	"Four Wooden Stakes"	Victor Rowan
1927	*The Demon Lover*	Dion Fortune
1933	"Shambleau"	C. L. Moore
	"Revelations in Black"	Carl Jacobi
1939	"The Cloak"	Robert Bloch
1941	"Over the River"	P. Schuyler Miller

Date	Title	Author
1949	"The Girl with the Hungry Eyes"	Fritz Leiber
1954	*I Am Legend*	Richard Matheson
1957	"The Living Dead"	Robert Bloch
1961	*Some of Your Blood*	Theodore Sturgeon
1972	*The Dracula Archives*	Raymond Rudorff
1974	*An Enquiry into the Existence of Vampires*	Marc Lovell
1975	*'Salem's Lot*	Stephen King
	The Dracula Tape	Fred Saberhagen
1976	*Interview with the Vampire*	Anne Rice
1977	*Bloodright*	Peter Tremayne
1978	*Hotel Transylvania*	Chelsea Quinn Yarbro
1980	*Unicorn Tapestry*	Suzy McKee Charnas
	Sabella, or the Bloodstone	Tanith Lee
1981	*The Keep*	F. Paul Wilson
	The Hunger	Whitley Strieber
	They Thirst	Robert McCammon
	Vampires of Nightworld	David Bischoff
1982	*The Delicate Dependency*	Michael Talbot
	Darkangel	Meredith Ann Pierce
	Fevre Dream	George R. Martin
1984	*I, Vampire*	Jody Scott
	Vampire Junction	S. P. Somtow
1985	*The Vampire Lestat*	Anne Rice
1988	*The Queen of the Damned*	Anne Rice
1990	*Out of the House of Life*	Chelsea Quinn Yarbro
1991	*Under the Fang* (Collection)	Robert McCammon, ed.
	The Ultimate Dracula (Collection)	Leonard Wolf, ed.
1992	*The Tale of the Body Thief*	Anne Rice

Lithuania The Baltic country that boasts a famous tale of vampirism, originally reported by a Captain Pokrovsky, a Russian-Lithuanian guards officer in 1905. Pokrovsky was forced to accept temporary banishment to his Lithuanian estates because of some vague political offense. A short while later, however, he spent some time with his uncle, enjoying his days with that nobleman's daughter, his cousin. One morning, while visiting the local peasants with this cousin, he came across a man whose health had begun to fail after his second marriage. Despite consuming red meats, he continued to deteriorate, prompting Pokrovsky to investigate the strange case. Summoning a doctor, the captain had the peasant examined. The physician diagnosed excessive blood loss, although there was no sign of a wound that could bring about such a condition. The man, however, did have two small punctures in his neck. There was no inflammation, as would have been expected with an insect or an animal bite. Various medicines were prescribed, and Pokrovsky returned home. A short time later he asked his cousin what had become of the man and was told that despite the tonics, healthy meals, and wine, the peasant had died. The wounds on his neck were much more severe at the time of his death, and the sudden disappearance of his widow had added to the fear of the locals, who suspected vampirism, although the woman had attended mass regularly. Pokrovsky believed that the woman had been drinking her spouse's blood during the night, acting unconsciously as a vampire. Another explanation that was given was of vampiric possession. The widow fled, defenseless against public reaction.

Liver An organ frequently mentioned in the determination of a person's possible status as a vampire or revenant. An undead's liver is said to be white in color, instead of the normal reddish brown. A white liver is found not only in the Slavic and German species of vampire. It is also said that witches' livers have the same pigmentation, as do women whose husbands die with suspicious frequency. The belief may have come from the custom of throwing bodies into rivers to see if they would float. Livers that are exposed to fresh water are said to turn white; examinations of such corpses would reveal whitened livers and thus provide a useful proof for vampire hunters. (See also *Jigarkhwar.*)

Live Vampires A term used to describe those Romanian persons who are destined to become members of the undead after death—at which time they will be "dead vampires"; the name is derived from the fact that they display definite vampiric tendencies while still alive. Live vampires, intertwined in folk belief with wizards and witches, have the ability to send out their souls to commit crimes and to wander at crossroads. Customarily, they also consort with reanimated corpses, dead vampires, and witches and sorcerers. The most common name for all vampires in Romania, whether dead or alive, is *strigoii* (fem. *strigoica*), although another name used is *moroii*. There is a minor tradition that *moroii* is more appropriate when describing the live vampire. Females are noted for their red faces, while males are bald.

Live vampires are most frequently women, using signs that give them power over living things. They take characteristics or attributes from animals such as the hen or lizard. Additionally, they can shape-change into horses, dogs, cats, and other species. Bees, too, suffer, for when the living vampires steal their "power," in this case honey, the bees cannot manufacture more and thus die. In villages the *moroii* can be detected through her bread. She steals the "power" of bread making from everyone else, combining their skills with her own. Live vampires can also offer to perform their powers for others for a fee.

"Living Dead, The" A 1967 short story by Robert Bloch, originally published in *Ellery Queen's Mystery Magazine,* also known under the title "Underground." A caveat to all those who would play the vampire, the tale relates how Eric Karon, a German collaborator in France during World War II, assumed the persona of the long dead Count Barsac, a French nobleman suspected of being a vampire. The disguise, donned to keep away the curious, shielded treasonous activities at the deserted Château Barsac—the use of a shortwave transmitter designed to help defeat the interests of France at the time. Years later, as the German army retreated in the face of the Allied forces, the dread "vampire" prepared to leave his haunt. Grown too accustomed to his nightly fun, he miscalculated and was captured by American soldiers, who turned him over to the local French, whom he had terrorized for years. Their response completed the moral of the story: "He realized there's such a thing as playing a role too well."

Living Fires Another name used for need-fires, found in those regions where pagan rituals continued even after Christianity had supposedly been instituted. (See *Need-fire* for additional details.)

Living Vampires: See *Live Vampires* and *Historical Vampires.*

Lobishomen A somewhat obscure vampire species found in Brazil, similar to the other main Brazilian vampire type, the *jaracaca,* in that it preys mainly on women. The *lobishomen* does not kill, however, preferring to draw out blood from its victims. Those women who survive its attack soon after exhibit definite nymphomaniacal tendencies. The *lobishomen* probably originated in Portugal, where there was a belief in *lobishomen,* a kind of werewolf or lycanthrope.

Locust A winged insect traditionally controlled by powerful members of the undead, part of the wide association of the vampire with plagues, destruction, and misery. Terrible swarms of the insects will descend upon crops, wiping out vast quantities of food. Plagues of locusts are virtually impossible to stop, spreading like an epidemic in a region. So, too, has the vampire been viewed as a plague carrier, blotting out life and property. The link between vampirism and locusts can be made more directly through the figure called the *kudlak,* a witch-vampire who is intent upon destroying village crops. The vampire can also transform itself into a locust or grasshopper.

London After Midnight A 1927 MGM film, starring Lon Chaney, Sr., and directed by Tod Browning, held to be the first vampire film ever made in the United States. A silent picture, it is an important lost film with only stills surviving of the original production. Based on the novel *The Hypnotist, London After Midnight* was actually a detective story in which a police officer (Chaney) pursues a killer through the city. At the same time, London is caught up in vampire hysteria as a member of the undead appears to be prowling the city's dark streets. At the film's climax, when the murderer is captured, it is revealed that there is no vampire, only the disguised hero, Chaney. His reputation for incredible makeup and shocking transformations was more than equaled here. Based on photographs of Chaney in full costume, he appeared with a mouth full of sharp teeth, disheveled hair, and bulging eyes, dressed in a tall black hat and a black cape in the shape of bat wings. A remake, *Mark of the Vampire,* was released in 1935, this time with sound and starring Bela Lugosi.

Loogaroo A type of witch-vampire found in the West Indies, also known as a *ligaroo* and closely associated with the *sucoyan.* In some areas it is said that the *loogaroo* is male while the *sucoyan* is female, although the terms have been used for both, and most frequently the *loogaroo* refers to an old hag. The name is an apparent derivation of the French *loup garou* (shape-changer), the tradition supposedly entering the Caribbean from Guinea and the Congo in Africa. The *loogaroo* is said to be a human, usually an old woman who has made a pact with the devil, receiving magical powers as long as she offers up blood from victims. Each night the *loogaroo* goes to the so-called Devil Tree or Jumbie Tree (the silk-cotton tree) and removes its skin, which is folded up neatly and hidden. The vampire then soars off into the night in the form of a sulfurous ball. It cannot be stopped by doors or windows, entering houses to drink the blood of inhabitants. One method of resistance, however, is to scatter rice and sand in front of the abode, forcing the *loogaroo* to stop and pick up each grain before proceeding. As this usually takes many hours, the dawn comes upon the vampire before its task can be completed, an idea echoed in many parts of the world. The *loogaroo* is subject to injury and is actually quite vulnerable while away from its skin. Should a person discover the skin during the night, it is recommended that he or she sprinkle salt on it. In that fashion the vampire will be unable to return to it and will cry out, "Kin, kin, you no know me!" With the dawn, the *loogaroo* will be visible to one and all, its disguise abandoned.

Lord Ruthven ou les Vampires A novel written by Cyprien Berard and published in February 1820 in Paris. This was a sequel to the then widely popular story "The Vampyre," by John Polidori. Very similar to the original in style, the novel was probably composed under the patronage of Charles Nodier, who was responsible for bringing Polidori's story to the stage later that year (in June). It was but one of the many versions, translations, or adaptations of the Polidori original that would appear.

Lory, Robert Author of a series of Dracula novels, published in the 1970s, intended to capitalize on the enduring popularity of the count. Dismissed by many critics, Lory's writing was aimed principally at the mass paperback audience; the entire group of novels was known under the title the Dracula Horror Series. The first installment, *Dracula Returns!* (1973), presented the revival of Dracula by a wheelchair-bound retired criminologist. He uses Dracula and his powers to solve various crimes. The other Lory books include *The Hand of Dracula* (1973), *Dracula's Brothers* (1973), *Dracula's Gold* (1973), *The Drums of Dracula* (1974), *The Witching of Dracula* (1974), *Dracula's Lost World* (1975), *Dracula's Disciple* (1975), and *Challenge to Dracula* (1975). Lory has also written two vampire short stories, "There's Something in the Soup" (1975) and "The Beat of Leather Wings" (1975).

Lost Boys, The A 1987 horror-comedy film, starring Dianne Wiest, Jason Patric, Edward Herrmann, Corey Haim, Kiefer Sutherland, Jami Gertz, Barnard Hughes, and Corey Feldman, directed by Joel Schumacher. *The Lost Boys,* which is set in the mythical town of Santa Carla, refers to a pack of teenage vampires who infest the city and surrounding area, preying on the public and assorted riffraff. The plot centers on the gradual seduction of a newcomer (Patric) and the resulting jealousy of the group's leader (Sutherland) toward the new member. When the mortal is saved by his brother, the ire of the vampire is aroused. Virtually the entire second half is devoted to the efforts of the vampires to exact revenge. The effects are first-rate, combined with broad gallows humor. The film is disliked by many vampirologists because of its abuse of vampire customs and traditions. (See *Films.*)

Louis One of the main characters in the Vampire Chronicles by Anne Rice. Appearing first in the novel *Interview with the Vampire* (1976), Louis was the main narrator, telling his life story to a young reporter in San Francisco. He was vampirized by the enigmatic Lestat and introduced to the world of the undead in a most brutal fashion. Louis is quite memorable for his fascinating innocence, a naiveté that has remained despite centuries of killing and feasting.

Love: See *Sex and Love.*

Love at First Bite A 1979 comedy film, ranked with *Abbott and Costello Meet Frankenstein* and *Dance of the Vampires* as one of the most successful spoofs of the horror genre. Starring George Hamilton, Susan Saint James, and Richard Benjamin, and directed by Stan Dragoti, it leaves no cliché unused as it follows Dracula's journey to America after his expulsion from Transylvania by the local Communist party. He travels to the strangest place imaginable, New York, meets a beautiful model (Saint James), and wins both her love and a battle of wits with a hopelessly neurotic psychiatrist, Van Helsing (Benjamin). As the count, Hamilton is perfect, speaking with a monstrous Bela Lugosi accent.

Lovecraft, H. P. A brilliant and imaginative writer and very influential figure in American horror literature, Lovecraft (1890–1937) is ranked in the first order of authors of the macabre and the weird. Howard Philips Lovecraft was born in Providence, Rhode Island, and became a specialist in Colonial New England, a region that later served as the setting for many of his tales. Most of his work appeared in the magazine *Weird Tales* (starting in 1923), although he remained largely obscure for most of his life. After his death the publisher Arkham House collected and promoted his output, and his genius was recognized. While not a prolific writer on vampires, he did use strange vampiric creatures. Among them were "The Hound" (1924), about an undead sorcerer who exacts revenge upon grave robbers; "The Shunned House" (1937); "Herbert West—Reanimator" (1922); "The Outsider" (1926); "The Tomb" (1926); "The Thing on the Doorstep" (1937); and "The Case of Charles Dexter Ward" (1941).

Lucy Westenra: See *Westenra, Lucy.*

Lugat A type of Albanian vampire, also known as the *kukuthi.* According to some folk accounts, it was similar in appearance to other undead types found in the Balkans and could be rendered harmless by hamstringing or by burning. Other sources, however, present the *lugat* as a much more formidable monster, virtually indestructible by the living, with one exception: the wolf, its great nemesis, was capable of attacking and biting off its leg. Humiliated, the *lugat* would retreat to its grave, never again to torment the district.

Lugosi, Bela Legendary horror star (1882–1956) who is still considered the most recognizable portrayer of Count Dracula, although fans of Christopher Lee would beg to differ. Lugosi was an excellent actor, but his career was stereotyped by his performance as the count. Born Béla Blasko in the now Romanian town of Lugos, he was the fourth child of a baker and farmer. He studied at the Academy of Theater Arts in Budapest, making his stage debut in a 1904 production of *Romeo and Juliet*. After touring with a large company in his native province, he appeared in several unknown films in Hungary and Germany, becoming unhappy with his prospects and moving to America in 1921 to work on the stage. In 1927, after several film roles, Lugosi returned to the stage, winning the role of Dracula in the New York production of Hamilton Deane and John Balderston's play. He then returned to Hollywood and appeared in several films, including *The Thirteenth Chair* (1929), directed by Tod Browning. When Lon Chaney, Browning's first choice for Count Dracula, died in 1930, the director picked Lugosi to play the part. He was paid $500 a week. Lugosi worked steadily over the next years, but having established the Hollywood prototype of the vampire, he found it increasingly difficult to escape the typecast of monster or mad scientist.

Some of his films were quite memorable, particularly *The Black Cat* (1934) and *Mark of the Vampire* (1935); many were terrible, including *The Ape Man* (1943) and *Scared to Death* (1948). Sadly, his only success in later years came with revivals of the play *Dracula*, in 1943, 1947, and 1951. For treatment of sciatica, Lugosi took and became addicted to morphine. In 1955 he publicly admitted his addiction but died while filming *Plan Nine from Outer Space* (on August 16, 1956), generally accepted as the worst movie ever made. At his request, he was buried in the long black cape from *Dracula*. Interestingly, the ring he wore as the count was later worn by Christopher Lee in his film outings as the renowned bloodsucker.

Lust for a Vampire The second installment of Hammer Films' so-called Karnstein Trilogy, based on Sheridan Le Fanu's Carmilla Karnstein. Starring Yutte Stensgaard, Ralph Bates, Barbara Jefford, Michael Johnson, and Mike Raven, directed by Jimmy Sangster, and released in 1971, this was a demonstration of how far Hammer Films had gone beyond the classic work "Carmilla" (1872). Resurrected by her parents, Carmilla, known as Mircalla (Stensgaard), is enrolled in a local girls' school, reviving the vampire killings that had ended with her death. The populace, fed up with the new murders, burns down Karnstein Castle, and Mircalla perishes on a burning wooden rafter.

The film is also known as *To Love a Vampire.* (See also *Twins of Evil* and *Vampire Lovers, The.*)

Lycanthropy: See *Werewolf.*

Macedonia A region in the Balkans, stretching from the Aegean Sea to Yugoslavia. Macedonian vampire beliefs represent the combination of Greek and Slavonic ideas, the names used include *vrykolakas* or *vampyras.* A person could become a vampire if a cat jumped over his or her corpse while awaiting burial. Relatives and friends thus took up the duty of watching over the corpse during the night before burial. Should a cat somehow jump over the body, immediate steps were taken. The dead person was pierced with two large sack needles. It was agreed that maintaining the watch was "good for the soul," in the hope that someone would do the same for them in time. Routine exhumations often revealed that loved ones were vampires. Their bodies were removed, burned in boiling oil, and had a long nail stuck through the navel. Mustard seeds were thrown on roof tiles, and doors were barred with thorns and branches. The Macedonian vampire is recognized by its hideous appearance, as it is said to look like a bull-skin full of blood, with eyes that gleam like coals in the dark. When feeding on sheep and cattle, it usually rides on the animal's back or shoulder. The two forces best able to fight these evil creatures are dervishes and Sabbatarians. (See *Vrykolakas.*)

Magic The practice of controlling or foreseeing events and nature through the use of spells, incantations, or supernatural agencies. Magic is commonly divided into two types, evil and good, described as black and white or as magic of the left or right hand. The association of magicians with vampires is an ancient one, as the use of blood was a component in many spells. During the Middle Ages, it was accepted in much of Europe that evil sorcerers were doomed to eternal damnation. From this came the view that they would return from the grave as vampires, a suitable punishment for turning from God. Some truly wicked sorcerers made pacts with the devil to be able to continue on in a kind of existence beyond the grave that would allow not only life, but the spread of evil in the shape of vampirism. Such a one was probably Count Dracula, described by Professor Van Helsing as a member of "a great and noble race, though now and again were scions who were held by the coevals to have had dealings with the Evil One. They learned his secrets in the Scholomance . . . where the devil claims the tenth scholar as his due." Vampire magicians are found all over the world, in Russia, the Balkans, India, and in Asia. Magic is also a powerful weapon in defeating the undead. For example, Bulgarian sorcerers could bottle a vampire. (See also *Sorcerers.*)

Malaysia: See *Bajang, Bottling the Vampire, Langsuir, Magic, Mati-anak, Pelesit, Penanggalan, Polong, Pontianak,* and *Witchcraft.*

Maldicion de los Karnsteins, La A 1963 Italian-Spanish film, released in the United States under the title *Terror in the Crypt,* translated as *The Curse of the Karnsteins,* starring Christopher Lee, Audrey Amber, Jose Campos, and Ursula Davis, directed by Camillo Mastrocinque. A somewhat lifeless version of "Carmilla," *Maldicion* is nevertheless distinguished by some excellent photography. Lee plays the role of Count Karnstein. (See also *Karnstein, Carmilla.*)

Malleus Maleficarum A famous theological treatise, written around 1486 and intended to be a handbook for the discovery and eradication of witches in Europe, authored by two members of the Dominican Order, Johann Springer and Henrich (Institoris) Kraemer. It was known in the German as *Der Hexenhammer* and in English as the *Witch Hammer* or *Hammer of the Witches.* The work—authorized by Pope Innocent VIII, who had found the many tales of witchcraft circulating throughout Christendom disturbing—served as one of the main sources of the witch hysteria that gripped Europe over the succeeding centuries. Deeply misogynist in tone, the *Malleus* used as its basis the biblical motto "You shall not permit a sorceress to live" (Ex. 22:18). So definitive was the work and so respected by experts that it was adopted by both Catholic and Protestant witch-hunters. It was influential in establishing vampirism as one of the worst manifestations of the devil and included some early tales of vampiric activity.

Manducation A technical term meaning "eating," referring to a corpse actually eating or chewing food or its own shroud, held by experts of the seventeenth and eighteenth centuries as proof concerning the existence and the unwholesome activities of the undead. Manducation was said to be the result of demonic infestation by the devil or by some demon, with the intent of making the living hate the dead by playing on fear that a loved one had led an immoral life or had come to doubt divine providence. Additionally, Satan wished to stir panic among the living so that bodies would become exhumed and plagues spread. The most detailed presentation of manducation was made by the theologian Philip Rohr in his 1679 treatise, *De Masticatione Mortuorum.*

Mandurugo A Filipino vampire found in the region of Capiz, said to appear as a beautiful woman during the day and as a foul flying fiend at night. The *mandurugo* ("bloodsucker") uses her beauty to attract and wed young men, thus providing herself with a constant blood supply. When not feasting secretly upon her husband, she flies away in the dark of night, hunting for prey until dawn, when the crowing of the cock signals her to return home. She then changes back into human form. A *mandurugo* was seen in 1992 during the Philippines presidential election.

"Man-Eating Tree, The" An 1881 short story by Phil Robinson, published originally in *Under the Punkah* (1881), notable as the first tale ever written about a vampire tree. This terrible creature, found in Africa, inhabits an otherwise empty glade of grass. Its leaves, described as being like "thick, helpless, fingerless hands (rather lips or tongues than hands) dumpled closely with little cuplike hollows," try to grab any living thing that comes near them. Other stories of vampire plants, grass, or trees include H. G. Wells's "The Flowering of the Strange Orchid" (1895) and "The Purple Terror" (1894) and Algernon Blackwood's "The Transfer" (1912).

Map, Walter English chronicler (d. ca. 1208) author of the history *De Nugis Curialium* (*On the Courtier's Trifles*), which preserved English folk traditions during the Middle Ages. Map was born in the area around Hereford and served in the government of King Henry II, eventually holding the post of archdeacon of Oxford. His work is a compilation of anecdotes, stories, and gossip, valued for its coverage of peculiar legends. Aside from mentioning the *Herlethengi,* Map discussed fictive fairy people and the dead who returned to life, among them the Enchanted Shoemaker of Constantinople, a vampire-demon that murdered three children, and a Welsh revenant.

Maple Useful as a source for stakes and thorns for the destruction of the undead. It is not as popular as hawthorn. Maple is found throughout northern regions, including Siberia and China.

Mara Known in the Slavic as *mora,* a terrible night visitor that crushes or oppresses its victims, normally taking the shape of a beautiful woman or a truly hideous old hag. *Mara* comes from the Anglo-Saxon verb *merran* (to "crush"), which also provides the root for nightmare (the *nicht mara*) and *mara* (a *succumbus* or *incubus*); the word was widely used in Iceland, Denmark, and Sweden. The *mara* was feared from ancient times, known to enter the room of sleepers and to bring them dreadful dreams. At times the creature appeared as a horse, placing its forehoofs on the sleeper's chest, glaring at the poor soul with gleaming red eyes. As with the *alp,* the *mara* has close associations with vampires through its nocturnal predations and, in some areas, its fondness for blood. According to the southern Slavs, once the *mara* drinks the blood of a man, she will fall in love with him, never leaving him and forever plaguing his slumbers. She is also fond of sucking the breasts of children. A number of vampire species are classified as variations on the *mara: ephialtes, langsuir, civitateo, alp,* and the *mora* of the Ontario, Canada, Kashubes, who hold to be the wandering spirit of an unbaptized dead girl, eager to suffocate people.

Mark of the Vampire A 1935 MGM film, director Tod Browning's remake of his 1927 silent classic, *London After Midnight,* starring Bela Lugosi, Lionel Barrymore, Elizabeth Allan, Carol Borland, and Lionel Atwill. *Mark of the Vampire* was intended to be Browning's comeback, as he had not directed since his 1932 *Freaks* and was eager to make a major hit equal to his 1931 *Dracula.* The film proved superior to *Dracula,* using vigorous pacing, improved performances, and a chillingly macabre atmosphere to tell the story of events in a Czechoslovakian castle. Browning reveals at the end of the film that there is no supernatural element involved, disappointing the audiences who had become fond of Dracula as a real entity.

Marquise of O A novel by the German playwright and poet Heinrich von Kleist (1777–1811), written in 1805 and considered an important work in creating the archetypal vampire in Gothic literature. A widow, the Marquise of O—— discovers that she is inexplicably pregnant. A Russian count who had saved her life months before, a man she considers an angel, turns out to be the father, having ravished her while she was unconscious. She throws holy water at him, suddenly believing him to be evil. In time, however, the two are united in love, and the count finds personal redemption. (See also *Literature.*)

Marshall, William: See *Blacula.*

Martin A controversial 1977 film by George Romero (creator of *The Night of the Living Dead* and other horror productions), starring John Amplas, Lincoln Maazel, Christine Forrest, and Tom Savini, *Martin* presents a complex psychological treatment of blood drinking and living vampirism. Martin, the blood addict, sedates his victims, rapes them, and then slashes their wrists. Some allusions to vampiric lore are incorporated into the film. (See also *Blood.*)

Masan A feared Indian vampire demon, possibly the ghost of a child or the spirit of a low-caste individual, that delights in tormenting and murdering children. The fiend can turn its victims green, red, and yellow, but the children normally just waste away. The *masan* can also curse the young with its shadow (similar to the German *nachzehrer*). It is attracted by water used to put out a cooking fire or the act of extinguishing a lamp with the fingers and then rubbing them on clothes. Should a woman allow part of her gown to drag behind her, the vampire will follow her home. The recommended way to free children from the *masan* is to weigh them in salt.

Masani A terrible female demon vampire of India, the spirit of burial grounds. She is black in appearance, with a hideous countenance. Her hunts are conducted at night, beginning with her emergence from the ashes of a funeral pyre. Anyone passing the burial site is attacked. (See *India.*)

Matheson, Richard Successful American writer (b. 1926) whose first story, "Born of Man and Woman," appeared in 1950. Among his other notable works are *Hell House* (1971), *Bid Time Return* (1975), and scripts for the television series "Twilight Zone" and "Star Trek." He earned immortality in the vampire genre for his novel *I Am Legend* (1954) and his short stories about vampires. The novel presents a grim, apocalyptic future in which plague has wiped out most of the earth, the survivors turned into vampires. The exception is the immune Robert Neville, who works to find a cure while hunting down the undead during the day. The novel was filmed twice, as *The Last Man on Earth* (1964) with Vincent Price and *The Omega Man* (1971) with Charlton Heston. His vampire short stories include "Drink My Red Blood" (1951), "Dress of White Silk" (1951), "The Funeral" (1955), "No Such Thing as a Vampire" (1959), and "First Anniversary" (1960).

Mati-anak Another name for the Malaysian species of vampire, the *pontianak*. (See *Pontianak* for details.)

Mau-Mau Ultraviolent Kikuyu rebels of Kenya during the 1950s who opposed British rule and conducted bloody ritual oaths to ensure the loyalty of members. The so-called Kikuyu Central Association used the name *mau-mau* to add a supernatural element to the struggle, which involved ritual cannibalism, vampirism, and animal and human slaughter, with both African and European victims. Oaths were taken by drinking blood and eating excrement, brains, or crushed bones. Starting in 1952, the British waged war upon the rebels with such vigor that by 1956, eleven thousand militants were slain and another twenty thousand placed in indoctrination camps.

Maupassant, Guy de French writer (1850–1893), author of more than three hundred short stories, known in full as Henry René Albert Guy de Maupassant. Raised in Normandy, he studied law in Paris and served in the Franco-Prussian War. Gustave Flaubert was a major influence on his works. Among de Maupassant's works was "The Horla," published in 1887, the classic tale of an invisible vampire that comes from Brazil and attaches itself to the individual narrating the story. Written in the first person, the tale describes how, with increasing horror, the man's life and sanity are destroyed. "The Horla" evidences de Maupassant's tendency toward the morbid and is viewed by scholars as a prefiguring of the writer's own madness, the result of a nervous condition brought on by syphilis. He went insane in 1891 and died in an asylum. A film version of "The Horla," *Diary of a Madman*, was made in 1963, with Vincent Price.

> Now I know, I can divine. The reign of man is over, and he has come. He who was feared by primitive man; whom disquieted priests exorcised; whom sorcerers evoked on dark nights, without having seen him appear, to whom the imagination of the transient masters of the world lent all the monstrous or graceful forms of gnomes, spirits, genii, fairies and familiar spirits. After the coarse conceptions of primitive fear, more clear-sighted men foresaw it more clearly. Mesmer divined it, and ten years ago physicians accurately discovered the nature of his power, even before he exercised it himself. They played with his new weapon of the Lord, the sway of a mysterious will over the human soul, which had become a slave. They called it magnetism, hypnotism, suggestion—what do I know? I have seen them amusing themselves like rash children with this horrible power! Woe to us! Woe to man! He has come, the—the—what does he call himself—the—I fancy that he is shouting his name to me and I do not hear him—the—yes—he is shouting it out—I am listening—I cannot—he repeats it—the Horla—I hear—the Horla—it is he—the Horla—he has come!
>
> Guy de Maupassant
> "The Horla" (1887)

Mavrodullu, G. A mid-nineteenth-century Romanian playwright who authored a work on the infamous Vlad Tepes (Vlad the Impaler). Its title was *Vladu Tzepesku, Drama Istorica in Cinci Acte,* and it was performed at Bucharest in 1856 or 1858. Such plays helped to reintroduce Vlad to Europe, leading to Bram Stoker's use of this historical figure as a source for *Dracula* (1897).

Maya One of the foremost cultures of Mesoamerica that was comparatively bloodless in its religious practices but possessed a fearsome bat god whose rule spread over much of Central America. The god was known to the Maya as Zotzilaha; depictions of this deity are found in temples and cities stretching across the Mayan realm. He was portrayed as a tall man with the head and wings of a bat, his face and teeth those of the vampire bat. In one hand was a severed head, in the other a heart, symbolizing his power over the living and the granting to him of the ultimate sacrifice—human life. Zotzilaha was later adopted by the Aztecs, who incorporated many of his attributes into their deity, Huitzilopochtli, a much more demanding god than that of the Maya. (See also *Mexico.*)

Mayflower Known commonly also as trailing arbutus, a popular flower in North America and Europe, characterized by its hairy evergreen leaves which often conceal the fragrant, early spring flowers. In England the hawthorn is also called mayflower. On the Isle of Man it was used to ward off evil, fastened to the doors of houses. It could also be applied in conjunction with rowan, which was fastened in cattle sheds and byres.

Mayne, Ferdy German actor, known also in full as Ferdinand Mayne, who appeared in many films, including such well-known works as *Where Eagles Dare* (1969) and *Conan the Destroyer* (1984). Mayne worked in several notable vampire films, playing a doctor in *The Vampire Lovers* (1970) and the following year portraying Count Dracula in the West German comedy *Happening Der Vampire* (released in the United States as *The Vampire Happening*). Directed by Freddie Francis, the latter film included many strange elements, such as the departure of a vampire via a helicopter, replete with a bat symbol on the side, à la Batman. Mayne's most famous role as an undead, however, was in the 1967 *Dance of the Vampires,* directed by Roman Polanski, in which he portrayed the wicked Count Krolock. He also starred in the 1983 *Frightmare,* playing a revived corpse who goes on a killing spree.

Mayo, Herbert A mid-nineteenth-century English surgeon who was professor of anatomy and physiology at King's College, professor of comparative anatomy in the Royal College of Surgeons in London, and senior surgeon of Middlesex Hospital. Mayo was also the author of a famous work, *On the Truths Contained in Popular Superstitions* (1851), devoting an entire chapter to the subject of vampirism. His analysis of vampire attacks attempts to establish a link between vampirism and superstitious autosuggestion, arguing that there rests an essentially psychological explanation for the many related characteristics associated with vampire feedings—elements such as anemia, neck bites, and the deathlike trance. Night visitations by dead loved ones or persons known to the victims were deemed part of the traditional sexual fantasy, associated closely with the blood kiss, the autoerotic act in which kissing becomes biting and blood drinking. Anemia, loss of appetite, and other symptoms could thus be explained either on psychological or medical grounds. Mayo's writings were an early attempt to bring some rational explanation to a subject that was still causing alarm in parts of Europe. He stated, however, that "the proper place of this subject falls in the midst of a philosophical disquisition." Montague Summers, in his *The Vampire, His Kith and Kin* (1928), discusses Mayo's writings in some detail, but from the perspective that the undead are an unearthly reality. (See also *Belgrade Vampire.*)

Medicine In ages past the vampire found a bitter enemy in the medical profession as the physician worked desperately to save victims of vampiric attack, participated in the hunt for and the destruction of the undead, and allied himself with churchmen, theologians, magistrates, and outraged peasants. A classic example of this was Dr. Johann Flückinger, who in 1732 helped liquidate a nest of vampires in Meduegna.

Gradually, however, the vampire came to be better understood, and as sympathetic writings appeared with attention paid to the vampire's point of view, a change of attitude took place. Physicians, always secretly fascinated with the way in which vampires functioned, not only aided some undead to ease the torment of their existence, but actually labored to find possible cures for their terrible conditions. Thus, Dr. Julia Hoffman, on the television show "Dark Shadows" (from 1966 to 1971 portrayed by Grayson Hall and from 1990 to 1991 by Barbara Steele) gave her time, services, and unrequited love to Barnabas Collins in an effort to cure him. Similar labors have been undertaken by physicians in such works as *Vampyr* (a novel by Jan Jennings) and *Nightlife* (a comedy film).

At the same time, of course, medicine and vampires have come together in infrequent but diabolical unions, creating what can be called medical vampirism. Such an alliance with its terrible results was seen in the short story "Good Lady Ducayne" (1896) and in the novel *Those Who Hunt the Night* (1988). Medical vampirism can manifest itself anywhere a person with even rudimentary medical knowledge has a desire or a predisposition to drink blood. Needles, syringes, scalpels, bandages, and transfusion equipment are all that are needed for virtually anyone to be a medical vampire—someone who lives on human or animal blood, drained from a host, perhaps without their knowledge and certainly without their consent. (See also *Blood.*)

Meduegna: See *Paole, Arnold.*

Melrose Vampire A priestly revenant who terrorized the area around Melrose Abbey and whose activities were recorded by the twelfth-century chronicler William of Newburgh, in his *Historia Rerum Anglicarum*. While still of the living, this cleric, chaplain to a lady of high rank, had done little to distinguish himself as a loyal servant of the Church. It was said that he acted almost as if he were a secular, earning the nickname *Hundeprest* (Dog Priest) because of his love of hunting with horse and hound. Not surprisingly, a short time after his death he began appearing, trying for several nights to gain entry to Melrose Abbey. He met with no success, owing to the sanctity of this great English monastery. So, defeated, he proceeded elsewhere, appearing one night in the chamber of the woman who had employed him while he lived. He shrieked and groaned obnoxiously, and the lady summoned a senior member of the abbey. Upon investigating the matter, the monk set out with another associate and with two brave-hearted laymen. That night they stood watch, retreating at midnight to a nearby lodge, where they warmed themselves by a fire. The senior monk, however, stood at his post, and as his companions departed, the undead cleric emerged from his slumber, facing the solitary enemy. Initially frightened, the monk soon recovered enough to use his ax to ward off attacks. With the monk at his heels, the revenant fled, seeking refuge in his grave, which opened up to receive him before closing again. Joined by the others, the monk ordered that the grave be opened first thing the next morning. The corpse inside appeared badly injured, and black blood poured from a wound, filling the tomb. The men moved the body to an area outside of the monastery, burned it, and scattered the ashes into the wind. (See also *England.*)

Menippus A pupil of the ancient philosopher Apollonius of Tyana, who was saved by his teacher from certain death at the hands of a terrible female vampire, an *empusa*. The story is told in *The Life of Apollonius of Tyana* by Philostratus.

Mercure Galant A late-seventeenth-century French newspaper or journal that, with the *Gleaner*, or *Glaneur Hollandois,* helped to spread the vampire craze that was sweeping across Europe. The *Mercure Galant,* in its 1693–1694 edition, devoted much of its space to the topic of vampires, reporting in lurid details the habits of such creatures. The vampires, it declared, made their appearance after lunch and remained until midnight. They drank the blood of people and cattle, sucking it through the nose, mouth, or, most commonly, the ears. So hungry were these living dead that they ate their own shrouds. Such tales were a source of intense interest to theologians and scientists. The result was an outpouring of vampire treatises in the eighteenth century.

Mérimée, Prosper: See *Guzla, La* and *Literature.*

Mesoamerica: See *America, Central.*

Mexico A Central American nation with a rich vampire tradition in both folklore and film. Among the many Aztec views was the deep-seated belief that the world's very survival was dependent upon the careful procurement of human sacrifices, in which hearts of victims were torn out and offered to the powerful sun god. These virtually endless rituals have come to identify the Aztecs with excessive brutality, imperialist expansion, and a morbid fascination with blood and death. Taken in their cosmological context, the sacrifices were absolutely essential, as were the activities of the priests of Tlaloc, the rain god, who offered up children to the god believing that the greater the cries of the infants during torture, the more generous the deity would be in giving rain. These priests were always distinguishable by their blood-soaked garments and blood-matted hair. With these pagan clerics were the *nahualli,* the feared magicians, and the *tlaciques,* witches among the Nahuatl of Mexico. The latter were deemed capable of turning into blood-drinking turkeys. Following the brutal massacre of the Aztec empire in 1521 by the Spanish, elements of European folklore were impressed upon Mexico, either being accepted outright or combined with the traditional native beliefs. Thus the stories of La Llorona, the Weeping Woman, which originated in Europe, soon spread throughout Mexico and beyond.

Mexico is also the home of one of the world's most prolific vampire film markets, dismissed by some students of the genre as poorly made, grotesque, and handicapped by bad acting. However, these films have achieved at times a genuine sense of atmosphere and have provided interesting movie cycles. The chief performer was German Robles, who appeared as Count Lavud in the 1950s and as Nostradamus in the 1960s. By far the oddest, and perhaps worst, of the movies were those featuring the masked wrestler Santo, a now legendary figure in Mexico, whose exploits in the ring, on the street, and on screen have encouraged millions of fans, many living in the poorest parts of Mexico. Often appearing with his fellow wrestler Blue Demon, Santo took on a bewildering array of villains in the films, including vampires. His "son" now makes public appearances to benefit charitable organizations and programs for the young.

Mikonos Also Mycona or Myconos, an island in the Aegean, south of Andros, the site of a gruesome vampire haunting that was reported by the French botanist Joseph Pitton de Tournefort, who traveled in Greece from 1700 to 1702. The affair was reported in his *Relations d'un Voyage du Levant.* This was a classic appearance by a *vrykolakas,* the Greek vampire species, and an interesting demonstration of Greek methods of destroying the undead. The vampire was originally a peasant of Mikonos, an unpleasant man who died by the hands of an unknown assailant. Two days after his burial he was seen in the streets, performing various tricks on his fellow villagers. As the attacks worsened, the local priests decided to wait for nine days to see if the vampire would settle down. On the tenth day a mass was celebrated, and the body was exhumed to have its heart removed. By custom, the organ had to be ripped out and incense burned to mask the stench. Clouds of smoke supposedly poured out of the body, and the flesh appeared still warm. The heart was burned, but still the vampire continued his attacks. The people panicked. They fasted, purified doors with holy water, conducted religious processions, and filled the mouth of the corpse with holy water. Some tried to stick swords into the grave, only to have an Albanian point out that such methods were useless. The man advised against Christian swords with cross handles, symbols that prevented the devil from leaving the corpse. He recommended that they use instead Turkish scimitars or sabers, but these proved equally ineffective. While some people contemplated fleeing Mikonos, others took the body to the small island of St. George, situated in the harbor. There the corpse was prepared with tar and set ablaze on a large pyre. This act, accomplished on January 1, 1701, put an end to the plague. People then declared that in this case the devil had overreached himself, and they wrote street songs and ballads mocking and ridiculing the Evil One. (See also *Greece.*)

Millet The general name given to certain grasses and cereals. One of the most commonly grown is the so-called hog millet (*Panicum miliaceum*), known even in ancient times. Millet has been used as a vampire preventive and as a protection against attack. In Bulgaria, where it ranked with garlic, it was placed or rubbed into the eyes, ears, and nostrils of a corpse to help ensure that the individual did not return. Elsewhere millet was scattered over graves and around the cemetery, even along the walkways of houses, forcing the vampire to collect the grain, seed by seed, perhaps allowed only one seed a year.

Mirrors Objects that vampires try to avoid and frequently seek to destroy. The assumed dislike of the vampire for mirrors is largely the product of fiction. Credit must be given to Bram Stoker, who had Dracula react violently to seeing Jonathan Harker's shaving mirror (he throws it out of a window). The vampire knows that it will cast no reflection, something that is bound to be noticed in time. Folkloric reasons for this aversion stem from the concept that a mirror also reflects a soul, and evil beings have no soul to reflect. It has also been argued that the bloodsuckers actually exist in two worlds, that of the living and that of the dead. As it is in neither world completely, it will not be seen in a mirror. Bulgarians turned the mirror toward the wall when a person died to prevent the death of another individual should the corpse be reflected. In Mecklenburg there was an idea that the corpse, seeing itself doubled, would fetch someone to take with it. The mirror can also prove a useful weapon for vampire repulsion. The undead will be deflected momentarily, affording the hunter time to draw more formidable weapons.

Mists Bodies of fog seen floating through the night, passing beneath doors, swirling into rooms, and transforming into vampires. Mists are said to be one of the ways in which the powerful undead are able to move about and to negotiate difficult-to-reach areas. Visually, the image of a vampire turning into mist, sailing along the ground, and then re-forming into human shape, is a powerful one. It has been developed in cinema more often than in fiction, mainly because of the opportunity it presents for special effects. The Universal film *Son of Dracula* (1943), with Lon Chaney, Jr., tapped into the mist concept, presenting Count Alucard entering a room in an impressive body of fog. This has been used repeatedly in such projects as *Dracula* (1979), *The Keep* (1983), *Fright Night II* (1989), and especially *Bram Stoker's Dracula* (1992). In legend, the mist is not a commonly mentioned aspect of vampires; only rarely, as in parts of Hungary or China, was it held to be a feared characteristic. There is, however, a clear link between such misty transformations and speculation as to how the undead leave their graves; misty forms are thought to billow out of the multiple holes found usually just above or around the coffin.

Mmbyu: See *Pacu Pati.*

Moderner Vampyre, Ein An 1882 novel, written by Ewald August König and published at Leipzig. The novel, despite its title, was not about vampires; the name was used only to attract a wider audience. The work is typical of the period as writers attempted to capitalize on the continuing vampire craze, both in fiction and on stage. Similar was the 1873 *Moderne Vampyr* by Franz Hirsch.

Mongolia A large Asian country dominated by the Gobi Desert in its middle regions. The Mongols, once the possessors of the largest empire in history, practiced a kind of ritualized cannibalism during their primitive eras in which warriors consumed a small portion of their fallen comrades in order to partake of their courage and skill in battle. Early Mongolian religion also possessed within its pantheon a fearsome vampire deity, known as the lord (god) of time. He was depicted in full demonic glory with sharp, evil teeth, the bones and skulls of dead and rotting corpses strewn about his storm-filled landscape. This was but one of numerous, terrible deities to be feared and placated. In his "Mortmain" (1940), Seabury Quinn featured a Mongolian vampire, the *ching shih* (a variation on the *kuang-shi*), who was created by sorcery. This monster was nearly impossible to slay, able to regenerate itself as long as a single fragment of its body remained. (See also *India.*)

Montenegro A Balkan region in southwestern Yugoslavia, situated on the Adriatic and bordering Albania. The Montenegrin vampire is traditionally called the *tenatz* and is usually found in the shape of a dead person, although in the past there was a tradition that a *tenatz* could also be a so-called live vampire. The process by which a person became a *tenatz* was known as *potentzio se*, the means of such an event typical of other regions, such as having a cat jump over a corpse. The *tenatz* will return from the grave to torment the living, although its bloodsucking habits are rarely mentioned. It can be destroyed by staking, burning, or hamstringing. By custom, priests must preside over the staking.

Moonlight The rays of the moon, seen most often in the films of the genre illuminating cemeteries as the undead come out of their lairs to feast upon the living. The vampire does not need the light of the moon, as its vision is reputed to equal that of the owl. The moon does figure in lore as affecting the undead. In Slavic lands, for example, it was held that any vampire killed by a silver bullet blessed by a priest should not be allowed to rest in moonlight, lest it be rejuvenated. This was especially true in periods of full moon, when its powers were magnified. The revivatory capacities of moonlight were used to great effect by James Malcolm Rymer in his famous 1847 epic, *Varney the Vampyre*, as well as in John Polidori's "The Vampyre" (1819).

Moore, C. L. A brilliant and innovative writer of fantasy and science fiction (b. 1911), known most for her contributions to the magazine *Weird Tales* as well as her subsequent science-fiction tales. Catherine Lucille Moore sold her first story, the famous "Shambleau," to *Weird Tales* in 1933. She married the writer Henry Kuttner in 1940, collaborating with him on numerous projects and ending her all-too-brief period of weird literature. After his death in 1958, she wrote for films and television. "Shambleau" introduced the well-known character Northwest Smith, a roguish warrior, survivor of a multitude of battles, and a traveler in space. The Shambleau is a Medusa-like creature that exists by "stoking itself up with the life forms of men." Smith's adventures continue in "Black Thirst" (1934) and "Tree of Life" (1936). Another character, Jirel of Joiry, encounters a vampiric entity in "Hellsgarde" (1939).

Mora: See *Mara.*

More, Henry English poet and philosopher (1614–1687) whose writings and pursuit of the metaphysics of Plato made him one of the main contributors to the school of thinkers known as the Cambridge Platonists. He authored many well-known treatises and became a fellow in Cambridge in 1639. His work *An Antidote Against Atheism* (1652), known completely as *An Antidote Against Atheism: or An Appeal to the Natural Faculties of the Mind of Men, Where There Be Not a God,* is a collection of stories about ghosts, witches, and vampires. More thus became one of the first English authors to record vampiric activities since the chroniclers of the twelfth century. Among his assembled tales are the Breslau Vampire and Johannes Cuntius, the so-called Pentsch Vampire.

Morgano A ballet that debuted on May 25, 1857, in Berlin, described as a *komische-zauber* (comical-magical) ballet. It was written by Paul Taglioni with music by J. Hertzel and was set in Hungary. The ballet tells of a young woman, Elsa, who is taken by a group of vampires led by Morgano. After dancing with them in their castle, she is saved by her lover, Retzki, who destroys Morgano with a consecrated sword. Another ballet, *Il Vampiro,* opened in Milan in 1861, written by Rotta, with music by Paola Giorza.

Morieve, Viscount de A terrible French vampire who was active for many years after the French Revolution, haunting his ancestral holdings. An aristocrat shrewd enough to keep his head during the Revolution, he waited for years to exact revenge upon the leaders of the local peasantry who had humiliated him at the time of the upheaval. At the end of the Revolutionary period he summoned the peasants to his estate and chopped off their heads. Soon, of course, he was assassinated. A short time after his burial, children began to disappear; their corpses were eventually discovered, with their throats torn and their bodies drained of blood. While his tomb was being repaired, the viscount supposedly killed more children, nine in one week. The terror caused by de Morieve continued for seventy-two years, ending only with the succession of a grandson to the title. He investigated the case with the help of a local priest, examining the corpse after opening the viscount's tomb. De Morieve was preserved, with soft, lifelike skin and protruding teeth. Taking immediate steps, the young viscount ordered the body removed and impaled with a whitethorn stake. Blood poured everywhere, and terrible screams issued from the corpse. A search of the family archives revealed that the original viscount had come from Persia, perhaps bringing with him a vampire taint. The story was first recorded in *Another Grey Ghost Book* by Jesse Adelaide Middleton. (See also *France.*)

Morlacchi A people living in Dalmatia, whose beliefs concerning vampires and other evil beings were preserved by the naturalist Giovanni Battista Alberto Fortis (1740–1803) in his *Viaggio in Dalmazia* (*Travels in Dalmatia*). The Morlacchi (also Morlachs) believed in vampires, as well as witches, fairies, and ghosts. The name that they gave to the undead was traditional for the region, *vukodlak,* a fiend who hunted the blood of children. Their most common methods of vampire prevention were slashing a corpse's hamstrings and sticking pins in its body. Morlacchi who feared that they might return from the grave left careful instructions for relatives to take all necessary steps to keep their bodies in the earth.

Mormo A hideous female vampirelike creature found in Greek mythology, said to be part of the train of the goddess Hecate and not quite as hideous as the *empusa*. Greek children were told stories about the *mormo* by their nurses, and in time she became a favored bugaboo rather than a terrible denizen of the underworld. In his *De Spectris* (1575), Louis Lavater included the *mormo* in his examination of vampire species in the ancient world. The *mormo* was also thought to be similar to the *lamia.*

Moroii A Romanian name for a kind of vampire, specifically a live vampire, as compared to the *strigoii,* or dead vampire. While *strigoii* is used by Romanians to refer to vampires of all types, *moroii* is considered a more appropriate term for the living variety. The *moroii* can be male or female. A male *moroii* is usually bald or balding; a female, red in the face. (For other details, see *Live Vampires* and *Strigoii;* see also *Romania.*)

"Morte Amoureuse, La": See *Gautier, Théophile.*

Mosquitoes Flying insects found virtually worldwide, known to suck blood from animals and humans as the female pierces the skin, injects its own salivary fluids, and then withdraws blood. Mosquitoes are known to transmit certain diseases and have been associated with vampires. In some regions it was believed that vampires could control mosquitoes or transform themselves into mosquitoes in order to enter homes and feed on victims. A famous tale about the origin of the mosquito recited by African Americans told of the mating of a witch with a devil, a union that resulted in children. The devil's wife exacted revenge by slaying the witch and turning the offspring into mosquitoes.

Motetz Dam A Hebrew word for "vampire," translated as "bloodsucker."

Moths: See *Butterflies.*

Movies: See *Films.*

Mullo Also *muli* and *mulo,* the Gypsy undead, synonymous with a ghost, held in horror because of its vicious, lustful nature. A *mullo* comes into being when a person dies of unnatural causes (many Gypsies view death itself as unnatural), by improper rites, or by sudden death. Having no set appearance or attributes, as these change from region to region, the creature can be invisible, or seemingly normal looking but lacking in certain digits, or have appendages of animals. In India they are described as having yellow or flaming hair. Among the Swedish Gypsies, the *mullo* can change into an animal, the wolf shape traditionally being the most common. An insatiable sexual appetite is frequently mentioned; thus a *mullo* will always return to its wife. The result of their union is called a *dhampir.* The lovers of such beings are exhausted, and female *mullos* can drive their male lovers to death from fatigue. Preventives for becoming one include piercing a corpse with a steel needle or driving a hawthorn stake through its leg. Also useful are bits of iron placed between the teeth, in the ears, nose, and between the fingers. Fishing nets, juniper pieces, thorns, and the rosary will all keep an abode safe from visitation, as will the use of charms and spells, or antivampire animals (such as black dogs, black cocks, and wolves). The theft of the left sock of the corpse or the firing of a gun by a *dhampir* will kill the *mullo,* as will pouring boiling oil on a grave, walking a horse over it several times, or pounding long stakes into the ground where the stomach and head of the corpse are located. (See *Gypsies.*)

Mulo: See *Mullo.*

Munch, Edvard Norwegian painter and printmaker (1863–1944) whose work displayed the influence of neoimpressionism, examining love and death through powerful symbols and psychological themes. His work is known for its original design and color. In 1895 Munch painted *Vampire,* a beautiful red-haired woman bending over a man's neck. A slightly different but equally striking lithograph was produced in 1895, an important variation on the original. August Strindberg wrote a prose-peom for the *Revue Blanche* on Munch's paintings:

> Golden rain falls on the unfortunate kneeling creature
> who craves of his evil genius the boon of death by the prick of
> a needle. Golden fibres which bind to earth and to suffering. A
> rain of blood flows in torrents over the accursed head of him

who seeks the misery, the divine misery of being loved, that is—of loving.

Murnau, F. W. German film director (1888–1931), one of the early proponents of German expressionism, most known today for his 1922 masterpiece, *Nosferatu.* F. W. Murnau was a pseudonym for Fredrich Wilhelm Plumpe. He studied at the universities of Heidelberg and Berlin, coming under the influence of Max Reinhardt, the theatrical director and innovator. After making propaganda films during World War I, Murnau embarked on a directorial career and in 1920 released his *Der Januskopf* (known in the United States as *Dr. Jekyll and Mr. Hyde*), starring Conrad Veidt and Bela Lugosi. He then discovered Bram Stoker's 1897 novel *Dracula,* a perfect vehicle for the screen, but preferred not to acquire the rights, as the novel was still copyrighted. Instead he changed the novel to a degree that he believed would protect him legally, entitling his work *Nosferatu* and using German rather than Transylvanian settings. His character Count Orlock was a terrifying creature closely linked to the legends of Eastern Europe rather than to Gothic literature. These adjustments, however, were ultimately superficial, and the Stoker estate mounted a legal challenge. Despite its many merits, *Nosferatu* was attacked as a blatant copy of *Dracula,* receiving only limited release as a result. A 1929 version called *Nosferatu the Vampire* was distributed in the United States, but by that year it was dated and did little to enhance Murnau's growing reputation. After many years of obscurity, *Nosferatu* is finally recognized as an immense cinematic achievement, ranked by many critics as one of the most effective films of the entire genre. Murnau utilized such technical innovations as shadowing and white trees against a black sky. (See *Nosferatu* for additional details.)

Muroni Also called *murony* and *muronul,* a kind of vampire found in the southern Romanian region of Wallachia. The *muroni* is very similar to the Romanian *strigoii,* although it is especially feared for its ability to transform itself into a variety of shapes, including cats, dogs, fleas, or spiders. While in these incarnations, the *muroni* slays easily, leaving behind marks that disguise its true nature. The only real clue is the fact that its victim is left completely drained of blood without the usual puncture marks. Anyone thus slain is doomed to become a vampire, and no preventives are available. The recommended methods of destroying the *muroni* are simple: Pound a long nail through the forehead or a stake through the heart.

Murray, Mina A major character in the novel *Dracula* by Bram Stoker. Mina Murray (later Mina Harker) is the symbolic "good" woman of the story, in contrast with Lucy, who succumbs to the wiles of Dracula and becomes a vampire. Mina rejects the unwholesome advances of the count, refuses many of the so-called New Woman ideas admired by Lucy, and even contemplates suicide rather than risking surrender to Dracula. Epitomizing Stoker's concept of Victorian morality, Mina is remarkably resilient, strong, and intelligent, playing an active role in defeating Dracula's plans and subjecting herself to Van Helsing's hypnotism in order to track the count through her mind link with him, which resulted from their exchange of blood. To many analysts of the novel, Mina represents as well the nurturing mother who cares for the hunters of Dracula and is rewarded with love and a child, while Lucy, who rejects her mothering instincts, is condemned to destruction at the hands of her would-be husband. Mina's child, however, has the blood of Dracula coursing through his veins. Two of the best portrayors of the Mina character in film were Kate Nelligan in the 1979 *Dracula*, and Winona Ryder in the 1992 hit *Bram Stoker's Dracula*. [See also *Dracula (Novel)* and *Westerna, Lucy.*]

Mustard Seed The product of the herbs of the genus *Brassica*, used for a number of purposes, including the creation of the condiment mustard and as a preventive against vampires. Mustard seeds have been applied in Eastern Europe in the same manner as millet, linen seeds, carrot seeds, and other items. They are to be sprinkled around graves or strewn along the roads leading to graveyards. Some believe that the vampire must eat the grain before proceeding on its terrible rounds, perhaps allowed by custom to only one grain a year. Others hold that the undead must pick up each grain before moving on, again limited to only one grain each year. Mustard seeds are either yellowish white or black (dark, reddish brown), but both are equally acceptable in fighting vampires; they are odorless when whole but have a pungent taste. Their value may stem from the traditional medicinal characteristics of mustard: mustard plasters for chest colds and mustard baths for relaxing. The Macedonians particularly use mustard seeds, honoring them as a symbol of the Christian faith.

Mutilation: See *Binding a Corpse* and *Piercing a Corpse.*

Myiciura, Mr. A tragic case of vampire hysteria in modern England and an example of how old-country traditions are not expunged by modern culture. The story appeared in the *Times* of London in January, 1973, detailing the curious demise of a Polish immigrant named Myiciura, in an article entitled "Immigrants' Fears of Vampires Led to Death." Police were summoned to the Stoke-on-Trent apartment of a sixty-eight-year-old retired pottery worker who had resided in England for twenty-five years. He was found dead, apparently the victim of accidentally choking on a clove of garlic. According to his landlady, the man was terrified of vampires, convinced that they were everywhere, especially in his neighborhood. He used pepper, salt, and garlic to protect himself. His body was found surrounded by bags and containers of salt, which was sprinkled on his blankets. Garlic was placed outside his window in a bowl and had been smeared in his door keyhole. The man had placed a clove in his mouth for added protection. He fell asleep and choked to death. (See also *Poland.*)

"Mysterious Stranger, The" An influential 1860 short story, written anonymously in German and then translated into English and published in the *Odds and Ends* magazine. The story bears a remarkable similarity to Bram Stoker's *Dracula* and has been considered a virtual prototype for the famed novel. Stoker must have used it in researching materials for his work, for in the villain Count Azzo he was given a clear example of the Romantic vampire type of Lord Ruthven, Varney the Vampire, and Carmilla. Set in the Carpathian Mountains, the tale foreshadows the plot of Stoker's *Dracula,* complete with a wandering knight and the destruction scene in a castle. (See also *Azzo, Count.*)

Now listen! I had walked up and down my room for a long time; I was excited—out of spirits—I do not know exactly what. It was almost midnight ere I lay down, but I could not sleep. I tossed about, and at length it was only from sheer exhaustion that I dropped off. But what a sleep it was! An inward fear ran through me perpetually. I saw a number of pictures before me, as I used to do in childish sickness. I do not know whether I was asleep or half awake. Then I dreamed, but as clearly as if I had been wide awake, that a sort of mist filled the room, and out of it stepped the knight Azzo. He gazed at me for a time, and then letting himself slowly down on one knee, imprinted a kiss on my throat. Long did his lips rest there, and I felt a slight pain, which always increased, until I could bear it no more. With all my strength I tried to force the vision from me, but succeeded only after a long struggle. No doubt I uttered a scream, for that awoke me from my trance. When I came a little to my senses I felt a sort of superstitious fear creeping over me—how great you may imagine when I tell you that, with my eyes open and awake, it appeared to me as if Azzo's figure were still by my bed, and then disappearing gradually into the mist, vanished at the door!

"You must have dreamed very heavily, my poor friend," began Bertha, but suddenly paused. She gazed with surprise at Franziska's throat. "Why, what is that?" she cried. "Just look: how extraordinary—a red streak on your throat!"

Anonymous
"The Mysterious Stranger" (1860)

Nabeshima, Cat of A terrible vampire demon of Japan who took the shape of a cat, murdering a courtesan and then focusing its attention on the prince of Hizen, a member of the Nabeshima family. The cat throttled the concubine O Toyo, assumed her shape, and subsequently spent every night with the prince, who grew more and more ill with each passing day. Doctors were unable to find a medicine that would bring relief, but they did notice that he worsened at night. Guards posted to keep watch fell asleep, and the perplexed ministers went to the chief priest of a nearby temple. While praying over the prince, the priest discovered a lowly soldier, Ito Soda, who begged to stand guard. When the magical spell fell on him, he stabbed his thigh to keep himself awake and saw a beautiful young woman enter the prince's chamber.

Soda's presence worked against her spells, and she was unable to feed. She tried to induce sleep upon Soda but failed, and the prince began to recover. Soda, meanwhile, was convinced that O Toyo was a vampire, and he went to her apartment, gaining entry by saying that he carried a message. As he neared the woman, he lunged with a dagger, but she flew across the room, seized a halberd, and assaulted him. When it became clear that she was not able to win, the woman turned into the cat, fled to the roof, and escaped into the mountains. Local inhabitants were tormented until the prince led a great hunt. The vampire cat was slain, but ever after the people of Nabeshima have been alert for the monster, last reported seen in 1929. (See also *Japan.*)

Nachzehrer A species of vampire found among the Kashubes of northern Europe and in parts of Germany, including Silesia and Bavaria. The *nachzehrer* (also *nachtzehrer*) is distinguishable in its coffin by its curious custom of holding the thumb of one hand in the other and keeping its left eye open. This creature is able to kill its relatives through a kind of long-range sympathetic magic. While in the grave it will devour its own shroud, piece by piece, moving on to feast on its own flesh. As this takes place, the surviving relatives will begin to waste away, their life force being drawn out. According to some Kashubes, the *nachzehrer* then leaves its coffin or tomb, often in the shape of a pig, and visits its family, drinking their blood. It is also able to ascend to a church belfry to ring the bells, bringing death to anyone who hears them. Another, less-known power of this vampire is the ability to bring death by causing its shadow to fall upon someone.

Those hunting the creature in the graveyard listen for grunting sounds, which it makes while munching on its grave clothes. The Bavarians believed that a *nachzehrer* could be created if a person was born with a caul or second skin. It can be destroyed by placing a coin in its mouth and by cutting off its head with an ax, while any name must be removed from the deceased's clothing. (See also *Decapitation* and *Caul*.)

Nadilla A ghoul that supposedly lived near Baghdad during the early fifteenth century, eventually marrying a handsome youth, Abdul-Hassan. Abdul-Hassan supposedly was the son of a wealthy merchant and destined for an arranged marriage. When told about the plans for his wedding, he asked to think about it and took a walk in the countryside. While wandering he heard a beautiful voice and discovered a stunningly attractive woman. Despite knowing nothing about her, Abdul-Hassan begged permission to marry her, and his father agreed reluctantly. Weeks of happiness followed the nuptials, marred only by the woman's refusal to eat at the evening meal. She claimed she was used to a frugal diet. Growing suspicious, Abdul-Hassan discovered that Nadilla, as the woman was called, went out at night, returning before dawn. He followed her, uncovering her terrible secret. She was a ghoul that went to the cemetery each night with her frightful companions to eat corpses. Abdul-Hassan confronted Nadilla the following night. She was unresponsive at first but at midnight tried to attack him when she believed he was asleep. She was impaled by Abdul with a sword, and her body was placed in a tomb. Three days later, however, Nadilla returned with superhuman strength, and Abdul-Hassan ran for his life. The following day he went to her tomb and found her body perfectly preserved, with large amounts of blood spilled in the coffin. Nadilla was placed on a pyre with spices and frankincense, her ashes scattered in the Tigris River.

Native Americans The numerous peoples found in America who had their own beliefs concerning the return of dead spirits, ghosts, or revenants. There are so many individual native traditions that it is impossible to detail them all, but several are quite noteworthy. The Ojibwa Indians accepted a kind of revival or resurrection in which a soul that could not enter the next world for whatever reason would return to its body, bringing it back to life. Specific vampire beings also existed, such as the Ojibwa man-eater or the Cherokee liver eaters. The nastiest Native American vampire was the creature who had a horn-shaped mouth, and was known to suck out people's brains through their ears. (See also *America, North; La Llorona; South, American;* and *Toad Woman*.)

Necrophagism Also necrophagy, a psychological term used to describe the consumption of pieces of the corpse of someone who has been terribly mutilated. Done often while in a state of frenzy, this deviant act can be differentiated from cannibalism in that it is most often directed (1) to a specific organ or body part of (2) a dead person, the victim normally having been murdered only moments before.

Necrophilia A severe mental disorder and sexual deviation involving the uncontrollable desire to engage in assorted sexual activities with a cadaver, normally performed by a male with an obsessive attitude about young women, toward whom he has a severe inferiority complex. The necrophiliac very closely monitors the obituaries and then digs up recently deceased women or breaks into their tombs. The deviance has been noted throughout history; evidence for it dates back to the writings of Herodotus (fifth century B.C.) and to the tyrant of Corinth, Periander (d. 585 B.C.). Cases of necrophilia were often mentioned in Europe in conjunction with terrible murderers—especially the so-called historical or living vampires—criminals who killed after rape and torture and then ate their victims. (See also *Necrophagism, Necrosadism,* and *Necrostuprum.*)

Necrosadism A mental disorder in which the sufferer has an uncontrollable urge to mutilate a human corpse, deriving from this act a sort of sexual or psychological release. The term was used early in this century by Dr. Alexis Epaulard, in a 1901 treatise on vampirism. Meaning sadism toward the dead, the behavior intends not pain, but the destruction of human flesh and organs. Such activities are often accompanied by necrophilia and cannibalism (or necrophagy). The most famous necrosadist was Sergeant Bertrand, the so-called vampire who terrorized Paris in the 1840s.

Necrostuprum A term used by psychologists for the act of stealing a corpse, normally part of a necrophiliac's plan to use a body for sexually deviant purposes. Necrostuprum is thus often a direct aspect of necrophilia and can lead to necrosadism. (See also *Body Snatching.*)

Need-fire The name given to certain bonfires found throughout much of Europe, kindled to save dying cattle and livestock and to serve as a form of ritual purification. Need-fire, also known as wildfire, is a lingering element of paganism, a holdover of beliefs that evil or witchcraft could be repulsed or prevented by driving a herd between roaring flames, the smoke and heat purging the wicked influences. It was said to be effective in times of plague, continuing well into the nineteenth century and used at times specifically as a remedy for vampire infestations. The Christians banned the need-fire when it was revived in the Middle Ages, but it survived in pastoral regions, where the lore was handed down orally. Witches and sorcerers were said to have sustained the secret knowledge about such things. In times of crisis it reappeared, as in the famous cattle plague of 1598 at Neustadt, near Marburg, or the 1792 sickness at Sternberg. Countries or regions in which such fires were used include Switzerland, Saxony, Mecklenburg, Hanover, Quendlinburg, Brunswick, Silesia, Sweden, Poland, Serbia, Bulgaria, England, Russia, and the Carpathian Mountains. (See also *Ustrel.*)

Nelapsi The name of a Slovak vampire in the Zemplin district of Czechoslovakia, probably a local term, describing an undead that can do serious harm to the living. The creature drinks human blood and massacres entire villages, including people and livestock. The *nelapsi* also has the ability to kill with one glance, slaying everyone visible to him from a church tower. Such a being can be detected, however, as the corpse carries certain telltale characteristics: the lack of rigor mortis in the grave, a normal-colored face, open eyes, and two curls in its hair. Should these features be present, it may be assumed that the corpse has two hearts, therefore two souls as well. Preventives include burial with coins, the use of enchanted herbs, the placing of Christian symbols in the coffin, and the pouring of millet or poppy seed into the mouth, nose, and along the path to the cemetery. When taking a corpse out of a house, the coffin should not hit the threshold and should be removed headfirst. More drastic measures vary from nailing the hair, limbs, and clothes to the coffin, to impaling the head or heart with a blackthorn or hawthorn stake (a hatpin will also do), to the lighting of a "new-fire" by rubbing sticks together. After the burial, the family members are urged to wash their hands.

Nepal A central Asian kingdom situated in the Himalayan Mountains between India and Tibet, its traditional capital found at Katmandu. Historically, the Nepalese have been Hindus, with Buddhists constituting a minority. As such, it was the recipient of Indian (or Indus Valley) beliefs concerning terrifying vampire deities, gods who shaped Nepalese conceptions of hell, nature, and death. Clearly the most horrible of these beings was the god of death. He is depicted with vampire fangs, standing on a base of human skeletons. Human skulls, polished and bleached, crown his head, and around his neck the god wears a garland of severed heads. (See also *Asia.*)

Neuntöter A German vampire species found especially in Saxony, traditionally a great carrier of plagues, usually seen during severe epidemics. The name *neuntöter* (the "nine-killer") comes from the generally held belief that it takes nine days for this vampire to be fully formed in the grave. The accepted method for destroying the *neuntöter* is to place lemon in its mouth. (See also *Germany.*)

New England The region that perpetuated English traditions concerning the devil's part in daily human affairs, the terrors of the supernatural, and the need to be ever alert to the perils of witchcraft. Thus, at Salem and elsewhere in the area, the Puritans and people of other faiths conducted trials of those accused of using magic or dabbling in the black arts. One of the well-known characteristics of witchcraft as practiced in New England, examined by many writers, was the drawing out, the use of, and the drinking of blood. Children were particularly common victims, suffering bite marks and loss of life energy. (See also *Exhumation, Plague, Ray Family Vampire,* and *Rhode Island.*)

New Guinea An island situated to the north of Australia, its capital at Papua, distinguished by its vast tropical jungles and mountain ranges. Among the Papuans, Melanesians, and Negritos who inhabit New Guinea, there are widely held beliefs concerning the power of blood. The liquid was said to possess powerful elements of the soul, so much so that villagers tried to make certain that not even a drop was allowed to fall into the hands of evil magicians or sorcerers. All bandages were carefully burned or thrown into the sea. One of the strongest fears in this context was that a magician might summon an evil spirit and then give it blood, thereby providing it with the means of having a corporeal existence. (See *Blood* and *Magic.*)

Night The time between dusk and dawn when evil is exalted and the powers of darkness are most active; also the period of activity for the vampire. There are, however, some species, such as those found in Poland and Russia, that are able to go out during the day. The use of the night as the exclusive time of terror for the vampire was not the product of folklore, as many undead reported in accounts dating to the seventeenth and eighteenth centuries were seen or felt both in the day and night. The most horrible of their cruelties, however, took place in the dark of night. A host of species haunt the living in the late evening or early morning.

Nightmare A horrible or terrifying dream, often accompanied by a feeling of oppression or a crushing sensation. The nightmare derived its name from the Anglo-Saxon *neaht* (or *nicht*) and *mara,* implying that there was a kind of evil spirit or being at work, the *mara* (known among the Slavs as *mora*) being closely associated with the *incubus* or *succubus.* This, in turn, connected terrible dreams with the attack of a vampire. Additionally, many of the reports concerning vampires (such as those of Arnold Paole or Peter Plogojowitz in the eighteenth century) included details of their appearances during the night while their victims were asleep. In his work *On the Nightmare* (1931) by Ernest Jones, the nightmare was examined in extensive psychoanalytic and folkloric detail. (See also *Old Hag.*)

Night Stalker, The A 1972 made-for-TV film, starring Darren McGavin, Claude Akins, Carol Lynley, and Barry Atwater, directed by John Llewellyn Moxey, produced by Dan Curtis, written by Richard Matheson, and adapted from an unpublished novel by Jeff Rice. *The Night Stalker* was, for ABC, the highest-rated television program in its time, remaining so for a number of years. It was set in Las Vegas, a city suddenly gripped by terror as a killer is on the loose. Kolchak (McGavin), the disheveled but dogged reporter, is convinced that the killer is a vampire, but he faces opposition from the local police and the Vegas establishment. The vampire Janos Skorzeny (Atwater) is hunted by Kolchak, who stakes him just as the police enter the scene. The following year Jeff Rice's novel was published, while McGavin went on to play Kolchak in a short-lived television series.

Nightwing The popular 1977 novel by Martin Cruz Smith, featuring vampire bats instead of vampires, although the animals are as dangerous and pestilential as any traditional bloodsucker. The bats are joined in their predations by humans—those pillaging the Indian nation by stripping it of its natural wealth and destroying its culture and heritage. The plot centers on the efforts of a local deputy, Youngman Duran, to contain a plague caused by the bats. Interlaced with his work are the struggles between the rural Native American groups and the arrival of a slightly mad vampire hunter, Hayden Paine.

Nightwing A 1979 Paramount film version of the novel by Martin Cruz Smith, starring Nick Mancuso, Kathryn Harrold, David Warner, and Stephen Macht, directed by Arthur Hiller. A plague of vampire bats descends upon a Hopi-Navajo reservation, first killing cattle and then attacking humans. David Warner's performance as a scientist obsessed with vampire bats is first-rate. The film is generally faithful to the original novel and offers stunning southwestern landscapes.

Nodier, Charles French writer, playwright, and organizer of the French Romantic movement in the early nineteenth century, largely responsible for bringing the earliest vampire drama to the stage, thereby beginning the European vampire craze. A leading Paris literary figure, Nodier (1780–1844) wrote a theatrical adaptation of the popular "The Vampyre" by John Polidori (1819) in 1820. The play, *Le Vampire, melodrame en trois actes avec un prologue,* opened at the Théâtre de la Porte-Saint Martin in Paris on June 13, 1820, and was an enormous success, spawning a host of similar plays and comedies elsewhere. His work was adapted that year in the James Planché production, *The Vampire, or the Bride of the Isles.* Nodier's 1821 novel, *Smarra, ou les Demons de la Nuit (Smarra, or the Demons of the Night),* demonstrated his skill in examining dreams.

Nosferatu Also *nosferat,* a decidedly lustful Romanian species of vampire associated with both the *incubus* and the *succubus,* said to be the illegitimate child of parents who are illegitimate. Shortly after its burial, the creature wakens, departs the grave, and embarks on a long and savage career. It sucks blood, but it also delights in tormenting and engaging in wild orgies with the living. The male *nosferatu* is able to impregnate women. The resulting children are born covered with hair and are destined to become witches or live vampires (the *moroii*). The vampire also dislikes recently married couples, making the male impotent and the bride barren. The best method of destroying the creature is by firing a shot into its grave or by impaling it on a stake. (See also *Romania.*)

Nosferatu In full, *Nosferatu, a Symphony of Horror* (from the original German, *Nosferatu, eine Symphonie des Grauens*), the 1922 classic silent film starring Max Schreck, photographed by Fritz Arno Wagner, and directed by F. W. Murnau. *Nosferatu* is ranked as one of the greatest vampire films ever made, despite its near total obscurity for decades (the result of a bitter legal campaign by Bram Stoker's widow, Florence, to stop its release). The work was unofficially based on Bram Stoker's *Dracula* (1897), with changes incorporated to prevent violation of the novel's copyright. Dracula thus became Count Orlock, or Orlok, and Whitby was changed to Bremen. Despite these superficial alterations, the heart of *Dracula* remains, and its presentation of evil is brilliantly captured. Florence Stoker obtained an injunction against Murnau, and the work was withdrawn in 1925, preserved in pirated copies despite the order to destroy all prints and negatives. It is now widely circulated and has received enormous praise from critics.

Nosferatu the Vampyre Known in the German as *Nosferatu, Phantom der Nacht,* a 1979 remake of the classic 1922 silent film by F. W. Murnau, *Nosferatu, eine Symphonie des Grauens.* The remake starred Klaus Kinski, Isabelle Adjani, and Bruno Ganz and was directed by Werner Herzog. This hypnotic homage to expressionism features Kinski as the loathsome Count Orlock, a vile, ratlike, pestilential creature in the direct tradition of Max Schreck, the star of the original. *Nosferatu* is generally faithful to Murnau's masterpiece, adding a number of its own touches while focusing on the unwholesome desires of the vampire for a beautiful woman. The obscenely disease-spreading qualities of the creature are brilliantly displayed in one scene as hordes of rats move through a once serene and safe town. Kinski's performance is also outstanding.

Nostradamus A vampire character in four Mexican films of the 1960s, starring the well-known Mexican actor German Robles. Nostradamus is supposedly a descendant of the famed sixteenth-century seer

Michel de Nostradamus. A totally evil vampire, he was distinguished by a completely black wardrobe, a Mephistophelian beard and mustache, and a thirst for blood. He was introduced in *La Maldicion de Nostradamus* (1960, *The Curse of Nostradamus*), in which he tried to create a cult of vampires but was destroyed in a landslide. His resurrection came in *La Sangre de Nostradamus* (*The Blood of Nostradamus*), with further adventures in *Nostradamus y el Genio de las Tinieblas* (1960, *Nostradamus and the Genie of Darkness*) and *Nostradamus y el Destructor de Mostruos* (*Nostradamus and the Destroyer of Monsters*). These astoundingly low-budget films were directed by Federico Curiel. (See also *Mexico.*)

Oats Various kinds of grasses of the genus *Avena*, grown and harvested for their grains and hay. Throughout parts of Eastern Europe and particularly in Russia, oats have long been counted among the grains used as preventives against vampires. Usually they are strewn around on the ground. (See also *Seeds.*)

Obayifo A kind of living vampire found among the Ashanti people on the Gold Coast in West Africa. The *obayifo* is said to be a male or female human, able to leave its body at night to travel about and cause harm of all kinds. The vampire's chief delight is to drink the blood of children, causing their slow, painful deaths. It also attacks crops, sucking out the sap and vital juices, thereby causing terrible blights, especially in cacao crops. Anyone can be an *obayifo*, although certain clues to their identity are available—an obsession with food, meat in particular, and constantly shifting eyes. While in flight at night, the vampire is phosphorescent. The name is derived from the Ashanti word *bayi*, meaning "sorcery." The *obayifo* is similar to the *loogaroo* of the West Indies.

Ohyn A species of Polish vampire, caused by the presence of teeth and a caul at birth. The only way that one can prevent such a child from becoming an *ohyn* is to extract the teeth of the infant, lest it die and awaken in the earth, and chew its own flesh and bones before feasting on relatives. (See also *Poland.*)

Oil, Boiling A liquid used frequently in the destruction of vampires, most notably those found in Greece, such as the *vrykolakas*. When a vampire is exhumed and removed from the coffin, the vampire hunters scald the body in oil before staking it. Boiling oil is also thrown on the dirt above the coffin, thereby sealing the ground from future vampiric habitation. (See also *Hearts* and *Oil, Holy*.)

Oil, Holy The consecrated liquids used by the Christian churches for sacramental purposes, including ordination, baptism, confirmation, consecration (of prelates), and burial. In fighting the undead, holy oils have been used to create deadly weapons against evil. Priests can anoint wooden stakes and daggers to be wielded against vampires, or consecrated holy oil can be thrown upon a vampire, but the substance is not always available and is a thick, viscous fluid limited in range. Holy water, easier to acquire and to throw, is the sacred liquid of choice among vampire hunters. (See *Destroying the Vampire*.)

Old Hag An English colloquialism for an ugly, shriveled woman or a psychological term used to describe a kind of night visitor that torments the sleeper. Throughout history, old women or hags have been connected with evil or malicious intent, many being feared as witches. Naturally, legend extends the dread of old hags to include vampires, particularly in Eastern Europe. In fiction, ancient crones have presented excellent subjects for treatment. The two most famous tales of old women exhibiting vampiric traits are "Good Lady Ducayne" (1896) by Mary Elizabeth Braddon and "The Room in the Tower" (1912) by E. F. Benson. In psychology, the old hag refers to a night fright, a terrible experience that a sleeper will later swear took place while he or she was awake during the night. The significance of this phenomenon is clear when one reads many of the accounts of vampires preserved through the years; sufferers often reported details of vampiric attack that were remarkably similar to an encounter with the old hag. (See *Nightmare*.)

Oldenburg A district of Lower Saxony in northern Germany, on the North Sea. In the nineteenth century, the people of Oldenburg had a firm belief that all corpses had to be buried very deep in the ground. Should a body be placed too close to the surface, the deceased would invariably become a revenant, chewing its way to the living. (See also *Germany*.)

Ossenfelder, Heinrich August An eighteenth-century minor poet of Germany who authored one of the earliest poems about vampires, *"Der Vampir,"* published in Leipzig in May, 1748, in *Der Naturforscher*. The poem was quite ahead of its time, including within the vampire motif the sophisticated concept that a vampirelike existence was much more than the Christianized dualism of good and evil that had previously been presented by writers and theologians. A translation of *"Der Vampir"* appeared in *The Vampire in Verse* (1985), edited by Steven Moore.

Out of the House of Life Another installment in the adventures of Le Comte de Saint-Germain, the vampire creation of Chelsea Quinn Yarbro, published in 1990. The novel reveals some of the earliest days in Saint-Germain's life, focusing on his time as a slave in ancient Egypt, where he worked in the House of Life, the repository of medical knowledge and teaching. The count's reminiscences are presented in the form of letters to his lover, Madelaine. She is a vampire also, taking part in an archaeological dig in Egypt.

"Over the River" A harrowing 1941 short story written by P. Schuyler Miller (1912–1974), first published in the fantasy magazine *Unknown* in April of that year. *Unknown* (later *Unknown Worlds*) was known for its satire and high-quality black humor, but "Over the River" served up a highly disturbing glimpse of the tortured, repulsive life of a vampire, told from the hazy, ghoulish perspective of a recently created revenant.

Ovid One of the foremost Latin poets (43 B.C.–A.D. 18) of the early Roman imperial age, also called the Augustan age. His vast output of poetry included *Ars amatoria* (Art of Love) and *Metamorphoses*, and in them he reflected the Roman traditions, even from his place of exile in the Black Sea. In his *Fasti* he presented certain views of the *strix*, an evil demon that sucked the blood of children. A more direct reference to vampirism came in his *Amores* (III, XIV, 34), appearing in Dryden's translations:

> Why do your locks and rumpled head-clothes show
> 'Tis more than usual sleep that made them so?
> Why are the kisses which he gave betray'd
> By the impression which his teeth has made?

Owl A nocturnal bird of prey found in most countries around the world, common in legend and folklore as the personification of wisdom, or the animal embodiment of Athena, or the sacred bird of some tribes of North America. As a creature of the night, the owl is also known for its acute vision, compared in parts of Eastern Europe to that of the vampire. Peasants in this region did not address the owl by name but used some other word, in fear that the owl was a transformed vampire. In Malaysia the night owl is held to be the embodiment of both the *langsuir* and her stillborn child, the *pontianak*. (See also *Birds*.)

Pacu Pati A powerful Indian vampire whose name means "master of the herd," known also as *mmbyu* (an earlier personification of death). The creature is deemed the lord of all beings of mischief, including varieties of ghouls, ghosts, and vampires. He is seen at night, surrounded by his terrible servants, frequenting cemeteries and places of execution. (See also *India.*)

Palance, Jack: See *Dracula* (*1973*).

"Pale-Faced Lady, The" An 1848 short story by Alexandre Dumas père, published as a subplot to the first portion of his multivolumed work *Thousand and One Phantoms,* in the section called "Une Journée à Fontenay-aux-Roses," translated into English as "The Pale-Faced Lady." The work was published in England as an individual tale, appearing in *In the Moonlight* (1848), reprinted as "The Carpathian Vampire" in the 1975 work *The Horror at Fontenay.* Dumas used the Carpathian Mountains and Moldavian life and customs while adopting a style very reminiscent of John Polidori ("The Vampyre," 1819). The vampire in this tale is a Moldavian nobleman named Kostaki, destroyed by a blessed sword.

Palm Hair One of the most unappealing characteristics of vampires, a trait that is largely fictional in origin. Bram Stoker mentioned palm hair in his novel *Dracula,* in Jonathan Harker's description of the count. There is no general folk tradition of palm hair being a regular attribute of the undead. Once Stoker used it, however, it became an accepted fact by such writers as Montague Summers.

Paole, Arnold One of the most famous vampires in history, whose story was given high press coverage. The case of Arnold Paole took place in 1727–1728 in the Serbian village of Meduegna, near Belgrade, although another epidemic broke out in 1732. Several prominent surgeon-officers from Belgrade investigated, including Johann Flückinger, who authored the report *Visum et Repertum* (*Seen and Discovered*), which was published throughout Europe and discussed on all social levels.

Paole returned to his native village in 1727 after a tour in the army, during which he was stationed in Greece and in the Levant. He settled down to a quiet life in Meduegna, but his neighbors began to view him with suspicion when he showed little interest in the highly eligible Mina, the daughter of a neighboring farmer. Under pressure, he wed the young woman, but there was always a shadow between them, and she finally asked him what troubled him. Paole then recounted a visitation from a vampire. The event took place when he was stationed in Greece. He destroyed the creature, resigned from the military, and returned home, feeling that he was forever after cursed.

A short time later Paole fell from a hay wagon, lingered for a brief period, and died. A month after that stories began spreading that Paole was wandering about. Officers were summoned from Belgrade, and on a cold, gray morning they exhumed his corpse. The body had moved to one side in its grave, its jaw was open, and blood was trickling from its mouth. The officers and the church sexton sprinkled garlic on the remains and drove a stake through its heart, whereupon a dreadful scream issued from the body and blood gushed forth. Four other nearby corpses were also exhumed and had whitethorn stakes driven through them before cremation with Paole.

Six years passed quietly, but then vampirism broke out again. Several individuals died from loss of blood, and the surgeons were summoned again from Belgrade. The lengthy report that followed included accounts of a ten-year-old girl, a villager named Stanko, and a seventeen-year-old girl who was found in "unmistakable" vampiric condition. Their heads were cut off and burned with their bodies by the local Gypsies. The ashes were thrown into the river Morava.

Passion of Dracula, The A successful play written by Bob Hall and David Richmond, opening off Broadway in 1977, the same year as the enormous Broadway hit *Dracula*, starring Frank Langella. The play was directed by Peter Bennett, with Christopher Birnau as Dracula. It was noted for its humor.

Pausanias An A.D. second-century Greek traveler who was the author of the important work *Descriptions of Greece*, a guide to the ruins found there. Aside from his invaluable preservation of details concerning the ancient Greek structures, Pausanias recorded some very interesting mythic elements. At Corinth, for example, he learned that the children of Medea were said to have returned from the dead to torment and slay infants, until on the advice of an oracle the citizens of Corinth gave yearly sacrifices to the slayers. Additionally, the Corinthians erected a statue in the shape of a *lamia*, a hideous woman, over the tomb of Medea's offspring. (See also *Greece*.)

Pelesit A mischievous Malaysian spirit-vampire, described normally as a house cricket said to be the plaything or the pet of the *polong*. Sent by a controlling agent, the *pelesit* invades the body of a victim, causing illness and death, often in conjunction with the *polong*. Victims rant about cats while suffering, revealing the presence of the *polong,* which can be questioned by a magician and forced to reveal the name of the controlling agent, speaking through the victim's voice. The agent, called the "mother" or the "father" of the *pelesit,* is then coerced into taking the creature back. Women are the most adroit at catching a *pelesit,* keeping it in a bottle and feeding it saffron rice or blood drawn from the fourth finger. Burial will end the creature's activities. There is also a charm that may compel the *pelesit* to leave a victim.

Penanggalan A dreadful Malaysian vampire, one of the most unique in the world because it flies about at night with only a head and neck, its intestines dangling beneath them. The creature is always a female and delights in sucking blood from children or women in labor, although men are not safe from it, either. The origins of the *penang-galan* are Asiatic, with one version identifying it as a woman who died in childbirth and returned to torment infants, crying out *"Mengi-lai!"* whenever a child is born. Another version states that she was a woman surprised by a man while performing a religious penance. She reacted by tearing her head off and her intestines out, and then flew off. The blood or water dripping from her intestines cause terrible sores. The *penanggalan* uses vast amounts of vinegar to shrink her bloated intestines so they will fit back into her body. These organs glow in the dark. Because of the presence of the vampire, women in childbirth are enclosed in houses decorated with special leaves, thistles with sharp thorns from the *jeruju.* The thorns will snare the intestines of the creature, holding her until dawn, when she is vulnerable. Author Seabury Quinn wrote a gruesome tale about a *penanggalan* called "The Malay Horror," which appeared in *Weird Tales* in 1933.

Pentsch Vampire The name given to Johannes Cuntius, a citizen of Pentsch in Silesia, whose story was told in *An Antidote Against Atheism* (1653) by Henry More. Cuntius, a well-respected alderman, was nearly sixty when one of his horses kicked him in a very vulnerable place. He displayed no sign of his injury, but he soon fell ill, indicating to others that he was guilty of so many sins that pardon from God was impossible. A short time later his body was attacked by a black cat as he lay dying. During his funeral a great tempest arose, ending only when he had been laid in the ground. Rumors, stories, and sightings of Cuntius quickly spread, and it was decided to exhume the body. Unlike those around it, his corpse was perfectly preserved. Taken to be burned, it seemed strangely heavy. With great difficulty the executioners placed Cuntius on the fire, but the flames failed to have any effect on the corpse. The executioner, now desperate, chopped up the body, this time with success, throwing the ashes into the river after successful cremation.

Petronius A Roman satirist (d. ca. A.D. 66) who earned the title *Arbiter* from Emperor Nero for his remarkable taste and sense of the elegant. He was well known for his luxurious and profligate life-style, losing favor with Nero eventually and committing suicide to avoid a more ghastly death. He was the author of the famed *Satyricon,* fragments of which still survive, including the "Dinner of Trimalchio," in which a tale of a werewolf and a vampire are recounted. Although the story is a flight of fancy, the episode provides a glimpse into the reputed activities of the old Roman night hag, a witchlike vampire called the *strix.*

Phantom, The An 1856 play written by Dion Boucicault (1822–1880) that was actually a revival of his earlier play *The Vampire* (which premiered originally in June 1852 in England). *The Phantom* proved successful in New York's Wallach Theatre, a number of modifications having been made in the plot for the staging. The play was presented in two acts, one set in the reign of King Charles II (1660–1685), the second approximately two hundred years later, with Boucicault playing the part of the villain, Alan Raby.

Phantom of Montparnasse: See *Bertrand, Sergeant.*

Philinnion A young female revenant in the second century A.D. who returned from the dead to visit Machates, a young man staying at the time with her parents. Her romantic tale was told by Phlegon of Tralles in his work *Concerning Wondrous Things,* but most of the early portions of the story are not extant. The tale begins with a nurse in the household discovering Machates in bed with a female who looks exactly like her recently buried charge, Philinnion. The parents are alerted and see the same thing but do nothing about it until morning. Machates, when asked, claims ignorance about the loss of the family daughter and says his lover's name is Philinnion. He tells them that she gave him a ring and left behind a ribbon. The piece of jewelry was, of course, the same item on the hand of the daughter when she was buried. The ribbon had been tied to her corpse in the tomb. Machates agrees to cooperate with the parents but on the second night he talks himself into believing that his lover is really alive and well. He gives a signal, however, and the parents come in to greet their returned daughter and are scolded by her in return:

> . . . Cruel are you to grudge me a visit with a guest in my own home, doing no harm to anyone. You will grieve sorely for your curiosity for I must now return to the place that is appointed to me. It was against the will of god that I came here.

The girl dies, and the family mourns as word of the episode spreads through town. Finally the tomb is investigated and is found empty.

The magistrates find the body in the family home and take it out to burn it, making sacrifices to the god Hermes Chthonius, said to lead souls to the underworld. The tale was famous during the period of the Roman Empire and was the basis for the Goethe ballad "Die Braut von Korinth" (1797, *The Bride of Corinth*).

Philippines: See *Aswang, Capiz, Danag, Flying, Mandurugo;* see also *Films.*

Philostratus: See *Apollonius of Tyana, Empusa,* and *Menippus.*

Phlegon: See *Philinnion.*

Photosensitivity An aversion to light, specifically the sun. (See *Sunlight* for details.)

Pick A two-headed tool used for digging, excavating, and impaling vampires; one of the many weapons chosen by vampire hunters, along with the mainstay, the wooden stake. The more common sexton's spade, nails, spikes, and so on are also employed. The specific advantages of the pick outweigh the obvious disadvantage of its extreme weight. The pick provides the means of digging into the soil of the grave, crushing the coffin, and impaling the body of the vampire with one powerful blow. According to some legends, such as those among the Yugoslavian Gypsies, the blood of the vampire will cause madness if it comes in contact with human skin; the pick offers the additional advantage of distance in performing the act. In the case of Russian vampires, the pick also helps ensure that impalement is accomplished with one blow, an essential element in the annihilation of the creatures. (See also *Destroying the Vampire.*)

Picture of Dorian Gray, The: See *Wilde, Oscar.*

Piercing a Corpse The act of impaling or mutilating a body in order to prevent the return of the deceased as a revenant or vampire. Corpse piercing is different from using a stake to impale an undead or decapitating it with a sexton's spade, as this act is a preventive measure, intended to make sure that a vampiric transformation does not take place at all. It is also different from corpse binding, as it involves the piercing of the flesh. The act has been practiced in many regions, especially the Balkans and Greece and in northern Europe, where nails were pounded into the heads of corpses. Stakes were hammered into the chest to pin the body to the grave, and studs or nails were also inserted into the feet, hair, and legs. This symbolic attaching of the corpse to the earth was believed to ensure eternal rest. Such acts were combined with the even more severe practice of decapitation or with the more simple placement of antievil substances in the grave, items such as grain, nets, garlic, or roses. Stakes can also be pounded into the earth above the grave to perform the same function, impaling the vampire as it attempts to rise from the earth. (See also *Preventing a Vampire* and *Stake, Wooden.*)

Pijavica A kind of Slovenian vampire found in parts of northwestern Yugoslavia, particularly in the region bordering Austria and Italy. The *pijavica* is created as a result of various evils having been perpetrated by the deceased during his or her mortal life, including incest—the worst possible offense and the one that most assuredly guarantees a person's return as a vampire. The creature can be destroyed by decapitation, its annihilation made complete by placing the head between the legs. The Croatian variation is the *pijawica,* the name in this case (as probably the *pijavica*) derived from *pit,* to drink.

Pisacha An Indian demon ranked among the country's many vampire species and often associated closely with the *rakshasa,* said to be a creature resulting from humanity's vices—the returned spirits of criminals, liars, adulterers, and those who died insane. It is also known in various parts of the country by other names: in the *Veda* they are called *kravyad,* or "eaters of raw flesh"; and in Kashmir they are known as *yaksha,* meaning "speeders," after certain demigods in the Ajanta and Elephanta caves of Buddhist Brahman lore. The term *pisacha-bhasha*—"goblin language"—has been applied to English as the Indians considered it total gibberish. The *pisacha* can cure diseases. Victims of illness sometimes go to a crossroads in an unkempt condition just before dawn with two large handfuls of rice. Putting them in the center of the crossroads, the ill return home without once looking back. This ceremony is repeated for days until the *pisacha* takes an interest, at which time it appears and says, "I will end your suffering." If the sick person is courteous and accepts the aid of the creature, it will be cured. The being also inflicts evil, as its favorite pastime is the eating of fresh corpses. (See also *India.*)

Plague The name given to several forms of epidemic diseases that caused severe depopulation in Europe and in parts of the Middle East throughout the Middle Ages and into the seventeenth century. The most famous outbreak was the Black Death, beginning in 1347 at Constantinople. Types of plagues include bubonic, pneumonic, and septicemic. Plagues and vampirism have been linked in many accounts dating to medieval times, the undead being blamed for bringing diseases to a village or a region. The first victim was invariably seen as the culprit. It was widely held that by staking and burning the corpse of the initial vampire, the other persons that he had infected and turned into undead (those who had also died from the plague) would quickly become quiet in their graves, and the epidemic would end. An excellent example of this type of thinking can be found in the case of the Berwick Vampire, reported by the twelfth-century English historian William of Newburgh.

Planché, James Robinson: See *Vampire, The (Planché).*

Plays: See table.

Pliny the Elder Famed Roman naturalist (A.D. 23–79) who died while recording the eruption of Mount Vesuvius. His only remaining work is the *Natural History* (in thirty-seven books), a vast collection of largely secondhand information on the world. Among his many stories are ones concerning the return of the dead and lycanthropy. Pliny subscribed to the theory that many who were thought dead were actually quite alive, eventually reviving in the tomb or just before cremation. Contemporary medicine simply lacked the skill to make the proper determination through symptoms. (On this subject see *Premature Burial.*)

Plogojowitz, Peter A well-known vampire who appeared in the village of Kisolava in Serbia in September 1725 and whose case was attested to by three officers of the imperial army. Plogojowitz, a farmer, died in September 1725 but apparently departed his grave three days later, appearing before his son and demanding food. He returned the next night, but the son refused this time and received a threatening look from Peter, who then left. By morning the son was dead. While accounts vary, within a few days nine other persons were also dead. Each complained of exhaustion and seemed to have lost large amounts of blood. They also dreamed of having been visited by Peter during the night. Alarmed, the parish priest wrote to the local magistrate, who communicated the news to a nearby commander of imperial troops. He soon arrived with two officers and an executioner and promptly exhumed the corpses of all who had died. Peter was discovered perfectly preserved, his mouth stained with blood. A stake was pounded into his chest, blood gushing everywhere. After the body was reduced to ashes on a pyre, the other bodies were reburied with the normal preventative measures, garlic and whitethorn being placed with each corpse in the grave. This case is notable because of the completeness of the official accounts involving the accepted aspects of vampire infestation. The story was reported in *Lettres Juives* by the marquis d'Argens, published in London in 1729 under the title *The Jewish Spy.*

Plays

Notable theatrical works on Dracula or on other vampires. Plays with a star (✪) are covered in detail in a separate entry.

Play	Author and Date
Almost the Bride of Dracula	Dennis Snee 1980
Bats Are Folks	Sneed Hearn n.d.
Beast of a Different Burden	Faith Whitehall 1974
Blood Pudding	Jeanne Youngson 1981
Boys and Ghouls Together	David Rogers n.d.
Bride of Frankenstein	Tim Kelly 1976
✪ *Cadet Buiteux, Vampire*	Désaugiers 1820
Carmilla	David Compton 1978
Carmilla	Wilford Leach 1975
✪ *Chastelard*	Algernon Swinburne 1865
Count Dracula	Ted Tiller 1972
Count Dracula, or a Musical Mania from Transylvania	Laurence O'Dwyer 1974
Countess Dracula!	Neal Du Brock 1980
Count Will Rise Again, or Dracula in Dixie	Dennis Snee 1980
Dearest Dracula	Margaret Hill, et al. 1965
Death at the Crossroads	Stephen Hotchner 1975
Dracula	Kingsley Day 1978
✪ *Dracula*	Hamilton Deane 1924
Dracula	Hamilton Deane and John Balderston 1927
Dracula	Stanley Eveling, Alan Jackson, et al. 1972
Dracula	Larry Ferguson 1973
Dracula	Stephen Hotchner n.d.
Dracula	Crane Johnson 1976
Dracula	John Mattera 1980
Dracula, a Modern Fable	Norman Beim 1978
Dracula, Baby!	Bruce Ronald and Claire Strauch 1969
✪ *Dracula, or the Undead*	Bram Stoker 1897
Dracula Doll, The	Jeanne Youngson 1980
Dracula: Sabbat	Leon Katz 1970
Dracula Sucks	Jerry Wheeler 1969
Dracula: The Musical?	Rick Abbot 1982
Dracula, The Vampire Play	Tim Kelly 1978
Dracula's Treasure	Dudley Saunders 1975

Play	Author and Date
✪ *Encore un Vampire*	Emile B. L. 1820
Escape from Dracula's Castle	Stephen Hotchner 1975
Fils Vampiri, Le	Paul Feval 1820
Frankenstein Slept Here	Tim Kelly n.d.
Ghoul Friend	Gene Donovan n.d.
✪ *I'm Sorry the Bridge Is Out, You'll Have to Spend the Night*	Sheldon Allman and Bob Pickett 1970
I was a Teenage Dracula	Gene Donovan 1958
Lady Dracula	Tim Kelly 1980
Love Bite	Monica Mobley n.d.
Mors Draculae	Warren Graves 1979
Night Fright	William A. Kuehl n.d.
✪ *Passion of Dracula, The*	Bob Hall, David Richmond 1979
✪ *Phantom, The*	Dion Boucicault 1856
✪ *Polichinel Vampire*	(unknown) 1822
Possession of Lucy Wenstrom, The	Stephen Hotchner 1975
Seven Wives of Dracula	Tim Kelly 1973
✪ *Vampire, Le*	Alexandre Dumas 1851
✪ *Vampire, Le*	Martinet 1820
✪ *Vampire, Le*	Martin Joseph Mengals 1826
✪ *Vampire, Le*	Charles Nodier 1820
✪ *Vampire, Le*	Scribe and Melesville 1820
✪ *Vampire, The*	Dion Boucicault 1851
✪ *Vampire, The*	Jose Levy 1909
✪ *Vampire, The*	R. Reece 1872
✪ *Vampire, The, or the Bride of the Isles*	James Robinson Planché 1820
Vampire, The, a Tragedy in Five Acts	Dorset, St. John 1831
Vampire Bride, The, or the Tenant of the Tomb	George Blink ca. 1820
Vampire's Bride, The, or the Perils of Cinderella	Maureen Exeter n.d.
✪ *Vampires ou les clair de lune, Les Trois*	Brazier, Gabriel and Armand 1820
✪ *Vampyr, Ein*	Ulrich Franks 1877
Young Dracula, or the Singing Bat	Tim Kelly 1975

Note: Revivals of *Dracula* are staged each year by professional, semiprofessional, and amateur companies.

P'o The name given by the Chinese to the second of two souls belonging to each person. The superior soul, the *hun,* partakes in the finest qualities of the spirits of goodness, while the *p'o* is the inferior, ranked with evil spirits and characterized by malevolence. In Chinese vampire lore, the *p'o* plays an important role in the creation of the undead. Should any part of the corpse remain intact or undestroyed, the *p'o* might be able to use this piece to pass forth from the tomb, becoming a vampire and making the fragment the base of its powers. The accidental exposure of whole body parts to the sun or the moon was a terrible event, as the *p'o* could be energized enough to go out and drink human blood, thus adding to its own vitality. (See also *China, Kuang-shi,* and *K'uei.*)

Poe, Edgar Allan American writer and critic (1809–1849), recognized as one of literature's greatest and most influential figures. This Boston native is credited with changing forever the horror tale, with such classics as "The Pit and the Pendulum" and "The Masque of the Red Death." Several of his stories are decidely vampiric, although the presentations are superbly subtle. In "The Oval Portrait" (1842), he depicts an artist who vampirically transfers the life essence of the model into his painting of her, draining her with each sitting until she dies at the moment he completes his work. A form of psychic vampirism is also at work in "Ligeia" (1838), in which a husband consumes the life of his wife, absorbing her essence into his unconscious until she returns to reclaim what he has taken. Other similar works are "Morella," "Berenice," and "The Oblong Box." In "The Fall of the House of Usher," the residence itself is a vampiric monster. Poe was the inspiration and model for a host of succeeding writers. In Manly Wade Wellman's story "When It was Moonlight" (1940), Poe is shown actually meeting a vampire. (See also *Premature Burial.*)

Poenari Castle: See *Castle Dracula.*

Poetry: See table.

Poland A Slavic country whose vampires, called *upior* (called also *upier,* male, and *upierzyca,* female), are known for their seemingly insatiable thirsts, no matter how much blood they consume. This thirst is visible when the *upior* is destroyed, as enormous quantities of blood pour out into the coffin. The *upior* is also characterized by a barbed tongue, the hours that it keeps (rising from noon until midnight), and its habit of consuming the winding sheet used in its funeral. The Poles have developed a number of preventives, such as prone burial, placing a willow cross under the armpits, chin, and chest, and using large amounts of earth to place the body deep within the ground. For added protection they consume blood bread made of vampire blood and flour. Staking and decapitation are recommended as well. An obscure species also recognized in Poland is the *vjiesce.*

Polichinel Vampire A comedy play first performed in 1822 at the Circus Maurice in Paris. The vampire portrayed was a type of puppet or buffoon, designed to provide entertainment and to reduce the dreaded creature to a figure of farce. This new characterization of vampires was inevitable, given its enormous popularity on the Parisian stage, the result of John Polidori's "The Vampyre" (1819) and Charles Nodier's theatrical adaptation of the work. According to contemporary accounts, the *Polichinel Vampire* was highly successful.

Polidori, John English writer and poet (1795–1821), physician to Lord Byron, and author of "The Vampyre; A Tale" (1819). After earning a degree from the University of Edinburgh at nineteen, he joined the literary society and was chosen by Byron's publisher to serve as Byron's medical practitioner and to keep a record of the poet's activities during an extended trip to the Continent in 1816. Quarrels soon erupted between Byron and Polidori, however, with Polidori alternating between states of hero worship and resentment at the cruel treatment given him by Byron. When the two reached Geneva on May 27, Polidori took an instant dislike to Mary Shelley (who had joined them with her husband), and he also felt decidedly inferior. This sense was probably heightened by the famous competition held at the Villa Diodati on Lake Geneva, when, during a period of terrible weather, each member of the party tried to write a ghost story. Polidori wrote what Mary called "a terrible idea about a skull-headed lady." She, of course, began *Frankenstein.* The quarrels continued, and Polidori was dismissed sometime after September 1816.

> It happened that in the midst of the dissipations attendant upon a London winter, there appeared at the various parties of the leaders of the *ton* a nobleman, more remarkable for his singularities than his rank. He gazed upon the mirth around him, as if he could not participate therein. Apparently, the light laughter of the fair only attracted his attention, that he might by a look quell it, and throw fear into those breasts where thoughtlessness reigned. Those who felt this sensation of awe, could not explain whence it arose; some attributed it to the dead grey eye, which, fixing upon the object's face, did not seem to penetrate, and at one glance to perceive through to the inward workings of the heart; but fell upon the cheek with a leaden ray that weighed upon the skin that it could not pass. His peculiarities caused him to be invited to every house; all wished to see him, and those who had been accustomed to violent excitement, and now felt the weight of ennui, were pleased at having something in their presence capable of

engaging their attention. In spite of the deadly hue of his face, which never gained a warmer tint, either from the blush of modesty, or from the strong emotions of passion, though its form and outline were beautiful, many of the female hunters after notoreity attempted to win his attentions, and gain, at least, some marks of what they might term affection. . . .

John Polidori
"The Vampyre; A Tale" (1819)

In an effort to get some type of literary revenge on Byron, Polidori took the framework of the tale that Byron had begun in the Villa Diodati and authored "The Vampyre," published in the *New Monthly Magazine* in April 1819. Lord Ruthven, the title character, bore more than a passing similiarity to Byron, so that Lady Caroline Lamb called Byron "Ruthven" in her Gothic satire *Glenarvon*. The story was first published under Byron's name, igniting a controversy that remains unsettled even today. Byron's connection to "The Vampyre" persisted even as Polidori tried desperately to claim his due credit; Polidori died in 1821, having seen his work go through multiple printings, translations into French, Spanish, German, and Swedish, and theatrical adaptations. Of "The Vampyre," Goethe ironically wrote that it was "the best thing Byron had written." (See *Byron, Lord,* and *"Vampyre, The"* for details.)

"Political Vampires" Also "Political Vampyres," an article that was reprinted in the London *Gentleman's Magazine* in May 1732, considered one of the earliest uses of the word *vampire* in the English language and following closely the March 1732 publication in the *London Journal* of an English translation of the report of the investigating committee looking into the case of Arnold Paole. "Political Vampires" was a social satire on the vampire hysteria gripping Europe at the time, comparing the evil of the undead to the more real terrors perpetrated by living vampires. As the article stated:

These *Vampyres* are said to torment and kill the living by sucking out all their Blood, and a ravenous Minister, in this part of the World, is compared to a Leech or Bloodsucker, and carries his Oppressions beyond the Grave, by anticipating the publick Revenues, and entailing a Perpetuity of Taxes, which must gradually drain the Body Politick of its Blood and Spirits. . . .

Polong A vampiric bottle imp or evil spirit of Malaysia, used by malicious mortals to bring illness and death to others. The *polong* is created by placing the blood of a murdered man into a bottle (*buli-buli*) with a long narrow neck, saying prayers over it, and reciting some arcane enchantment. Seven days later, or perhaps within two weeks, the sound of chirping birds emerges from the bottle. At this point the creator cuts a finger and inserts it into the bottle for the newly hatched *polong* to suck, a process repeated each day to strengthen the bond. When matured, the *polong* will attack on command, with the creator settling old quarrels or gaining money by renting out its assassin for particular murders. The *polong* has a pet or plaything, called the *pelesit,* a spirit that enters the victim and prepares the way. Afflicted mortals go quickly insane, ripping off clothing, biting friends, and becoming quite ill. Medicine men trained in relieving this condition are summoned to try to learn from the *polong* the name of its creator. As the spirits vary in individual powers, the magicians' efforts may succeed or may lead to silence or the false condemnation of innocents. Murder by a *polong* is made evident when great amounts of blood issue from the mouth of the corpse, which also bears many bruises. When seen by the human eye, the *polong* looks like a tiny female, a mannequin no bigger than the top joint of the little finger. Aside from bottling the creature or ordering it out of a victim, there are few remedies against its pernicious attacks. Removal of the creator can be attempted, as can the recitation of charms. One such charm is intended to neutralize the *polong,* the other to destroy it. The latter charm is addressed to the *pelesit,* in an attempt to reach the more fearful creature. (See also *Malaysia.*)

Poltergeist A mischievous spirit or agency that makes strange or inexplicable noises, throws objects, causes mayhem in homes, torments families, starts fires, and causes damage. Poltergeists are recognized today as entities that focus on a young person, around the age of puberty, with attacks increasing or ceasing as a result of external influences, such as the presence of certain family members. The activities of the *poltergeist* have been routinely associated with the predations of vampires, the most obvious case being that of the so-called Vampire of Belgrade. (See *Belgrade* for details.)

Polycrites A vampire of the ancient world whose story was recorded by the early nineteenth-century writer Colin de Plancy in his *Dictionnaire Infernal* (1818). According to this tale, Polycrites was a respected citizen of Thermon in Aetolia (a part of ancient Greece) who was chosen to be governor of the country. He served for three years, at the end of which time he married. Four days after a union with a woman from Locris, he died. His wife was with child and gave birth eventually to a hermaphrodite, a sexless infant said by the augurs of Aetolia to be an omen of terrible things to come—a civil war between the Aetolians and the Locri. The only way to spare both sides such a disaster was to burn both the child and mother. On the appointed day, however, just as the fire was about to be lit, Polycrites appeared, pale and hideous, dressed in a bloodstained robe. The people fled, but Polycrites called them back, threatening the worst possible calamity if they burned his wife and offspring. Seeing that the people did not believe him, he grabbed his own child and began to eat it. Horrified, the crowds threw stones at him, to no avail. The city leaders sent a delegation to the Oracle at Delphi to decipher the meaning of such an event. Polycrites disappeared, but the child's head, the only part of its body that remained whole, announced that horrible disasters awaited them all. The prophecy, of course, came true in time.

Polynesia One of the main regions of the Pacific Ocean, stretching in a pyramidal shape across some 110,000 square miles. Included in Polynesia are the Hawaiian Islands, Samoa, Tonga, Easter Island, and New Zealand. Throughout Polynesia, tales concerning returning ghosts, spirits, and revenants are quite common, and the stories passed on orally. Very often the revenant comes to a family or village in order to accomplish some goal. In Hawaii, for example, the returner will complain about improper burial or grave disturbances. Revenants will also reveal (and punish) their slayers or point out to a surviving relative that he or she is acting evilly. Vengeance is a powerful reason for a revenant to haunt a village, and tales found in Hawaii, the Cook Islands, Easter Island, and Rotuma describe such acts. Easter Island is especially noted for its bloodthirsty undead. A type of Polynesian vampire is the *tü*.

Pomerania Known in the German as Pommern, a province in northern Germany, in Prussia, along the Baltic Sea. The Pomeranians had two different vampire customs. In burials they often placed a songbook in the coffin to provide the deceased with some sort of entertainment. Such a diversion would keep the creature from chewing as well. As another means of protection, they took part of the shroud of the revenant, dipped it in some of the revenant's blood, and squeezed it into a glass of brandy, which was then consumed, rendering the drinker invulnerable to attack.

Pontianak Also *mati-anak*, the stillborn child of a female vampire, the *langsuir* of Malaysia, taken probably from the term for stillborn, *mati-beranak*. Such an infant will become a bloodsucker, and care has to be taken with its burial. Hen's eggs are placed under each armpit, a needle is stabbed into the palm of each hand, and glass beads are put into the mouth. In conjunction with these preventives (the same used for the *langsuir*), a charm is designed to help it find eternal rest. The *pontianak* was featured in a number of Malaysian films, such as the 1958 *Anak Pontianak* (*Son of the Vampire*).

Poetry

Major contributions to vampire poetry.

Date	Work	Poet
1748	*Der Vampir*	Heinrich August Ossenfelder
1773	*Lenore*	Gottfied August Bürger
1797	*Die Braut von Korinth*	Johann Wolfgang von Goethe
	"Christabel"	Samuel Taylor Coleridge
1800	"Thalaba the Destroyer"	Robert Southey
1810	"The Vampyre"	John Stagg
1813	"The Giaour"	Lord Byron
1819	*La Belle Dame Sans Merci*	John Keats
1820	"Lamia"	John Keats
1833	"The Vampire Bride"	Henry Liddell
1836	*La Morte Amoureuse*	Théophile Gautier
1845	"The Vampyre"	James Clerk Maxwell
1857	*Le Vampire*	Charles Baudelaire
	Les Metamorphoses du Vampire	Charles Baudelaire
1897	"The Vampire"	Rudyard Kipling

Other Vampire Poems

"The Vampyre" by Vasile Alecsandri
"The Vampire" by Arthur Symons
"The Vampire" by Madison Cawein
"Le Belle Morte" by Conrad Aiken
"The Vampires Won't Vampire for Me" by F. Scott Fitzgerald
"Enter the Vampire" by Clement Wood
"Stephen's Vampire Poem" by James Joyce
"The Vampire: 1914" by Conrad Aiken
"Vampire" by Bertrande Harry Snell
"Oil and Blood" by William Butler Yeats
"To His Mistress, Dead and Darkly Return'd" by Roger Johnson
"Vampyre" by Stephen Spera
"The Vampire's Love Song" by Margaret Keyes and Jeanne Youngson

These and other lesser-known works can be found in the collection *The Vampire in Verse* (1985), edited by Steven Moore.

Poppy Seeds The seeds of the poppy plant, genus *Papaver*, known for its beautiful but short-lived flowers. The seeds are associated with sleep and rest, related to the narcotic nature of the plant itself. They have been used in many regions to quiet revenants, strewn on graveyard paths. (See also *Sleep, Vampiric.*)

Porphyria The name given to several diseases that are caused by a metabolic disorder from a deficiency in the enzyme needed for synthesis of heme (heme proteins functions as oxygen carriers during respiration). Porphyria, called incorrectly the vampire disease, is extremely rare, manifesting itself in one of a number of disorders. Victims often suffer from severe photosensitivity, lack of pigmentation, chemical imbalances, and other potentially severe conditions. Forms of the disease may vary, but the main ones are acute intermittent porphyria (AIP), congenital erythropoietic porphyria (CEP), erythropoietic protoporphyria (EPP), porphyria cutania tardata (PCT), and variegate porphyria (VP). The term is derived from the Greek for "purple," as purple urine is one of the common characteristics, the liquid turning dark red after standing in light; under ultraviolet light it turns fluorescent. This symptom can be useful in convincing physicians that a serious medical problem is present, as many doctors fail to diagnose the disease for various reasons, often preferring to assume a psychological cause. Porphyria victims also are faced with the frequent association of the disease with vampirism, the result of symptoms that cause paleness and even fangs. Porphyria remains a rare but serious disease throughout the world. (See *Dolphin, Dr. David.*)

Portugal The Iberian country that has only a limited vampire tradition. Except for witches, the Portuguese have been terrorized over the years only by a female species of the undead known as the *bruxsa*. (See also *Spain.*)

Potentzio se: See *Montenegro.*

Potsherd A piece of broken earthenware, used in parts of Europe as a means of preventing the return of the dead. On the island of Chios potsherds were placed on the lips of a suspected corpse during a funeral; put there by the priest, the piece was inscribed with the legend "Jesus Christ conquers." In Prussia, among the branch of the Kashubes found there, a potsherd was put into the mouth of the deceased to provide the corpse with something on which to bite instead of surviving family members.

Powers of the Vampire: See table.

Pregnant Women Frequent and tragic victims of the evils of vampirism, who either die from the attacks of the undead or give birth to children doomed to carry on the blood-drinking legacy of the mother's assailant. Pregnant women are prime victims for becoming future vampires themselves (particularly in Asia) should they suffer the misfortune of dying before, during, or immediately after childbirth. The spirit known as the *langsuir* (Malaysian) is an example. The Romanians have long held traditions about women with children being menaced by vampires. Should a Romanian vampire cast its eyes upon a pregnant woman, especially one past her sixth month, her child is certain to enter the ranks of the undead. The only way to avoid such a calamity is to seek the blessing of the Church. The eating of salt during pregnancy is considered another preventive. (See also *Becoming a Vampire.*)

Premature Burial The tragic and horrifying event of burying people while they are still alive. Those who woke up in the grave or tomb and managed to free themselves from the earth were greeted with terror, revulsion, and hysteria and were called vampires come back to prey upon the living. Premature burial contributed to the spread of vampire fears in Europe. It was simply not possible for the physicians in the past to determine the true state of an individual, particularly patients in a coma or in a cataleptic state. In the Balkans and Eastern Europe, as well as in other regions, cremation was used along with corpse mutilation as a guarantor of death. Bavarians adopted a waiting period, placing the corpse in a death hut to determine its true status. Dr. Franz Hartmann, in his 1896 work, *Premature Burial,* provided morbid details about accidental interment. Edgar Allan Poe brilliantly captured the grotesque nature of living inhumation with such stories as "The Cask of Amantillado," "Berenice," and "The Premature Burial."

Prest, Thomas Preskett An enormously prolific and urbane English writer (1810–1859) who was thought for many years to be the author of *Varney the Vampyre, or the Feast of Blood,* published in 109 weekly installments from 1845 to 1847, running into nearly nine hundred pages and weaving astonishingly lengthy stories into the basic plot. His other novels, including *Sweeney Todd, the Demon Barber of Fleet Street,* were of similar length and convoluted themes, thus making Prest the obvious candidate for author of *Varney the Vampyre.* Late in the century, however, studies of the writings and notebooks of James Malcolm Rymer caused right of authorship to pass from Prest to Rymer.

Powers of the Vampire

Commonly attributed abilities of the undead.
(Note: not all vampires possess the powers
listed; see separate species for details.)

Common Attributes

Create other vampires: Some believe the vampire can choose to
create more of its kind; others think that it takes three bites to be
effective.

Flight: The *bruxsa, langsuir,* and *aswang* can fly; other vampires
change shape to fly.

Misting or vaporizing: Gives the vampire access to places
considered secure or hard to reach.

Strength: Equal to that of many men; increases with age.

Hypnosis: Useful in luring and ensnaring victims.

Change in size or dimensions: Good for tight spots, as seen in
Dracula with Lucy.

Control the elements: Power extends over wind, rain, and other
natural forces.

Control of animals: Power extends over many creatures, including
insects, rats, fleas, and bats.

Eternal life: Varies in length; not all vampires are immortal.

Scale walls: Vampires are as nimble as spiders.

Transformation: Vampires can turn into bats, cats, dogs, wolves,
butterflies, insects, rats, birds, fleas, mice, and locusts.

Drain life force or psychic energy: An attribute of the psychic
vampire.

Less Common Attributes

Causing blights and crop failures: Vampires are opposed in this
activity by the *kresnik.*

Causing plagues or epidemics: The result of killing so many people.

Siring children: The offspring are called *dhampirs* in some regions.

Causing impotence: A power of the *nosferatu.*

Stealing organs: A power of the *jigarkhwar* (takes the liver) and
upier (takes the heart).

Preventing a Vampire

Common steps to ensure that a corpse does not return from the grave.

Preburial or Corpse Preparation

Adhere to proper rituals
Destroy the vampire who caused the person's death
Close all windows (in some areas, open the windows)
Prevent animals from jumping over the corpse
Prevent moonlight from falling on the corpse
Prevent shadows from falling on the corpse
Cover all mirrors
Place coins in mouth
Place garlic in mouth
Cover all standing water
Close the eyes of the corpse
Remove the corpse through a hole cut into wall of house
Mutilate the corpse by hamstringing, removing the heart, piercing with thorns, placing thorns in the mouth, pounding a stake in the chest, pounding nails into various body parts, sticking a sickle into the heart
Pour incense into the eyes, ears, and nose
Place a songbook (hymns only), a cross, or a brick under the chin
Bind the corpse by tying the mouth shut, tying legs or feet together, welding the toes together, wrapping in a carpet, or wrapping in nets
Decapitate the corpse and place the head under the arm or between the legs or bury it in a separate grave
Cremate the corpse
Stretch a dead cat or dog across the threshold

Burial

Inter in prone position
Place candles, towels, fishnets, sickles, knives, thorns, daggers, and nails within the coffin, and/or stakes to pierce the corpse should it attempt to rise; also millet, oats, garlic, incense, food, crosses, and/or wild roses
Place seeds, sand, thorns, roses, millet, garlic, and/or stones on or near the grave
Bury at a crossroads
Place long poles, stakes, or thorns in the dirt of the grave

Pret Also *paret* and *pretni,* in the feminine, a type of Indian ghost or spirit, classified as a general soul that has been separated from the body or as a potentially malicious vampirelike ghostly body of a deformed child or one that died at birth. The *pret* was believed to wander the earth for one year following its burial. It was the size of a man's thumb, weak and sad, not allowed to drink water because of a ban put on it by Varuna, the deity of water. Villagers gave the creature food and drink, dangling vessels of milk with small holes cut into them to allow the liquid to drip. The *pret* sipped the milk in midair, not allowed to touch the ground. The *pret* as the spirit of a deformed individual was feared because it was likely to become a *bhut,* an evil vampirelike being. The *pret* remains benign as long as it is not pestered and is given food offerings. At Gaya, for example, pilgrims make such offerings at *pret-sila, pret's* rock, in the hopes that Yama, the lord of death, will not treat the souls of the departed too badly. A procession of *prets* will cause madness and death to anyone who sees it. (See *India.*)

Preventing a Vampire: See table.

Price, Vincent American actor (b. 1911) who remains the most popular performer in horror films of all time. Price was born in Missouri, attended Yale and later the University of London. The first of his multitude of horror films was *The Invisible Man Returns* (1940). He also did the voice-over for the Invisible Man in *Abbott and Costello Meet Frankenstein* (1943). After his successful work in such mainstream classics as *Laura* (1944), *The Three Musketeers* (1948), and others, his career in horror blossomed with the 1958 *The Fly.* Price's films featuring vampires or the undead include *The Last Man on Earth* (1964; based on Richard Matheson's novel *I Am Legend*), *The Oblong Box* (1969), *The Monster Club* (1975), and a 1963 film adaptation of the Guy de Maupassant tale "The Horla": *Diary of a Madman.* On television he has played Dracula on "The Carol Burnett Show" and had vampiric roles on "F-Troop" and "The Snoop Sisters." Price was also the host of *Dracula, The Great Undead,* a 1982 documentary.

Priculics A legendary vampire in Wallachia who was said to appear during the day as a handsome young man. By night, however, the creature was transformed into a large black dog that drank the blood of those it encountered. Some experts on Romanian folklore argue that the *priculics* has no vampiric attributes and is associated solely with the werewolf. *Priculics* is also another name for the *varcolaci.*

Prone Burial The term used to describe the process of burying a person facedown as a means of preventing the body from rising as a revenant or vampire. Obscure in its origins, the custom has been used by the Celts, stemming from the belief in the so-called *widdershins,* reversing the direction of something that is going to enter the spirit world. Throughout Eastern Europe many burials were made in this manner in the belief that a corpse transformed into a vampire would dig into the earth instead of finding its way to the surface. Additionally, the Silesians, accepting the concept that the gaze of a corpse was fatal, turned the body toward the earth to escape such a fate.

Protection from Vampires: See table.

Psychic Vampires One of the most potentially dangerous of all vampire species, as these creatures feed upon the psychic energies of their victims, leaving them exhausted. Continued feedings can lead to permanent debilitation, even to death. In the past, young humans and animals were believed capable of stealing life and were kept apart from adults, especially in sleep periods. Various occult experts, such as A. Osborne Eaves and Franz Hartmann, wrote about the phenomenon, along with ways of resisting such assaults. Hartmann described the typical psychic vampire as having a hand that feels clammy and cadaverous. Eaves recommended protecting oneself by imaging a protective barrier of white mist beyond the person's own aura and by applying incense or garlic in a room. Keeping the hands closed in public was also thought to be beneficial.

The dangers of this form of vampirism were detailed in several works, including Eaves's *Modern Vampirism: Its Dangers and How to Avoid Them* (1904) and Dion Fortune's *Psychic Self-Defense* (1930). Naturally, fiction writers found the idea enticing. The earliest tale concerning such vampires was Webber's *Spiritual Vampirism* (1853), featuring a psychic vampire, Etherial Softdown. Other entries were "A Borrowed Mouth" (1886) by Frank Stockton, *Clara Militch* (1882) by Ivan Turgenev, and *The Princess Daphne* (1888) by Edward Heron-Allen. There followed classics on the subject: "The Parasite" (1891) by Sir Arthur Conan Doyle, "Luella Miller" (1903) by Mary Wilkins-Freeman, "The Transfer" (1912) by Algernon Blackwood, "The Girl with the Hungry Eyes" (1949) by Fritz Leiber, "The Mindworm" (1950) by C. M. Kornbluth, and "Try a Dull Knife" (1968) by Harlan Ellison. Psychic attacks are deemed so common that they have crossed the bounds of pure vampire literature into mainstream horror, as with Poe's works. A little-known film, *One Dark Night* (1982), dealt with psychic predations, as did *Lifeforce* (1985).

Protection from Vampires

Common means of securing safety from vampiric attack.

Method	Remarks
Garlic	Most common protective herb, used on windows, doors, around neck, possibly under armpits; mixed with water it can be sprinkled or sprayed throughout an area.
Holly	Placed around house.
Fishnets	Placed on windows or doors or in graves to distract vampires who are obsessive about untangling objects.
Seeds	Seeds such as mustard or poppy are sprinkled on yards and walkways.
Grain	Oats, millets, and other grains are sprinkled on yards and walkways.
Holy water	Vials can be thrown at vampires, poured into graves or coffins, or sprinkled on doors, windows, thresholds, and other areas.
Juniper	Logs kept in house for their antievil powers.
Bells	Constant ringing will drive away the undead.
Candles	An abundance of light deters vampires, especially if candles have been blessed.
Incense	Incense of the Latin rite preferred over the Eastern varieties, but both are acceptable and offer powerful protection.
Tar	Crosses are painted with tar on doors and windows.
Knives	Stab the vampire in the heart; also useful against the *mara*.

Method	Remarks
Mirrors	Placed on doors because they really annoy vampires when they cannot see their own reflection in them.
Stakes or pins	Used to impale or pierce, but care must be taken to avoid spurting blood.
Magic or witchcraft	Potent protections, but can be performed only by the trained.
Appeasement with blood	Rarely useful, but a method for stalling until help or the dawn arrives.
Crosses or crucifixes	The traditional method; the use of such sacramentals can hold vampires at bay or can render a gravesite useless to them.
Icons	Particularly effective among Byzantine or Orthodox vampires.
Eating of blood bread	A method used in Poland.
Burial of wine	A method used in Transylvania, not known in many other regions.
Drinking blood brandy	A method used in Pomerania.
Consecrated host	This sacramental is hard to come by and should be handled with care, lest sin of blasphemy cause user more problems than the visits of a vampire.
Prayer	Always helpful.

Pumpkin Along with watermelon, a fruit that is deemed capable of becoming a vampire, albeit not a very dangerous one. The belief in vampire pumpkins is found among the Gypsies of the Balkans, particularly those of the Muslim faith. According to their traditions, any pumpkin kept more than ten days or after Christmas will come alive, rolling around on the ground and growling. People naturally have little fear of the creatures. One of the main indications that a pumpkin is about to undergo a vampiric transformation (or has just completed it) is the appearance of a drop of blood on it.

Quarry, Robert American actor whose career was highlighted by his vampire roles, especially his portrayal of the modern fiend Count Yorga. He first played the part in the 1970 film *Count Yorga Vampire,* reappearing in the 1971 *Return of Count Yorga.* Having brought to a close his Yorga period, Quarry took on a new character, Khorda, a vampire who arrives in California and becomes a guru of sorts in the 1972 American International release *The Deathmaster.* He also made a brief appearance in the 1974 Vincent Price vehicle *Madhouse.*

Queen of the Damned Book three of the Vampire Chronicles by Anne Rice, continuing the wildly successful epic started in *Interview with the Vampire* (1976) and *The Vampire Lestat* (1985). This 1988 novel presents the culmination of the themes developed in the previous novels. Central to the plot is the awakening of Queen Akasha, the royal vampire who, with her consort, had been cared for over the centuries by the Roman undead Marius. Akasha proceeds to liquidate every vampire on the planet, with a few exceptions: those too old or too powerful to destroy, and the loves of Lestat, the vampire rock star whose songs about the "gift" and "Those Who Must Be Kept" had brought her out of her slumber.

Quinn, Seabury American writer (1889–1969) who held the distinction of being the most prolific contributor of short stories to the magazine *Weird Tales,* authoring some 145 stories from 1923 to 1952. He boasted that he never received a rejection slip. Among his works are numerous vampire stories, the first being "The Man Who Cast No Shadow" (1927), which featured the criminologist Jules de Grandin, who is assisted by his able companion Dr. Trowbridge and opposed by Count Czerny. De Grandin returned in "Restless Souls" (1928), a love story between a vampiress and a terminally ill young man. Other vampire tales include "The Silver Countess" (1929), "Satan's Stepson" (1931), "Malay Horror" (1933), featuring a *penanggalan,* "The Black Orchid" (1935), "A Rival from the Grave" (1936), "Pledged to the Dead" (1937), "The Poltergeist of Swan Upping" (1939), "Clair de Lune" (1947), and "Vampire Kith and Kin" (1949). (See *Weird Tales.*)

Rakshasa A powerful species of Indian vampire, considered a type of demon, goblin, or ogre. Mentioned in the Veda, its name means "the injurer," and it is an enemy of all humanity. The *rakshasa* (also *rakhas* or *rachhas*) can change its form at will, appearing as a dog, owl, vulture, or some other creature, arriving at night and fleeing before dawn. When seen in their natural state, they are stained with blood and have adamantine teeth, matted hair, and five feet. The *rakshasa* wear tinkling bells tied to his body and has a blue throat. The female, known as the *rakshasi,* assumes the form of a beautiful woman, luring men to their deaths. In modern folklore, the *rakshasa* live in trees, inducing vomiting and indigestion to all who trespass on their territory at night. A young boy will be transformed into a *rakshasa* if he can be induced to eat human brains.

Ramanga A type of living vampire found among the Betsileo tribe of Madagascar. The *ramanga* is a person who lives outside the normal boundaries of society, performing grisly services for the chiefs of the tribe. Whenever a nobleman or noblewoman had his or her nails clipped or endured some medical treatment in which blood was spilled, the *ramanga* was expected to eat the nail clippings and to drink the blood. Should a *ramanga* not be in attendance, the clippings and the blood were carefully preserved until the return of the ceremonial vampire.

Ranftius, Michael An eighteenth-century German theologian and academic who authored several treatises on vampires. Ranftius wrote *De Masticatione Mortuorum in Tumulus Liber* (*On the Eating Dead*), published in Leipzig in 1728, and *Tractatus von dem Kauen und Schmatzen der Todten in Gräbern* (*Treatise on the Chewing and Eating of the Dead in Their Graves*), 1734, also published at Leipzig. In the first work Ranftius discussed the grim subject of manduction (corpses eating their shrouds or parts of their bodies). In his time he was ranked with other vampire experts such as Zopfius, Rohr, and de Schertz.

Rat A rodent, two most common species of which are the brown house rat (*Rattus norwegicus*) and the black house rat (*Rattus rattus*). Such animals have long been associated with the spread of epidemics, including rabies, tularemia, rat-bite fever, typhus, and the bubonic plague, carrying the germs of these diseases in their fleas. Rats have also been associated with vampires, as both are unclean carriers of disease, preferring dark, dank places and feeding on the wastes of society, be it garbage or the most unfortunate or defenseless of the living. They also symbolize death and disaster. Vampires are said to be able to transform into rodents, an image used effectively in movies and stemming from the English folklore belief that a soul departs a corpse in the form of a mouse or a bee. In the films *Nosferatu* (1922) and *Nosferatu the Vampyre* (1979), rats were used to represent the pestilential activities of the vampire villains.

Raven A highly intelligent member of the crow family found in North America and northern Europe and Asia; a carrion eater not necessarily deemed an evil bird. Its cousin, the crow, is honored for its ability to fight vampires. The raven can serve as a familiar for a witch or sorcerer and can be a suitable shape for a vampire, because of its dark wings, ability to fly, keen eyesight, sharp beak, and predisposition to blood and to the flesh of the dead or dying. (See also *Birds.*)

Ray Family Vampire A North American story of an undead who tormented the Ray family of Connecticut, originally reported in an 1854 article in the *Norwich Courier*. The events took place in Jewett and started with the death of Horace Ray, the family patriarch. Ray died of consumption and was given the usual burial, but over the next few years his sons wasted away, two of them dying in 1852. By the time of the third son's demise, the remaining family members were convinced that the three had perished from vampire attacks. At first the eldest brothers, not Horace, were deemed the culprits. Officials gave permission in June 1854 to exhume the corpses, which were burned to ashes, ending the epidemic. It has been said that consumption had been at work, a disease often confused with vampiric activities, but the Jewett Vampire was also held responsible. (See also *Exhumation.*)

Reanimation The return of life to a corpse; reengaging or resuscitating a body. While reanimation is most often associated with voodoo practices, or with the foul experiments of Frankenstein as presented in Mary Shelley's 1818 novel, it has also played an important role in the theological discussions concerning vampires. According to many of the learned, pseudoscientific treatises of the early to middle eighteenth century, Satan was considered responsible for bringing a kind of unlife to the dead. Other theories concerning reanimation include resuscitation by sorcery, the return of the person's soul to the body after a brief period of wandering incorporeally, and the inhabitation of a corpse by another wandering soul. The term *reanimation* can also be applied to the process by which a person becomes a member of the undead. (For details on this process, see *Transformations into a Vampire;* see also *Demons, Satan,* and *Voodoo.*)

Red Hair Said to be a leading indication that an individual is a vampire. The Greeks, Serbs, Bulgarians, and Romanians believed that red was the hair color of vampires, joining often with blue eyes, another vampiric attribute. Judas Iscariot was described as having red hair; thus came the clan of vampires known as the Children of Judas.

Renfield One of the most memorable characters in the novel *Dracula* by Bram Stoker (1897). A mental patient in the asylum of Dr. John Seward, Renfield becomes linked to the terrible activities of Count Dracula in England. First mentioned in Dr. Seward's journal in chapter 8, Renfield deteriorates mentally as Dracula begins his invasion of England, his zoophagous appetite increasing as the count approaches the isle. He consumes flies, spiders, a blowfly, and sparrows, asking for but not receiving a kitten. At one point Renfield escapes and is caught running toward Carfax, where Dracula has stored his boxes of earth. Promised the souls of thousands of rats and animals, he allows Dracula to enter his room, only to have his back broken and his skull crushed. An example of the sensitivity of the mentally ill to evil, Renfield also represents the victims of vampiric manipulation. In the 1931 film version of the novel by Tod Browning, Renfield was played brilliantly by Dwight Frye. Another memorable Renfield was Tom Waits in *Bram Stoker's Dracula* (1992). Subsequent to 1931, a Renfield-type servant appeared as an aide to Dracula or another powerful vampire, often continuing the original zoophagous tastes. Modern works, however, portray this servant as a monster, only slightly less dangerous than his master. Excellent examples of this are found in Stephen King's *'Salem's Lot* (1979) and in the films *Fright Night* (1985) and *Fright Night II* (1989).

Return of Count Yorga A 1971 American International film starring Robert Quarry, Mariette Hartley, Roger Perry, and George Macready, directed by Bob Kelljan. The sequel to the highly profitable *Count Yorga, Vampire* (1970), this is an equally campy film that relies upon audience familiarity with the villain. It is not clear how Yorga was revived after his death by a broomstick in the previous adventure, but this time he takes up residence beside an orphanage, surrounded by his vampire harem and taking an interest in one of the orphanage workers, Cynthia Nelson (Hartley), who is engaged to the hero, a doctor (Perry). (See *Films.*)

Return of the Vampire A 1944 Columbia film starring Bela Lugosi, Nina Foch, Frieda Inescort, and Matt Willis, directed by Lew Landers. The film, though not a sequel, appears to take up in the middle of a werewolf movie, in which Andreas Obry (Willis) summons his vampire master, Armand Tesla (Lugosi), to prey on a young woman in a nearby sanitarium. Set in 1918, the first segment ends with Tesla being impaled; but the plot starts over again, many years later, when two civil defense workers revive the vampire during the blitz. The *Return of the Vampire* marked a rehabilitation of sorts for Lugosi, who came back to a major studio after years with less impressive production companies. (See *Films.*)

"Revelation in Black" The most famous short story by Carl Jacobi (b. 1908), originally appearing in *Weird Tales* in April 1933. Victorian in style, the tale presents a customer in 'Giovanni Larla-Antiques,' who browses through various items, before discovering, with the help of Larla himself, a book on horror, measuring four inches by five inches, bound in black velvet, each corner protected by ivory triangles. Unwilling to sell it, Larla allows the man to borrow the tome, but with dire warnings. Adventures ensue as the book casts a spell over the man. He comes upon vampires and has to destroy them.

Revenant A broad term that can be used to differentiate a reanimated or wandering undead from a vampire. The word is from the French *revenir,* meaning "to come again," and implies that a revenant is someone who has "returned" from the dead. A revenant does not necessarily mean a vampire, and indeed originally the word meant a restless ghost or spirit who returned endlessly to the scene of a terrible incident (murder or accident) where he or she either was slain or slew someone else. Such souls could find no rest until an exorcism was performed. Similarly, the Greeks viewed the revenant as a reanimated body of a loved one, who rarely attacked the living; violence was normally only part of revenge. The definition could thus be applied to most cases of vampirism reported in the Middle Ages and in the treatises of the seventeenth and eighteenth centuries when many of the returning dead were quite unthreatening. As the Church clarified its position on excommunication and the supposed infestation of a corpse by evil spirits, revenants took on more sinister characteristics and were confused with vampires.

Revenge of Dracula The second in a series of novels by Peter Tremayne, who presented the character of Count Dracula in several different stories while remaining generally faithful to the description and nature of the bloodsucker as created by Bram Stoker. Published in 1978, *Revenge of Dracula* proposes that Dracula was the descendant of a cult of serpent worshipers, the cult of Draco, who sought immortality through magical rites. As with his other novels, *Bloodright* (1977) and *Dracula My Love* (1980), Tremayne's Dracula writings carefully adhere to Stoker's style in particular and to Gothic literary elements generally.

Rhode Island The site of numerous tales of vampiric infestations, most often the result of deaths from consumption but attributed to demonic forces. In 1874 the *Providence Journal* reported the case of William Rose, a resident of Placedale, whose daughter had died. He began to waste away. Blaming his child, he dug her up, cut out her heart, and burned it to ashes. A similar tale was recounted in 1892 about the Brown family of Exeter. George Brown lost his wife to consumption and watched his daughters waste away as well. A brother fell ill before fleeing to Colorado Springs, where he recovered. After returning to Rhode Island, he again became sick. George finally took the drastic step of exhuming his wife and two daughters, discovering one somewhat preserved, her heart and liver dripping blood. These organs were cremated to end the epidemic. (See also *New England.*)

Rice, Anne American-born writer (b. 1941) of horror and the supernatural, currently the undisputed queen of vampire literature through her monumentally best-selling series of novels known collectively as the Vampire Chronicles. Born Anne O'Brien in New Orleans, she graduated from San Francisco State University and published her first novel, *Interview with the Vampire,* in 1976. It became the most successful vampire story of the latter twentieth century, now ranked only behind Bram Stoker's *Dracula* in popularity. This was followed by *The Vampire Lestat* (1985), *Queen of the Damned* (1988), and *The Tale of the Body Thief* (1992). Her novels, including such nonvampiric tales as *The Mummy* and *The Witching Hour,* single her out as the foremost practitioner of the Gothic style in the modern age. (See also individual novels for details about her writings.)

Richard, Father François A Jesuit priest of the mid-seventeenth century who lived on the island of Santorini (Thera) for many years, where he wrote the *Relation du ce qui s'est passé à Sant-Erini Isle de'Archipel* (1657, *Relating What Occurred on the Island of Santorini in the Archipelago*), published in Paris. He presented interesting details about Santorini and its vampires, doing much to advance the notion that the island was the most vampire-infested spot on earth. In chapter 15, Father Richard attributes these undead to the evil devices of

Satan and demons, proclaiming that the evil spirits animated bodies and preserved them in order to accomplish some evil purpose.

Robles, German A well-known Mexican actor who became the foremost vampire performer in Central and South America, particularly in Mexico. He first played an undead in the 1957 *El Castillo de los Monstruos*, portraying a Dracula look-alike. In 1959 he embarked on a long career in vampire cycles, starting with *El Vampiro*, in which he played Count Lavud. The next year he returned in *El Ataud del Vampiro*, a sequel. Having gained stardom, Robles began a new series of films, the Nostradamus movies, facing Professor Duran (Domingo Soles) as his foe. The four Nostradamus films were *La Maldicion de Nostradamus* (1960, *The Curse of Nostradamus*), *Le Sangre de Nostradamus* (1960, *The Blood of Nostradamus*), *Nostradamus y el Genio de las Tinieblas* (1960, *Nostradamus and the Genie of Darkness*), and *Nostradamus y el Destructor de Monstruos* (1961, *Nostradamus and the Destroyer of Monsters*). Robles also appeared in the Argentinian production *El Vampiro Aechecho* (See also *Mexico* and *Nostradamus.*)

Rohl, Christopher An early-eighteenth-century German theologian whose full name was Johann Christopher Rohl. With Johann Hertel he authored the extensive vampire treatise *Dissertatio de Hominibus post Mortem Sanguisugis* (*Dissertation on the Bloodsucking Dead*), published at Leipzig in 1732. It was ranked with the works of Zopfius, Harenberg, and Rohr.

Rohmer, Sax English writer (d. 1959) best known for his fiendish creation Dr. Fu Manchu, the Chinese criminal mastermind. Rohmer also wrote novels with an occult theme, often depicting vampires. His *Brood of the Witch Queen* (1918) features the discovery by the young heir of a wealthy family that his ancestor was a vampire. Another novel, *Grey Face* (1924), offers up a killer distinguished by its horribly cadaverous face.

Rohr, Philip A late-seventeenth-century German writer and expert on the undead who wrote *De Masticatione Mortuorum* (*On the Chewing Dead*), a pseudoscientific treatise on vampirism published in 1679 at Leipzig, that made a contribution to the concept of manducation, the eating of shrouds and food in the grave. (See *Manducation.*)

Romania A southeastern European nation, historically divided into Transylvania, Moldavia, and Wallachia, although it has faced foreign invasions and occupation from the Romans (who called it Dacia) to the Hungarians and Ottoman Turks. Romania possesses one of the greatest bodies of folklore in the world, with many traditions varying from district to district and from village to village. Their customs enabled the villages and communities to remain stable in the midst of constant foreign intervention and rampant domestic political disarray. This vast folklore extended to the vampire and included precise rules to prevent the return of a corpse, regulations that maintained the social order and curtailed the hysteria so often found in other lands. In researching *Dracula* (1897), Bram Stoker tapped into this mine of superstition, succeeding so brilliantly that Romania was forever after closely associated with vampires, many people believing that the undead originated in this beautiful, mountainous land.

Such an assumption is logical (if not historically accurate), given the wide variety of species found throughout Romania. The most common type is the *strigoii,* known as the "dead vampire," compared to the "live vampire," the *moroii.* There are also the *muroni, zmeu, nosferatu, priculics,* and the *varcolaci.* The latter can cause eclipses by "eating" the sun and the moon. Each has its own method of destruction. The *nosferatu,* for example, can be staked, but it can also be killed by having a bullet fired into its chest. Unfortunately, just as there are many ways to slay Romanian undead, so too is there a host of ways for corpses to become vampires, including suicide, witchcraft, being a seventh son, having a cat jump over the corpse, having a vampire stare at an unborn child, and even having an expectant mother fail to consume enough salt.

Romania has also had some local rulers who are ranked among the bloodiest in history, most notably Vlad Tepes (Vlad the Impaler, 1431–1476) and Elizabeth Bathory (1560–1614). Vlad, of course, has been singled out as a major figure in the formation of Romanian nationalism; most Romanians hold the view that he was the victim of wicked propaganda. The novel *Dracula* was thus banned by the government. However, a trickle of tourists searching for vampires began to flow into Romania, even at the height of the Communist regime. Tours were conducted to Bistritz, the Borgo Pass, and Transylvania and this convinced the dictator Ceausescu that such business could be profitable. Today the Communists are gone, but the vampires remain, and the Romanian government proudly offers tours throughout Dracula country. Included in the reasonably priced package tour is a copy of Bram Stoker's *Dracula.*

Rome, Ancient: See *Ancient Vampires, Italy, Lemuria,* and *Strix.*

"Room in the Tower, The" A 1912 short story by E. F. Benson, published originally in *The Room in the Tower and Other Stories,* subsequently included in numerous anthologies and remaining one of the finest works of the entire vampire genre. For sheer dread the work has few equals. It centers around the recurring nightmare of a young man, who dreamed for fifteen years about entering the house of a friend and learning that he must stay in a certain room. Each time he is told, "Jock will show you your room. I have given you the room in the tower." Upon seeing his lodgings, he wakens in terror. Inevitably, of course, his nightmare comes true in hair-raising fashion. (For an excerpt, see *Benson, E. F.*)

Ropes Used in many regions to bind or tie the dead in their graves in the hope that the deceased will be held fast. The Saxons of Transylvania believed that such treatment would inhibit the passage of the corpse to the next world; they removed ropes and even the strap holding the chin in place. Ropes with knots were also used, in the belief that vampires had a compulsion to undo knots and were thus distracted from feasting on the living. (See *Binding a Corpse* and *Knots.*)

Rosary A string of beads used in the Catholic church and in other Eastern churches to aid in the recitation of prescribed prayers. The Russian version is called the *vertitza* (string) or *lievstoka* (ladder). The Eastern Orthodox version is the *kombologion* (chaplet), and the Romanian rosary is the *matanie*. The rosary can be ranked with other well-known weapons against vampires, having the advantage of including a crucifix or cross and wooden beads, preferably fashioned out of trees with antivampiric properties (such as the ash or maple). Additionally, the spiritual power of the rosary is spread throughout the beads, each representing a sacred prayer. The spiritual protection is thus more complete and more difficult for a vampire to penetrate. (See also *Cross* and *Crucifix.*)

Roses A common but beautiful flower with occult meanings and spiritual significance, ranging from beauty, to love, to blood. Among the Rosicrucians it is said to be a symbol of transcendental spirituality. A prevailing theory among occultists holds that the petals and fragrance of the rose are a terrible bane to all evil, including witches, werewolves, and vampires. Its aroma repels them, and its flowers burn them like acid. In Romania, specifically in Transylvania, a branch of the wild rose was placed across the body to prevent its return as a vampire. Placed upon a grave, the rose will supposedly trap a vampire within the earth.

Rowan A small tree, also known as the mountain ash, held in high esteem in parts of Europe for its powers against evil, including witches, vampires, and other mythical beasts. Rowan was used on the Isle of Man to make crosses, which were fastened onto cattle sheds and byres to offer protection from vampiric attack or sorcerous enchantments.

Rowan, Victor: See *"Four Wooden Stakes."*

Russia A land steeped in legend and folklore, with an ancient vampire cult that remained strong for centuries, imprinting itself upon the people and their tales. The Russian name for vampire, *upyr* (or *upir*), was joined over time by many others as local species developed, including the *viesczy* of the Kashubes, the *veripard* of the Estonians, *upior* and *wampir* in Ukraine, and *upar* in Byelorus. The term *upur* probably appeared first in the region of Great Russia. Sources mention early belief in blood-drinking spirits and demons, although *upyr* was first used pejoratively for a Novgorodian prince (in 1247), but appeared consistently over the next centuries until it was established that the *upyr* was an undead creature of evil. There was near universal agreement that vampires were beings of malevolence, to be feared and destroyed.

Reverend Montague Summers, in his grim treatise *The Vampire in Europe* (1929), declared that in the Russian traditions was found "a note of something deformed, as it were, something curiously diseased and unclean, a rank wealth of grotesque and fetid details which but serve to intensify the loathliness and horror." This is partly true, as the Russian people, long suffering and historically deeply religious, had a genuine dread of the returning dead. Like the Romanians, they also believed in a host of causes for such beings, including witchcraft, suicide, immorality, and a variety of curses at birth that produced a predisposition toward vampirism after death. By far the most unique cause was leaving the corpse exposed to the bitter winds of the vast Steppes. Heresy was listed as another reason for persons to come back from the grave, those vampires known variously as *erestun, eretik,* and *eretica.*

Russian folktales kept the undead ever present in the minds of the people. The innumerable stories were collected and preserved by Russian scholars, the chief of them being Alexander Afanasief, who was the inspiration for W. R. S. Ralston's *Russian Folktales* (1873). Included in his compilation were the vampire tales "The Dog and the Corpse," "The Shroud," "The Coffin-Lid," "The Two Corpses," and "The Soldier and the Vampire." Russian vampires figured in Susan Petrey's short stories on the *varkela,* a Steppes tribe of blood drinkers with retractable fangs; her works appeared in the *Magazine of Fantasy and Science Fiction* from 1979 to 1983. Another idea was used in *Red Snow,* an episode on the revived "Twilight Zone" in 1985, with producer Philip De Guere. This television show presented a colony of exiled vampires in Siberia and starred George Dzundza and Victoria Tennant. (See also *Heretics, Icon,* and *Inovercy.*)

Ruthven, Lord The main character of John Polidori's 1819 classic tale, "The Vampyre," one of the most important figures in the development of the modern vampire. He marks the introduction to the literature of his day of a type of irresistible demon lover, a merciless predator who is evil, reprehensible, and deadly and at the same time attractive, desirable, and aristocratic in appearance. The first of the so-called Byronic vampires, Ruthven was patterned on Lord Byron himself, a means of achieving literary revenge for the indignities that Polidori had once suffered at the hands of the noble poet. The vampire parodies Lord Byron in many ways, both being pale-faced, exceedingly handsome, astoundingly successful with women, and utterly cruel, particularly to those who loved him. Polidori's creation was a complete success, attaching to vampires a romantic image, a nobility that reversed the folkloric concepts of such beings as peasants who clawed their way out of the muck to wander about in bloody gore, wrapped only in a blood-soaked shroud. Once unleashed onto the Continent, Polidori's vampire launched a vast number of imitators, reinforcing the Byronic image and guaranteeing its acceptance as the public's idea of a vampire. The influence of Lord Ruthven was seen in writings and theatrical productions throughout the nineteenth century. (See *Polidori, John* and *"Vampyre, The"* for additional details.)

Rymer, James Malcolm A highly prolific writer (1814–1881) of the Victorian age in England, now considered the author of the popular novel *Varney the Vampyre, or the Feast of Blood,* written from 1845 to 1847 and published in 109 installments. Rymer was a writer of the "penny dreadful," a type of common literature read by the masses at the time. Writing for the usual payment of one penny per line, Rymer was a master at drawing out a story to earn more money. He also wrote the lengthy novels *The Black Monk* and *Ada the Betrayed. Varney the Vampyre* was his longest and most successful work, coming in at a stunning 868 pages of turgid prose. Credit for the work was originally given to Thomas Preskett Prest, an equally prodigious scribbler, but modern research now points to Rymer.

> The red glare of the fire continues. It throws up the tall gaunt figure in hideous relief against the long window. It shows, too, upon the one portrait that is in the chamber, and that portrait appears to fix its eyes upon the attempting intruder, while the flickering light from the fire makes it look fearfully life-like. A small pane of glass is broken, and the form from without introduces a long gaunt hand, which seems utterly destitute of flesh. The fastening is removed, and one-half of the window, which opens like folding doors, is swung wide open upon its hinges. . . .
> The figure turns half around, and the light falls upon the face. It is perfectly white—perfectly bloodless. The eyes look like polished tin; the lips are drawn back, and the principal feature next to those dreadful eyes is the teeth—the fearful-looking teeth—projecting like those of some wild animal, hideously, glaringly white, and fang-like. It

approaches the bed with a strange, gliding movement. It clashes together the long nails that literally appear to hang from the finger ends. No sound comes from its lips.

James Malcolm Rymer
Varney the Vampyre (1847)

Sabbatarians The name applied to someone born on a Saturday who is said to possess certain powers such as being able to see ghosts and spirits. Sabbatarians were credited with having a definite influence over vampires and were useful in hunting down the undead. This was especially true in Greece and in Macedonia, where the Sabbatarians fought against the *vrykolakas,* aided often by a kind of natal spirit, a fetch dog. These hounds were also commonly found in Iceland, where they were known as the *fylgja.* Sabbatarian twins could be used to protect Gypsy villages—male and female twins, wearing their underclothing inside out, could drive away vampires. (See also *Dhampir.*)

Saberhagen, Fred Highly respected American writer (b. 1930) of science fiction and fantasy, author of a series of novels on Count Dracula in which the vampire created by Bram Stoker (in 1897) is transformed into a hero. Saberhagen's books place the count in a number of different settings throughout history, meeting such memorable figures as Leonardo da Vinci, Merlin, and Sherlock Holmes. The first volume was *The Dracula Tape* (1975), followed by *The Holmes-Dracula File* (1978), which presented the idea that Holmes was Dracula's half nephew, *An Old Friend of the Family* (1979), *Thorn* (1980), *Dominion* (1982), *A Matter of Taste* (1990), and *A Question of Time* (1992).

Sacrifices: See *Food Offerings* and *Gods, Vampire.*

Saint-Germain Chronicles, The A collection of five short stories published in 1983 featuring the vampire Le Comte de Saint-Germain, the literary creation of Chelsea Quinn Yarbro. The character of this ancient, wise, and irresistible vampire is based on the enigmatic Comte Rakoczy de Saint-Germain. The stories include "Spider's Glass,"

"Cabin 33," "Art Songs," "Seat Partner," and "Renewal," each presenting the hero in a different situation. There is also an essay in which Yarbro answers the questions most asked by her fans concerning the count's ancient origins.

Saint-Germain, Le Comte de In full, Rakoczy, comte de Saint-Germain, a historical figure transformed by Chelsea Quinn Yarbro into a literary vampire hero, first appearing in the novel *Hotel Transylvania* (1978). Saint-Germain (ca. 1696–1784) amazed Europe with his legendary exploits, knowledge of the occult and alchemy, and apparent immortality. Yarbro's character is also an alchemist who became a vampire and survived over the centuries despite brushes with dangerous foes. Learned, compassionate, and seductively sensual, this Saint-Germain moves about during the day by placing dirt in the heels of his shoes and feeds by drinking small amounts of blood from women who provide it in return for his incredible romantic abilities. He is an intriguing amalgam of Count Dracula and the count of Monte Cristo, with elements of the historical figure Saint-Germain retained to maintain a sense of reality.

'Salem's Lot The popular 1975 novel by Stephen King, who consciously patterned his story on Bram Stoker's *Dracula* (1897). *'Salem's Lot* supposedly originated in answer to the question of what would happen if a vampire settled in a small American town. The answer is one of King's best novels, especially for aficionados of his skill in presenting gruesome scenes and introducing total and absolute evil into the lives of average people, in this case inhabitants of the small New England town of 'Salem's Lot. A writer, Ben Mears, returns to his hometown and starts research on a house that has stayed in his mind since childhood as a dreadful memory. He begins to notice that the town is dying as if a plague has descended, and he notes that two strangers have taken possession of the house that haunts him. Convincing the townspeople that vampires have invaded the house and 'Salem's Lot, Ben organizes a hunt to find and destroy the bloodsucker Barlow, but he is hampered by Barlow's servant. One by one the hunters are viciously murdered until Mears and a young friend are left to face the wrath of Barlow alone. The novel was presented as a television movie in 1979.

'Salem's Lot A 1979 made-for-TV film that brought Stephen King's novel *'Salem's Lot* to the small screen; it starred David Soul, James Mason, Bonnie Bedelia, Lance Kerwin, and Reggie Nalder as Barlow, the vampire. The film was directed by horror maven Tobe Hooper and is generally faithful to the King original. Several changes include the greater use of the house just outside of town as a center for diabolical

forces and the changing of the Barlow figure from a Dracula-like villain to a grotesque *nosferatu* that has no dialogue.

Salic Law The so-called *lex Salica* in the Latin, the code established by the Salian Franks who conquered Gaul in the fifth century. It was first issued by Clovis ca. 507–511 and was twice reissued by his successors, including as a proclamation by Charlemagne. Aside from some elements of civil law, the Salic law was a long list of crimes and punishments. Among these were pronouncements against vampirism, a reaction to the fear that was rampant in the early ninth century concerning such creatures. Charlemagne, when he reissued Clovis's laws, was concerned that pagan and Christian rites were being mixed. The Saxons, for example, misunderstood the Christian term *body and blood of Christ* and burned and executed old women whom they suspected of witchcraft or sorcery. The Salic law pronounced a death sentence on anyone burning a suspected vampire, termed a *striges:* a severe measure used to end the hysteria. (See also *Laws About Vampires, Malleus Maleficarum,* and *Witchcraft.*)

Salt Sodium chloride, used in preserving and seasoning, also a symbol of purity and the holy influence of goodness in life. The ancient world associated the substance with mythical properties, and as a result salt was used in the preparation of Christian holy water and was ranked as a potent bane of witches, for anything evil cannot touch it. In some parts of Europe salt was thrown into coffins to prevent invasion by evil spirits. The antivampiric purposes of salt are obscure, the most attested connection found in Romania, where pregnant women were encouraged to eat salt lest their unborn children become vampires. (See *Protection from Vampires;* see also *Myicuira, Mr.*)

Samos Vampire A humorous tale recorded by John Lawson in his 1909 study, *Modern Greek Folklore and Ancient Greek Religion,* concerning a farm hand on the island of Samos. A simple laborer who was devoted to his former master died one day and soon returned as a *vrykolakas,* the Greek species of vampire. Unbeknownst to the farmer, this returned laborer rose from the grave each night to supplement the farm work being done during the day. Thus, after dark, he led the oxen from the stall and guided them in their plowing. Naturally the farmer was perplexed by the astounding progress being made in the fields, but his cattle seemed on the verge of death from exhaustion. His neighbors, suspecting that there was something strange going on, kept watch and saw the *vrykolakas* in action. They opened the grave, found the laborer quite preserved, and burned him.

Sanguisuga A Latin term meaning "bloodsucking" that was used in the Vulgate (a translation of the Bible) to explain a passage in the book of Proverbs (30:15) making reference to a bloodsucking demon, the aluga. *Sanguisuga* was also in the titles and texts of several eighteenth-century pseudoscientific treatises on vampires, including the *Dissertatio de Hominibus post Mortem Sanguisuga* (1732, *Dissertation on the Bloodsucking Dead*) by Johann Christopher Rohl and Johann Hertel, and the *Dissertatio de Cadaveribus Sanguisuga* (1732, *Dissertation on Bloodsucking Cadavers*) by Johann Christian Stock.

Santorini A Greek island in the Aegean Sea, a member of the Cyclades, also known as Thera, traditionally the most vampire-infested site in the world. The phrase "taking vampires to Santorini" was used in the same way as "carrying coals to Newcastle." The reason for this abundance of the undead is probably rooted in the antiseptic soil that prevents swift decomposition of corpses. Thus, persons who had been buried for some time were discovered to be remarkably preserved when exhumed. They were deemed vampires by the local populace, of the species known as *vrykolakas* (or *vrykolatios*), described in the 1900 *Handbook for Travellers in Greece*. Not surprisingly, the island inhabitants became the foremost experts in Europe in destroying the undead; troublesome vampires were carried to Santorini to be dealt with there. Various accounts of travelers to the region mention the island's reputation. Montague Summers, who visited Santorini in 1906–1907, was a case in point. Father François Richard also spread the word, as did Paul Lucas in his *Voyage au Levant* (1705).

Satan The prime source of evil in the world, responsible for the ills of humanity and also, according to many theologians and experts in centuries past, the creator of vampires. The work of Satan was considered a terrible reality by theologians of the Christian church throughout history, especially in the Middle Ages. Thomas Aquinas, for example, wrote that Satan could create bodies out of the air and could give them any shape or form, a concept that lent credence to stories of devils inhabiting corpses. In the seventeenth and eighteenth centuries, treatises of German vampire experts used Satan as a recurring figure in explaining the generation of the undead. (See also *Demons* and *Excommunication*.)

Satanic Rites of Dracula Also called *Count Dracula and His Vampire Bride*, a 1974 Hammer Films release marking the last time Christopher Lee would portray Dracula for the English studio and the last time he would do battle with Peter Cushing as Dr. Van Helsing. Known originally as *Dracula Is Alive and Well and Living in London*, this installment of the long-running cycle continued to have Dracula in a modern setting, as established in *Dracula A.D. 1972*. The story is a fairly clever thriller about a world-threatening plague. Alan Gibson directed.

Saturday A day of the week traditionally said to be holy and held most sacred to the Virgin Mary, the Mother of God, and thus a time of little evil activity, even for some vampires. According to tradition, the Cretan species, called the *katakhana,* as well as the Greek variety, the *vrykolakas,* were able to sleep in the ground only on Saturdays during daylight. It was thus common practice in many regions to hunt for the creatures on Saturdays, especially if they were very dangerous. Persons born on Saturdays were called Sabbatarians, and they were deemed to possess powers against the undead, especially if they were twins. (See *Sabbatarians* for other details.)

Saxo Grammaticus A late-twelfth-century historian whose *Gesta Danorum* was the earliest history of the Danes, marking their entry into world literature. Among the brilliant Latin prose offerings of the work, dealing with legends about the Danish kings, are two accounts of the returning dead, both dispatched by means familiar to vampire hunters. In book one, Saxo wrote of Mith-othin, a trickster and juggler who tried to fool barbarian people into believing that he was a god. When Odin, the real god, returned, the trickster fled to Finland but was killed there by the inhabitants. He was not satisfied, however, and soon was causing death to anyone who entered his barrow. Spreading evil and disease, Mith-othin was exhumed, beheaded, and impaled on a stake. Book two includes the tale of Aswid and Asmund. Aswid died and was buried with his dog and his horse, while Asmund died and was provided with food offerings. Asmund later appeared, stating that the spirit of Aswid had returned to its body and had eaten both his horse and dog. Still not satisfied, Aswid had begun to consume Asmund, taking his ear. Asmund himself ended the problem by cutting off Aswid's head and putting a stake in him. These stories stand as some of the earliest medieval references to vampires.

Scandinavia: See *Denmark, Dogs, Grettis Saga,* and *Mara.*

Scars of Dracula A 1970 Hammer Films release, starring Christopher Lee as Dracula, Dennis Waterman, Jenny Hanley, Christopher Matthews, and Patrick Troughton. The film followed the profitable 1969 production *Taste the Blood of Dracula,* in which Dracula is destroyed in a church, but writer John Elder (a pseudonym for Anthony Hinds) and director Roy Ward Baker chose not to make this a sequel and placed the count's dusty remains back in his castle, where he is revived by a vampire bat that splashes blood on his powdered corpse. The story then centers mainly on the harrowing experiences of Simon, a young man (Waterman) who opposes Dracula's plans to make his fiancée, Sarah (Hanley), his vampire bride. This was the last Dracula film by Hammer set in the nineteenth century. (See *Films.*)

Schertz, Karl Ferdinand de An early-eighteenth-century lawyer who was author of the *Magia Posthuma,* an early dissertation on vampires published at Olmutz and Osnabruck. As a legalist, de Schertz wrote his study from the perspective of law, declaring that should a person suspected of having returned as a vampire be proven guilty of crimes such as cruelty to the living or making terrible noises, the cremation of the body would be quite acceptable. Among the tales recorded in *Magia Posthuma* was one concerning a woman who came back from the grave to attack people and animals. He also wrote of the famed Blow (or Blau) Vampire. Interestingly, a review of *Magia Posthuma* was included by Dom Augustin Calmet in his 1748 treatise *Dissertation sur les Apparitions,* an early example of how learned experts on the undead used each other to spread stories and theories about vampires.

Schreck, Max German character actor (1879–1936) who earned virtual screen immortality for his portrayal of Count Orlock in the 1922 masterpiece *Nosferatu,* directed by F. W. Murnau. A member of the Max Reinhardt theatrical company, Schreck was blessed with a very appropriate name, for *schreck* means "terror" in German. This was not a stage name, as has been suggested over the years. Schreck established arguably the most hideous version of a vampire that has ever been seen in film. Following *Nosferatu,* he had character roles in other films but never matched his triumph as Orlock.

Science Fiction A major genre of literature that inevitably welcomed the undead into its vast gallery of speculation and imagination. As the vampire is a being that defies description, its uncertain origins and potential manifestations make it ideally suited to the science-fiction field. Some sci-fi writers examine the possibility that vampires are actually extraterrestrials or members of alien races on earth for particular purposes. Others postulate that the undead are of this world, but members of an entirely different species. Still others present the idea of vampirism as a disease that is passed on through feedings that infect and transform the body of the victim. The forms vampires take are restricted only by the imagination; the more bizarre the vampire, the more intriguing it becomes. Probably the most famous sci-fi vampire novel is Colin Wilson's *The Space Vampire* (1976), in which aliens take over bodies in order to feed on life energies. Other works in this same vein include H. G. Wells's "The Flowering of the Strange Orchid" (1894); Sewell Wright's "Vampires of Space" (1932); C. L. Moore's "Shambleau" (1933) and "Black Thirst" (1934); A. E. Van Vogt's "Asylum" (1942); Ray Bradbury's "Pillar of Fire" (1948); Richard F. Watson's "Vampires from Outer Space" (1959); Tanith Lee's *Sabella, or the Blood Stone* (1980); Susan Petrey's "Spareen" stories; and Meredith Ann Pierce's *The Darkangel* (1982). Alien vampires also figure in science-fiction films: *The Thing* (1951, 1983), *It! The Terror Beyond Space* (1958), *Planet of the Vampires* (1965), and *Lifeforce* (1985).

Scotland A land long tormented by the evils of witchcraft, ghosts, and the terrible vampire known as the *baobhan-sith*, steeped in the dark past of the Picts and others, who had many stories of unearthly beings. Aside from infamous witches, there was Redcap, so called because of his habit of dipping his cap in blood, preferably human. He haunted ruined castles and attacked unwary travelers. His predations could be resisted by words from the Scriptures or by a cross-handled sword. Redcap assumes various forms in different regions of Scotland and is considered a figure of good luck in some. The *baobhan-sith*, however, was a terrible fiend who sucked the blood out of unsuspecting men. The play *The Vampire, or the Bride of the Isles* (1820) by James Robinson Planché was set in Scotland. (See also *Fealaar, Vampire of* and *Swinburne, Algernon.*)

Scott, Sir Walter Scottish inventor (1771–1832) of the so-called historical novel, author of such works as *Waverley* (1814), *Guy Mannering* (1815), *Old Mortality* (1816), and *The Heart of Midlothian* (1818). His contribution to the vampire genre came in 1794 with his translation of Gottfried Bürger's ballad *Lenore* (1773). Scott also translated the Icelandic *Eyrbyggia Saga*, which includes an account of several vampires who killed off nearly twenty servants in a household in the year 1000. He also made a reference to vampirism in *Rokeby:*

> For like the bat of Indian brakes,
> Her pinions for the womb she makes,
> And soothing thus the dreamer's pains
> She drinks the life blood from his veins.

Season of the Dead A term used to describe those days of each year when the dead were said to leave their graves and spend time among the living. The season of the dead was normally fall, most often in November, and was closely linked to the widespread feast of All Souls' Day (November 2 or, if the second fell on a Sunday, November 3). Various traditions were observed throughout Europe as part of the season, including the eating of soul-cakes. Care was taken not to do anything that might offend the dead, such as slamming doors or windows. Empty chairs were placed at the hearth or at the table, and graves were decorated with flowers and food offerings. (See also *Calendar.*)

Seeds Any of a wide number of granular substances used to prevent acts of vampirism or to hinder the progress and activities of the undead. Seeds are intended to play upon the obsessive nature of the revenants, in this case a need to count things on the ground or to pick them up. Additionally, individual seed types have specific traits or powers. Effective seeds include mustard, linen, carrot, poppy, rice, sand, oats, and millet.

Senses, Vampiric The often overpowering sensations encountered by the undead as a result of their preternatural powers. Vampires possess senses quite different from those of living humans as the undead developed specific abilities for survival in a world of night. This landscape is alive with challenges and dangers, many of which are posed by the main source of vampire food, humans. While shown romantically in stories and novels as still possessing human characteristics, the vampire is nevertheless a truly alien life form, functioning on a separate plane of existence. It stands to reason, therefore, that its senses should be equally unique. The sight of the vampire is suited to the dark, probably along the infrared spectrum. Its hearing is the formidable combination of that possessed by the owl and the echo sensitivity of the bat, made more acute when in the form of that flying mammal. Taste is centered almost exclusively on blood, although it is clear that both taste and smell can be oriented to more mundane matters, such as cooking, for Count Dracula provided Jonathan Harker with an "excellent roast chicken" (presumably not prepared with garlic), salad, cheese, and a bottle of old Tokay. The sense of touch in vampires is highly acute; the beating of a human heart can be felt through walls and from a distance of many miles. The strongest of all the senses, of course, is that of smell. The blood coursing through human veins tantalizes the vampire, which envisions its warmth and smells its tempting aroma, even as it feels blood throbbing in each body. The skill in distinguishing different persons by their blood scent or even by their thought processes gives the vampire total advantage over its prey. The undead also have the ability to sense the emanations of good and evil, knowing to avoid certain areas where goodness prevails or to enter sites known to be evil. (See also *Powers of the Vampire.*)

Serbia The eastern region of Yugoslavia, with its capital at Belgrade, it serves as one of the cradles of vampirism in Europe. Serbia is distinguished as the land in which several historical vampire epidemics took place—for example, those of Arnold Paole in Meduegna and Peter Plogojowitz in Kisolava. The main species of undead in Serbia are the *vampir* and *vukodlak*. The latter is a term that originally meant "werewolf," eventually coming into use as a name for vampires. The Serbian *vampir* is one of the varieties common in folklore, found perfectly preserved in its grave and setting out after dark to feast upon local communities. It can be destroyed by staking, preferably with whitethorn. Decapitation and cremation are also recommended.

Vampires were long known in Serbia, their fabled predations spread by Slavic and Gypsy peoples in the area. So feared were they during the Middle Ages that the Serbian ruler Stephen Dusan (reigned 1331–1351) issued decrees to curb the vampire hunts of the time. Among the interesting traditions found in Serbia are the painting of tar in the shape of a cross to guard against attack; vampiric transformations into butterflies; and the idea that an undead must be destroyed within thirty years lest it become mortal, traveling the world under a different name.

Seven Spirits Demons who terrorized Babylonians, reappearing later in a slightly altered form in the magical traditions of both Syria and Palestine. In his study *The Devils and Evil Spirits of Babylonia* (1903), R. Campbell Thompson recorded an incantation that was used against them:

> Seven are they!
> Knowing no care,
> They grind the land like corn;
> Knowing no mercy
> They rage against mankind:
> They spill their blood like rain,
> Devouring their flesh (and) sucking their veins. . . .

Seventh Sons In Romania, those persons born seventh are deemed fated to become vampires. The seventh son of a seventh son, a truly cursed individual, can be detected at birth by the presence of a small tail. This belief contradicts Gaelic and English views that seventh sons (or generally the seventh child of a family) are born with certain positive powers, such as remarkable luck and healing. The occult nature of the seventh child, including an affinity for the spirit world, is interpreted by the Romanians as an unavoidable attraction to vampirism after death.

Sex and Love One of the powerful elements in the allure of the undead, combining the sensuality of death, the tempting aspects of a demon lover, and the wild casting away of inhibitions and restraining moralities. The vampire in fiction and folklore possess a definite capacity to elicit potent sexual responses from enemies and victims alike.

The undead pose a kind of spiritual eroticism, summoning a mortal to share in an intimacy that goes beyond the physical sexual act. A mortal who shares in the undead experience embarks upon a physical and spiritual journey whose conduit is the most potent of substances, blood. Sex with a vampire is based in part on physical sensation but is also rooted in the passing of a soul into the realm of the undead, as a mortal undergoes seduction, acceptance, and the partial death of the physical form—a metaphysical intimacy unobtainable between mortals.

The recognition of this spiritual eroticism is truly ancient, as exemplified in such figures as Lilith and Kali. Among the most feared of demons were the *incubus* and the *succubus,* precisely because of their relentless sexual pursuit, driving victims to their deaths out of sheer exhaustion. The folklore of vampires arose out of this tradition. The Gypsy vampire, the *mullo,* is very libidinous, while species around the world use the lure of sex as a fatal trap. Vampires are frequently women and are a reflection of the misogynist natures of the cultures in which they are found. While vampires are seemingly lustful, some even capable of fathering children, they are also sources of great love. Several revenants came back from the grave to aid their families and friends—the shoemaker in Constantinople made shoes for his children, while a farmer on Samos tilled the soil at night.

Sex in vampire fiction and film has been both overt and covert. Subtlety has usually worked to far greater effect than blatant sexual content. The lesbianism of *Dracula's Daughter* (1936) is considered far more disturbing than in the more obvious Karnstein Trilogy of Hammer Films or the wild sex vampires of France's Jean Rollin. Readers also generally prefer to read the stylish sex in *The Hunger* (1981) by Whitley Strieber or *Live Girls* (1987) by Roy Garton to the *Adult Verson of Dracula* or *Monster Sex Stories. Dracula* and "Carmilla" remain, of course, two classic sensual works that function on numerous sexual levels. Love that would put mortals to shame has been often presented in literary vampiric romances: Saint-Germain and Madeleine de Montalia in the stories of Chelsea Quinn Yarbro, Marius and Pandora and Armand and Daniel in the Vampire Chronicles of Anne Rice, and Valen and James in Jan Jennings's *Vampyr.* Even Dracula found his own in *Dracula, My Love* (1980) by Peter Tremayne, and in *Dracula in Love* (1979) by John Shirley. (See also *Blood.*)

Shadows A leading means of detecting the vampire in the contemporary imagination, for the undead cast no shadow, even in moonlight. There is virtually no folk tradition supporting the concept that a vampire has no shadow, and it is once more Bram Stoker who deserves the credit for providing Count Dracula with this intriguing attribute. The idea of a shadow being absent is quite logical, for the vampire has an inherently noncorporeal nature. In folklore, vampires possess shadows and even use them to deadly effect. The *nachzehrer* and *masan,* for example, cause death to anyone who falls within their shadows. Other vampires can be detected because their shadows set off sparks in the darkness. There is a tradition that a shadow should not pass over a corpse, lest the deceased return from the dead. Among the Slavs, this prohibition was amended to male shadows only. Gypsies believed that vampires were like shadows, an extension of the idea that the undead could take the shape of mist. In the film *Nosferatu* (1922), F. W. Murnau ignored the growing idea of shadowless vampires and gave Count Orlock one that stretched dramatically across walls, buildings, and entire streets—an image that perfectly set in motion the impact of his pestilential activities and served as a bold cinematic embodiment of the impressionistic style of the film. The 1992 *Bram Stoker's Dracula* offered homage to Murnau and *Nosferatu* by providing the count with a remarkable shadow, first seen when Dracula greets Jonathan Harker in a scene reminiscent of the arrival of Count Orlock. An extension of Dracula's malevolent will, the shadow seems to have a life of its own, acting out the count's unconscious thoughts or desires. At one point, for example, the shadow symbolically tries to strangle Harker when it becomes clear to the count that he is a rival for Mina's affections. (See also *Detecting the Vampire.*)

"Shambleau": See *Moore, C. L.*

Sherlock Holmes: See *Holmes, Sherlock.*

Sherlock Holmes vs. Dracula A 1978 work by Loren D. Estleman in which the legendary detective encounters the infamous vampire. The story is fairly conventional and is written as one of the stories penned by Dr. John Watson. Estleman weaves his Holmesian plot around the original Stoker novel *Dracula* (1897). As one critic commented, the book is better than the title would indicate.

Shrouds A dressing for the undead, usually composed of one long piece of white cloth. In previous centuries the shroud was the customary wrapping for the deceased and thus was the most common attire for folkloric vampires. In European burial customs, it was important not to allow the shroud to touch the face of the corpse in order to avoid manducation, the act of a corpse eating its shroud or its own flesh. Aside from the distasteful image of a dead person consuming its own shroud or limbs, the chewing of the funerary cloth could also curse the surviving family. This belief was very strong in and around Mecklenburg. (See also *Preventing a Vampire.*)

Sickle An implement with a sharp curved or crescent-shaped blade on a short handle. In Romania, Hungary, and the Balkans it was used as a vampire preventive; from as early as the ninth century corpses were buried with sickles. Specific reasons vary for believing the impalement has powers that keep the dead from rising. In Transylvania it was thought to keep the body from swelling; in Hungary it was believed to prick a bloated corpse; and in Yugoslavia, where they tied sickles around the neck of the dead, it was intended to decapitate a revenant if it decided to rise. The Romanians felt that unmarried persons faced the greatest risk of becoming vampires (the *strigoii*), so a sickle was plunged into the hearts of their corpses.

Silesia A historical region stretching across southeastern Germany, southwestern Poland, and in parts of former Czechoslovakia. Silesia was the site of two famous revenant cases, the Breslau and the Pentsch vampires.

Silver A metallic element revered in alchemy as the symbol of the moon and of the goddess Diana. Because of its white, lustrous, and often pure nature, silver is considered a formidable bane to evil of all kinds, especially to the devil. Crosses made of pure silver are supposedly much more powerful in providing protection than other ones, especially against vampires. Silver is famous in fiction and films as the metal used for bullets that mortally wound vampires, werewolves, and their assorted companions of the dark.

Silver Bullet A weapon more commonly used in destroying the werewolf than the vampire but one that is nevertheless potentially applicable to the undead. The original folkloric bullet was not required to be made of silver, a substance beyond the reach of most villagers. Silver or otherwise, shots fired into a grave slew the vampire, as did bullets striking the heart of a *nosferatu*. Gunshots fired into the air chased away vampires in some regions. One clear reference to silver bullets was found in Serbia, where coins with crosses could be broken up, loaded into a shotgun, and blown into a revenant. (See *Destroying the Vampire.*)

Sleep, Vampiric The slumber of the undead, usually from dawn until dusk, the time when the vampire is most vulnerable to attack and destruction. The fact that vampires must return to their coffins or seek the cover of darkness to rest during daylight hours is now a commonly accepted idea, found more in literature and in film than in folklore. There are, of course, many examples of the required sleep period in the tales of vampires throughout Europe. In Russian folklore, for example, the hero is routinely saved from certain death by the coming of dawn, when the vampire falls to the ground, seemingly unlifeless. On Crete, the *katakhana* is allowed to find rest in the ground only once a week, on Saturdays.

As with other vampiric attributes, the vampire's sleep is a literary development owing much to Bram Stoker's *Dracula*. Jonathan Harker finds the count at rest in one of his fifty boxes. A vampire must sleep as a means of restoring its energies; perhaps it is the way in which blood is absorbed into the body and spirit, filling the corpse with the vital forces of its unlife. This desperate need for sleep is coupled with the question of how much control the undead has over the arrival of such a state. At dawn, the vampire must retire out of concern for the sun's potentially damaging power and also because at the crowing of the cock and at the breaking of the dawn he or she may fall unconscious. In *The Hunger* (1981), Miriam Blaylock always prepared to rest, knowing that the time of sleep could not be resisted and would come, welcome or not, regardless of the dangers. (See also *Destroying the Vampire.*)

Sleepwalking The phenomenon in which a person moves about while still in the grip of sleep. Sleepwalking can be partly responsible for causing a relative, usually a brother, to become a vampire. Should a person die and have a brother who sleepwalks, there is a strong likelihood that the deceased will return. This strange concept probably stems from the link between sleep and death, with the brother figure epitomizing the walking dead.

Smith, Clark Ashton One of the foremost contributors to the famed magazine *Weird Tales* during the 1930s, along with H. P. Lovecraft and Seabury Quinn. Originally a poet, Smith (1893–1961) composed verse for the magazine and then sold his first short story in May 1930, "The End of the Story." This tale was set in a nonexistent French region and depicts an eighteenth-century law student falling victim to a beautiful vampire. "A Rendezvous at Averoigne" (1931) depicted the same fictional setting with a haunted castle infested by vampires. "The Vaults of the Yoh-Vombis" (1932) offered up Martian vampires with an appetite for human brains. Smith's most gruesome story by far was "The Seed from the Sepulchre" (1933), featuring a South American plant that invades a flower lover with its vampiric spores, transforming the human into a grotesque plant. Other tales include "The Death of Ilalotha" (1937), "The Enchantress of Sylaire" (1941), "The Testament of Athammaus" (1932), "The Invisible City" (1932), and "The Epiphany of Death" (1934). (See also *Weird Tales.*)

Smith, Martin Cruz: See *Nightwing,* the novel.

Snakes Animals of the reptile family that symbolize rebirth or regeneration as well as primordial evil or sin. The snake and the vampire have only limited connections, although their union in Yugoslavia, most notably in the folklore of the Muslim Gypsies, is greatly feared. According to this tradition, snakes are included in the list of animals that can become vampires, with the added warning that of all nature's creatures, the serpent vampire is the one most to be feared. The idea of a snake or serpent as an immortal being is derived from its ability to shed its skin. Its evil nature is a common aspect of the

Judeo-Christian ideologies and of Islam, because of the Old Testament accounts. (See *Animals*.)

Socks Items of clothing that can be used to destroy a vampire or at least to drive it away, especially in the traditions of the Gypsies of Eastern Europe. It relies upon the obsessive nature of the vampire toward certain items, such as seeds, grains, or its own clothes. Vampire hunters steal the left sock from the grave of an offending vampire, fill it with rocks or dirt from the grave, and throw it outside the village boundary, preferably into running water. The undead will awaken, miss his sock, and start searching for it, even enduring water in order to retrieve it. The vampire, of course, drowns when he enters the water. (See also *Destroying the Vampire*.)

Sorcerers: See *Magic*.

Soul-cakes A type of bun or bread that is baked and eaten in honor of the dead, probably as a means of imparting food or sustenance to the deceased or as a means of appeasing the visiting dead while allowing them to partake of family life one night each year. Soul-cakes were common in Belgium, as well as in Bohemia, southern Germany, Austria, and parts of England. They were baked on November 1, the feast of All Saints, and eaten the following day. Normally they were made of the finest white flour, although variations included the use of saffron. They were shaped into human form and had currants for eyes. In England the cakes were called "dirge-loafs" and were baked on or around the feast of St. Jude or St. Simeon (October 28), Jude being the revered patron of hopeless causes.

Soul-Recalling Hair A belief found in China that a cat, especially the tiger, has the ability to bring back the souls of the deceased because it possesses a hair in its tail with such magical power. After dragging a victim into a mountain cave, the cat would wave its tail in the air over the dying or dead individual. Once the poor victim died, the soul would suddenly return to the body, bringing great pleasure to the cat because it meant that its meal would suffer twice. Starting with the wild tiger, this soul-recalling ability was soon viewed as inherent to all cats, and thus the Chinese were careful to keep all household felines away from corpses, lest they jump over the body. This tradition spread widely and is now an accepted phobia all over the world. (See *Jumping over the Corpse*.)

South, American A region of the United States that received the cultural imprint of Europe, Africa, and the Caribbean. The slave populations of the South retained many of the folkloric traditions of Africa, transplanting the concepts of voodoo and Africa vampires into the New World. Among these was a fear of old women who stayed alive by sucking the blood of children. Thus was the West Indies *loogaroo* reborn in America. Vampire fears were not restricted to the slave population, of course, as among the white population there were many folk tales of giant bloodsucking creatures who preyed on visitors to the swamps. The most famous tale of an undead in the South was the bell witch.

Southey, Robert English poet and historian (1774–1843) who earned the title of poet laureate in 1813, considered a master of prose and poetry. In July 1799 he began writing his high-Gothic vampire ballad, "Thalaba the Destroyer," completing it at Cintra in 1800. Southey researched vampirism for the work, studying accounts of the case of Arnold Paole and the writings of Pitton de Tournefort. He commented on both in the notes of his own edition (1837–1838). A theatrical version of "Thalaba" opened on August 18, 1823, at the Royal Coburg in London.

Spain The Iberian country with only a limited vampire tradition, known, however, for its contribution to the vampire genre through its films. Spanish folklore reports evil vampirelike witches, similar to the Italian *striges,* who attack children, often sucking their blood or trying to carry them off to perform even more diabolical rites. Such creatures often mount roofs and tear at the tiles, trying to get into the rooms of children. The Catholic clergy of Spain serve as the chief opponents of these witches, armed with the Bible and holy water. The Spanish cinema has distinguished itself with a vigorous treatment of the vampire theme. One of the most successful directors of these productions was Leon Klimovsky, who created *La Noche de Walpurgis* (1970, *Walpurgis Night*), *La Orgia Nocturna de los Vampiros* (1973, *The Vampire's Night Orgy*), and *La Saga de los Draculas* (1973). Other Spanish films include *El Vampiro de la Autopista* (1970), *La Llamada del Vampiro* (1971), *Noche del Terror Ciego* (1973), and *El Gran Amor del Conde Dracula* (1973). The leading Spanish actor in horror during the early 1970s was the very muscular Paul Naschy.

Spiders Predatory insects often compared to the vampire because of their method of luring their prey, entrapping it, and then sucking the life out of it, leaving only an empty shell of a carcass. Vampires can supposedly transform themselves into spiders. The similarities between the undead and the arachnid are obvious, without any shapeshifting or transformation: the vampire can crawl along walls and down the sharpest cliff faces with the agility of a spider.

Spikes Weapons that can be used to prevent a vampire from rising from its grave, often made of hawthorn or of iron. Spikes differ from stakes insofar as they are intended to be pounded not into the vampire, but into the ground. They supposedly impale the vampire when it tries to rise out of the earth. (See *Stake, Wooden;* see also *Preventing a Vampire.*)

Spiritual Vampires: See *Psychic Vampires.*

Stagg, John English poet who authored the ballad "The Vampyre" (1810), which included as well a discussion on vampirism in its prologue. This work preceded John Polidori's "The Vampyre" (1819) by nearly a decade and was a superbly Gothic creation in the tradition of Bürger's *Lenore* (1773). The ballad tells of Gertrude, who is worried about her lord, Herman, whose face is "deadly pale," and wonders at "the fading crimson of his cheek." Herman tells her of the dreadful nightly visitations of his young friend Sigismund, who was recently buried but who comes forth each night to drink his blood. He predicts to Gertrude that he will die that night. Keeping watch, Gertrude beholds the specter of Sigismund, who is dispatched in the usual manner after being discovered "still warm as life, and undecay'd."

Stake, Wooden The primary and most effective weapon in the destruction of the undead, an absolutely essential component of any vampire hunter's kit. Wooden stakes have been the weapons of choice for centuries, serving in Eastern Europe and especially the Balkans as the prescribed means of preventing the creation of a vampire or ending the reign of terror of one of the undead. As a preventive, the stake can be pounded into the earth above the grave or it can be placed in the coffin on top of the corpse or in a position to prick the body if it bloats and begins to transform. As anyone who has seen a vampire film knows, the stake's main purpose is to be hammered into the chest of an undead, accompanied by harrowing howling from the fiend and gratuitous amounts of blood. This pounding represents spiritually and symbolically the final severing of the body from its spirit, the irreversible fixing of the corpse to the earth, and the death of the body in a material sense, thus allowing the spirit to depart to find rest. The recommended length of the stake is about two to two and one-half feet, with a smooth, flat top and a very sharp point. The woods suggested for use are ash, juniper, buckthorn, whitethorn, or hawthorn, the latter the best possible choice. In some cases the recitation of prayers will add a spiritual dimension to the act of impalement. A hammer or mallet is normally used to pound the stake into the chest of the vampire, as the deed should be accomplished in one movement to avoid angering the undead or allowing it to respond. Using more than one blow to accomplish the deed will revive the vampire according to some traditions, especially the Russian ones concerning the *upir*. (See also *Destroying the Vampire* for alternative methods.)

Stephen Dusan: See *Laws About Vampires* and *Serbia*.

Stock, Johann Christian An eighteenth-century German expert on vampirism who authored a treatise on the undead, published in 1732 at Jena. The work was entitled *Dissertatio de Cadaveribus Sanguisugia* (*Dissertation on the Bloodsucking Dead*) and was not as well known as other studies, such as those by Philip Rohr, Zopfius, or Rohl.

Stoker, Bram Irish writer, theater manager, and father of modern vampires through his immortal creation, *Dracula* (1897). Stoker (1847–1912) was born in Dublin, the son of Abraham and Charlotte Stoker. A sickly child, he was not expected to survive and spent most of his early years confined to bed. Ironically, he grew into a fine athlete, but his long convalescence exposed him to his mother's Irish folkloric tales and details of the horrible cholera epidemic in Sligo in 1832. A shy person, he was uncomfortable around people and preferred reading the many books in the household to socializing. Early on he expressed a desire to be a writer and in November 1864 entered Trinity College.

During his college years Stoker attended a performance of the Theatre Royal, where he saw the great actor Henry Irving. His fascination with Irving led to his becoming a drama critic for the *Dublin Mail* in 1871. At the same time, he began writing the so-called penny dreadfuls; his first novel, *The Primrose Path* (1875), was serialized in the *Shamrock*. The following year he met Irving, who had a profound influence on Stoker, the writer using Irving's Mephistophelian stage appearance as one of the models of Dracula.

Stoker subsequently served as acting manager of the Lyceum Theatre in London. He continued to write while working in the theater, authoring a series of allegorical children's stories, *Under the Sunset* (1881), that included one episode inspired by his mother's cholera account. *Dracula* was published in 1897, at the end of one of Stoker's most productive periods. It was long believed that he wrote the novel hastily, supposedly beginning it in August 1895 while on a holiday at Cruden Bay. Recent studies, however, indicate that he probably initiated his research as early as 1890. Already impressed by Le Fanu's "Carmilla" (1872), Stoker met Arminius Vambery, an expert on folklore, in 1890 and no doubt gained useful information from him. He conducted research at the British Museum as well. His research took him to many locales included in the novel, such as Whitby Harbor, where, interestingly, several shipwrecks had occurred, most notably that of the Russian schooner *Dimetry* in 1885, a perfect prefiguring of the *Demeter* in *Dracula*. He also visited the London Zoo and acquired extensive research on medicine, folklore, the supernatural, and Transylvania. Stoker originally thought of locating his story in Styria, as did Le Fanu, but his early studies led him instead to the "Land Beyond the Forest," the literal translation of Transylvania. In Whitby in 1890, he read the *Account of the Principalities of Wallachia and Moldavia* by William Wilkinson, a onetime consul in Bucharest. In the work he was introduced to Vlad Tepes, known as Vlad the Impaler, once ruler in the region; he was also called Dracula, meaning "son of Dracul." By 1892 Stoker's notes contain clear references to Count Vlad. In May 1897 the novel was published in London.

Stoker wrote other novels and short stories, including *The Mystery of the Sea* (1901), on witchcraft; The Jewel of the Seven Stars (1903), about a mummy; *The Lady of the Shroud* (1909); and *The Lair of the White Worm* (1911), his last work. He has been the subject of numerous biographies that examine his emotional and psychological state while writing *Dracula*. His widow, Florence, was a dedicated defender of his estate and copyrights, as men such as film director F. W. Murnau discovered. (See also *Dracula* and *"Dracula's Guest."*)

> The moonlight was so bright that through the thick yellow blind the room was light enough to see. On the bed beside the window lay Jonathan Harker, his face flushed and breathing heavily as though in a stupor. Kneeling on the near edge of the bed facing outwards was the white-clad figure of his wife. By her side stood a tall, thin man, clad in black. His face was turned from us, but the instant we saw we all recognized the Count—in every way, even to the scar on his forehead. With his left hand he held both Mrs. Harker's hands, keeping them away with her arms at full tension; his right hand gripped her by the back of the neck, forcing her face down on his bosom. Her white nightdress was smeared with blood, and a thin stream trickled down the man's bare breast which was shown by his torn-open dress. The attitude of the two had a terrible resemblance to a child forcing a kitten's nose into a saucer of white milk to compel it to drink. As we burst into the room, the Count turned his face, and the hellish look that I heard described seemed to leap into it. His eyes flamed red with devilish passion; the great nostrils of the white aquiline nose opened wide and quivered at the edge; and the white sharp teeth, behind the full lips of the blood dripping mouth, chomped together like those of a wild beast. With a wrench, which threw his victim back upon the bed as though hurled from a height, he turned and sprang at us.

Bram Stoker
Dracula (1897)

Stregoni benefici An Italian variation on the Istrian (Dalmatian) name for the *kresnik,* the good vampire or mortal enemy of the evil *kudlak.* The name means "beneficial vampire" and indicates a belief that there were certain undead who were on the side of goodness. (See also *Dhampir.*)

Strength, Vampiric A much-studied attribute of the vampire, generally said to be many times that of mortals. As the undead are supernatural or preternatural creatures, empowered by a combination of the spirit and the flesh, they possess the physical strength of beings quite untethered to this plane of existence. No longer constrained by the earthly limitations of mortality, the vampire has vast resources of energy into which it can tap at will, although the conduit of this resource appears to be blood. Should the vampire be deprived of this crucial liquid, its strength will diminish until it is pitifully emaciated and hopelessly weak. Precisely how strong the vampire can become is subject to much speculation, particularly in the hands of novelists.

Strieber, Whitley: See *Hunger, The,* the novel.

Striges A name for a kind of witch (usually female) who could transform at night into a terrible crow and drink the blood of humans, especially children. The name, used also for a *lamia* and for a bird, came most likely from the Roman *strix,* a blood-drinking bird of the night. Some rank them with actual vampires, but such a classification would probably have to be of the living variety (the so-called live vampire), as they were clearly alive while active. (See also *Strix* and *Witchcraft.*)

Strigoii The most common species of vampire found in Romania, known as a "dead vampire" as compared with the "living" variety, the *moroii.* The *strigoii* (feminine *strigoica*) will consort with the *moroii,* who join the ranks of their undead cousins upon death. The ways of becoming a *strigoii* are traditionally numerous: suicide, witchcraft, criminal activities, perjury, death at the hand of a vampire, being the seventh son, being born with a caul, having a cat jump over one's corpse, being stared at in the womb by a vampire, or dying unmarried with an unrequited love. Additionally, the ropes used in burial must be placed near the body and should not fall into the possession of a practitioner of black magic who might use them to turn a relative into a vampire. A body that is transforming into a *strigoii* will have its left eye open and staring. The recommended preventives against such a change include a sickle stabbed through the heart of the corpse and the sticking of nine spindles into the ground to pierce the creature as it rises. Wine also figures in creating a powerful shield against attack. The *strigoii*'s distinguishing features include red hair, blue eyes, and the presence of two hearts. (See also *Live Vampires* and *Romania.*)

Strix A kind of screech owl known to the Romans, who attributed to it the ability to drink the blood of young children. Over time, the name *strix* became associated more directly with vampirism, evolving probably into *striges,* a kind of witch-vampire that was mentioned in various medieval laws and edicts. The *striges* supposedly could transform itself into the night bird.

Sturgeon, Theodore American writer of science fiction, fantasy, and horror (1918–1985) whose early works appeared in the magazines *Unknown* and *Weird Tales.* Born Edward Hamilton Waldo, Sturgeon made several contributions to vampire literature, including the chilling 1961 novel *Some of Your Blood,* viewed by many critics as his best work. This is a gruesome tale that features an orphaned youth who vampirizes women by drinking their menstrual blood. Sturgeon also wrote the vampire tales "The Professor's Teddy Bear" (1948), "The Music (1953), and "So Near the Darkness" (1955).

Styria Known in the German as Steiermark, a region in southeastern and central Austria noted for its mountains and its mountain resorts. Styria was immortalized in vampire lore by Sheridan Le Fanu's "Carmilla" (1872). Bram Stoker originally considered setting his novel *Dracula* (1897) in Styria. In his homage to Le Fanu in an early portion of *Dracula* (later published as "Dracula's Guest"), Stoker wrote of Jonathan Harker's adventure near Munich, where an enormous wolf sits upon him by the tomb of a noblewoman that bears the following inscription:

> Countess Dolingen of Gratz
> In Styria
> Sought and Found Death
> 1801.

(See also *Austria.*)

Succubus A female demon, the feminine to the male *incubus,* a night fiend that visits men in their sleep to torment their dreams and to engage in sexual relations. The *succubus,* like the *incubus,* has definite vampiric characteristics, including its nighttime activities that render a victim totally exhausted and weakened by incessant carnal performances. The demon is also quite similar to such female vampire spirits as the *mara* and the Gypsy *mullo,* the latter said to carry on romances with young men without their knowledge, the only evidence of their nocturnal orgies being acute, potentially fatal fatigue. The *Malleus Maleficarum* and the writer Walter Map both made mention of the *succubus;* Map wrote of the demon Meridiana. (See also *Incubus* and *Nightmare.*)

Sucoyan: See *Loogaroo* and *West Indies.*

Suicides Those humans who take their own lives, becoming prime candidates for the ranks of vampires and revenants. The view of the Christian church has long been that suicide is in direct contradiction with the will of God. Suicides were thus shunned by mourners, denied proper burial, and feared after death. In England they were buried at crossroads in the belief that their souls would wander until they received proper burial in holy ground. As such an abode would never be afforded them, a stake was pounded into their chests before interment to prevent evil spirits from making use of the body. This practice was continued until the reign of King George IV (ruled 1820–1830), when private burial was allowed. (See *Crossroads.*)

Summers, Montague English cleric, Gothic scholar, and a leading figure in the study of the occult in the early twentieth century. Summers (1880–1947) is more respected today for his literary accomplishments than for his sizable contributions to the study of the supernatural. He is the author of two of the most famous works on vampires ever written: *The Vampire, His Kith and Kin* (1928) and *The Vampire in Europe* (1929). Summers's life remains quite obscure, although he was well known in London's literary circles. He was ordained a deacon in the Church of England in 1908. A year later he began studying for the Roman Catholic priesthood but was never ordained, perhaps for reasons related to his early life, when he may have dabbled in necromancy and sorcery. It is possible that he was ordained in Italy by an obscure sect, but if so, it was never recognized by the Church, although he wore elaborate clerical dress.

Summers's works on the supernatural include *A History of Witchcraft* (1926), the introduction to the reissue of *The Discovery of Witches* by the infamous Witchfinder General Matthew Hopkins, and others seemingly written in the strict orthodox tradition of the Catholic church but not given the seal of approval by Church authorities. In 1934 he published a study on the werewolf. *The Vampire in Europe* and *The Vampire, His Kith and Kin* are two complementary works that cover fairly distinct areas with only limited overlapping. The longer and more complex of the two, *The Vampire, His Kith and Kin* contains extensive footnotes and excerpts in Greek, Latin, French, and German. Such materials reduce the value of the books to general readers, who rarely boast Greek as a second language. Of particular interest was Summers's total belief in the reality of what he was writing about, a perspective that makes the books intriguing. His own autobiography, *The Galanty Show*, was finally published in 1980.

Sun: See *Sunlight.*

Sundal bolong: See *Java.*

Sunlight The rays of the sun that must be avoided by the vampire because they bring absolute, irrevocable destruction. In common contemporary thinking, where fiction and folklore have been combined, all vampires are severely photosensitive, and the unwillingness of a person to go out into the sunlight or even to face bright lights can be taken as an indication that vampirism is at work. It is often disappointing to readers of vampiric works to learn that the undead of folklore had little fear of the sun. Some vampires, those of Poland and Russia, often prowled during the day, from noon until midnight, and there is no mention of any of them erupting in flames with the coming of dawn. Bram Stoker, one of the great innovators and contributors to modern vampire lore, has Count Dracula appear twice in the daytime without any ill effect.

   Nosferatu (1922), F. W. Murnau's important film, first used sunlight as a useful means of dispatching the undead, working on the principle that the vampire is a creature of night and evil, therefore vulnerable to the sun. Such a response provided for the use of special effects in films, with the undead collapsing and burning. A host of other films followed suit, such as *The Horror of Dracula* (1958), *Dracula* (1979), and *Fright Night* and *Fright Night II* (1985, 1989). An interesting moment came in *Vampire* (1979), a made-for-TV movie with Richard Lynch, as the vampire, late returning to his lair, barely outruns the sun, and his clothes start to smoke.

Sunset The time of day that heralds the coming of darkness, the moment when vampires stir in their graves and the last instant of the day that the vampire hunter can destroy them. In the war against vampires, there are few more terrifying sensations for the hunter than to see the sun dipping below the trees and shadows stretching across the landscape. (See also *Sleep, Vampiric.*)

Swawmx A vampire deity long worshiped in Burma. (See also *Gods, Vampire.*)

Swinburne, Algernon English poet (1837–1909) the author of some twenty-five volumes of poetry, including *Atalanta in Calydon* (1865), *A Song of Italy* (1867), and *Songs Before Sunrise* (1871). Three of his poetic dramas examined Mary, Queen of Scots, and one of them, *Chastelard* (1865), presented her as a kind of vampire. Mary, of course, is ultimately destroyed by beheading, a fitting death given the fact that decapitation is an accepted form of vampiric destruction. Swinburne wrote *Chastelard* under the influence of the writings of the Marquis de Sade, especially *Juliette* and *Justine.*

Swords Weapons used against vampires. Swords can impale vampires, although a good blade would be wasted where a wooden stake would do and could be left in the cadaver. Sword handles in the shape of crosses can be wielded as protection should a vampire manage to snap the blade in a hand-to-hand scuffle. The two parts of a broken blade can also be retrieved and held in the form of a cross, as in *Dracula—Prince of Darkness* (1965) with Christopher Lee. Some swords, however, are seemingly haunted or thrive on blood. Historically there are blades, including the Uesugi types of Japan, and swords of the Norse berserkers and the Gurkha blades, that could not be put into their scabbards until blood had been drawn, lest they turn on their masters. The most terrifying blade of literature was Stormbringer, the weapon of Elric of Melnibone in the *Elric Saga* by Michael Moorcock. The blade devoured the souls of men and had a companion called Mournblade. Swords have been used effectively in vampire movies, such as *Captain Kronos: Vampire Hunter* (1974). (See also *"Pale-Faced Lady, The"*; see also *Mikonos.*)

Talamaur The name given to a kind of living vampire found in the Banks Islands, near Australia. Either male or female, the *talamaur* could communicate with ghosts, establishing a close relationship with a deceased individual and making it a kind of dread familiar, or a servant that could be sent to affect the living. Someone suspected of being a *talamaur* was seized and forced to endure the smell of burning leaves until it confessed that it was the master of a spirit, surrendering the name or names of those creatures being used and the living individual who was the intended victim. Another kind of *talamaur* was an individual who could send out his or her soul to consume the lingering life essence contained in a new corpse. The approach of a *talamaur* could be detected by a scratching at the door and a rustling sound near the corpse.

Tale of the Body Thief, The The fourth installment of Anne Rice's Vampire Chronicles, published in 1992, and again written from the perspective of the virtually indestructible vampire Lestat de Lioncourt. Raglan James, a body thief, offers Lestat the opportunity to be mortal once more, for a few days, in return for hundreds of millions of dollars and the use of his vampire body. Lestat, ever seeking new adventures and suffering from melancholy, agrees to the bargain. James, it seems, can steal bodies by driving out the so-called higher soul and then inhabiting the body. But Lestat has difficulty recovering his vampire self from the body thief, and learns a few hard lessons about humanity along the way. Throughout the story, considerable attention is also given to the mortal David Talbot, head of the Talamasca, an organization devoted to occult research. Some readers will be disappointed by the near total absence of other vampires from the Chronicles who formed a rich tapestry of the undead in the previous novels.

Tar A viscous substance distilled from coal and used as a shield against vampires in many regions; also a protection from witchcraft and sorcery. Tar is applied with a brush to outer doors or posts in the shape of a cross, and its antievil properties are derived from its potent odor, said to be strong enough to keep vampires at bay.

Taste the Blood of Dracula A 1969 Hammer Films release, starring Christopher Lee as Dracula, with Ralph Bates, Linda Hayden, Anthony Corlan, and Roy Kinnear, directed by Peter Sasdy. Like *Dracula Has Risen from the Grave* (1968), the previous entry in the cycle, the film aimed at younger audiences. The central theme revolves around the count's desire for revenge against three mortals who offended him by killing his servant. The climax takes place in an abandoned church, where Alice (Hayden), the daughter of one of the victims, is rescued by her lover (Corlan), who causes Dracula to crumble into dust in the midst of prayers, hymns, and holy candles, toppled by grace. (See *Films.*)

Taxim A revolting type of revenant found in parts of Eastern Europe, also called the "walking dead," the reanimated body of a deceased who can find no eternal release until he or she has satisfied a desire for vengeance. What makes the *taxim* so terrible is the fact that, unlike vampires or most other revenants, it is a decomposed creature, a rotted corpse driven on by its spirit. There are few remedies available in the face of the *taxim*, as it exists for only one purpose—to make others pay for their sins against it while it lived—and it cannot be appeased with less. The pulp horror magazines have made good use of this revenant.

Teeth: See *Fangs* and *Ohyn;* see also *Detecting the Vampire.*

Tempting Fate A 1982 novel by Chelsea Quinn Yarbro featuring the aristocratic bloodsucker Le Comte de Saint-Germain. The vampire is trapped in Russia during the Russian Revolution but escapes into the night while aiding a noblewoman. Saint-Germain also rescues the woman from the clutches of the Nazis. *Tempting Fate* was followed by the 1983 collection, *The Saint-Germain Chronicles.*

Terror in the Crypt: See *Maldicion de los Karnsteins, La.*

"Thalaba the Destroyer": See *Southey, Robert.*

Theater: See *Plays.*

Theodore of Gaza Noted Greek humanist and translator of Aristotle (d. 1478) who researched in Italy and worked to revive the study of the classics. In *History of the Spectres* (1586), Pierre Le Loyer recounted a story involving Theodore and a small holding in Abruzzi, Italy. A farmer, given a cottage under the care of Theodore, unearthed an ancient urn containing ashes. That night he was visited in his dreams by a terrifying man who demanded to be immediately reburied where he had been found, and who promised dire consequences if he was refused. The farmer shrugged off the warnings until his son, normally vigorous, sickened and died, looking as if he had been drained of blood. That evening the father was again visited, but this time the specter was bloated with blood and predicted the death of yet another son. Horrified, the farmer went to Theodore, who took the urn and put it back into the earth in the exact spot where it had been originally uncovered.

They Thirst A 1981 novel by Robert R. McCammon, featuring a centuries-old vampire who, in the form of a teenager, terrorizes Los Angeles. Memorable because of its ambitious plot, it is one of the few works featuring a vampire as the centerpiece of a massive disaster.

Thorns Sharp spines from a wide variety of shrubs, such as the hawthorn, used for centuries as protective weapons against vampires wherever traditions concerning corpse piercing and impalement were prevalent. In Romania it was customary to wrap the head and feet of a corpse with thorns. Additionally, thorns or briers were placed inside a coffin near the head as part of the ritual, which included pounding a nail into the skull of the deceased. The Slavs inserted thorns into the tongues of corpses to keep them from sucking. Thorns could also be scattered in coffins or on graves to catch the shrouds of the rising dead and pin them to the earth. An interesting use of the hawthorn was depicted in the *Satanic Rites of Dracula* (1974), when Dracula (played by Christopher Lee) chases Van Helsing (Peter Cushing), who leads him into the thornbushes, assuring the vampire's destruction. (See also *Destroying the Vampire* and *Protection from Vampires.*)

Threshold An entrance that vampires cannot cross without the express permission of the occupant. This means that people remain safe as long as they do not provide hospitality for the undead. Once entry has been secured, however, it is difficult to be rid of the guest. Normally vampires are invited into abodes because no one has recognized their true natures. Once inside, the vampire uses its formidable powers to its own advantage. The concept of the threshold in vampire lore probably evolved out of the Christian tradition that the devil cannot go where he is not welcome.

Thousand and One Nights: See *Aluga, Amine,* and *Ghoul.*

Tibet The mountainous central Asian land, isolated from the world, that has been historically steeped in Buddhism and its lore. There are a multitude of spirits, demons, gods, and cults in this lore, including vampiric fiends. The Tibetans adhere to the precepts of cremation, holding that the simple burning of a corpse serves as an invitation for the soul to return as a vampire in search of blood. Blood offerings have been made in many temples, usually decorated with magnificent but hair-raising frescoes and sculptures of the supernatural abode of their deities. Among the most fearsome of the Tibetan vampires is *bhayankara,* known simply as the "awful," who receives blood sacrifices. Given the age of Tibetan vampire traditions, dating to the earliest days of Hindu and Buddhist religious expansion, if not earlier, it has been postulated by some that Tibet is the real home of the vampire. Anyone who has visited the Himalayan monasteries and seen Tibetan religious art probably shares this view. (See also *Nepal.*)

Tieck, Johann Ludwig: See *"Wake Not the Dead."*

Tlaciques Vampire-witches found among the Nahuatl Indians of Mexico, similar to the West Indian *loogaroo,* as they can turn into balls of flame. The *tlaciques* are also able to transform into turkeys in order to suck the blood of humans without being discovered. (See *Mexico;* see also *Civatateo.*)

Toad Woman A Native American version of the European and later Mesoamerican figure of La Llorona, the "Weeping Woman." Toad Woman was found among the Penobscots of the Algonquin nation of central Maine and described as a terrible seducer of men and the slayer of children. One story states that she entered a camp and moaned that she had lost her child. After asking to hold the infant of a woman in the camp, she was handed the child but was driven away by its father before she could claim it. She ran off in tears to hunt another victim. The Native Americans of the Pacific Northwest had a similar figure, called the Frog Woman. (See *Native Americans.*)

Tolstoy, Alexis Properly Count Aleksei Konstantinovich Tolstoi (1817–1875), Russian nobleman, cousin of Leo Tolstoy, and author of several notable vampire stories. Tolstoy was a lifelong student of Russian and Slavic folklore and was influenced by German Romanticism, both of which were reflected in his first literary work, "Upyr" (1841, "The Vampire"). He subsequently wrote three additional stories in French concerning the undead: "The Family of the Vourdalak," "The Reunion after Three Hundred Years," and "Amena." "The Family of the Vourdalak" (1847) is the best known and most popular of his writings, now a classic of the genre. It utilizes a powerful sexual allegory with peasant folklore of the kind used by Prosper Mérimée in his own creation, *La Guzla.* Tolstoy sometimes wrote under the name Kranorogsky, taken from Krassny Rog, the Tolstoy family estate.

"Tomb of Sarah, The" A riveting short story by F. G. Loring, published in the December 1900 *Pall Mall* magazine, with a conventional plot but a stylish presentation of terrifying activities on the part of a female vampire, Sarah. She is unearthed accidentally by workmen and soon feeds on the residents of the nearby English village. A favorite among vampire readers, the story has been included in various anthologies and collections.

Tools, Vampire Usually agricultural implements that have become empowered with a vampiric spirit, albeit not a particularly dangerous one. The idea is found among the Gypsies, particularly the Muslim Gypsies of Yugoslavia, who believe that this happens when tools are not used for a set period of time, normally three years. The two most common vampire tools are the wooden knot used as a yoke and a wooden rod for tying sheaves of wheat.

Totenlaut Translated from the German as "death cry," the traditional groan or moan heard coming out of a vampire when it is staked. This is normally accompanied by thrashing about and by appalling amounts of blood spurting into the air. It is a common event, mentioned in accounts of vampiric destructions in previous centuries. Medically the sound is caused by the stake being pushed into the thoracic cavity, thereby forcing air out of a corpse. The same thing can happen when a body is moved, thus giving rise to the tradition that vampires or revenants will make protests when being moved from their graves. (See *Destroying the Vampire.*)

Tournefort, Joseph Pitton de A noted French botanist and traveler (1656–1708) who wrote *Relations d'un Voyage du Levant* (1717, *Account of a Voyage in the Levant*), published in Paris and based on his travels in Greece and elsewhere from 1700 to 1702. The work helped to preserve important traditions related to vampires, especially their destruction. His account was centered on his experiences on the island of Mikonos. (See *Greece, Mikonos,* and *Richard, Father François.*)

"Transfer, The" A famous short story by Algernon Blackwood, published in 1912 in *Pan's Garden,* presenting two formidable psychic vampires. One of them, Mr. Frene, is described as "a supreme, unconscious artist in the science of taking the fruits of others' work and living—for his own advantage. He vampirized, unknowingly, no doubt, everyone with whom he came in contact; left them exhausted, tired, listless." Against him is the "Forbidden Corner," a patch of barren earth in which nothing will grow even though the rest of the garden is verdant and beautiful. (See *Blackwood, Algernon* for an excerpt.)

Transformations, Vampiric The adoption of animal shapes of which a vampire is deemed capable; the most common transformation today is into the shape of the bat, which is reflected in the dress of the modern vampire, who wears a cloak cut in the rough shape of bat wings. Vampires can also take the shape of birds, rats, flies, locusts, dogs, mice, wolves, and fleas. Additionally, the vampire can transform itself into a mist or even into dancing lights, similar to the will-o'-the-wisp. (See also *Appearance, Vampiric.*)

Transformations into a Vampire The process by which a person can become a member of the undead, one of the greatest and most important mystical rites of vampiric lore. Through it a corpse is changed into a creature that has fangs or a barbed tongue, glowing red eyes, taloned hands, and preternatural abilities and powers. Concepts concerning the process of transformation are highly varied. Theologians hold that it is caused by demonic infestations spreading like an infection from person to person, from corpse to corpse. Some Muslim Gypsies accepted the notion that the vampire came to life on a Tuesday, beginning its gruesome rounds on the following Thursday. Others claim a vampire rose three, seven, or forty days after burial.

Modern theories vary. As it is generally agreed that the powers of the vampire emanate from within, from a type of unlife or antilife, it has been argued that this negative energy is also responsible for creating the undead; blood is the catalyst for the perpetuation of this negative source, and the vampiric attributes develop or evolve to suit the specific needs of hunger and survival. Equally intriguing, however, is the theory that vampirism is a disease caused by a virulent virus. This virus theory rests at the heart of the medical efforts to cure the vampire, the characteristics being physical rather than spiritual. Regardless of the direct cause, the actual experience of turning into a vampire can be quite alarming, given the sensations of fangs developing, vision enhancing, strength increasing, and an insatiable thirst for blood erupting and taking over.

The transformation is complete when the vampire rises for its first taste of blood; hence weapons are inserted into the coffin or onto the gravesite to halt it at this point. Some cultures place much importance on eliminating the vampire in the early stages lest it become so powerful that nothing will end its career. The transformation process offers unlimited opportunities for literary images and devices. A very interesting passage into vampirehood was presented by Michael Romkey in *I, Vampire* (1990). (See also *Becoming a Vampire.*)

Transylvania Known in the Romanian as Transilvania or Ardeal and in the Hungarian as Erdely, one of the main regions of Romania, with Wallachia and Moldavia, although much of its history was dominated by Hungary. Transylvania (which translates as "Land Beyond the Forest") was virtually unknown in the West in the centuries prior to the publication of Bram Stoker's *Dracula* (1897). In conducting research for his novel, Stoker received folkloric information on Romania from Arminius Vambery and found in Transylvania a land rich in superstitions and ideally suited as the home of his major character. His knowledge was enhanced as well by the book *The Land Beyond the Forest* (1885) by Emily Gerard.

Thanks to *Dracula*, the complex political struggles of Transylvania have been neglected by the West in favor of the vampire myth. The public association of Transylvania with the abode of the undead is complete. It is now a common caricature, in fact, that all vampires speak with a Transylvanian accent, the result of Bela Lugosi's thick pronunciation. He spoke with a Hungarian, not a Romanian, accent, but movie audiences did not know the difference. Although Count Dracula never lived, Transylvania was ruled by bloody historical figures, such as Vlad Tepes (Vlad the Impaler, 1431–1476). Elizabeth Bathory (1560–1614) was another individual who perpetuated the aura of vampirism in the area. The region has been used in such movies as *Transylvania 6-5000* (1985), *Transylvania Twist* (1989), and the many film versions of the novel, especially *Bram Stoker's Dracula* (1992). (See also *Romania.*)

Travel, Vampiric The manner in which a vampire moves about. The vampire is beset by severe limitations concerning travel because of its need to sleep in a coffin or box filled with its native soil. Such logistical problems enhance cinematic and literary presentations, as they force vampires to rely upon a human seneschal to arrange matters, especially when a prolonged journey is involved. Shipboard journeys, for example, often demand that rats and other animals be slain for blood, as a rapidly diminishing passenger list on a liner would result in an immediate investigation with potentially dire consequences. Bram Stoker used the limitations to advantage in describing Dracula's journey to England. Other authors have devised similarly dramatic images and sequences. The use of dirt in shoes, the ability of older vampires to reduce their need for blood, and other innovations have added new luster to the modern tales.

Travels of Three English Gentlemen A travelogue written around 1734 and published in London in volume four of the *Harleian Miscellany* (1745), in which the word *vampyre* was used for one of the first times in the English language. The book noted: "These Vampyres, said to infest some Parts of this Country [a reference to Laubach, Carniola] . . . are supposed to be the Bodies of deceased Persons, animated by evil Spirits, which come out of Graves, in the Night-time, suck the Blood of many of the Living, and thereby destroy them." (See also *"Political Vampires."*)

Tremayne, Peter Author of several novels and short stories featuring Count Dracula or his fictional ancestors. Tremayne created a well-known and well-written series of novels imitating the style of Victorian literature. His first effort was *Dracula Unborn* (1977, known in the United States as *Bloodright: Memoirs of Mircea, Son to Dracula*), featuring Vlad Tepes's son, who struggles to avoid the vampiric fate of his relatives. Two other novels followed: *The Revenge of Dracula* (1978) and *Dracula, My Love* (1980). Tremayne's short stories include "Dracula's Chair" (1980), "The Hungry Grass" (1981, a novella), and "The Samhain Feis" (1986).

"True Story of a Vampire" An 1894 short story written by Stanislaus Eric, Count Stenbock, published in London in *Studies of Death*. The poorly written work is remembered today mostly for its content and because of the eccentricities of its author. The vampire, Count Vardalek, is one of the earliest examples of a literary undead choosing as its prey a member of its own sex, an idea developed previously in the 1872 masterpiece "Carmilla." Vardalek visits the castle of an old baron named Wronski, developing a predatory passion for the young man Gabriel. The youth wastes away slowly as Vardalek's attentions increase, dying finally after receiving a passionate kiss from the vampire. Stenbock was a slightly demented Russian nobleman who lived in England and authored some remarkable works in verse. He slept in a coffin and always ate his meals with his pet toad on his shoulder.

Twins Identical or similar siblings, honored among the Gypsies for their powers over vampires. The twins, however, must meet certain traditional requirements: they must be born on a Saturday, wear their underclothes inside out, and preferably be brother and sister instead of same-sex twins. Should these regulations be fulfilled, the twins can protect their own village. Among the Muslim Gypsies of Yugoslavia, twins are supposedly able to see vampires, even though their version of the vampire is invisible to most.

Twins of Evil A 1972 Hammer Films release, the final installment in the so-called Karnstein Trilogy, starring Madeleine Collinson, Mary Collinson, Peter Cushing, and Damien Thomas, directed by John Hough. This was originally announced as *The Gemini Twins* and the *Virgin Vampires* and was one of Hammer's goriest productions, with an emphasis on sex and unrestrained libido. The tale involves twins who arrive at Karnstein to live with their uncle, the leader of a force of witch-hunters (Cushing). Count Karnstein, the local noble, revives his ancestress, Mircalla, who vampirizes him. He then seduces and transforms Frieda, one of the twins, into an undead; Frieda revels in her new state. The pure twin, Maria, is almost killed by mistake but is saved as the count and Frieda are destroyed. (See *Films.*)

Tympaniaios A Greek term meaning "drumlike," used to describe the *vrykolakas,* referring to its traditional appearance. Its skin is bloated like a drum, a characteristic that made it easy to identify in the grave. In its original meaning, *tympaniaios* was a name for a revenant or returning dead, generally not feared and treated with respect. As *vrykolakas* came into wide use in Greece, implying a ferocious, bloodsucking vampire, the definition was changed to fit this evil species. (See also *Detecting the Vampire.*)

Ubour The most common species of vampire in Bulgaria, although others recognized there include the *vapir* and the *vurkolak.* The *ubour* is created when a person meets a violent, sudden death, when a cat jumps over a corpse, or when a spirit refuses to leave its body by sheer force of will. The corpse remains in the ground for forty days, bloated and filled with a gelatinous substance until a skeleton forms. Once risen, the *ubour* causes all kinds of mischief, drinking blood only when other nourishment (regular food and dung) is not available. Its destruction is usually undertaken by a trained vampire killer known as the *vampirdzhija*. This sorcerer can detect the *ubour* before it has formed and can destroy it after it has risen, most commonly by bottling. This type of vampire has only one nostril, possesses a barbed tongue, and emits sparks during the night.

Uncle Helleborus: See *Austria.*

Upior or *Upier* An eastern Slavic name for "vampire," used most often in Poland. It differs from other species in Eastern Europe (except for the *upyr*) by sleeping much of the night, rising only between noon and midnight, and is distinguished by its dangerous barbed tongue, which it uses to consume vast amounts of blood. Its thirst is quite legendary among the undead. Indeed, this creature has a particular fascination with blood: the *upior* sleeps in it, drinks it, and literally explodes with it when staked. A person can be prevented from becoming an *upior* by being buried facedown with a cross of willow placed under the armpits, chest, or chin. Destruction of an *upior* is possible by staking or by decapitation. It is possible to become immune to attack by the *upior* by mixing vampire blood with flour and consuming the substance in the form of baked blood bread. (See also *Myiciura, Mr.*)

Upir Also *opir,* a vampire species found in the Ukraine. It is generally similar to the Russian type, *upyr,* but it is distinguished by its habit of eating large amounts of fish. This name is also used for the vampires in some regions of Czechoslovakia.

Upor A Byelorussian vampire species whose name is a variation on the traditional Russian *upyr.* This creature is noted for its ability to assume various forms and to ride horses.

Upyr One of the most common vampire species of Russia. The traditions relating to this species vary from region to region but are found most developed in Ukraine and White Russia. The *upyr* has a fairly blood-thirsty nature, sucking first the blood of children and then proceeding to their parents. They have teeth like iron that they use to chew their way through obstacles, especially during the winter when their hands freeze in the cold earth. As with the Kashubian and Polish vampires, the *upyr* wanders during the day, usually from noon until midnight. When trying to destroy it, it is suggested that a thread somehow be hooked to one of its buttons so that it can be traced back to its lair. Once discovered, holy water should be sprinkled about in large amounts and a stake pounded into the creature's chest. Care must be taken, however, that only one strike accomplish the deed, for two strikes will bring the *upyr* back to life in a somewhat testy mood, and the hunters may perish as a result. The *upyr* is also feared as a heart devourer, and it can be destroyed as well by decapitation (with one blow) and by cremation. (See also *Russia.*)

Ustrel A thirsty species of vampire in Bulgaria that preys exclusively on cattle, thought to be the returned spirit of a Christian child who was born on a Saturday but died before receiving baptism. Nine days after burial, the child claws its way out of the grave and searches for a herd of cattle. These poor beasts then serve his blood needs, and within ten days the *ustrel* is strong enough to remain aboveground, nestled in the horns of an animal or between the hind legs of a mulch cow. This vampire always starts feeding on the fattest, healthiest animals, moving down the ranks and leaving bloated carcasses in its wake. Need-fires will rid the herd of the creature, which will drop off when the herd is moved through the flames. For several days, however, no man or woman can approach the remains of the fire, or the *ustrel* will call out his or her name and follow him or her home. If left alone, the *ustrel* will eventually be destroyed by a wolf.

Utukku A Babylonian spirit, considered by some to be a kind of vampirelike phantom; also viewed as a demon. Generally it is the spirit of a dead person that has come from the grave for a particular reason. Much more feared is the *ekimmu,* the departed spirit. (See *Babylonia;* see also *Ekimmu.*)

Vambery, Arminius Hungarian scholar and traveler (d. 1913) who probably influenced Bram Stoker in the writing of *Dracula* (1897). Vambery met Stoker at the Beefsteak Club Room on April 30, 1890, after a performance by Henry Irving in the play *The Dead Heart.* They met again two years later in Dublin, where Vambery received an honorary degree at Trinity College. He provided Stoker with details concerning Vlad Tepes, who became the model for Count Dracula, and no doubt pointed him in the right direction about researching vampire customs and traditions. While no written record of their association has survived, and Vambery made no mention of any assistance on his part, a compliment was paid to the professor in *Dracula*, when Professor Van Helsing mentions his "friend, Arminius, of Buda-Pesh University [Budapest]." (See also *Stoker, Bram.*)

Vampir Also *vampyr*, generally the European spelling for "vampire," listed by Montague Summers as a Magyar word of Slavonic origin that appears in a wide variety of lands, including Russia, Poland, Hungary, Serbia, Bulgaria, and Czechoslovakia—essentially anywhere there has been a Slavic influence. The term spread to surrounding countries, so that *vampyr* is found in Denmark and Sweden as well as other lands. (See also *Vampire.*)

Vampire One of the most unique beings in the world, surviving from the darkest times in history, existing for millennia among mortals, feeding on them and using them to create more of its own kind in order to ensure the continuation of the species, perhaps in preparation for a final struggle between the living and the undead. The vampire is a very personal entity, with highly defined traits and characteristics, well known throughout the world. All people share traditions and knowledge about the vampire's appearance, activities, and powers. The vampire has been developed in literary and cinematic treatments evolving over the centuries into a glamorous being, but its roots in folklore remain primitive and bestial.

The word *vampire* (*vampir, vampyre*) has hazy origins, although scholars generally agree that it can be traced to the Slavic languages, with debates continuing as to its etymological sources. The word may have come from the Lithuanian *wempti* ("to drink"), or from the root *pi* ("to drink"), with the prefix *va* or *av*. Other suggested roots have included the Turkish *uber* ("witch") and the Serbo-Croatian *pirati* ("to blow"). Cognate forms developed, so that there can be found in Serbo-Croatian the term *vampir, upyr* in the Russian, *upior* in the Polish, and *upir* in the Byelorussian. Some scholars prefer the concept that *upir* is older than *vampir*, an eastern Slavic name that spread westward into the Balkans, where it was adopted by the southern Slavs and received vigorous circulation. The word *vampire* (or *vampyre*) arrived in the English language with two 1732 publications: the March translation of a report by the investigators looking into the case of Arnold Paole of Meduegna and the May release of the article "Political Vampires."

It is as difficult to define a vampire as it is to trace the origins of its name. For example, *Webster's International Dictionary* defines a vampire as "a bloodsucking ghost or reanimated body of a dead person, a soul or reanimated body of a dead person, believed to come from the grave and wander about by night sucking the blood of persons asleep. . . ." This definition does not include psychic or astral vampires or those peculiar species that are nonhuman. A broad definition was humbly offered by Brian Frost in *The Monster with a Thousand Faces* (1989), proposing that a vampire is "fundamentally a parasitic force or being, malevolent and self-seeking by nature, whose paramount desire is to absorb the life-force or to ingest the vital fluids of a living organism in order to sate its perverse hunger and to perpetuate its unnatural existence."

There are as many theories about the home of the undead as there are species. Many regions and countries have been suggested over the years as the cradle of vampirism. Some vampirologists hold Egypt to be their birthplace; others believe it to be India, China, Russia, Mesopotamia, and, of course, Romania (or Transylvania). The Transylvanian theory stems largely from the worldwide success of Bram Stoker's *Dracula* (1897) and its setting of the dread vampire cult of Count Dracula in the "Land Beyond the Forest." Because of the novel, stage versions, and film adaptations, many people readily state their opinion that the thirsty bloodsucker began in Romania—after all, don't all vampires sound like Bela Lugosi?—even if evidence to support this is limited.

Religious or semidivine bloodsuckers were an integral part of the ancient cults and were potent elements in formative religions and pantheons in the old and new worlds where divine approbation, blood, and the earth that gave life and food were inextricably linked. The survival of the vampire concept in the ancient world and beyond was probably a result of these ties to nature and the soil. By custom, it emerged from the ground, and was often limited by natural forces—the sun, water, and fire—but it could also control parts of nature—wind, rain, clouds, and even animals. For centuries, the vampire dominated the superstitions and fears of peasants as well as Church leaders and "learned" men steeped in the pseudoscience of their time, chained by rigid theological doctrine and folk belief.

The discovery of the vampire as a suitable motif for literary creations by the members of the Romantic movement released the undead from the boundaries of their primitive and essentially rural environment. Still rooted in the age-old terrors of death, blood, and the grave, the vampire began suddenly to function in the social, intellectual, and even political world. It has since proven remarkably adaptable to the demands of new generations, each of whom see in it something compelling, alluring, and desirable.

Where once the vampire was the corporeal embodiment of satanic activity in the world, today it is the reflection of the contemporary society's morbid preoccupations with aging and death. The undead serve as cultural metaphors of elusive immortality and victory over life. The vampire has achieved eternal life without the attainment of spiritual perfection or salvation. Here are beings who have conquered death, who have turned the tables on the suffering of daily living, and who have come to function outside the boundaries of society. For them actions have no moral limitations imposed from without, and there is no personal responsibility for deeds, regardless of how objectionable. They are sensual, irresistible, and immune to the horrifying aspects of the twentieth century: violence, drugs, AIDS, disease, famine, and financial and social chaos. Being a vampire signifies membership in this most select body of beings the world has ever known, a belonging best described by Robert Aickman in his 1975 "Pages from a Young Girl's Journal": "How I rejoice when I think about the new life which spreads before me into infinity, the new ocean which already laps at my feet, the new vessel with the purple sail and the red oars upon which I shall at any moment embark! . . . Soon, soon, new force will be mine, fire that is inconceivable. . . ."

Vampire, Le (**Dumas**) An 1851 production that opened in Paris at the Ambigu-Comique on December 20, written by Alexandre Dumas père in collaboration with Maquet. Dumas's *Le Vampire* was a new production of the enormously successful *Le Vampire* originally staged by Charles Nodier in 1820. Dumas's play featured the now famous Lord Ruthven, here called Lord Ruthwen, played by M. Arnault. Ruthwen is killed and revived by the rays of the moon but is ultimately destroyed by a sword that has been rubbed with a special ointment and blessed by a priest. (See *Dumas, Alexandre*, for details.)

Vampire, Le (**Martinet**) A burlesque or vaudeville that was written in Paris (1820) by Martinet. Known in full as *Le Vampire, Melodrame en Trois Actes, Paroles de Pierre de la Fosse de la rue des Morts* (*The Vampire, a Melodrama in Three Acts, Words by Pierre de la Fosse of the rue de Morts*), this farce was one of several presented at the time, comically capitalizing on the popularity of "The Vampyre" by John Polidori (1819) and the Nodier stage adaptation (1820). (See also *Plays.*)

Vampire, Le (**Mengals**) A comedy written by Martin Joseph Mengals that opened in the Ghent Theatre in Paris, on March 1, 1826, similar to the many comedies found on the Parisian stage at the time. It was based loosely on John Polidori's "The Vampyre" (1819) and its theatrical adaptation by Charles Nodier. (See also *Plays.*)

Vampire, Le (**Nodier**) The play written by Charles Nodier in 1820. (See *Nodier, Charles* for details.)

Vampire, Le (**Scribe**) A one-act vaudeville comedy, produced at the Vaudeville in Paris on June 15, 1820, written by Scribe and Melesville and set in Hungary. The inspiration again was John Polidori's "The Vampyre" (1819). This play, in turn, served as the basis for the German production of *Ein Vampyr*, 1877, by Ulrick Franks.

"Vampire, The" A short story by a Czech writer, Jan Neruda, first published in English in *Czechoslovakian Stories* (1920), then republished at Neruda's behest in *Great Short Stories of the World* (1927) and collected in *The Dracula Book of Great Vampire Stories* (1977). Ranked as a minor classic, the tale features a young artist who bears the title nickname because he invariably chooses subjects who are ill or weak. They die soon after he paints them.

Vampire, The **(Boucicault):** See *Phantom, The.*

Vampire, The **(Levy)** A "two-scene sketch" that was performed on September 27, 1909, at the Paragon Theatre in London, translated by Jose Levy from C. le Vylars and Pierre Souvestre's French. According to the review in *The Stage* several days later, it was "conceived in the grand Guignol vein." The play featured a young man, Harry le Strang, who is vampirized by his lover, who returns as an undead after having killed herself. (See also *Plays.*)

Vampire, The **(Planché)** In full, *The Vampire, or the Bride of the Isles,* an adaptation of Charles Nodier's *Le Vampire,* written by James Robinson Planché (1796–1880), the British playwright and antiquarian. *The Vampire* opened on August 9, 1820, at the Lyceum in London and was an immediate success, in large measure because of the "vampire trap" that was invented for the production—a device that allowed the actor to disappear from the stage, much to the amazement of the bemused audience. In his own memoirs, *Recollections and Reflections,* Planché wrote of his disappointment in this Nodier adaptation because of the manager's refusal to allow him to change the setting of the play from Scotland to a "place in the East of Europe," bemoaning "the usual recklessness of French dramatists" in placing the play in a country "where the superstition never existed." In 1829 Planché staged another vampire work, an adaptation of *Der Vampyr,* an opera produced originally at Leipzig with Hungary as the setting. This new production, with libretto by Planché, opened at the Lyceum on August 25, 1829, and ran for only sixty days.

Vampire, The **(Reece)** A comedy burlesque written by R. Reece that opened at the Royal Strand Theatre on August 18, 1872, in London. It was advertised as "a Bit of Moonshine in Three Rays," and was supposedly based on "a German legend, Lord Byron's story, and a Boucicaultian drama" (*The Phantom* by Dion Boucicault). The villain of the play is not a vampire but a plagiarist who survives by picking people's brains and stealing their ideas so that he can use their efforts to continue the weekly installments of his "penny dreadfuls" and other writings. As in the original, he haunts Raby Castle atop the Peak of Snowden, preying on lady novelists. The makeup worn by

Edward Terry in the title role was described as "extraordinary." (See also *Plays*.)

Vampire Bats The most famous of the subspecies of bat, found throughout Central and South America and the Caribbean. The term *vampire bat* is used for several species of the bat known collectively as family *Desmontidae*. These include *Desmodus rotundus, Desmodus rufus,* and *Diphylla ecaudata*. All are pure blood drinkers and earned their vampire connotation from Europeans, who were horrified to discover that such night creatures actually survived on the blood of the living.

The vampire bat has been more important in fiction than in folklore, assuming an interesting if not pivotal role in several films: *Kiss of the Vampire* (1963), in which bats destroy a cult of vampires; *Scars of Dracula* (1970), where a bat wipes out a village and revives the count; as well as *Dracula* (1931), *Dracula* (1979), *Son of Dracula* (1943), and, of course, *Nightwing* (1979). The novel by Martin Cruz Smith on which *Nightwing* was based remains the best work ever on the horror of the vampire bat. The association of the bat with the undead is now so common that it needs virtually no comment, save that the reputation of the *Desmontidae* has caused persecution of numerous other, beneficial species. The transformation of a vampire into a bat has been one of the great subjects of vampiric caricatures, featured in the works of Charles Addams and others and in such humorous shows as the television anthology "Night Gallery."

Vampire Cats: See *Nabeshima, Cat of* and *Cats*.

Vampire Circus A lurid 1971 Hammer Films production starring John Moulder Brown, Thorley Walters, Adrienne Corri, and Laurence Payne, directed by Robert Young. This departure from Hammer's usual Dracula fare presents a wandering circus troupe that brings vampirism to unsuspecting audiences. The circus metes out vengeance especially on a small Serbian village that in the past had destroyed a member of the undead, the evil Count Mitterhouse. *Vampire Circus* is as much an allegory as a horror film, using symbolic sexuality to examine the seduction and death of the villagers.

Vampire Junction A 1984 novel by S. P. Somtow (Somtow Sucharitkul), distinguished by its treatment of the vampire in the modern world. The undead in question assumes the disguise of a young rock star. This particular motif was also used by Anne Rice in her novel *The Vampire Lestat* (1985). A sequel, *Valentine*, was published in 1992.

Vampire Lestat, The The 1985 sequel to *Interview with the Vampire* (1976) by Anne Rice, continuing the Vampire Chronicles, a monumentally best-selling series of novels. In *The Vampire Lestat* the bloodsucker Lestat de Lioncourt moves into a position of prominence in Rice's writings, telling of his own life and adventures in Gothic manner, with spiritual and philosophical overtones, as did the character Louis in *Interview*. Lestat proves in many ways a much more compelling figure than Louis, in part because of his natural proclivities for outrageousness and his own deep obsession with good and evil. He is transformed into a vampire by the alchemist Magnus; saves his dying mother, Gabrielle; sets out to discover the mother and father of the undead (known simply as "They Who Must Be Kept"); and ultimately becomes a rock star. A comic book version of the novel was published in 1991.

Vampire Lovers The first entry in the Hammer Films Karnstein Trilogy of films, based loosely on Sheridan Le Fanu's "Carmilla" and starring Ingrid Pitt, Madeline Smith, Peter Cushing, Pippa Steele, Douglas Wilmer, and Ferdy Mayne, directed by Roy Ward Baker and released in 1970. Pitt, in her first vampire role, portrays the lesbian vampire Carmilla Karnstein with considerable enthusiasm, emphasizing the sensuality of the creature who is able to seduce her victims, transform into a cat, and instantly reappear somewhere else. Carmilla vampirizes several females before drawing attention to herself by choosing Emma Morton (Smith) as her next victim. A doctor (Mayne) deduces that a vampire is at work and takes his fears to those who can do something about it—the general (Cushing), the father of a victim (Steele), Emma's fiancé, and an experienced vampire hunter, Baron Hartog (Wilmer).

Vampires, ou le Clair de Lune, Les Trois A one-act farce performed in 1820 at the Variétes in Paris, written by Brazier, Gabriel, and Armand. The character M. Gobetout, an avid reader of vampire stories, is featured. One night while reading, he sees three shadowy figures and assumes that they are vampires. A little later he discovers his two daughters and the maid actually dining with these fiends. In fact, they are not conducting a tryst with vampires at all, but are consorting with their lovers and a valet, and the comedy centers on Gobetout's misunderstanding. One line supposedly brought thunderous ovations from the French audiences: "*Les vampires . . . il nous viennent d'Angleterre. . . .*" ("The vampires . . . they come to us from England. . . .)

Vampire Tapestry A highly respected work by the feminist writer Suzy McKee Charnas, published in 1980, it is actually a collection of five related or connected novellas featuring the stunning vampire Edward Lewis Weyland. Among the tales are two of Charnas's best-known stories: "The Ancient Mind at Work" (1979) and "Unicorn Tapestry" (1980).

Vampirella A highly voluptuous and scantily clad comic book character created by the Warren Publishing Company. One of the most successful comic characters, she is noted for her considerable physical endowments and the sensational nature of the stories in which she is involved. Her magazine was introduced in 1969 as "the coolest Girl meets Ghoul mag on the market!" Vampirella was later used in a series of novels by Ron Goulart, *Bloodstalk* (1976), *Blood Wedding* (1976), *Deathgame,* (1976), and *Snakegod* (1976). (See also *Comic Books.*)

Vampiri, I An Italian opera by the Neapolitan composer Silvestro di Palma, performed at the Teatro San Carlo in 1800. This work is notable because it appeared some nineteen years before the publication of John Polidori's "The Vampyre." For its inspiration, *I Vampiri* relied on the vampire treatise *Dissertazione sopra I Vampiri* (1744) by Giuseppe Davanzati.

Vampirism The act of being a vampire, involving the taking of blood, of psychic energy, or of some other power in order to survive or to increase personal vitality. While most people today associate vampirism with the traditional bloodsucker, there are, in fact, various types and degrees of activities performed by them. Psychic predations involve the draining from victims of their spiritual, mental, physical, and life essences, leaving them weakened or even dead. Sexual vampirism is actually quite common and entails the ceaseless need for sexual conquest, manipulation, and abuse. Other, less defined forms can range from political vampirism to financial vampirism, in which person or even institutions feed off society. Compared to some of these, which involve social ills and the degradation of entire peoples, the blood-drinking variety of vampirism seems tame to some. The most common vampirism in the modern world involves people who drink blood for psychosexual satisfaction. (See also *Vampire.*)

Vampiro, Il An obscure ballet by Rotta, with music by Paolo Giorza, performed in Milan in 1861. (For a similar work, see *Morgano.*)

Vampyr The 1932 classic French film directed by the Danish-born Carl Dreyer and starring Baron Nicholas de Gunzburg (who was listed as "Julian West" in the credits), Sybille Schmitz, Maurice Schutz, and Rena Mandel. Known in England as *The Strange Adventure of David Gray*, it was made independently by Dreyer with the help of his friends—various writers, poets, musicians, and artists—and was paid for by Baron de Gunzburg. The film is notably unconventional and is a masterpiece of mood and subtlety, photographed through gauze by Rudolph Maté. Its psychological depth and disturbing imagery were lost on audiences that expected another *Dracula* (which had been released the year before). *Vampyr* was based loosely on "Carmilla."

Vampyr, Der An opera advertised as a "grosse romantic Oper" ("great romantic opera") produced at Leipzig, Germany, on March 28 or 29, 1828, written by Wilhelm August Wohlbrück, with music by his brother-in-law, Henrich August Marschner. The work was so successful that James Robinson Planché made a free adaptation of it in August 1829 that opened at the Lyceum in London, the site of Planché's earlier success, *The Vampire, or the Bride of the Isles* (1820).

Vampyr, Ein An 1877 play in German, written by Ulrick Franks (Ulla Wolf) and presented in Vienna. A farce, it was based on *Le Vampire* (1820), by Scribe and Melesville.

Vampyre A variant spelling of vampire that endured into the nineteenth century and is seen periodically even today. "Vampyre" is quite acceptable, in some ways perhaps superior to "vampire," as its use is more closely connected to the Latin *vampyrus*, to John Polidori's title for his short story "The Vampyre" (1819), and to the works of experts of previous centuries, including Zopfius, Rohl, and Ranft. As the word *vampire* came into more common usage with the translation of such Eastern European names as *upior, upyr, vampir,* and *vapir* into English, vampyre became less common. It is certainly more exotic, echoing faintly the dark origins of the word. Some writers prefer vampyre or vampyr for their literary creations, using it to differentiate their undead from either the fanciful cinematic variety or a more violent species of bloodsucker. (See also *Vampire.*)

"Vampyre of the Fens" Also "A Vampire of the Fens," an obscure Anglo-Saxon poem from around the eleventh century whose title would have been added at a later date, after the word *vampyre* came into use. It is considered by some scholars to be the first vampire poem in European literature.

"Vampyre, The" The 1819 short story by Dr. John Polidori, first published in *The Monthly Magazine* in England, known in full as "The Vampyre; a Tale." It was based on an unfinished vampire short story by Lord Byron, told to Polidori and others at the Villa Diodati on the banks of Lake Geneva in 1816. Pirating this fragment as the framework of a novel, Polidori wrote "The Vampyre" as a means of gaining revenge upon Byron for the treatment he had received at the poet's hands. Lord Ruthven, the villain, bore more than a passing resemblance to Byron and became a highly influential model for the so-called Byronic vampires of literature.

"The Vampyre" begins with the introduction of Ruthven to polite society in London and the arrival of the orphaned Aubrey, a romantic and naive young man who attracts the vampire. Aubrey, refusing to recognize the evil in front of him, dooms himself and causes the death of his love, Ianthe, in Athens at the hands of a vampire. Almost killed at the same moment, Aubrey is nursed back to health by Ruthven. The two journey into the Greek countryside, where an attack by robbers leaves the vampire mortally wounded. He revives in moonlight. Aubrey then discovers evidence that Ruthven was implicated in Ianthe's murder and returns to England, knowing that his companion is a vampire.

Ruthven, known by this time as the Earl of Marsden, appears in London and, to Aubrey's horror, becomes engaged to the young man's sister. Begging her not to marry Ruthven, Aubrey, now believed to be mad, bursts a blood vessel. On his deathbed he begs his guardians to save the young woman, but when they rush to her rescue they discover, too late, that she is dead, that Ruthven is missing, and that "Aubrey's sister had glutted the thirst of a Vampyre!" (See also *Byron, Lord; Polidori, John; and Ruthven, Lord.*)

Van Helsing, Abraham A major character in Bram Stoker's novel *Dracula* (1897), who has come to represent the classic vampire hunter: learned, driven, forcefully compassionate, and blessed with luck and determination. A famous Dutch physician from Amsterdam, specializing in "obscure diseases," Van Helsing provided leadership for the forces opposing Count Dracula. He was named after Stoker's father, Abraham, and the scholar Arminius Vambery, who served as the professor's model. Summoned by Dr. Seward to England, Van Helsing is unable to save Lucy Westenra but is thereafter very aggressive in pursuing Dracula, the vampire king. He uses a variety of weapons, the most potent being a consecrated host, a blending of spirituality with the rigors of science observed, too, in his use of the cross with trains, a recorder, and telegrams.

The two most famous actors portraying Van Helsing in the great cinematic productions of the novel were Edward Van Sloan and Peter Cushing, the latter appearing in the Hammer films. Sir Laurence Olivier has also graced the role with his talents, and Anthony Hopkins has taken him on in a 1992 production.

Van Sloan, Edward American actor (1882–1964) who appeared in many horror films and was best known for his portrayal of Professor Abraham Van Helsing in *Dracula,* both on the stage and in the 1931 movie. He played the professor for the first time in 1927, opposite Bela Lugosi in the stage version of the 1897 novel by Bram Stoker, written by Hamilton Deane and John Balderston. Four years later he and Lugosi reprised their roles for the 1931 Universal classic, *Dracula.* Van Sloan became stereotyped along with Lugosi. After playing the learned Dr. Waldman in *Frankenstein* (1931) and Dr. Muller in *The*

Mummy (1932), Van Sloan returned to the Van Helsing role in *Dracula's Daughter* (1936). (See also *Dracula.*)

Varcolaci A mythical vampire species found in Romania that ranks with the most powerful of the undead because of its ability to "eat" the sun and the moon. Traditions vary as to what exactly the *varcolaci* are. They have been depicted as smaller than dogs, as dragons, or as animals with many mouths. They can originate as the souls of unbaptized children, those cursed by God, or the children of unmarried persons. They can also be created when women spin at midnight without a candle or when people place a porridge stick into a fire, even if a person sweeps the house at sunset, directing the accumulated dust and dirt toward the sun. The *varcolaci* may also appear as humans, with pale faces and dry skin. *Varcolaci* cause eclipses when their bodies drop into a deep sleep and their spirit goes into the sky to munch their way across the heavens. They can travel on the thread used in the midnight spinning, going where they wish as long as the cord remains unbroken. Another name in use for these beings is *priculics.* (See also *Romania.*)

Varney, Sir Francis The title character in the mammoth epic *Varney the Vampyre, or the Feast of Blood* (1847), most likely written by James Malcolm Rymer. Despite the near universal disdain for the novel, Sir Francis Varney remains one of the most influential vampires of literary history, an early embodiment of the modern vampire image: a reprehensible, cadaverous, cruel misanthrope who attacks beautiful maidens. The successor to John Polidori's Lord Ruthven, Varney has somewhat obscure beginnings since Rymer, who earned extra money by stretching out his story, provided his character with several inconsistent and contradictory origins. The most logical has Varney beginning his life as Marmaduke Bannesworth, a man who committed suicide and returned as a vampire. Throughout the adventure Varney is slain by hanging, staking, shooting, and a host of other grim methods, but the moon's rays restore him with awful regularity. At the request of Edwin Lloyd, the publisher who felt that Varney had run his course after some 868 pages of story, Rymer had his character leap into Mount Vesuvius. He was described in the tale as tall, with huge eyes like tin, and "cold and clammy like a corpse."

Varney the Vampyre Known in full as *Varney the Vampyre, or the Feast of Blood,* an 1847 epic published originally in 109 weekly sections. The first vampire novel in the English language, *Varney* was presented anonymously, authorship remaining in doubt for many years until Thomas Preskett Prest was designated its creator, a claim made by Reverend Montague Summers. Modern scholarship has made it a near certainty that the author was in fact James Malcolm Rymer. A massive and unwieldly work (it is 868 pages long, divided into 220 chapters), the novel is not easy reading for an audience of today. Repetitive episodes, bad prose typical of the "penny dreadful" (the tales carried in magazines and newspapers at the time), and the length itself caused the novel to decline in popularity until its rerelease in the early 1970s. Some critics, such as Summers, praised the novel, preferring it to Bram Stoker's *Dracula* (1897). *Varney* certainly had an influence on Stoker, and Francis Varney, the successor to Lord Ruthven, bequeathed many of his characteristics to Count Dracula. (See also previous entry.)

Verzeni, Vincenzo A so-called living vampire in Italy, who in 1872 was arrested for murder and corpse mutilation. He also drank human blood. Convicted, Verzeni was sentenced to life imprisonment. (See also *Historical Vampires.*)

Vetala A type of Indian vampire, also considered a demon, even a chief of demons, known in some regions as the *baital*, the *baitala*, or the *vetal*. This creature is described variously as being white, green, or wheat-colored and astride a green horse. It can also appear as an old hag, sucking the blood of women—customarily only those who are drunk or insane. Other traditions hold that the *vetala* is not actually malevolent. It can be seen at night in silver-and-gold cloth decorated with elephants and horses, a torch in one hand and a sword in the other. The *vetala* is best known from the *Vetala-panchavinsati* (or the *Baital-Pachisi*), a collection of folktales told by a *vetala* to King Vikramaditya. These stories were adapted for the West by Richard Burton in *Vikram and the Vampire, or, Tales of Hindu Devilry* (1870).

Vieszcy: See *Kashubes.*

Vikram and the Vampire: See *Vetala.*

Vinegar A liquid used as a vampire preventive. After decapitating a vampire, the head can be boiled in a vat of vinegar. The grisly practice of heart extraction can be culminated by cooking or sautéing the diced organ in vinegar; the cooked heart is then burned to ashes or replaced in the chest cavity. The *penanggalan,* a Malaysian species of vampire, uses vinegar to shrink its intestines in order to fit back into its body. (See *Destroying the Vampire.*)

Vision, Vampiric The eyesight of a vampire, said to be superior to that of mortals, even in the dark, and open to speculation of vampirologists and writers. Precisely how the undead see perfectly in the night is unknown; even Bram Stoker, creator of so much of the modern lore, was unable to give a proper explanation. In describing vampiric vision in *Dracula*, Professor Van Helsing states: "He can see in the dark—no small power this, in a world which is one-half shut from the light." Some have suggested that a vampire can adjust its vision to the infrared spectrum when required to do so. The creature can return to regular vision when entering a lighted area. Others suggest that the vampire has vision more akin to the bat, relying upon echo sensitivity to its environment, coupled with a perfected sense of smell that focuses on the blood of the living. The eyes of vampires are remarkable organs, traditionally described as glowing like coals from the pits of hell. With them, vampires are able to penetrate into the very souls of victims, holding them in a hypnotic thrall as they close in for the kill.

Vlad Dracul A Wallachian *voivode* (warlord or prince) (d. 1447), the father of Vlad Tepes (Vlad the Impaler). Dracul was born sometime before 1395, the illegitimate son of Prince Mircea of Wallachia. His reigns lasted from 1436 to 1442 and from the spring of 1443 to 1447. He vacillated between supporting the Hungarians and maintaining neutrality with the Turks, even though he was a member of the Order of the Dragon, which obliged him to aid Christendom. By 1447 the Hungarian ruler Janos Hunyadi decided to end Vlad's reign, marching into Transylvania and laying siege to Tirgoviste, one of Dracul's cities. Dracul fled and, like his son, was assassinated in the marshes near Bucharest. Vlad Tepes (b. 1431) eventually claimed the Wallachian throne, earning the title Dracula (son of Dracul) and Tepes (the Impaler). The meaning of the word *Dracul* is debated by scholars. (See *Dracula*.)

Vlad Dracula: See *Vlad Tepes*.

Vlad the Impaler The nickname given to Vlad Dracula (1431–1476), ruler of Wallachia, because of his habit of executing his enemies and subjects on an array of spikes and other implements of torture. (See next entry for additional details.)

Vlad Tepes Also called Vlad Dracula (1431–1476), ruler of Wallachia, with the title of *voivode* (warlord or prince), Vlad Tepes(pronounced tse-pesh) acquired a fearsome reputation as a result of his immense cruelty and the propaganda that was spread throughout Europe to discredit him in the decades following his death. In Romania, Vlad has been honored historically as a symbol of nationalism, as the ruler who defeated the Ottoman Turks and proved independent-minded in the face of Hungarian ascendancy. He was born in the Transylvanian town of Sighisoara, son of the formidable Vlad Dracul, Prince of Wallachia (d. 1447). Vlad and his younger brother, Radu, spent several years as hostages of the Turks, learning from them firsthand a lesson of terror, humiliation, and oppression. Briefly in 1448, with the approval of the Ottomans, Vlad claimed power in Wallachia but was soon overthrown, fleeing to Moldavia and the safety of the Hungarians.

In 1456 he returned to Wallachia with the support of the Hungarians, embarking on a reign that lasted until 1462. During that time Vlad campaigned against the Turks, built Castle Dracula with slave labor, and massacred thousands of his subjects by a variety of fiendishly diabolical methods, the most common device being the stake (hence his domestic title Tepes, the Impaler). By 1462 the wrath of the Ottomans was felt in Wallachia, and Vlad again fled to Hungary, where King Matthias Corvinus, fearing the man's restlessness and willpower, imprisoned him. After twelve years he was allowed his freedom (1474), although it was not until November 1476 that he once more assumed the rank of *voivode*. His enemies were far too numerous by that time, and Vlad was killed.

After death, however, Vlad assumed a definitive role in the legends of Romania, as wild rumors erupted about his demise and his corpse. His headless body was supposedly buried at Snagov, near Bucharest, but tales persisted that the grave was empty, Vlad having risen. Like the German ruler Frederick Barbarossa, it was said Vlad had not died but had gone into hiding to await the day of his needed return. The triumphs of this *voivode* overshadowed his penchant for slaughtering those around him, but grisly tales of his murders were circulating throughout Europe, published by German pamphleteers.

In searching for a model for his vampire character, Bram Stoker inevitably stumbled upon the shadowy figure of Vlad, perhaps coming across the information as early as 1890 and possibly under the influence of the scholar Arminius Vambery. Vlad fit the mold perfectly: he died under mysterious circumstances, he was decapitated, his body was apparently never recovered, and he relished impaling people. Even the name Dracula (or Dracul) had occult connotations. The associations of Vlad with vampirism were nonexistent, but Stoker deftly handled that deficiency by declaring outright through the words of another character, Van Helsing, that Dracula was, in truth, Vlad Tepes. Thus an ambitious nobleman who had perished some four hundred years before was catapulted back into the European limelight, once more the victim of propaganda. Whereas Vlad had earlier been accused of shedding the blood of innocents, he was now accused of drinking it. Interestingly, Stoker originally titled his novel *The Un-Dead*. At the last moment either he or his publisher changed it to *Dracula*.

Volkodlak A term for a vampire found in Slovenia. The word also refers to a werewolf, demonstrating the close association in some regions between these two creatures of the night. (See *Werewolf*.)

Voltaire Assumed name of François Marie Arouet (1694–1778), French philosopher and writer and leading figure of the Enlightenment. Among his vast output of works was the *Dictionnaire Philosophique* (1764), in which Voltaire expressed surprise that in his seemingly intellectual era there should be people who believed in vampires and that the learned doctors of the Sorbonne should actually give their approval to treatises about the undead. He added, mirroring the 1732 article "Political Vampires":

> What! Vampires in our Eighteenth Century? yes . . . in Poland, Hungary, Silesia, Moravia, Austria and Lorraine—there was no discussion of vampires in London, or even Paris. I must admit that in these two cities there were speculators, tax officials and businessmen who sucked the blood of the people in broad daylight, but they were not dead (although they were corrupted enough). These real bloodsuckers did not live in cemeteries: they preferred beautiful palaces. . . .

Voodoo Also *vodun,* a term first used by Haitians in Louisiana, probably taken from Dahomey in West Africa. *Voodoo* is an amalgam of occult African practices with elements of Roman Catholic rituals. A highly complex system, it is noted for its formidable sorcerers who practice various forms of magic, including necromancy, spell casting, and hexing. Blood forms part of the rituals that connect *voodoo* to vampirism. Additionally, zombies created by *voodoo* consume human flesh and have been ranked with primitive vampires. (See also *Zombies.*)

Vourdalak A species of vampire found in Russia, known in Russian folklore as a beautiful but evil woman or female spirit. The *vourdalak* was used by Alexis Tolstoy in his 1847 short story "The Family of the Vourdalak."

Vrykolakas The main vampire species of Greece, Macedonia, and the Aegean region, also *vroukalakas* and *brucolocas.* The name was used originally in Slavic regions to denote a werewolf, its vampiric connotations rising out of the belief that werewolves upon death came back as members of the undead. As the Slavic culture penetrated into Greece and the Aegean, the demon-ridden *vrykolakas* gradually replaced the indigenous Greek revenant, which was considered a fairly peaceful being until that time, ultimately emerging as the preeminent species in Greece.

The *vrykolakas* is created in several fashions: improper burial, an immoral life, death without baptism, or eating the flesh of a sheep killed by a wolf, among others. It goes about in the dark, knocking at doors and calling out the name of someone inside. Should that unlucky person respond, death comes quickly. It is customary in some regions not to answer a knock or a call the first time; the *vrykolakas*, being impatient, will not wait around to repeat itself, and moves on. The vampire strikes by seating itself upon and crushing a sleeping victim. All who die by its hand become vampires. The passage of time makes it more audacious and powerful, so there is a need for haste in destroying the fiend. Villagers who have had enough of its predations will wait until Saturday, the one day this vampire is allowed to rest in the earth. After exhuming the suspected corpse, they decapitate it or impale it on a spike. The lifting of a ban of excommunication is also useful. For particularly stubborn specimens of this species, exile to a small uninhabited island is recommended. All of its creations—the secondhand vampires—will cease to exist when the *vrykolakas* is exterminated.

Vrykolatios A vampire species found on the island of Santorini (Thera). It is a combination vampire and ghoul, mentioned in the 1900 *Handbook for Travellers in Greece*. With such creatures—described as fiends that "banquet on the living"—active on the island, the inhabitants of Santorini became the foremost experts in the various methods of destroying vampires.

Vukodlak A Serbian term for "vampire," derived from the word for werewolf, as the werewolf is associated with the undead in Slavic folklore. Werewolves are believed to return after death as members of the vampire species. Over time, as the vampire connotations outpaced the lycanthropic ones, the *vukodlak* was used more and more frequently in its present sense. In some parts of Yugoslavia, the *vukodlak* remains a werewolf; stories about persons turning into wolves and devouring sheep continued to circulate until the late nineteenth century.

Wagner, Peter A late-fifteenth-century printer at Nuremberg who, around 1488, published a type of newsletter on Vlad Tepes (Vlad the Impaler). The publication covered the terrible deeds of Dracole Wayda (Prince Dracula) and helped spread his reputation for cruelty throughout the West. Copies of the work currently reside in Munich, Bucharest, Stuttgart, and elsewhere.

"Wake Not the Dead" A tale written by Johann Ludwig Tieck in Germany in 1800, but not published in English until 1823, when it was included in the three-volume anthology *Popular Tales and Romances of the Northern Nations.* Tieck, a folklorist and prominent member of the late Romantic movement, presents one of the first memorable vampiresses of literature in the character of Brunhilda, a woman long dead who is restored to life by a sorcerer, hired by her husband, Walter. Brunhilda, however, cannot "keep up the genial glow of vitality" and is driven to derive nourishment from human blood, taken "whilst yet warm from the veins of youth." A dreadful *lamia,* she chooses innocent children as her victims until finally turning on her mortal "spell-enthralled" husband. With its sexual symbolism and allegory, "Wake Not the Dead" is a classic story, one that influenced its own era.

Wales The rugged, mountainous home of a most unique vampire, a chair that thirsts for blood. A tale included in many collections of Welsh folklore relates how a minister visiting a family that lived in a converted farmhouse sat on a chair for a time and discovered later that he had teeth marks on his hands and sides. It was claimed that the farmer who owned the chair had come back as a vampire. Another version notes that the minister discovered that his horse carried the same marks. The current resident of the legendary house told his victimized guest that two ministers had been attacked in recent times, but never their horses. (See also *Map, Walter.*)

Wallachia Also Walachia, with Moldavia and Transylvania, one of the historic divisions of Romania, found between the Transylvanian Alps and the Danube. In 1290 a princely line of rulers bearing the title *voivode* (warlord or prince) was established. This dynasty, called in history the Draculesti, was to produce rulers who managed to survive the many dangers posed by the Ottoman Turks dominating the Balkans at the time. Born to the Draculesti were two particularly noted *voivodes,* Vlad II Dracul (d. 1447) and Vlad III Tepes (Vlad the Impaler, 1431–1476), known also as Dracula (son of Dracul). Wallachia, like the rest of Romania, was haunted by a wide variety of vampires, including the *strigoii, moroii, varcolaci, zmeu,* and *nosferatu.* The *muroni* was a local species. Because of the extensiveness of its traditions, particularly in the area of Oltenia (Lesser Wallachia), the region is preferred by some vampirologists over Transylvania as the home of the vampire.

Walpurgis Night A festival held on May 1 in honor of the eighth-century English abbess and missionary, Saint Walpurgis (also Walburga). She eventually was confused in legends with the pagan fertility goddess Waldbourg, and Walpurgis Night became a time of great activity for witches—even though the occasion was supposed to celebrate the moving of the saint's relics to Eichstätt. Vampires on this night were said to be very dangerous, and Bohemians took measures to prevent their predations by placing hawthorn and wild roses around stables to entangle them and frustrate their evils. Walpurgis Night, steeped in folklore, was a suitable setting for a vampire story, used in the Spanish film *La Noche de Walpurgis* (1972), starring Paul Naschy, Gaby Fuchs, and Barbara Capell.

Water, Holy Water that has been blessed by a cleric, thereby made sacred and possessing powerful antievil properties. It has many functions with respect to the undead. First, it will burn a vampire like a terrible acid, leaving severe scars. Holy water may even destroy recently created vampires. Second, holy water can serve as a detection device for evil. If poured on ground that is under diabolical influence, the water will boil and smoke. If the liquid is poured into an empty coffin, it can seal it forever from vampiric habitation. The water can also be sprinkled onto a grave, having much the same effect. A final value was depicted in the film *'Salem's Lot* (1979), in which vials of glowing holy water told the living that the undead were near.

Water and Vampires A possible bane to the undead, often prominent in folklore. As with witches, the vampire is unable to swim or to cross running water, as water acts as a purifier, washing away evil and sin. In Greece, troublesome revenants were "exiled" to small uninhabited islands (surrounded by water), thus isolating them and keeping them from their sources of nourishment. In some regions, the soul was thought to be thirsty so offerings of water were placed near graves to keep the deceased from wandering in search of it. A trial by water, called the *iudicium aquae,* was sometimes used to see if a corpse had joined the ranks of the undead: if a body floated, it was a vampire. Out of such bizarre folk traditions came the belief that running water destroys a vampire or at least renders it paralyzed. In *Dracula, A.D. 1972* (1972), the vampire Johnny Alucard is destroyed by falling into a bathtub, accidentally turning on the shower. This is one of the most unique vampire exterminations in film. In *Dracula—Prince of Darkness* (1965), Count Dracula is trapped and imprisoned beneath the ice in a frozen stream until accidentally released in *Dracula Has Risen from the Grave* (1968).

Watermelons Like pumpkins, these fruit can become vampires; they are not considered very dangerous, particularly because they have no teeth. Watermelon vampires are found among the Muslim Gypsies of Yugoslavia. Virtually any kind of melon is susceptible, transforming if kept for more than ten days or for too long a period after Christmas. They make growling sounds, are stained with traces of blood, and roll around to pester the living.

Weeping Woman: See *La Llorona;* see also *Toad Woman.*

Weird Tales The foremost magazine of fantasy, horror, and weird fiction, it served as the publishing home of some of the century's best writers of fantasy and science fiction until going out of business in 1954. The magazine released a special vampire issue in July 1947, with illustrations by Lee Brown Coye. *Weird Tales* was the greatest of the so-called pulp magazines, outlasting such rivals as *Terror Tales, Horror Stories, Uncanny Tales, Mystery Tales,* and *Strange Tales.* First published in March 1923, the magazine offered readers a dizzying array of horror stories, featuring ghouls, vampires, werewolves, mutants, evil houses, tombs, rats, bats, spiders, and sorcerers of the worst kind. Many vampire tales that have subsequently become classics were first printed in the magazine. Originally edited by Farnsworth Wright (until his death in 1940), *Weird Tales* began with reprints of great writers including Edgar Allan Poe, Arthur Conan Doyle, Daniel Defoe, and Edward Bulwer-Lytton. Over the next three decades it attracted such masters as C. L. Moore, Robert Bloch, H. P. Lovecraft, Clark Ashton Smith, August Derleth, Fritz Leiber, Ray Bradbury, and Seabury Quinn, the most prolific of all contributors.

Wellman, Manly Wade American writer (d. 1986) of short stories and novels of horror and the supernatural, whose works appeared in the *Magazine of Fantasy and Science Fiction* and the well-known pulp magazine *Weird Tales.* Wellman was born in Portuguese West Africa and later worked as a reporter. His numerous vampire stories were immensely popular and included two classics: "School for the Unspeakable" (1937) and "The Devil Is Not Mocked" (1943). The former tells of the Nazi occupation of a castle in Transylvania and the latter of a closed school inhabited by vampires. His other vampire tales were "Fearful Rock" (1934), "The Horrors Undying" (1936), "When It Was Moonlight" (1940), "Coven" (1942), "The Last Grave of Lill Warren" (1951), "You Know the Tale of Hoph" (1962), and "Hundred Years Gone" (1978).

Wells, H. G. English author (1866–1946) and speculative writer of such classics as *The Time Machine* (1895), *The Invisible Man* (1897), and *The War of the Worlds* (1898). His contribution to vampire literature was a botanical bloodsucker in the short story "The Flowering of the Strange Orchid" (1894), set on the Andaman Islands, perhaps chosen after their use in the Sherlock Holmes mystery *The Sign of Four* (1890). (See also *"Man-Eating Tree, The."*)

Werewolf A kind of lycanthrope found, like the vampire, throughout the world, but causing particular alarm in Europe, where some thirty thousand cases were reported between 1520 and 1630. Not surprisingly, there has been a close association of lycanthropy with vampirism, including the widely held belief that any poor soul dying while under the curse of the werewolf was condemned to return as a vampire. Thus, in Slavic territories, many names used initially for werewolves came to be applied to the undead: *vrykolakas, vukodlak, vurkodlak,* and *volkodlak.* French demonologists wrote of a unique werewolf, known as the *loublin,* that was found in cemeteries, digging up corpses so as to consume them—an activity also attributed to werewolves (not to mention vampires) in other lands. In Montenegro, there was direct evidence that all vampires must spend time as wolves. In Greece, anyone who ate a sheep slain by a wolf would return as a vampire. The compatability of the vampire and the lycanthrope was examined by Ronald Chetwynd Hayes in his story "The Werewolf and the Vampire" (1975). (See also *Transformations, Vampiric.*)

Westenra, Lucy From the novel *Dracula* (1897) by Bram Stoker, a character who dies from the attacks of the count, returning as a vampiress, a truly dreadful creature of the night known to her victims as the "Bloofer Lady." Lucy represents the repressed aspects of the Victorian woman, the so-called New Woman whose longing for greater personal freedoms and a place in the world poses a threat to the male-dominated society of the time. At one point Lucy laments that she cannot marry three men, recanting immediately but showing that if given the opportunity, she would shed her inhibitions and succumb to her desires. The opportunity arises with the arrival of Dracula, an incestuous father figure who first slays her mother and then introduces her to the dark world of the vampire, where her hidden sensuality erupts into full flower. Her feeding on children is her final rejection of the role of nurturing mother. The seduction and transformation of Lucy is a major episode in the first half of *Dracula,* though it ends with her destruction by a stake delivered by her fiancé, Arthur Holmwood, on the very day of their planned wedding. Lucy provided the inspiration for similar characters in subsequent vampire films: women who secretly long to be vampirized, succumb to the attack, and then relish their new existence. But such creatures are merely used as instruments by the vampire, his true object of desire being the more virtuous woman who naturally opposes his evil.

West Indies A broad archipelago separating the Caribbean from the Atlantic Ocean, whose vampire lore was based on West African traditions brought with the slave trade. Sorcerers were greatly feared and were known to be stealers of hearts, mercilessly slaying anyone who offended them. The most well-known vampire species by far was the *loogaroo,* also associated with the *sucoyan,* said in some places to be the female version of the species.

Weyland, Edward Lewis The vampire character introduced in *The Vampire Tapestry* (1980) by Suzy McKee Charnas, a collection of novellas compiled into one volume. Weyland is a unique species of vampire, awakening into the modern world after half a century of sleep and assuming the persona of a professor of anthropology. He meets the formidable vampire Saint-Germain in "The Advocate," in a later collection, *Under the Fang* (1991).

"What Was It?" An 1859 tale by Fitz-James O'Brien, published in *Harper's New Monthly Magazine*, this Cork, Ireland, native's best work. The story is a variation on Guy de Maupassant's "The Horla" (1887), in which people are attacked by an invisible vampire when they sleep in a certain room.

Whiskey A liquor known as *rachia* in Romania, where it was used to prevent a *strigoii* from returning home to feast upon relatives. A bottle of whiskey would be buried with the corpse; the surviving family members would then declare: "Drink this and go away, and don't come home!" While the vampire drinks the whiskey and prepares to travel to some other village, the family members go home in silence. Should they speak, the spell is broken and they are susceptible to attack. (See also *Wine.*)

White Lady, The Known in the German as Die Weisse Frau, this legend possibly influenced the Weeping Woman or La Llorona, a woman guilty of infanticide and condemned to return from the dead for her crimes. The earliest references to the White Lady are from the late fifteenth century; one account, included in the *Chronologia Monasteriorum Germaniae Praecipuorum* (1552), tells of the widow of the count of Orlamünde, who murdered her two children in the hope of winning the favors of another handsome and powerful nobleman.

Over succeeding years the early story developed into the more well-known Weisse Frau. Centered in Cologne, this tale concerns a tanner's daughter who was seduced and impregnated by a disreputable knight who pretended to be a tanner himself. Not only did he refuse to marry her, he scorned and mocked her and his child. She became so outraged that she threw the child under his horse, stole his sword, and stabbed him to death. While she was in prison, her sanity departed and she hanged herself. Her body was buried without ceremony. After that night, between the hours of midnight and 1 A.M., she appeared at the very spot of the murders, dressed in white. Anyone speaking to her died soon after, victims of her terrible curse.

Whitethorn A species of the hawthorn, *Crataegus laevigata*, with white flowers, possessed of potent antievil properties. It has been carved into stakes and has been placed in coffins with garlic to ensure that a corpse remains free of vampiric infection. Whitethorn was used in the latter fashion during the 1725 epidemic caused by Peter Plogojowitz in Kisolova. (See also *Stake, Wooden.*)

Wilde, Oscar Dublin-born English writer (1854–1900), the author of poems, novels, comedies, and fairy tales, including *Lady Windermere's Fan* (1892) and *The Importance of Being Earnest* (1895). Wilde also wrote *The Picture of Dorian Gray* (1891), presenting in a highly literary fashion a parasitic vampire who brings suffering to those around him while remaining outwardly unchanged. A painting of him, hidden away, reflects his true moral state, the image becoming more horrible as his sins increase.

William of Malmesbury English chronicler (d. ca. 1143), Benedictine monk, and author of a history of England, *Gesta Regnum Anglorum* (1120). In this work he makes mention of the belief common at the time that men who died in a state of sin were condemned to return from the dead and to wander the earth, their bodies reanimated by the devil. (See *Reanimation.*)

William of Newburgh English chronicler and member of a priory at Newburgh (1136–ca. 1198), also known as William of Newbury, the author of the *Historia Rerum Anglicarum,* composed between 1196 ad 1198. He examined several stories of revenants, including episodes in Buckinghamshire, Berwick, Melrose, and Alnwick Castle. (See individual entries for details.)

Williamson, J. N. Author of a series of novels featuring the vampire Lamia Zacharius, who slays her victims literally by taking them for a ride in her death mobile. His four highly sensational works are *Death-Coach* (1981), *Death-Angel* (1981), *Death-School* (1982), and *Death-Doctor* (1982). Williamson also contributed the short story "Herrenrasse" to the anthology *Under the Fang* (1991).

Will-o'-the-Wisp Also *Ignis fatuus* ("foolish fire"), elf-fire, friar's lanthorn, or walking-fire, a flamelike phosphorescent light seen flittering over marshy ground, fooling many people who try to follow it and thus become lost in the marshes. The will-o'-the-wisp is caused by gases given off by decaying vegetable matter, but in folklore it became a living entity, often with malicious intent. The vampire associations with the will-o'-the-wisp include the idea that some species of the Eastern European undead, such as the *ubour* of Bulgaria, give off sparks or actually appear as luminescent specks of light. An excellent example of this was seen in Scotland's Vampire of Fealaar. (See also *Transformations, Vampiric.*)

Wine A liquor used in Romania to prevent attacks by the *strigoii*, a species of vampire. A bottle of wine buried near a grave at the interment of a suspected undead is dug up six weeks later and shared by family members. Whoever partakes of that wine will be protected from vampiric attacks. The Bulgarians boiled wine and threw it onto the remains of an exhumed and impaled corpse to drive out the infesting demon. In Serbia, the heart of the vampire was cut out, boiled in wine, and then placed back in the chest cavity. (See also *Destroying the Vampire*.)

Witchcraft The practice of magic or sorcery. Witches and warlocks have been closely associated with vampires in folklore, from service to Hecate, the ancient goddess of the underworld, to inclusion in the *Malleus Maleficarum*, a treatise on evils that were dangerous to mankind. (For details, see following entries: WITCHES OR WITCHLIKE VAMPIRE SPECIES: the *Bajang, Bell Witch, Bruxsa, Chordewa, Civatateo, Empusas, Estrie, Female Vampires, Impundulu, Jigarkhwar, Lamia, Loogaroo, Moroii, Nadilla, Obayifo, Old Hag, Pelesit, Penanggalan, Polong, Striges, Strigoii, Strix, Talamaur*, and *Tlaciques*. WITCH-RELATED SUBJECTS: *Abruzzi, Black Mass, Black Sunday, Bottling a Vampire, Bulgaria, Christianity, Crossroads, Exhumation, Flying, Greece, Gypsies, Hecate, Heretics, Italy, Kali, Laws About Vampires, Magic, Malleus Maleficarum, Need-fire, New England, Nightmare, Portugal, Romania, Russia, Salic Law, Scotland, Spain*, and *Walpurgis Night*.)

Wolfsbane Also wolfsbay, any of several plants of the aconite genus *Aconitum*, including *A. napellus*, providing a poisonous alkaloid used in medicine, with several colorful garden varieties, and *A. Lycoctonum*, with hood-shaped purplish blue flowers. Credited with definite antievil powers, the plant has been wielded against vampires in certain parts of Europe, especially Germany, and used in a manner similar to garlic—for example, placed in front of doors or windows.

Wolves Powerful carnivores, the most common species of which, the gray or timber wolf (*Canis lupus*), was once found throughout Europe, Asia, and North America. In Slavic and Gypsy folklore, wolves are reported to be avowed enemies of the vampire, while in other regions there is a close association between the two. In Romania, Gypsy villages were supposedly protected by white wolves that stood guard in cemeteries and devoured any vampires that emerged from the ground. Other Gypsy communities used wolves to attack vampires as well; the Yugoslavian Gypsies of the Kosovo region held that all vampires were doomed to wander the earth until finally meeting a wolf, which would tear them to pieces. A tribe in Montenegro was of the opinion that all vampires must spend some time as a wolf. (See also *Animals, Dogs, "Dracula's Guest," Lugat*, and *Transformations, Vampiric*.)

Wood: See *Stakes, Wooden;* see also *Ash, Aspen, Blackthorn, Buckthorn, Cross, Dogrose, Hawthorn, Holly, Juniper, Linden, Maple, Piercing a Corpse, Rowan, Spikes, Thorns,* and *Whitethorn.*

Wooden Stakes: See *Stake, Wooden.*

Wool To prevent a corpse from returning, wool is stuffed into the mouth in a practice similar to that of forcing jade, coins, or garlic into bodily openings. The tradition was found especially in the Balkans, among the Gypsies, and also among the Peruvians, who used the material in their mummification processes.

Wright, Dudley English historian (1868–1949) and author of *Vampires and Vampirism* (1914), a popularly written treatise on the undead. It was enlarged and rereleased in 1924, and then republished in 1973 under the title *The Book of Vampires*. Wright, an expert on Freemasons, thus produced the first treatise in the English language on vampires, which covered essentially the same material covered by Montague Summers in his two studies on the undead: *Vampire, His Kith and Kin* (1928) and *The Vampire in Europe* (1929).

Wurdalak: See *Vourdalak;* see also *Tolstoy, Alexis.*

Xloptuny Another name used by the Russians for the vampire species of the *erestun* or *erestuny.*

X.L.: See *"Kiss of Judas, A."*

Yarbro, Chelsea Quinn American writer (b. 1942) best known for her creation Le Comte de Saint-Germain, the ancient immortal whom she introduced in the 1978 novel *Hotel Transylvania*. This was followed by *The Palace* (1978), *Blood Games* (1979), *Path of the Eclipse* (1981), *Tempting Fate* (1982), and *The Saint-Germain Chronicles* (1983), a collection of short stories. After an absence of several years, Saint-Germain returned in *A Flame in Byzantium* (1987), although the story focused on Atta Olivia Clemens, his love who departed mortal life in *Blood Games*. Olivia is also the main character in *Crusader's Torch* (1988), but Saint-Germain was featured more prominently in *Candles for D'Artagnan* (1989), *Out of the House of Life* (1990), and *Darker Jewels* (1993). Yarbro also wrote the short story "Disturb Not My Slumbering Fair" (1978) and the novels *Dead and Buried* (1980) and *Nomads* (1989).

Yugoslavia: See *Albania, Croatia, Macedonia, Montenegro,* and *Serbia;* see also *Gypsies* and individual entries.

Z

Zmeu A ghostly vampirelike figure found in Moldavia. The *zmeu* took the form of a long flame that each night entered the room of a young girl or widow. Once inside, the flame became a man, who promptly seduced the female. Among the Transylvanians, the *zmeu* was found in the shape of a young girl, a maiden of the woods who had no back. She tempted shepherds by offering to lead them and their sheep to green pastures if they would make love to her. The recommended way of preserving one's virtue in this case was to carry a mixture of garlic, celandine (an herb from the poppy family), and candle wax.

Zombie More properly *zombi,* a term found originally among the Niger and Congo tribes of Africa. *Zombi* was a snake deity in West Africa but was applied by practitioners of *voodoo* in the West Indies to the magical power of reanimating a corpse. The most common understanding of zombie is a body that has a kind of life restored to it by magical means, or a living person under the complete control of a magician. Zombies differ from vampires in that they do not require blood, are mute, are not necessarily well preserved, and derive their strength from magic alone. As zombies have been portrayed as flesh eaters, some rank them with vampires and ghouls, an image reinforced by George Romero's many "living dead" films. (See also *Voodoo.*)

Zopfius, Johann Heinrich A prominent eighteenth-century German expert on vampires, who, with Karl Francis von Dalen, wrote the *Dissertatio de Vampyris* (1733, *Dissertation on the Vampires*, also *Dissertatio de Vampyris Serviensibus*), published at Halle. Von Dalen (also van Dalen) is little known, but Zopfius was the head instructor in the local gymnasium, or school. His treatise became widely read in England as the result of the publication in London in 1745 of *The Travels of Three English Gentlemen*, which included translated excerpts of the work. (See *Dissertatio de Vampyris* for an excerpt.)

APPENDIXES

Appendix 1

Short Stories

For those interested in classic or favorite stories, finding them can prove difficult as the original sources are not always available. Readers are therefore encouraged to consult the many anthologies or collections that have been published over the years. These works are recommended:

Blaisdell, Elinore, ed. *Tales of the Undead, Vampires and Visitants.* London: Crowell, 1947.

Bond, Edlyne, ed. *Dark Fires: Impressions from Dark Shadows.* Lawndale, CA: Phantom Press, 1980.

Bradbury, Ray. *October Country.* New York: Ballantine, 1955.

Carter, M. L. *Curse of the Undead.* New York: Fawcett, 1970.

Chapek-Carleton, Lori, ed. *Dracula.* East Lansing, MI: T'Kuhtian, 1980.

Chetwynd-Hayes, Ronald. *The Fantastic World of Kamtellar.* London: Kimber, 1980.

Collins, Barnabas and Quentin, ed. *The Dark Shadows Book of Vampires and Werewolves.* New York: Paperback Library, 1970.

Collins, Charles, M., ed. *A Feast of Blood,* New York: Avon, 1967.

Dalby, Richard, ed. *Dracula's Brood.* Wellingborough, Northamptonshire: Aquarian, 1987.

Dark Dominion, The. New York: Paperback Library, 1970.

Dark Shadows Book of Vampires and Werewolves. New York: Paperback Library, 1970.

Datlow, Ellen, ed. *Blood Is Not Enough.* New York: William Morrow, 1989.

Dickie, James, ed. *The Undead.* London: Pan, 1975.

Elwood, Roger, ed. *Monster Tales: Vampires, Werewolves and Things.* Chicago: Rand McNally, 1973.

———. *Vampires, Werewolves, and Other Monsters.* New York: Curtis, 1974.

Frayling, Christopher, ed. *The Vampyre: A Bedside Companion.* New York: Scribner's, 1978.

Greenberg, Martin H., ed. *Vamps.* New York: DAW Books, 1987.

———. *Dracula—Prince of Darkness.* New York: DAW Books, 1992.

———. *Taste of Blood, A.* New York: Dorset Press, 1992.

Haining, Peter, ed. *The Dracula Scrapbook.* New York: Bramhall House, 1977.

———. *The Ghouls.* New York: Stein and Day, 1971.

————. *The Midnight People*. New York: Popular Library, 1968.

————. *Vampire: Chilling Tales of the Undead*. London: Target, 1985.

Howard, Robert Ervin. *Skull-Face and Others*. Sauk City, WI: Arkham House, 1947.

Hunt, William, ed. *Chosen Haunts*. North Riverside, IL: Pandora Publications, 1981.

Jones, Stephen, ed. *The Mammoth Book of Vampires*. New York: Carroll and Graf, 1992.

Lankester, Eric. *Vampire, Vampire, Take Another Bite On Me*. Holland: 1972.

McCammon, Robert, ed. *The Horror Writers of America Present Under The Fang*. New York: Pocket Books, 1991.

McNally, Raymond T., ed. *A Clutch of Vampires*. New York: New York Graphic Society, 1974.

Moore, Steven, ed. *The Vampire in Verse: An Anthology*. New York: Count Dracula Fan Club, 1985.

Moskowitz, Sam, ed. *Horrors Unknown*. New York: Walker and Company, 1971.

Parry, Michael, ed. *The Rivals of Dracula*. London: Corgi, 1977.

Perkowski, Jan, ed. *Vampires of the Slavs*. Columbus, OH: Slavica Publishers, 1976.

Resch, Kathy, ed. *Decades*. Santa Clara, CA: Pentagram, 1977.

Robinson, Richard, ed. *The Best of the World of Dark Shadows*. Dardanelles, AR: Imperial, 1979.

Ryan, Alan, ed. *The Penguin Book of Vampire Stories*. New York: Doubleday, 1987.

Shepard, Leslie, ed. *The Dracula Book of Great Vampire Stories*. Secaucus, NJ: Citadel, 1977.

Stoker, Bram. *Dracula's Guest and Other Weird Tales*. London: Routledge, 1914.

Tolstoy, Alexis. *Vampires: Stories of the Supernatural*. New York: Hawthorn, 1969.

Underwood, Peter, ed. *The Vampire's Bedside Companion*. London: Leslie Frewin, 1975.

Varma, Devendra P., ed. *Voices from the Vaults*. Toronto: Key Porter, 1987.

Volta, Ornella, and Valeria Riva, eds. *The Vampire: An Anthology*. London: Neville Spearman, 1963.

Winfield, Chester, et al. *Monster Sex Stories*. New York: Gallery Press, 1972.

Wolf, Leonard, ed. *The Ultimate Dracula*. New York: Dell, 1991.

Youngson, Jeanne, ed. *A Child's Garden of Vampires*. Chicago: Adams Press, 1980.

————. *Count Dracula and the Unicorn*. Chicago: Adams Press, 1978.

———. *The Count Dracula Book of Classic Vampire Tales.* Chicago: Adams Press, 1981.

———. *The Further Perils of Dracula.* Chicago: Adams Press, 1979.

———. *Vampire Babies.* Chicago: Adams Press, 1986.

Youngson, Jeanne, and Peter Tremayne. *Freak Show Vampire and the Hungry Grass.* New York: Count Dracula Fan Club, 1981.

Appendix 2

Novels

The following are novels that have appeared over the past years, above and beyond those listed under the *Literature* entry. They represent the continuing fascination with vampirism and the many ways in which writers have explored the landscape of the undead. Dozens of new novels are published each year.

Alexander, Jan. *Blood Moon.*New York: Lancer, 1970.

Ascher, Eugene. *To Kill a Corpse.* London: World Distributors, 1946.

Asprin, Robert. *Myth-ing Persons.* Norfolk, VA: Donning, 1984.

Baker, Scott, *Dhampire.* New York: Pocket Books, 1982.

———. *Nightchild.* New York: Berkley, 1979.

Baker, Sharon. *Burning Tears of Sassurum.* New York: Avon, 1988.

——. *Journey to Membliar.* New York: Avon, 1987.

Barnes, Linda. *Blood Will Have Blood.* New York: Avon, 1982.

Bergstrom, Elaine. *Daughter of the Night.* New York: Jove, 1992.

Bischoff, David. *Nightworld.* New York: Ballantine, 1979.

Bloch, Robert. *It's All in Your Mind.* New York: Modern Library, 1971.

Bradbury, Ray. *Something Wicked This Way Comes.* New York: Simon & Schuster, 1962.

Bradley, Marion Zimmer. *Falcons of Narabelda.* New York: Ace, 1964.

Brett, Stephen. *The Vampire Chase.* New York: Manor, 1979.

Brite, Poppy. *Lost Souls.* New York: Delacorte, 1992.

Brown, Carter. *So What Killed the Vampire?* New York: Signet, 1966.

Brunelle, Jan. *Death on Tour: Chill Module.* Cleveland, OH: Pacesetter, 1985.

Burke, Norah. *The Scarlet Vampire.* London: S. Paul, 1936.

Butler, Octavia. *Mind of My Mind.* New York: Doubleday, 1977.

———. *Patternmaster.* New York: Doubleday, 1976.

———. *Wild Seed.* New York: Doubleday, 1976.

Campton, David. *The Vampyre,* London: Beaver/Arrow, 1986.

Carew, Henry. *The Vampires of the Andes.* London: Harrold, 1925.

Charles, Robert. *Flowers of Evil.* London: Futura, 1981.

Charnas, Suzy McKee. *The Silver Glove*. New York: Bantam, 1988.

Chetwynd-Hayes, Ronald. *Dracula's Children*. London: William Kimber, 1987.

———. *The House of Dracula*. London: William Kimber, 1987.

———. *The Partaker*. London: William Kimber, 1980.

Coffman, Virginia. *The Vampyre of Moura*. New York: Ace, 1970.

Corelli, Marie. *The Soul of Lilith*. London: Richard Bentley and Son, 1892.

———. *Ziska*. London: Simpkin, Marshall, 1987.

Cullum, Ridgwell. *The Vampire of N'Gobi*. London: Chapman and Hall, 1935.

Daniels, Les. *The Black Castle*. New York: Scribner's, 1978.

———. *Citizen Vampire*. New York: Scribner's, 1981.

———. *The Silver Skull*. New York: Scribner's 1979.

———. *Yellow Fog*. West Kingston, RI: Donald M. Grant, 1986.

Daniels, Philip. *The Dracula Murders*. London: Robert Hale, 1983.

Dear, Ian. *Village of Blood*. London: New English Library, 1975.

De la Mare, Walter. *The Return*. London: Arnold, 1910.

De Weese, Gene. *The Wanting Factor*. New York: Playboy, 1980.

Dillard, J. M. *Bloodthirst*. "Star Trek," no. 37. New York: Pocket Books, 1987.

———. *Demons*. "Star Trek," no. 30. New York: Pocket Books, 1986.

Dobbin, Muriel. *A Taste for Power*. New York: Richard Marek, 1980.

Dreadstone, Carl. *Dracula's Daughter*. New York: Berkley, 1977.

Duigon, Lee. *Lifeblood*. New York: Pinnacle, 1988.

Eliot, Marc. *How Dear the Dawn*. New York: Ballantine, 1987.

Engstrom, Elizabeth. *Black Ambrosia*. New York: Tom Doherty, 1988.

Estleman, Loren D. *Sherlock Holmes vs. Dracula: The Adventure of the Sanguinary Count*. New York: Doubleday, 1978.

Farrington, Geoffrey. *The Revenants*. London: Dedalus, 1983.

Frederick, Otto. *Count Dracula's Canadian Affair*. New York: Pageant, 1960.

Garden, Nancy. *Prisoner of Vampires*. New York: Farrar, Strauss and Giroux, 1984.

Garton, Roy. *Live Girls*. New York: Pocket Books, 1987.

Gibbons, Cromwell. *The Bat Woman*. New York: World, 1938.

Giles, Raymond. *Night of the Vampire*. New York: Avon, 1969.

Glut, Donald. *Frankenstein Meets Dracula*. London: New English Library, 1977.

Grant, Charles L. *The Soft Whisper of the Dead*. West Kingston, RI: Donald M. Grant, 1982.

Hambly, Barbara. *Those Who Hunt the Night*. New York: Ballantine, 1988.

Horler, Sydney. *The Vampire*. London: Hutchinson, 1935.

Hurwood, Bernhardt J. *By Blood Alone*. New York: Charter, 1979.

Huson, Paul. *The Keepsake*. New York: Warner, 1981.

Jennings, Jan. *Vampyr*. New York: Pinnacle, 1981.

Johnson, Ken. *Hounds of Dracula*. New York: New American, 1977.

Kahn, James. *Time's Dark Laughter*. New York: Ballantine, 1982.

Kapralov, Yuri. *Castle Dubrava*. New York: E. P. Dutton, 1982.

Karlova, Irina. *Dreadful Hollow*. London: Hurst and Blackett, 1942.

Kast, P. *The Vampires of Alfama*. London: W. H. Allen, 1977.

Killough, Lee. *Blood Hunt*. New York: Tom Doherty, 1987.

Knight, Malory. *Dracutwig*. New York: Award, 1969.

Koontz, Dean R. *The Haunted Earth*. New York: Lancer, 1973.

Kurtz, Katherine. *The Legacy of Lehr*. New York: Byron, 1986.

Lory, Robert. *The Dracula Horror Series*, 1–8. New York: Pinnacle, 1973–1975.

Lumley, Brian. *Necroscope Series*, I–V. New York: Tom Doherty, 1986–1991.

Mannheim, Karl. *Vampires of Venus*. New York: Pemberton, 1952.

Marryat, Florence. *The Blood of the Vampire*. London: Hutchinson, 1897.

Matson, Norman. *Bats in the Belfry*. New York: Doubleday, 1943.

McKenney, Kenneth. *The Moonchild*. New York: Simon & Schuster, 1978.

Norton, Andre. *Perilous Dreams*. New York: DAW Books, 1976.

Ptacek, Kathryn. *Blood Autumn*. New York: Tom Doherty, 1985.

———. *In Silence Sealed*. New York: Tom Doherty, 1988.

Randolphe, Arabella, *The Vampire Tapes*. New York: Berkley, 1977.

Raven, Simon. *Doctors Wear Scarlet*. New York: Simon & Schuster, 1960.

Rechy, John. *The Vampires*. New York: Grove, 1971.

Rice, Jeff. *The Night Stalker*. New York: Pocket Books, 1973.

Romkey, Michael. *I, Vampire*, Ballantine, 1990.

Ronson, Mark. *Blood Thirst.* London: Hamlyn, 1979.

Ross, Marilyn. *Barnabas Collins Series.* "Dark Shadows," no. 1–32. New York: Paperback Library, 1970–1972.

Russo, John. *The Awakening.* New York: Pocket Books, 1983.

Saberhagen, Fred. *Dominion.* New York: Pinnacle, 1982.

———. *The Holmes-Dracula File.* New York: Ace, 1978.

———. *Matter of Taste, A.* New York: Tor, 1990.

———. *An Old Friend of the Family.* New York: Ace, 1979.

———. *Question of Time, A.* New York: Tor, 1992.

———. *Thorn.* New York: Ace, 1980.

Samuels, Victor. *The Vampire Women.* New York: Popular Library, 1973.

Saralegui, Jorge. *Last Rites.* New York: Chartres, 1985.

Salem, Richard. *New Blood.* New York: Tor, 1982.

Saxon, Peter. *Brother Blood.* New York: Belmont, 1970.

———. *The Darkest Night.* New York: Paperback Library, 1967.

———. *Vampire's Moon.* New York: Belmont, 1970.

———. *The Vampires of Finistere.* New York: Berkley, 1970.

Scarborough, Elizabeth. *The Goldcamp Vampire.* New York: Bantam, 1987.

Shirley, John. *Dracula in Love.* New York: Kensington, 1979.

Sloane, William. *The Unquiet Corpse.* New York: Dell, 1956.

Smith, Martin Cruz. *Nightwing.* New York: W. W. Norton, 1977.

Stevenson, Florence. *The Curse of the Concullens.* New York: New American Library, 1972.

Stewart, Desmond. *The Vampire of Mons.* New York: Harper & Row, 1976.

Tem, Steve Rasnic. *Excavation.* New York: Avon, 1987.

Tyson, John Aubrey. *The Barge of Haunted Lives.* New York: Macmillan, 1923.

Valdemi, Maria. *The Demon Lover.* New York: Pinnacle, 1981.

Veley, Charles. *Night Whispers.* New York: Doubleday, 1980.

Viereck, George. *The House of the Vampire.* New York: Moffat, Yard, 1907.

Wallace, Ian. *The Lucifer Comet.* New York: DAW Books, 1980.

Walters, R. R. *Ludlow's Mill.* New York: Tom Doherty, 1981.

Whalen, Patrick. *Monastery.* New York: Pocket Books, 1988.

Williamson, J. N. *Death-Angel.* New York: Kensington, 1981.

———. *Death-Coach.* New York: Kensington, 1982.

———. *Death-Doctor.* New York: Kensington, 1982.

———. *Death-School.* New York: Kensington, 1982.

Wilson, Colin. *The Mind Parasites.* Sauk City, WI: Arkham House, 1967.

———. *The Space Vampires.* New York: Random House, 1976.

X, Madeline. *I Am a Vampire.* Hoboken, NJ: Essex, 1974.

Zimmer, Paul Edwin. *Blood of the Colyn Muir.* New York: Avon, 1988.

Appendix 3

Suggested Reading List

The following are books selected from the hundreds that were consulted in the preparation of this work. Readers are encouraged to use these many excellent studies, although some may be hard to find given their age or the limited numbers in which they were printed. If a favorite book is not included here, the reader is requested to write so that it might be included in later editions.

Abbott, C. F. *Macedonian Folklore.* Chicago: Argonaut, 1969.

Arens, W. *The Man-Eating Myth.* Oxford: Oxford University Press, 1979.

Barber, Paul. *Vampires, Burial, and Death.* New Haven: Yale University Press, 1988.

Bleiler, E. F. *The Guide to Supernatural Fiction.* Kent, OH: Kent State University, 1983.

Brunas, Michael, et al. *Universal Horrors, the Studio's Classic Films, 1931–1946.* London: McFarland, 1990.

Butler, Ivan. *Horror in the Cinema.* New York: A. S. Barnes 1967.

Carter, Margaret. *Dracula, the Vampire and the Critics.* Ann Arbor: UMI Research Press, 1989.

———. *The Vampire in Literature, a Critical Bibliography.* Ann Arbor: UMI Research Press, 1989.

Copper, Basil. *The Vampire in Legend, Fact and Art.* New York: Citadel Press, 1973.

Corliss, William. *Handbook of Unusual Natural Phenomena.* Glen Arm, MD: The Sourcebook Project, 1977.

Crooke, William. *Religion and Folklore in Northern India.* Oxford: Oxford University Press, 1926.

De Groot, J.J.M. *The Religious System of China.* The Hague: 1892–1910.

Dolphin, David. "Werewolves and Vampires," abstract of a paper, 1985.

Dorson, Richard. *America in Legend.* New York: Pantheon, 1973.

Faivre, Tony. *Les Vampires.* Paris: Le Terrain Vague, 1971.

Farson, Daniel. *The Man Who Wrote Dracula.* London: Michael Joseph, 1975.

Florescu, Radu, and R. T. McNally. *Dracula, a Biography of the Impaler.* New York: Hawthorn, 1973.

Frazer, J. G. *The Golden Bough,* vol. 10. London: Macmillan, 1930.

Friedland, Nat. *The Occult Explosion.* New York: G. P. Putnam's Sons, 1972.

Frost, Brian. *The Monster with a Thousand Faces.* Bowling Green: Bowling Green State University Press, 1989.

Garden, Nancy. *Vampires*. New York: J. B. Lippincott, 1973.

Ginzberg, Louis. *Legends of the Jews*. New York: Simon & Schuster, 1961.

Glut, Donald. *The Dracula Book*. Metuchen, NJ: Scarecrow, 1975.

————. *True Vampires of History*. New York: H.C. Publishers, 1971.

Groome, Francis. *Gypsy Folk Tales*. London: Hurst and Blackett, 1899.

Guiley, Rosemary. *Vampires Among Us*. New York: Pocket Books, 1991.

Haining, Peter. *The Dracula Centenary Book*. London: Souvenir, 1987.

————. *The Dracula Scrapbook*. New York: Bramhall House, 1977.

Hillyer, Vincent. *Vampires*. Los Banos, CA: Loose Change, 1988.

Hoyt, Olga. *Lust For Blood*. New York: Stein and Day, 1984.

Hufford, David. *The Terror That Comes in the Night*. Philadelphia: University of Pennsylvania Press, 1982.

Hurwood, Bernhardt J. *Passport to the Supernatural*. New York: Taplinger, 1972.

————. *Vampires*. New York: Quick Fox, 1981.

Jones, Ernest. *On the Nightmare*. New York: Liveright, 1971.

Kittredge, George. *Witchcraft in Old and New England*. Cambridge: Harvard University Press, 1929.

Lawson, John. *Modern Greek Folklore and Ancient Greek Religion*. New York: University Books, 1964.

Leatherdale, Clive. *Dracula, the Novel and the Legend*. Wellingborough: The Aquarian Press, 1987.

————. *The Origins of Dracula*. London: William Kimber, 1987.

Leland, Charles. *Gypsy Sorcery and Fortune-Telling*. New York: Dover, 1971.

Ludlam, Harry. *A Biography of Dracula*. London: W. Foulsham and Co., 1962.

Mackenzie, Andrew. *Dracula Country: Travels and Folk Beliefs in Romania*. London: Arthur Baker, Ltd., 1977.

Mackenzie, D. *Scottish Folklore and Folk Life*. London: 1935.

Masters, Anthony. *The Natural History of the Vampire*. New York: G. P. Putnam's Sons, 1972.

Masters, R.E.L., and Eduard Lea. *Sex Crimes in History*. New York: Julian, 1963.

McNally, Raymond T. *Dracula Was a Woman*. New York: McGraw-Hill, 1983.

McNally, Raymond T., and Radu Florescu. *In Search of Dracula*. Greenwich, CT: N.Y. Graphic Society, 1972.

Myles, Douglas. *Prince Dracula.* New York: McGraw-Hill, 1988.

Noll, Richard. *Vampires, Werewolves and Demons: Twentieth-Century Reports in the Psychiatric Literature.* New York: Brunner/Mazel, 1992.

Oinas, Felix. *Essays on Russian Folklore and Mythology.* Columbus, OH: Slavica Publishers, 1985.

Olson, Kiki. *How to Get a Date with a Vampire (And What to Do With Him Once You've Got Him).* New York: Contemporary, 1992.

Owen, Mary Alicia. *Voodoo Tales.* New York: G. P. Putnam's Sons, 1893; reprinted: Books for Libraries Press, 1971.

Page, Carol. *Blood Lust.* New York: Harper-Collins, 1991.

Perkowski, Jan. *The Darkling, A Treatise on Slavic Vampirism.* Columbus, OH: Slavica Publishers, 1989.

———. *Vampire of the Slavs.* Columbus, OH: Slavica Publishers, 1976.

Pirie, David. *The Vampire Cinema.* Leicester: Galley Press, 1977.

Puckett, Newbell. *Folk Beliefs of the Southern Negro.* New York: Negro University Press, 1969.

Ralston, W.R.S. *Russian Folktales.* London: Smith, Elder and Co., 1873; reprinted: Arno Press, 1977.

Ramos, Maximo. *Creatures of the Philippine Lower Mythology.* Philippines: University of Philippines Press, 1971.

Reed, Donald. *The Vampire on the Screen.* Inglewood, CA: Wagon and Star Publishers, 1965.

Reed, Toni. *Demon-Lovers and their Victims in British Fiction.* Lexington: The University Press of Kentucky, 1988.

Riccardo, Martin. *The Lure of the Vampire.* Chicago: Adams Press, 1983.

———. *Vampires Unearthed.* New York: Garland, 1983.

Robertson, R. Macdonald. *Selected Highland Folktales.* Edinburgh: Oliver and Boyd, 1961.

Ronay, Gabriel. *The Truth About Dracula.* New York: Stein and Day, 1972.

Roth, Phyllis, *Bram Stoker.* Boston: Twayne, 1982.

Schroeder, Aribert. *Vampirismus.* Frankfurt: Akademische Verlagsgesellschaft, 1973.

Senf. Carol. *The Vampire in Nineteenth-Century English Literature.* Bowling Green: Bowling Green State University Press, 1988.

Senn, Harry. *The Werewolf and Vampire in Romania.* Boulder, CO: Colorado University Press, 1982.

Skal, David. *Hollywood Gothic.* New York: W. W. Norton, 1990.

Skeat, Walter. *Malay Magic.* London: Macmillan, 1900.

Skinner, Charles. *Myths and Legends of Our Own Land.* Philadelphia: J. B. Lippincott & Co., 1896.

Smith, W. Ramsay. *Myths and Legends of the Australian Aborigines.* New York: Farrar and Rinehart, n.d.

Summers, Montague. *The Vampire, His Kith and Kin.* London: Routledge & Kegan Paul, 1928.

———. *The Vampire in Europe.* London: Routledge & Kegan Paul, 1929.

———. *The Werewolf.* New York: E. P. Dutton, 1934.

Toor, Frances. *A Treasury of Mexican Folkways.* New York: Crown Publishers, 1947.

Trachtenberg, Joshua. *Jewish Magic and Superstition.* New York: Meridian, 1961.

Trigg, Elwood. *Gypsy Demons and Divinities.* Secaucus, NJ: Citadel Press, 1973.

Twitchell, James B. *Dreadful Pleasures: An Anthology of Modern Horror.* New York: Oxford University Press, 1985.

———. *The Living Dead: The Vampire in Romantic Literature.* Durham, NC: Duke University Press, 1985.

Ursini, James, and Alain Silver. *The Vampire Film.* New York: A. S. Barnes, 1975.

Volta, Ornella. *Le Vampire.* Paris: Jean-Jacques Pauvert, 1962.

Waller, Gregory. *The Living and the Undead: From Stoker's Dracula to Romero's Dawn of the Dead.* Champaign, IL: University of Illinois, 1986.

Willoughby-Meade, G. *Chinese Ghouls and Goblins.* New York: 1928.

Wolf, Leonard. *The Annotated Dracula.* New York: Clarkson N. Potter, 1975.

———. *A Dream of Dracula.* Boston: Little, Brown and Co., 1972.

Wright, Dudley. *Vampires and Vampirism.* London: William Rider and Son, 1914.

X, Madeline. *How to Become a Vampire in Six Easy Lessons.* Chicago: Adams Press, 1985.

Appendix 4

Vampire Societies and Organizations

There are many organizations around the world that are devoted to the study and appreciation of vampires, Dracula, Gothic literature, and all things related. The following is a list of the major groups. Some other societies, also functioning and active, have requested that they not be included, so as to discourage public inquiries.

Anne Rice's Vampire Lestat Fan Club
    Sue Quiroz, founding member
    Teresa Simmons, president
    P.O. Box 58277
    New Orleans, LA 70158-8277   Fees: $10 annually; $15 international.

The Bram Stoker Society
    Albert Power
    227 Rochester Avenue
    Dun Laoghaire
    County Dublin, Ireland   Fees: $10 for U.S.; £5 for U.K.

The British Dracula Society
    R. J. Leake
    36 Elliston House
    100 Wellington Street
    Woolich, London, England SE 18
    Founded in 1973 by Bruce Wightman and Bernard Davies. Membership is upon approval of the committee. One of the oldest and most prestigious of the societies.

The British Vampyre Society
    Allen Gittens
    38 Westcroft
    Chippenham Wilts
    England SN 14 OLY
    Send $4 for a sample newsletter and membership information.

The Count Dracula Fan Club
    29 Washington Square West
    Penthouse North
    New York, NY 10011
    The fee to join is $50 ($35 annual renewal), $65 internationally. This is the largest society in America, with a *Dracula News Journal* and the Dracula Museum, which contains an extensive collection of memorabilia, costumes, books, photographs, and scripts. It was founded by Dr. Jeanne Youngson, who is always happy to assist interested persons in learning more about vampires and has devoted her life to the appreciation of the undead.

The Count Dracula Society
    334 West 54th Street
    Los Angeles, CA 90037
    (213) 752-5811
    Membership fees vary, depending upon category. The first of the societies, it
    was founded in 1962 by Dr. Donald A. Reed, who is also the head of the
    Academy of Science Fiction Fantasy and Horror Films.

The Count Ken Fan Club
    Ken Gilbert
    12 Palmer Street
    Salem, MA 01970
    Send $4 for a sample newsletter and membership information.

Dark Shadows Festival
    P.O. Box 92
    Maplewood, NJ 07040
    An excellent source for information on the "Dark Shadows" series, its actors,
    episodes, and conventions.

The Miss Lucy Westenra Society of the Undead
    Lewis Sanders
    125 Taylor Street
    Jackson, TN 38301   Fee:$10 annually.

The Quincey P. Morris Dracula Society
    Charlotte Simsen
    P.O. Box 381
    Ocean Gate, NJ 08740 $15.99 to join.
    A society founded in the 1970s by Charlotte Simsen, named after the only
    American in the novel *Dracula*. Also publishes *Transfusion*, a quarterly
    newsletter.

The Vampires Archives of Istanbul
    Giovanni Scognamillo
    PostacilarSokak 13/13
    Beyoglu, Istanbul, Turkey
    There are no members, as the archives is devoted to research on vampires.

Vampire Information Exchange
    Eric Held
    Box 328
    Brooklyn, NY 11229-0328
    Send $4 for a sample newsletter and for membership information.

Realm of the Vampire
    P.O. Box 517
    Metairie, LA 70004-0517
    Fee: $22 annually.
    Enclose S.A.S.E. with all correspondence.

The Dracula Experience
    9 Marine Parade
    Whitby Y021 3PR